Advance Pr<!-- -->... E-mails and
Other business Documents

I have been teaching Business English for about 14 years now and I recommend all your books to my students – *Model Business Letters* included. So far we have enjoyed good pass rates for the exams. Some students tell me they keep *Model Business Letters* handy in the office even after completing the course. The letters are relevant, simple to read and easy to understand, and that is the most effective form of communication!

Teresa Long, Lecturer, Thames Business School, Singapore

Model Business Letters is essential reading for everyone in business today, a guide that not only tells you how to write well, but also gives hundreds of examples too. I'm sure the 6thedition will fly off bookstores shelves everywhere. Well done!

Gordon Clark, Managing Director, Out of Obscurity, California, USA (www.outofobscurity.com)

It is not so much a book, as a really practical 'hands on' reference guide covering a comprehensive range of day to day issues which arise in business. A must in today's hectic business world and I would suggest very helpful to the smaller business in particular. Good luck with your new edition.

Ian Gange ACIB, Area Manager, HSBC, UK

Shirley, your workshops on business writing skills are fabulous. You are a natural presenter, making difficult things simple and bringing everyone into your world of writing. I have never had so much fun learning how to write better business letters! With *Model Business Letters* you have done the same thing – it's an easy-to-read, comprehensive but clear guide that will be indispensable for businessmen and woman all over the world.

Ricky Lien, Trainer, Mindset Media, Sydney, Australia

Model Business Letters has become the 'gold standard' for millions of people whose personal and professional success becomes increasingly dependent on effective business writing. With this new edition, Shirley has done it again – another fabulous book on business communication, which will become an invaluable reference for people all over the world.

K C See, CEO, The Quest Group, Kuala Lumpur, Malaysia

Model Business Letters is one of the most popular books in our Training Library, and everyone who borrows it sends back a glowing report. It's an excellent reference book for anyone in business – whether self-employed or working as a manager, secretary, PA or administrator. Good luck with your 6th edition.

Pamela Aitcheson, MIQPS, IQPS Training Library Manager (Institute of Qualified Private Secretaries, UK, www.iqps.org)

For many years Shirley has provided sound advice and practical guidelines on how to strengthen communication skills in all her popular books and workshops. Here is another book that is right on target, and set to become the industry's benchmark for successful business writing.

Alan Hill, Managing Director, Ward Hi-Tech Ltd, Sheffield, UK

In this 21st century world of increasingly faceless communication, our writing is more important than ever. As we are often judged by the way we write, it makes sense to learn to write well. In *Model Business Letters*, Shirley has come up with a desk reference tool that provides all the help anyone needs, as well as models we can adapt as necessary. Another runaway international success, without doubt!

Steven Seek, Managing Director, JobsDB.com, Singapore

Shirley has a unique ability to write in a straight forward, clear way that is easily understandable. No wonder her books are popular in countries all over the world. She does exactly the same thing in her training, with her friendly and participative approach that makes everyone feel like she's teaching them personally, one-to-one.

Sam Loo, Manager, Learner's Choice International, Singapore

People who learn to write well are increasing their value to the company, helping to create and enhance the company's corporate image and playing a major part in its success. With so many executives and managers *now composing their own correspondence*, Model Business Letters contains essential guidance that will help people all over the world to upgrade their writing skills and thus help them to achieve these aims.

Joy Chan, Executive Assistant to the Senior Vice President, HP Services Asia Pacific, Singapore

The impact and efficiency of our staff has been greatly enhanced by Shirley's workshop 'Transform your Business Writing Skills'. With *Model Business Letters*, we have a comprehensive oracle for writing clear and persuasive business correspondence – it's a must-have for every desktop in the 21st century.

Sukvender Kaur, Training & Communication Officer, IOI Properties Berhad, Johor Bahru, Malaysia

I have been searching for a simple yet effective book that deals with writing business letters and I have finally found one. Model Business Letters has been an invaluable help to me and I have, in fact, recommended it to Japanese buinessmen who wish to improve their written correspondence. The layout is simple and easy to follow and the models are in clear, plain English. The book is even being used as a text for non-native speakers of English, and both teachers and student speak very highly of it. I certainly advise anyone who wants to write professional yet uncluttered business documents to buy this book.

Michelle Sumura, Managing Director, "Let's Go Australia", Perth, Western Australia

If you're looking for 'enlightenment' on how to have a refreshing change to your business writing, don't go looking for a Bodhi Tree. Just pick up one of Shirley's books or, better yet, attend her inspiring workshops! She will exorcise the 'dinosaur' style of writing out of you!

Jacintha Shyamala Davis, Skills Coordinator, OPUS IT Services Pte. Ltd, Singapore

We use *Model Business Letters* with our students frequently, and find it a very practical and well-presented book, with lots of useful sample documents. Our students find the book very helpful, as well as your monthly e-mail newsletters, which are so interesting and informative. I know the 6th edition of *Model Business Letters* will be even more valuable!

Elaine Howard, Kudos Training, Surrey, UK (Top UK Secretary winner for 2000 and 2001)

Shirley's books, her training workshops, her website and her monthly e-newsletter all provide inspiration and valuable guidance on how to write well. She teaches us in a practical, fun and straight forward way how to ditch the boring, standard clichés and other stuffy formalities that have no place in modern 21st century business writing. Good luck with *Model Business Letters* 6th edition – it's bound to be a runaway success!

Ajitha Gunaratna- Freelance Trainer, Communication Skills. Sri Lanka

At ELS Language Centers in Malaysia we use many of Shirley's books to help teach business communication. Shirley has a special talent of giving explanations that are straight forward, simple and clear – this natural, friendly style is what makes her training workshops so successful too. The new edition of *Model Business Letters* is sure to be another great success.

Chee Yin Fair, Centre Director, Johor Bahru branch, ELS Language Centres, Malaysia

Congratulations Shirley on your 6th edition of *Model Business Letters*. Twenty years have gone by since you first joined our teaching staff. I am glad that you are reaching out to a wider audience. I pray that more people in business can be converted to follow your preaching – the Guru in Business Communication.

Rose Yeo, Principal/Owner, SSTC Education Centre, Singapore

Booksellers tell me that while their shelves are full of books on business writing, it is *Model Business Letters* that sells and sells, so they never hesitate to stock it well. Not many other business writing books can claim to have sold over 350,000 copies to! I once had to write an important and urgent Press Release for the launch of a new book. Without fail, I found just what I needed in *Model Business Letters* and it did the job superbly. Well done Shirley.

Leslie LIM Boon Hup, Regional Sales Manager, STP Distributors (Books), Singapore

Model Business Letters – it is so inspiring, the bible of business communication. Everyone should always have one of the books on their desk.

Delphine Ang, Business Development Manager, Partners Conference Event Management Pte Ltd, Singapore

Model
Business
Letters,
E-mails

& Other
Business
Documents

FT Prentice Hall

FINANCIAL TIMES

In an increasingly competitive world, we believe it's quality of thinking that will give you the edge – an idea that opens new doors, a technique that solves a problem, or an insight that simply makes sense of it all. The more you know, the smarter and faster you can go.

That's why we work with the best minds in business and finance to bring cutting-edge thinking and best learning practice to a global market.

Under a range of leading imprints, including *Financial Times Prentice Hall*, we create world-class print publications and electronic products bringing our readers knowledge, skills and understanding which can be applied whether studying or at work.

To find out more about Pearson Education publications, or tell us about the books you'd like to find, you can visit us at
www.pearsoned.co.uk

PEARSON

Education

Model
Business
Letters,
E-mails

& Other Business Documents

Sixth Edition

Shirley Taylor

Originally written in 1971 by

L Gartside

Former Chief Examiner in Commercial Subjects
College of Preceptors

FT Prentice Hall
FINANCIAL TIMES

An imprint of **Pearson Education**

London • New York • Toronto • Sydney • Tokyo • Singapore
Hong Kong • Cape Town • Madrid • Paris • Amsterdam • Munich • Milan

PEARSON EDUCATION LIMITED

Head Office:
Edinburgh Gate
Harlow CM20 2JE
Tel: +44 (0)1279 623623
Fax: +44 (0)1279 431059
Website: www.pearsoned.co.uk

First published in Great Britain in 1992
Sixth edition published 2004

© Pearson Education Limited 2004

The right of Shirley Taylor to be identified as Author
of this Work has been asserted by her in accordance
with the Copyright, Designs and Patents Act 1988.

ISBN 978-0-273-67524-2

British Library Cataloguing in Publication Data
A CIP catalogue record for this book can be obtained from the British Library

15 14 13

Cartoon illustrations by Tim Major
Typeset by Northern Phototypesetting Co Ltd, Bolton
Printed and bound in China
GCC/13

The Publishers' policy is to use paper manufactured from sustainable forests.

About the author

Shirley Taylor is author of several popular, best-selling books. Her first book, *Communication for Business*, published in 1991, is now in its third edition and is used in colleges all over the world. Since then Shirley has written many other successful books, including best-sellers *Model Business Letters*, *Essential Communication Skills*, *Pocket Business Communicator*, *The Secretary in Training* and *Guide to Effective E-mail*.

A trained teacher from the UK, Shirley took up her first teaching post in Singapore in 1983, where she spent several years as Training Consultant and Lecturer teaching on secretarial and business studies courses. She has also worked as Head of Department and Senior Lecturer in Bahrain, as well as in the UK and Canada.

Shirley is based in Singapore now, having set up her own business, Shirley Taylor Training and Consultancy, and she enjoys conducting her popular training programmes, workshops and seminars all over Asia. Shirley is also regularly asked to speak at international conferences.

Shirley writes a monthly e-newsletter called 'Shirley Says' with articles, tips and quizzes on modern business writing. To sign up for this popular e-newsletter, type your name in the sign-up box on Shirley's home page, www.shirleytaylor.com.

Shirley can be contacted on e-mail: shirley@shirleytaylor.com.

Contents

Unit 3 CREATIVE AND PERSUASIVE DOCUMENTS

Preface to the first edition

By Leonard Gartside

Few business transactions are carried through successfully without correspondence at some point. Enquiries must be answered, quotations given, orders placed, complaints dealt with, transport and insurance arranged and accounts settled. Letters must be written to customers, salesmen, agents, suppliers, bankers, shipowners and many others; they cover every conceivable phase of business activity. They are the firm's silent salesmen and, often enough, represent its only contact with the outside world. Hence the need to create a good impression, not only of the writer's firm but also of the writer himself as an efficient person eager to be of service.

In the pages that follow are to be found over five hundred specimen letters dealing with a comprehensive range of transactions of the kind handled in business every day. They are represented, not as models to be copied, for no two business situations are ever quite alike, but rather as examples written in the modern English style to illustrate the accepted principles of good business writing.

Every business letter is written to a purpose; each has its own special aim, and one of the features of this book is its use of explanation to show how the various letters set out to achieve their aims. Basic legal principles relevant to different types of transaction are also touched upon, but only where there is a need to clarify legal relationships. Where the book is used in class, the letters provide material for teachers who may wish to enlarge on these matters and the exercises the means for students to apply in practice what they have been taught.

The many letters included are written in the straightforward and meaningful style of the modern age and should be of special help to the overseas user, and especially to students in schools and colleges where commercial correspondence is taught either as a general business accomplishment or as a preparation for the various examinations.

November 1971 *L.G.*

Preface to the sixth edition

By Shirley Taylor

'With reference to your letter'

'Enclosed herewith please find'

'I am writing to inform you'

'Please be advised'

Are you still writing letters and e-mails using the same old standard, boring clichés? In today's fast-paced business world with its focus on effective communication, these stuffy formalities make your writing unnecessarily complicated and impersonal. Yet each office has someone who is intoxicated with the exuberance of their own verbosity. Phrases like 'We have received your letter' and 'Kindly be advised' and 'Please find enclosed herewith' are recycled regularly. For such people, all correspondence has to be peppered with these standard clichés made up by our great-grandfathers. What a paradox to use such convoluted language in today's business world, which runs at 2000 beats a minute!

With the ever-increasing speed of technological change, we all need to stay up to date with new equipment and new computer programs. As soon as a new version of a popular program becomes available, we must learn it. When some new technology comes out, we have to have it. In line with technological developments, the way business is conducted generally has changed immensely over the past couple of decades. Business is being conducted in a much more informal way – a natural, more relaxed language is being used in meetings and conferences. But what's happened to our business writing skills? Many people are still using a style more suited to our great-grandfathers than to 21st-century businessmen and women.

It seems we are writing more than ever. Most managers are creating their own communications – letters, memos, faxes, reports, articles, marketing materials, and especially e-mails. In this global age, speed is often the key to successful negotiations, so writing effectively under these circumstances can be very demanding.

E-mail has promised us a future of minimum effort and maximum communication. Where once words were the signs of ideas, now words are being replaced by signs themselves ;-). Despite this, there is one huge anomaly that holds out against this torrent of speed and ultra-efficiency. Despite the growth of e-mail and the new jargon it has introduced, it seems our skill in business writing has evolved very little. Age-old conventions are still being dredged up from the very core of our beings. Somewhere deep within each of us there seems to be a hoard of standard phrases and old-fashioned clichés that are just shouting out to be included even in today's modern e-mails.

'As spoken in our telecon …', 'Please revert to me on this matter …', 'Kindly furnish us with this information …', 'The above-mentioned goods …', 'at your soonest convenience …', 'for your reference and perusal'. The list is endless!

Including stuffy formalities like this in business writing serves only to obscure the real meaning, and spinning out sentences makes them intolerably long. The reader often ends up searching for the real meaning in this haystack of rhetoric.

This is 2003, not 1903! The speed of sound is old hat today. People want the speed of thought! If you are still peppering your writing with these standard, boring clichés, then you aren't doing yourself or your company any favours – and you are certainly not helping your readers. Such phrases have only one place in today's business language: the trash bin.

In *Model Business Letters, E-mails and Other Business Documents* you will find none of these stuffy formalities and great-grandfather writing. This comprehensive reference book is full of examples of modern business writing, tips and techniques and useful guidelines that will help you to communicate effectively.

Effective communication gives a professional impression of you and of your organisation. Effective communication helps to get things done. Writing effectively is perhaps the most demanding work we do. Writing requires imagination, creativity, organisation, careful planning and many other skills if a message is to be effective and get results. In today's fast-paced business world, there should be no room for yesterday's old-fashioned, long-winded jargon.

Today's business language should be proactive, stimulating, interesting, and most of all it should reflect your personality. Instead of using boring clichés that have been around for decades, the key is to write in a natural style, as if you were having a conversation. The golden rule of all communications is mentioned regularly throughout *Model Business Letters, E-mails and Other Business Documents*: 'Remember! If you wouldn't say it, don't write it!'

The Internet has made it possible for us to communicate with people from all over the world. The only way those people can form an opinion of us is by looking at the way we write. I hope this book will help you to learn to write well.

Shirley Taylor
September 2003

Introduction

This book is for you if you want to ditch the boring standard clichés that have been peppering written communications for decades. This book is for you if you are tired of using the same stuffy formalities like 'Please be advised …', 'for your reference and perusal …', 'I would like to inform you …', and so on. This book is for you if you want your writing to give a good impression of you and your organisation. This book is for you if you want to learn how to write as you speak, how to write in a natural style, how to make your writing proactive, interesting. This book is for you if you want your writing to be a reflection of your personality instead of filled with old-fashioned jargon designed by our great-grandfathers that has been overused and abused for decades.

Model Business Letters, E-mails and Other Business Documents is a one-stop shop for all your business communications. It is a guide that not only tells you how to do it but also gives you examples that you can lift straight off the page and adapt for your own use. It is an invaluable oracle for writing clear and persuasive business correspondence.

WHO SHOULD USE THIS BOOK?

Many people will find this book useful:

- **Executives and managers who regularly compose their own correspondence.** Many managers now compose their own correspondence on their desk-top or portable PC. These ready-to-use documents can be copied or adapted to meet your precise needs. They will help you to say what you want to say and to achieve the desired results. You will be able to save time and do your job better, more effectively and easily, without scratching your head for ages thinking about what to write.
- **Overseas users.** Past editions of this book have been sold extensively from India to Indonesia, from Malaysia to the Maldives, from Singapore to Sri Lanka, from Hong Kong to Harrogate, from Shanghai to Sheffield, from Toronto to Thailand. Overseas users will appreciate the value of this comprehensive resource book. It will be especially useful in dealing with international business transactions using modern business language.
- **Students and lecturers.** Students following a business, professional, secretarial or administrative examination course often need to compose business letters and other business documents. You will find the guidelines,

theory, specimen documents, 4 point plans, definitions and checklists particularly useful in learning how to compose your own effective communications.

HOW IS THE BOOK ORGANISED?

I have organised the book so that you can hop around to whatever topics interest you. Just dip in whenever you face a blank page, and hopefully you will find some inspiration to get you started and some useful tips to help you finish the task.

The first unit is a must for everyone. **Written communication – an overview** discusses the importance of attractive presentation of business documents, including fully blocked layout and open punctuation – a 'modern' style that is now, believe it or not, over 30 years old! Unit 1 also discusses my 4 point plan for structuring your messages, the 7 deadly sins of modern business writing, the top 10 rules of good writing, and my checklist for effective business writing in the 21st century. Also featured in Unit 1 is a completely rewritten unit on e-mail, including the top 10 complaints about e-mail in practice, how you can make e-mail work for you not against you, and the netiquette that has evolved from this wonderful invention.

Unit 2 Routine business documents contains just that – enquiries, orders, quotations, invoices, all the correspondence making up a standard business transaction.

Unit 3 Creative and persuasive documents contains a lot of new material not in previous editions. Many documents today require creativity and imagination if they are to be successful, so this chapter looks at the specific writing skills involved in complaints, reports, notices and advertisements, circulars, sales letters, press releases, and much more.

Unit 4 Classified business letters contains some special documents used in business, such as minutes, personnel correspondence, secretarial and administrative correspondence, international trade and banking.

SPECIAL FEATURES

- As each new document is introduced, the format is illustrated in a specimen document, with notes highlighting every aspect of document presentation.
- Each section contains full explanations, discussion and theory regarding the various documents concerned.
- Many specimen letters are boxed and include marginal notes that discuss important features of the text.
- 4 point plans encourage you to plan and structure your own communications effectively.
- Definitions of special terminology or phrases are placed in footnotes on the relevant pages.

Look out for these special icons:

TIP: Throughout the book there are over 100 top tips for effective communication.

WEBWATCH: I have included some notes about some websites that I find particularly useful.

CHECKLIST: At the end of each chapter there is a checklist to remind you of the key points to remember.

WHAT'S WRONG? Take a look at these examples of poor business writing.

These are followed by **WHAT'S RIGHT?** to show you how they should have been done.

FINAL WORD

I hope this reference book, with its emphasis on high-quality presentation, structure, language and tone, helps you to convey your messages appropriately and effectively. Remember that in so doing you will not only be helping to create and enhance the corporate image of your organisation, you will also be increasing your value to the company and playing a major part in its success.

By picking up this book you have already shown a desire to learn more about modern business writing. The solid advice and practical guidelines, combined with hundreds of sample documents, will show you how to develop effective written communication skills. The rest is up to you.

Good luck!

Shirley Taylor

Please note: For reasons of consistency and simplicity and to avoid confusion, we have used the UK -ise spelling convention throughout this book. Readers should also be familiar with the -ize convention used in many countries worldwide.

Unit 1

Written communication – an overview

There are many modern communication methods available today, but the traditional business letter remains an important means of sending printed messages. As the business letter acts as an ambassador for the company, it is vital that it gives a good first impression. In this respect, it is good business practice to ensure good quality stationery and printing of the letterheaded paper. The business letter also conveys an impression of the company in many other ways:

Presentation Structure Language and Tone

Developments in technology have made it possible for us to have instant communication all over the world. Speed is now becoming the key to successful business communications. As a result, fax messages and e-mail are taking the place of many business letters. E-mails are also phasing out the use of internal memos, although they still remain popular in some companies. All these methods of written communication will be discussed in this unit.

Whatever method you choose to convey your printed message – letter, fax, e-mail, memo, etc – your aim should be to ensure a high standard in all the important areas named above: presentation, structure, language and tone. Remember the importance of the 'first impression'. By setting high standards in the important area of written communications you will be helping to create and enhance the corporate image of your organisation.

Very often nowadays instead of a secretary being asked to type documents for signature by the employer, it is the employer who is keying in their own text and sending messages straight to recipients. Although very often it makes sense in terms of time and energy for the employer to prepare his/her own communications, it is also good practice to allow a secretary to 'tidy them up'. The boss may be an expert in his/her own field or specialism, but the secretary is more often than not the expert in presentation, layout and structure.

In today's competitive business world, high communication standards are vital. Therefore it is essential to ensure that the need for speed does not result in a decline in the standards of communications. Instead, the constant advances in technology should help us to improve and enhance our business communications, and thereby maximise business potential.

In this unit these three aspects – presentation, structure, language and tone – will be considered in detail, along with correct layout of letters, fax messages, memos and e-mail.

 Good writing is like any other endeavour. The more you put into it, the more you will get back.

Presentation of business documents

PRINTED STATIONERY

Attractive and consistent presentation of your business documents is vital if they are to make a good impression.

Your printed stationery should be of good quality, especially when being used for sending to external contacts. For internal documents the stationery does not need to be of such high quality.

The paper your company uses for its printed correspondence will express the personality of your company. Your letterhead will show:

- a logo or graphic symbol identifying your company
- the company's name
- the full postal address
- contact numbers – telephone, fax, e-mail address
- the url or website address
- registered number or registered office. When the registered office is different to that shown in the address section, it is usual to show the registered address, normally at the foot of the notepaper, along with the registered number.

It is usual to engage experts to design a letterhead, especially an eye-catching logo with which the company can be identified.

Here are two examples of letterheaded paper.

The letterhead
shows:

Logo

Company name

Address

Contact details

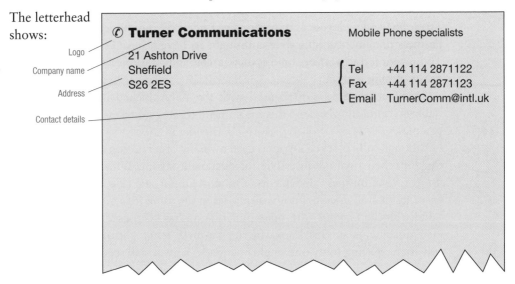

Turner Communications   Mobile Phone specialists

21 Ashton Drive
Sheffield
S26 2ES

Tel   +44 114 2871122
Fax   +44 114 2871123
Email   TurnerComm@intl.uk

The company name is
displayed attractively
at the top left

The address and
contact details are
neatly placed at the
top right

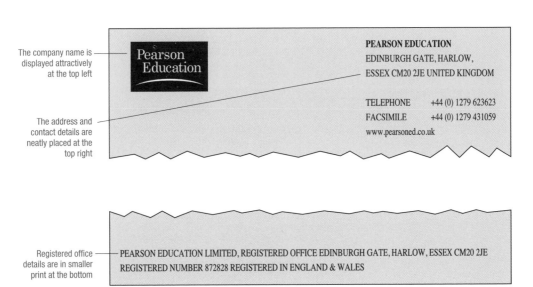

PEARSON EDUCATION
EDINBURGH GATE, HARLOW,
ESSEX CM20 2JE UNITED KINGDOM

TELEPHONE   +44 (0) 1279 623623
FACSIMILE   +44 (0) 1279 431059
www.pearsoned.co.uk

Registered office
details are in smaller
print at the bottom

PEARSON EDUCATION LIMITED, REGISTERED OFFICE EDINBURGH GATE, HARLOW, ESSEX CM20 2JE
REGISTERED NUMBER 872828 REGISTERED IN ENGLAND & WALES

FULLY BLOCKED STYLE WITH OPEN PUNCTUATION

The fully blocked layout is now the most widely used method of display for all business documents. This style is thought to have a businesslike appearance. This layout reduces typing time as there are no indentations for new paragraphs or the closing section.

Open punctuation is often used with the fully blocked layout. Again this reduces typing time because there is no need for any unnecessary full stops and commas.

Although fully blocked layout is used by many organisations, some still prefer to adopt their own inhouse style for document layout. Whichever layout you use for your business documents, the most important rule is consistency, ie ensuring that all documents are displayed in the same format.

Fully blocked layout with open punctuation has been used for all the specimen documents in this book. In the business letter shown here, note the consistent spacing (only one single line space) between all sections of the letter.

 The Chinese would say good presentation is good feng shui!

FT Prentice Hall
FINANCIAL TIMES

Financial Times Prentice Hall
Edinburgh Gate
Harlow, Essex
CM20 2JE
UNITED KINGDOM
Telephone: +44 (0)1279 623623
Facsimile: +44 (0)1279 431059

Letterheaded paper

Reference
(initials of writer/typist,
sometimes a filing
reference)

ST/PJ

Date (day, month, year)

12 November 200—

Inside address (name,
title, company, full
address, postal code)

Mr Alan Hill
General Manager
Long Printing Co Ltd
34 Wood Lane
London
WC1 8TJ

Salutation

Dear Alan

Heading
(to give an instant idea
of the theme)

FULLY BLOCKED LETTER LAYOUT

This layout has become firmly established as the most popular way of setting out letters, fax messages, memos, reports – in fact all business communications. The main feature of fully blocked style is that all lines begin at the left-hand margin.

Body of letter
(one line space between
paragraphs)

Open punctuation is usually used with the fully blocked layout. This means that no punctuation marks are necessary in the reference, date, inside address, salutation and closing section. Of course essential punctuation must still be used in the text of the message itself. However, remember to use commas minimally today; they should be used only when their omission would make the sense of the message unclear.

Consistency is important in layout and spacing of all documents. It is usual to leave just one clear line space between each section.

I enclose some other examples of fully blocked layout as used in fax messages and memoranda.

Most people agree that this layout is very attractive and easy to produce as well as businesslike.

Complimentary close

Yours sincerely

Shirley Taylor

Name of sender

SHIRLEY TAYLOR (Miss)

Sender's designation or
department

Training Specialist

Enc (if anything is
enclosed)

Enc

Show if any copies
are circulated
(if more than one, use
alphabetical order)

Copy   Pradeep Jethi, Publisher
        Amelia Lakin, Acquisitions Executive

CONTINUATION PAGES

Some companies have printed continuation sheets that are used for second or subsequent pages of business letters. Such printed continuation sheets usually show just the company's name and logo. If printed continuation sheets are not available, the second or subsequent page should be typed on plain paper of a similar quality to that of the letterhead.

When a second or subsequent page is necessary, always include certain details at the top of the continuation sheet. These details are necessary for reference purposes in case the first and subsequent pages are separated in any way:

- page number
- date
- name of addressee.

When a continuation sheet is necessary, remember the following guidelines:

- It is not necessary to include anything at the foot of the previous page to indicate that a further page follows. The fact that there is no closing section or signature should make this quite obvious.
- A continuation page should contain at least three or four lines of typing as well as the usual closing section.
- Do not leave one line of a paragraph either at the bottom of the previous page or at the top of the next page. Try to start a new page with a new paragraph.

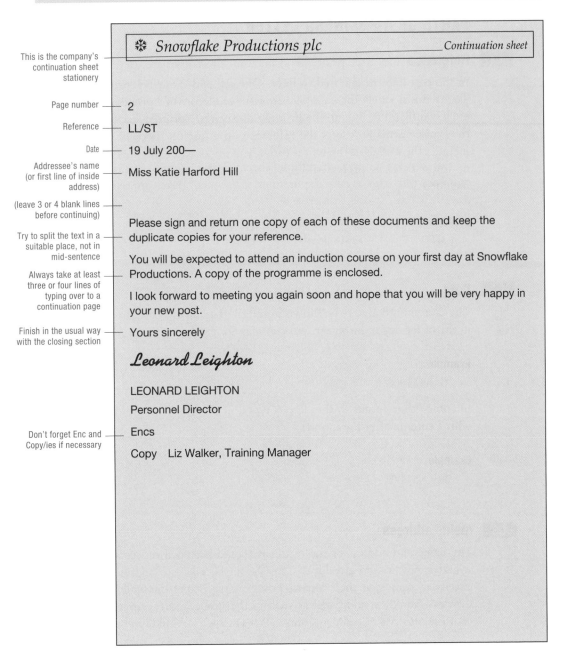

❄ *Snowflake Productions plc* _____ *Continuation sheet*

This is the company's continuation sheet stationery

Page number — 2

Reference — LL/ST

Date — 19 July 200—

Addressee's name (or first line of inside address) — Miss Katie Harford Hill

(leave 3 or 4 blank lines before continuing) —

Try to split the text in a suitable place, not in mid-sentence — Please sign and return one copy of each of these documents and keep the duplicate copies for your reference.

Always take at least three or four lines of typing over to a continuation page — You will be expected to attend an induction course on your first day at Snowflake Productions. A copy of the programme is enclosed.

I look forward to meeting you again soon and hope that you will be very happy in your new post.

Finish in the usual way with the closing section — Yours sincerely

Leonard Leighton

LEONARD LEIGHTON
Personnel Director

Don't forget Enc and Copy/ies if necessary — Encs

Copy   Liz Walker, Training Manager

TIP   **You don't need a line on which to sign your name. You get past that stage at five years old!**

PARTS OF A BUSINESS LETTER

1.1 Reference

In the past letterheads used to have 'Our ref' and 'Your ref' printed on them. Today this is rarely the case because with modern word processors and printers it is difficult to line up the printing on such pre-printed stationery. Instead, the typist normally inserts the reference on a line on its own. The reference includes the initials of the writer (usually in upper case) and the typist (in upper or lower case, as preferred). A file or departmental reference may also be included.

Examples

GBD/ST   GBD/st/Per1   GBD/ST/134

1.2 Date

The date should always be shown in full. In the UK it is usual to show the date in the order day/month/year. No commas are used.

Example

12 July 2003

In some other countries the date is typed in the order month/day/year, often with a comma after the month.

Example

July 12, 2003

1.3 Inside address

The name and address of the recipient should be typed on separate lines as it would appear on an envelope. Care should be taken to address the recipient exactly as they sign their letters. For example, a person signing as 'Douglas Cowles' should be addressed as such in the inside address, preceded with the courtesy title 'Mr'. To address him as 'Mr D Cowles' would not be appropriate.

Example

Mr Douglas Cowles
General Manager
Cowles Engineering Co Ltd
12 Bracken Hill
Manchester
M60 8AS

When writing letters overseas, the name of the country should be shown on the final line of this section. As the letter will be sent by airmail, this should be indicated one clear line space above the inside address. Again note that the appropriate courtesy title (Mr/Mrs/Miss/Ms) should always be shown:

Example

AIRMAIL

Mr Doug Allen
Eagle Press Inc
24 South Bank
Toronto
Ontario
Canada M4J 7LK

1.4 Special markings

If a letter is confidential it is usual to include this as part of the inside address, one clear line space above it. This may be typed in upper case or in initial capitals with underscore.

Example

CONFIDENTIAL

Miss Iris Tan
Personnel Director
Soft Toys plc
21 Windsor Road
Birmingham
B2 5JT

Some decades ago an attention line was used when the writer simply wanted to ensure that the letter ended up on a certain person's desk, even though the letter was addressed to the company in general, and always began 'Dear Sirs'.

Example

FOR THE ATTENTION OF MR JOHN TAYLER, SALES MANAGER

Garden Supplies Ltd
24 Amber Street
Sheffield
S44 9DJ

Dear Sirs

In today's business letters, it should rarely be necessary to use an attention line. When you know the name of the person you are writing to, the name of the recipient should be included in the inside address, and a personalised salutation will be used.

1.5 Salutation

If the recipient's name has been used in the inside address, it is usual to use a personal salutation.

Example

Dear Mr Leighton   Dear Douglas   Dear Miss Tan   Dear Rosehannah

If your letter is addressed generally to an organisation and not to a specific person, the more formal salutation 'Dear Sirs' should be used.

Example

Dear Sirs

If your letter is addressed to a head of department or the head of an organisation whose name is not known, then it would be more appropriate to use a salutation as shown here.

Example

Dear Sir or Madam

1.6 Heading

A heading gives a brief indication of the content of the letter. It is usually placed one clear line space after the salutation. Upper case is generally used, although initial capitals with underscore may be used if preferred.

Example

Dear Mrs Marshall

INTERNATIONAL CONFERENCE – 24 AUGUST 2003

1.7 Complimentary close

It is customary to end the letter in a polite way by using a complimentary close. The two most common closes are 'Yours faithfully' (used only with Dear Sir/Sirs/Sir or Madam) and 'Yours sincerely' (used with personalised salutations).

Examples

Dear Sir
Dear Sirs   } Yours faithfully
Dear Madam
Dear Sir or Madam

Dear Mr Leighton
Dear Mrs Yap   } Yours sincerely
Dear Caroline
Dear Sam

1.8   Name of sender and designation

After the complimentary close 4 or 5 clear spaces should be left so that the letter can be signed. The name of the sender should then be inserted in whatever style is preferred – upper case, or initial capitals only. The sender's designation or department should be shown directly beneath his/her name. In these examples note that the title 'Mr' is never shown when the writer is male. However, it is usual to add a courtesy title for a female; this is shown in brackets after her name.

Examples

Yours faithfully   Yours sincerely

PATRICK ASHE   LESLEY BOLAN (Mrs)
Chairman   General Manager

When a letter has to be signed on behalf of the sender, it is usual to write 'for' or 'pp' in front of the sender's printed name; 'pp' is an abbreviation for per procurationem, which simply means 'on behalf of'.

Example

Yours faithfully

Shirley Johnson

for EDWARD NATHAN
Chairman

1.9   Enclosures

There are many different methods of indicating that an enclosure is being sent along with a letter:

- Affix a coloured 'enclosure' sticker usually in the bottom left-hand corner of the letter.
- Type three dots in the left-hand margin on the line where the enclosure is mentioned in the body of the letter.
- Type 'Enc' or 'Encs' at the foot of the letter, leaving one clear line space after the sender's designation. This is the most common form of indicating enclosures.

Example

Yours sincerely

LINDA PATERSON (Mrs)
Marketing Manager

Enc

1.10 Copies

When a copy of a letter is to be sent to a third party (usually someone in the sender's organisation) this may be indicated by typing 'cc' (copy circulated or courtesy copy) or 'Copy' followed by the name and designation of the copy recipient. If there are two or more copy recipients, it is usual to show these in alphabetical order.

Example

> Copy Ravi Gopal, General Manager
> Ashley Ow Yong, Company Secretary
> Candice Reeves, Accountant

If the writer does not wish the recipient of the letter to know that a third person is receiving a copy of the letter, then 'bcc' (blind courtesy copy) is used. This should not be shown on the top of the letter, only on the file copy and bcc copy/ies.

Example

> bcc   Mr Gordon Clark, Chief Executive

 Don't send a cc to everyone you know – just send them to people who need to know.

OPEN PUNCTUATION

Open punctuation is commonly used with fully blocked layout. Only punctuation marks that are essential to ensure good grammatical sense are included within the main body of the message itself. All other commas and full stops are omitted, especially in the presentational aspects like the date, inside address, etc.

 With commas, the rule is now less rather than more.

1.11 Dates

	NOT
25 September 2003	25th September, 2003
14 July 2004	July 14th, 2004

1.12 Names and addresses

Mr G P Ashe
Chief Executive
Ashe Publications Pte Ltd
#03-45 Ashe Towers
212 Holland Avenue
Singapore 2535

no full stops

no commas at the end of lines

1.13 Salutation

Dear Patrick

no comma

1.14 Complimentary close

Yours sincerely

no comma

1.15 Abbreviations

NOT

Mr	eg	Mr.	e.g.
Dr	ie	Dr.	i.e.
BA	pm	B.A.	p.m.
IBM	am	I.B.M.	a.m.
MRT		M.R.T.	
NB		N.B.	
PS		P.S.	

1.16 Times and numbers

NOT

9.30 am		9.30 a.m.	9.30am
0950		09.50 am	
1400		14:00	

1	8	1.	8)
2	9	2.	9)
3	10	3.	10)

TIP **Use open punctuation and remove a lot of the clutter from your writing and presentation.**

MEMOS

A memo is a written message from one person to another (or several people) within the same organisation. Memos (or memoranda) serve several purposes:

- to provide information
- to request information
- to inform of actions, decisions
- to request actions, decisions.

Some companies have pre-printed forms for internal memos but very often templates are saved on word processing systems. The typist then only has to insert the relevant details alongside the given headings.

1.17 Format

The following format is an easy, clear method for displaying internal memos.

Emphasise the word MEMORANDUM	**MEMORANDUM**
Insert the recipient's name and designation	*To* Christine Winters, Administrative Assistant
The sender's name and designation	*From* Sally Yap, PA to Chairman
A reference (initials of sender and typist)	*Ref* SY/JJ
Date of issue	*Date* 14 August 200—
No salutation is necessary	
Subject heading – clearly state the topic of the message	INHOUSE DOCUMENT FORMATS

Many congratulations on recently joining the staff in the Chairman's office. I hope you will be very happy here.

I am enclosing a booklet explaining the company's general rules regarding document formats. However, I thought it would be helpful if I summarised the rules for ease of reference.

1   DOCUMENT FORMATS

All documents should be presented in the fully blocked format using open punctuation. Specimen letters, fax messages, memoranda and other documents are included in the booklet. These examples should guide you in our requirements.

2   SIGNATURE BLOCK (LETTERS)

In outgoing letters it is usual practice to display the sender's name in capitals and the title directly underneath in lower case with initial capitals.

3   NUMBERED ITEMS

In reports and other documents it is often necessary to number items. In such cases the numbers should be displayed alone with no full stops or brackets. Subsequent numbering should be decimal, ie 3.1, 3.2, etc.

I hope these guidelines will be useful and that you will study the layouts shown in your booklet. If you have any questions please do not hesitate to ask me.

Sally Yap

Enc

Copy   Personnel Department

The body of the memo should be separated into paragraphs, reaching a relevant conclusion and close

No complimentary close is necessary

Leave space for signature (the sender's name and designation are at the top so it is not necessary to repeat these details here)

Enc (if appropriate)

Copy/ies (if appropriate)

TIP Set a high standard in all your correspondence – high standards in correspondence suggest a high standard in business generally.

FAX MESSAGES

A fax machine is a relatively inexpensive essential item of equipment for any business. Fax messages may be sent between branches of the same company or to external business associates. Today many communications which would normally be sent by letter are in fact sent by fax. When referring to the model letters in this book, therefore, the text of the messages may be used in fax communications or indeed as e-mail messages.

1.18 Printed form or template

Many companies have a standard printed form for use when sending fax messages. Very often a template is designed for calling up on computers and word processors. Operators need then just key in the relevant information. Here is an example of how a printed fax form or a template might be designed.

Fax

To	From
Company	Date
Fax No	No of Pages (including this page)

1.19 **Fully blocked style**

When a pre-printed form is not available, the fully blocked style may be used in preparing a fax message, as shown in this example.

Letterheaded paper

© **Turner Communications**   Mobile Phone specialists

21 Ashton Drive
Sheffield   Tel   +44 114 2871122
S26 2ES   Fax   +44 114 2871123
                                       Email TurnerComm@intl.uk

Include the main heading 'FAX MESSAGE'

FAX MESSAGE

These headings are important so that all the essential details can be inserted alongside

To	Susan Gingell, General Manager
Company	Asia Communication (Singapore) Pte Ltd
Fax Number	65 6767677
From	Low Chwee Leong, Managing Director
Ref	LCL/DA
Date	6 June 200—

It is important to state the number of pages being sent

Number of Pages
(including this page)   1

A salutation may be included if preferred

The heading should state the main topic of the fax message

VISIT TO SINGAPORE

Thank you for calling this morning regarding my trip to Singapore next month. I am very grateful to you for offering to meet me at the airport and drive me to my hotel.

The body of the fax message should be composed similarly to a business letter

I will be arriving on flight SQ101 on Monday 8 July at 1830 hours. Accommodation has been arranged for me at the Supreme International Hotel, Scotts Road.

I will be travelling up to Kuala Lumpur on Sunday 14 July on MH989 which departs from Singapore Changi Airport Terminal 2 at 1545 hours.

A complimentary close is not necessary

I look forward to meeting you.

Low Chwee Leong

 TIP   **You are being judged on how you write – so learn to write well!**

CHECKLIST

☐ Design an attractive letterhead with a unique logo for your company's letterheaded paper.

☐ Use consistent layout for all your business documents – fully blocked style with open punctuation is the most popular.

☐ Leave just one line space between each section of your documents. Be consistent in this aspect too.

☐ Include the sender's name and title in the address section – an 'attention line' is not necessary.

☐ If there is an appropriate heading, use it. If not, leave it out.

☐ Remember to indicate when something is enclosed by putting 'Enc' at the end.

☐ Use Copy or cc (courtesy copy) when other people receive copies.

☐ When a letter, memo or fax is continued onto a second page, do not type anything at the foot of the first page.

☐ At the head of a continuation sheet (fully blocked at the left margin) show the page number, date and name of addressee.

☐ Your business documents reflect an impression of you and your company – make sure it's a good one.

Structuring your communications

4 point plan

Checklist

Whether you are composing a business letter, a fax message, a memo or an e-mail, the general rules for structuring the body of the message are the same. A well-structured document written in good business language is the core of effective communication. This section will help you to get past that blank page and start creating well-structured documents that will achieve your objectives.

4 POINT PLAN

Many communications are short and routine. You can write or dictate them without any special thinking or preparation. However, documents that are not so routine need more thought and careful planning. I first suggested this 4 point plan in *Communication for Business*. It provides a useful but simple framework for structuring all written communications, and is illustrated simply here:

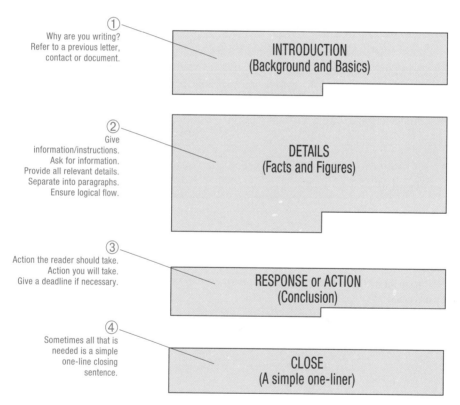

① Why are you writing? Refer to a previous letter, contact or document.

INTRODUCTION
(Background and Basics)

② Give information/instructions. Ask for information. Provide all relevant details. Separate into paragraphs. Ensure logical flow.

DETAILS
(Facts and Figures)

③ Action the reader should take. Action you will take. Give a deadline if necessary.

RESPONSE or ACTION
(Conclusion)

④ Sometimes all that is needed is a simple one-line closing sentence.

CLOSE
(A simple one-liner)

Let's look at this 4 point plan in more detail:

1 Opening or introduction

The first paragraph will state the reason for the communication, basically setting the scene. It may:

- acknowledge previous correspondence
- refer to a meeting or contact
- provide an introduction to the matter being discussed.

Examples

Thank you for your letter of …
It was good to meet you again at last week's conference.
We wish to hold our annual conference at a London hotel in September.

Beware beginning a sentence with 'Further to your letter of …' This should always be continued as shown:

Further to your letter of 12 July, I am sorry for the delay in attending to this matter.

2 Central section (details)

This main part of the message gives all the information that the recipient needs to know. Alternatively you may be requesting information, sometimes both. Details should be stated simply and clearly, with separate paragraphs used for individual sections. This section should flow logically to a natural conclusion.

3 Conclusion (Action or Response)

This section draws the message to a logical conclusion. It may:

- state the action expected from the recipient
- state the action you will take as a result of the details provided.

Examples

Please let me have full details of the costs involved together with some sample menus.

If payment is not received within seven days this matter will be placed in the hands of our solicitor.

4 Close

A simple one-line closing sentence is usually all that is necessary to conclude a message. This should be relevant to the content of the message.

Examples

I look forward to meeting you soon.

I look forward to seeing you at next month's conference.

A prompt reply would be appreciated.

Please let me know if you need any further information.

 Closes such as these are incomplete and should not be used:

Hope to hear from you soon.
Looking forward to hearing from you.

The 4 point plan for structuring all written messages is illustrated in this letter.

Institute of Secretaries
Wilson House, West Street, London SW1 2AR

Telephone 020 8987 2432
Fax 020 8987 2556

LD/ST

12 May 2004

Miss Ong Lee Fong
15 Windsor Road
Manchester
M2 9GJ

Dear Lee Fong

2004 SECRETARIES CONFERENCE, 8/9 OCTOBER 2004

Opening (give a brief introduction) — As a valued member of the Institute of Secretaries, I have pleasure in inviting you to attend our special conference to be held at the Clifton Hotel, London on Tuesday/Wednesday 8/9 October 2004.

This intensive, practical conference for professional secretaries aims to:

Details (separate paragraphs, flowing logically) —
- increase your managerial and office productivity
- improve your communication skills
- bring you up to date with the latest technology and techniques
- enable networking with other secretaries

Leave one blank line everywhere except the signature space — The seminar is power-packed with a distinguished panel of professional speakers who will give expert advice on many useful topics. A programme is enclosed giving full details of this seminar which I know you will not want to miss.

Conclusion (action expected from the recipient) — If you would like to join us please complete the enclosed registration form and return it to me before 30 June with your fee of £50 per person.

Close (a simple closing statement) — I look forward to seeing you again at this exciting conference.

Yours sincerely

Louise Dunscombe

LOUISE DUNSCOMBE (Mrs)

Conference Secretary

Encs

This e-mail message gives another example of the 4 point plan.

From	johnwang@stelectronics.co.sg
Date	14:10:03 12:30:45
To	suzieliu@videoworks.com
CC	
Subject	24th anniversary video

Dear Suzie

Intro — Thank you for inviting me to visit your studios last week. I was most impressed by your new facilities.

Details — I am delighted that you can accept our invitation to produce a video to celebrate the company's 25th anniversary. This is a very special landmark in our history, and it is important that this video portrays both past, present and future.

Action — You promised to let me have a draft outlining your thoughts for this special video. I look forward to receiving this before 30 October together with your approximate costings.

If you need any further information please give me a call on 2757272.

Close — Best wishes

John Wang
Marketing Manager
ST Electronics
www.stelectronics.co.sg

 TIP Study all the documents in this book as good examples of using the 4 point plan.

CHECKLIST

☐ Remember: a well-structured business document is the core of effective communication.

☐ Use a subject heading to give the main gist of your message.

☐ Refer to a previous letter, contact or document in the first paragraph – the Introduction.

☐ Compose the central section (details) so that each point follows in a sensible order, and make sure the information flows logically from point to point.

☐ Separate the message into paragraphs, leaving one blank line between each section.

☐ Conclude your message by stating what action you expect the reader to take after reading your message.

☐ Be sure to include a deadline for any response, if this is appropriate.

☐ Your close may simply be a one-liner, whatever is relevant to the situation.

☐ Proofread your message carefully and take a while to consider whether it is structured appropriately and that all the details are arranged logically.

☐ Read through your final message as if you were the reader – imagine how the reader will feel when receiving it. If anything is not right, make the necessary changes.

Language and tone

The weakest link in your business writing

10 steps to good business writing

Checklist

The secret of composing good business communications is to use plain language, as if you are having a 'conversation in writing'. Simply, it means putting across your message in a natural way, using a courteous style. General business practice is to use an informal style of writing rather than being too formal.

In all communications it is essential to ensure correct grammar, spelling and punctuation. However, you need more than an ability to structure sentences correctly. Your aim is to transfer thoughts and ideas from one person to another, so you must always remember that you are dealing with a person as well as a situation. The document chosen as well as the approach and the tone used will all be determined by the person who will receive the message.

Put yourself in the place of the recipient and imagine how they will accept what is written in the tone used. Anticipate the recipient's needs, wishes, interests, problems. Consider the best way of dealing with the specific situation.

Whether you choose to write a business letter, a fax, a memo or an e-mail, remember the following points:

- Choose the method of communication carefully.
- Create the document thoughtfully.
- Present the document so that it looks good and gives an impression of efficiency and reliability.

- Use a format that is neat, easy to read and structured logically.
- Use appropriate tone, considering the circumstances, the situation and the recipient.
- Ensure your message is accurate in terms of grammar, spelling and punctuation.

TIP Remember the 3Rs – guide the Reader towards the Response you expect, and you will achieve the right Results!

THE WEAKEST LINK IN YOUR BUSINESS WRITING

My mother is a big fan of the popular game show 'The Weakest Link', which has earned international success. It's a great show, in which contestants have to identify the weakest link from their fellow players and get rid of them as quickly as possible.

What a great principle, and one we can all easily use to improve our business writing skills and enhance corporate image. Business today is being conducted in a very informal way – in meetings and conferences we are using a natural, more relaxed language rather than stilted, formal language that was used several decades ago. So how come many people are still using business writing that is more suited to our great-grandfathers than to 21st-century businessmen and women? Here is what I believe to be 7 of the weakest links that I would like to eliminate from 21st-century business writing.

1 So many young people with so many old-fashioned expressions

When will people realise that business language has changed? Expressions like 'Please be informed', 'Kindly be advised', 'I would like to bring to your attention' and 'I am writing to advise you' should have been relegated to the recycle bin way before the turn of the new millennium. Unfortunately today's writing is still full of centuries-old expressions like these, not to mention even worse ones such as 'Enclosed herewith please find our catalogue for your reference and perusal', 'With reference to your above-mentioned order', 'Further to the telecon today between your goodself and the undersigned'. This type of writing is BORING! People are using these standard clichés simply because everyone else uses them, and because they have been used for centuries. Please! Put some thought and personality and some feeling into your writing.

Instead of	Say
We refer to your letter of 21st October 2004.	Thank you for your letter of 21 October.
As spoken in our telecon today.	Thank you for calling me this morning.
Please revert to me soonest possible.	I hope to hear from you soon.
Should you require any further clarification please do not hesitate to contact the undersigned.	Please give me a call on 2874722 if you have any questions.

2 So many long-winded expressions

Long words and long expressions, long sentences and long paragraphs will impress no one – they will only confuse. Later in this section I will talk about the KISS principle – Keep. It Short and Simple! Instead of 'I should be very grateful', why not simply say 'Please' (definitely not Kindly!). Use short words like *buy*, *try*, *start* and *end* instead of *purchase*, *endeavour*, *commence* and *terminate*. Remember to KISS in your business writing – use short words, simple expressions, short sentences and short paragraphs that are clear and concise.

3 Let's get more active

Our great-grandfathers used passive voice in writing because they didn't want to show who was responsible for anything. They preferred to use long sentences that beat about the bush but never revealed what was really happening and who was really responsible. Today's business writers should use active voice, which is more alive, more focused, more personalised and much more interesting and clear.

Instead of	*Say*
Arrangements have been made for a repeat order to be despatched to you immediately.	I have arranged for a repeat order to be sent to you today.
The cause of your complaint has been investigated.	I have looked into this matter.
The seminar will be conducted by Adrian Chan.	Adrian Chan will conduct the seminar.
Sales of the X101 have exceeded all expectations.	X101 sales have gone sky high.

 TIP **Put some thought and personality and feeling into your writing.**

4 Colons Colons Colons

Why is it that many people have to put a line of colons in any list? It looks so cluttered and messy. Let's get rid of all the clutter in our business writing, and make it look neat, clean and well organised.

❌
Date	: 29 November 2003 (Thursday)
Time	: 9.00am to 5.00pm
Venue	: Sheraton Towers Hotel

✓
Date	Thursday 29 November 2003
Time	9.00 am to 5.00 pm
Venue	Sheraton Towers Hotel

5 Attention!

Our great-grandfathers invented the attention line (and they were not lazy – they wrote it in full, 'For the attention of ...') because they were merely directing the letter to the desk of a real person, not writing personally to that person. In those days, even with the attention line, letters still began 'Dear Sirs' and the wording was formal and passive, as if talking to the company as a whole, not to a real individual person. Over the years the attention line has been very much misused and lazy writers have abbreviated it to 'Attention' or even 'Attn'. Attention lines today are being incorporated (wrongly) in personal letters with personal salutations such as 'Dear John', 'Dear Mr Tan'. Let's put the attention line in the recycle bin and relegate it firmly to the last century where it belongs. We rarely need it today. If you know the person to whom you are writing, and if you want to use a personal salutation, incorporate the addressee's name and title into the address section.

Attn   :   Leslie Lim Boon Hup

STP Distributors Pte Ltd (Books)
30 Old Toh Tuck Road #05-02
Singapore 597654

Mr Leslie Lim Boon Hup
Product and Sales Manager
STP Distributors Pte Ltd (Books)
30 Old Toh Tuck Road #05-02
Singapore 597654

6 Do you really need a line to sign your name on?

I thought it was only children who needed a line on which to write. Would managers really go into a fit if there was no line on which to sign their name? Would they really sit there and wonder where to put their signature? I really doubt it. Surely the space between 'Yours sincerely' and the writer's name/title is indication enough that this is where the signature goes? Again, this is something that we simply don't need. Get rid of the line and let's get rid of even more clutter in our writing.

Yours sincerely

Tan Lee Hong
Managing Director

7 Thank you!

Why do so many people need to say 'Thank you' at the end of a message? Thank you for what? For reading my letter? Please! Stop wasting time and printer ink. If you have been courteous throughout your communication (and let's face it, no matter what the circumstances, your writing should always be courteous) there should be no need to keep saying 'Thank you' over and over again just because someone read your letter or e-mail.

In today's fast-paced business world, there should be no room for yesterday's old-fashioned, long-winded jargon. Ditch the boring clichés that have been around for decades. Put some life into your business writing by using a natural, relaxed, friendly style. Put some zip into your presentation by using a style that is more proactive, stimulating and interesting – writing that reflects your personality. This is 2003, not 1903!

Thank you. (kidding☺)

 TIP Instead of using boring clichés that have been around for decades, the key is to write in a natural style, as if you are having a conversation.

10 STEPS TO GOOD BUSINESS WRITING

Now that we have looked at things you should not do in your writing, let's take a look at my top 10 rules of good business writing. If you follow these rules you will be helping yourself to become a better business writer.

1 Remember your ABC

Good written communication results when you say exactly what you want to say using an appropriate tone. Your message must meet these essential specifications:

Accurate   Check facts carefully
Include all relevant details
Proofread thoroughly

Brief   Keep sentences short
Use simple expressions
Use non-technical language

Clear   Use plain, simple English
Write in an easy, natural style
Avoid formality or familiarity

2 Be courteous and considerate

Courtesy does not mean using old-fashioned expressions like 'your kind consideration' or 'your esteemed order'. It means showing consideration for your correspondent and being empathetic – that means showing respect for your reader's feelings. Writing in a courteous style enables a request to be refused without killing all hope of future business. It allows a refusal to be made without ruining a friendship. Courtesy also means:

● Reply promptly to all communications – answer on the same day if possible.
● If you cannot answer immediately, write a brief note and explain why. This will create goodwill.
● Understand and respect the recipient's point of view.
● Resist the temptation to reply as if your correspondent is wrong.

- If you feel some comments are unfair, be tactful and try not to cause offence.
- Resist the temptation to reply to an offensive letter in a similar tone. Instead, answer courteously and do not lower your dignity.

 TIP **Why do you need to say 'Thank you' at the end of a message? Be courteous throughout your message and skip all these redundant closes.**

3 Use appropriate tone

If your message is to achieve its purpose the tone must be appropriate. The tone of your message reflects the spirit in which you put your message across. Even when writing a complaint or replying to one, your message can be conveyed in a way so as not to be rude or cause offence. Ignoring the need to use an appropriate tone could result in a message that sounds aggressive, tactless, curt, rude, sarcastic or offensive. This will not meet your desired objectives.

Instead of	*Say*
We cannot do anything about your problem.	Unfortunately we are unable to help you on this occasion.
This problem would not have happened if you had connected the wires properly.	The problem may be resolved by connecting the wires as shown in the handbook.
Your television's guarantee is up, so you will have to pay for it to be fixed.	Your television's guarantee has ended, so unfortunately you must bear the cost of any repairs.
I am writing to complain because I was very unhappy with the way I was treated in your store today.	I was most unhappy with the standard of service I received in your store today.

You alter your tone of voice to convey messages in different ways. Much of what you say is also interpreted through non-verbal clues – eye contact, gestures, inflections of the voice, etc. This type of 'reading between the lines' is not possible with the written word. Therefore it is vital to choose your words carefully. You can be firm or friendly, persuasive or conciliatory – it depends on the impression you wish to convey. It is important to try to get the tone right because using the wrong tone could cause real offence to your reader.

Here are some expressions to avoid in your business writing:

- Your failure to reply …
- You did not see …
- We must insist …
- You should not expect to …
- Your refusal to co-operate …
- You have ignored …

- This is not our fault ...
- I can assure you ...
- You failed to ...
- I have received your complaint ...

The Plain English Campaign has an interesting section called 'The A to Z of Alternative Words'. This contains hundreds of alternatives to the pompous words and phrases that litter official writing.

www.plainenglish.co.uk/plainenglishguide

4 Write naturally and sincerely

Try to show a genuine interest in your reader and his/her problems. Your message should sound sincere while written in your own style. Write naturally, as if you are having a conversation.

Instead of	Say
I have pleasuring in informing you	I am pleased to tell you
We do not anticipate any increase in prices	We do not expect prices to rise
I should be grateful if you would be good enough to advise us	Please let me know
Please favour us with a prompt reply	I hope to receive a prompt reply
Please revert to us soonest	I hope to hear from you soon

5 Remember the KISS principle

Business people today have many documents to read. A message that is direct and straight to the point – while retaining courtesy – will be appreciated. As you work on developing your writing ability, you should constantly practise your KISSing skills. KISS stands for:

Keep

It

Short and

Simple

KISS means instead of long or complex words, use short ones:

Instead of	Say
commence	start
regarding	about
purchase	buy
utilise	use
require	need
endeavour, attempt	try
terminate	end
state	say
expedite	hurry, speed up
advise, inform	tell
visualise	see
despatch	send
assist	help
sufficient	enough
kindly	please

KISS also means instead of long phrases, use one word where appropriate:

I should be glad if you would	please
in spite of the fact that	despite
with regard to	about
at the present moment in time	now
conduct an investigation	investigate
in view of the fact that	as ... because
in the event that	if
in the very near future	soon
at a later date	later
we would like to ask you to	please

Research has been conducted into the degree of understanding of sentences of different lengths. Take a look at these figures:

Number of words in the sentence	Percentage of people who will understand on the first reading
7–10 words	95%
15–20 words	75%
27 words or more	4%

You can meet the KISS objectives by using sentences that contain 7–20 words.

For an excellent website containing lots of information about words, punctuation, grammar, usage, dictionary, thesaurus, etc, check out Merriem-Webster Online.

www.m-w.com

Avoid these phrases altogether:

I have noticed that
It has come to my attention that
I am pleased to inform you that
I am writing to let you know that
I must inform you that
Please be informed that
Please be advised that
Thanking you in anticipation
Thank you and regards
Kindest regards

If you include stuffy formalities in your business writing, you will obscure the meaning and make sentences intolerably long. The reader will end up searching for the real meaning in your haystack of rhetoric.

6 Use modern terminology

Old-fashioned phrases add nothing to your meaning. Such unnecessary, long-winded phrases are likely to give a poor impression of the writer and may even lead to confusion. A good business message will use no more words than are necessary to convey a clear and accurate message.

Instead of	Say
We are in receipt of your letter of 12 June	Thank you for your letter of 12 June
We have received your letter of 12 June	Thank you for your letter of 12 June
Enclosed herewith you will find ... Please find enclosed ...	I enclose ...
Please be good enough to advise me ...	Please let me know ...
Please be reminded ...	Please remember ...
... the above-mentioned goods	... these goods

TIP Today's business language should be proactive, stimulating, interesting and, most of all, it should reflect your personality.

7 Include essential details

If the recipient of your message must ask a question, or if something is unclear, then something has been omitted from your message. Do not leave anything to chance. Include all essential information.

Instead of	*Say*
My flight arrives at 3.30 on Wednesday.	My flight BA 121 from London Heathrow should arrive at Singapore Changi Airport at 1530 on Wednesday 12 June.
I thoroughly enjoyed your article in last month's newsletter.	I thoroughly enjoyed your article on *feng shui* in last month's company newsletter.
Our Sales Manager will contact you soon.	Mr John Matthews, our Sales Manager, will contact you soon.

Be consistent

Consistency is not only important in the way your message is presented, it is important within the message itself.

Instead of	*Say*
The people attending will be John Wilson, G Turner, Mandy Harrison and Bob from Sales.	The people attending the next committee meeting will be John Wilson, Gloria Turner, Mandy Harrison and Bob Turner.
I confirm my reservation of a single room on 16/7 and a double room on 17 Oct.	I confirm my reservation of a single room on 16 July and a double room on 17 October.

9 Use active not passive voice

'Voice' is a grammatical term that refers to whether the subject of the sentence is acting or receiving the action. Using active voice can considerably improve your writing style. Active voice makes your writing more interesting, more lively and more ... well, active!

Check out these two examples of a similar message:

Active voice: Tim played the violin.

Here, the subject is the actor, Tim. You can almost see Tim playing the violin, totally absorbed in his music. The sentence is alive and interesting.

Passive voice: The violin was played by Tim.

Here, the subject is the violin. The action is gone. The emphasis has been moved from the subject performing the action to the subject receiving the action. It is not so easy to visualise what is happening. The sentence is dull and boring.

Here are some tips that may help you to tell when a sentence is passive:

- Watch for sentences that start with the action rather than the actor. Sentences that start with the action are often passive.
- Watch for various forms of the verb 'to be' such as – is, are, was, were, will be, have been, should be, etc. These verbs may not always indicate that the sentence is passive, but they often give you a clue.

Passive voice was preferred by our great-grandfathers because they did not want to show any responsibility in their writing. It also created a distance between the writer and the reader. Yes, passive voice was perfect for our great-grandfathers.

Our writing today, however, should show responsibility, and it should be more personal and natural, more focused. Remember my golden rule 'If you wouldn't say it, don't write it!'

Instead of	*Say*
The design of our new systems was simplified by the use of hydraulics.	The use of hydraulics simplified the design of our new systems.
The new system was developed by our staff.	Our staff developed the new system.
The investigation has been concluded by our client, and the paperwork has been signed.	Our client has concluded the investigation and signed the paperwork.
The cheque was presented to the charity by the Prince of Wales.	The Prince of Wales presented the cheque to the charity.

 Use active voice in your writing. This is more alive, more focused, more personal – much more interesting and a lot clearer.

Is passive voice ever appropriate? Yes, there are some occasions when passive voice would be more appropriate.

- It may be better to make a particularly important noun the subject of the sentence, thus giving it extra emphasis.

  Example: It would be better to say:

  Our restaurant has been recommended by all the leading hotels in Singapore.

  This emphasises 'our restaurant' rather than:

  All the leading hotels in Singapore recommend our service.

- When you want to place the focus on the action, not the actor.

  Example: *The noise was heard all over the island.*
  Here, the emphasis is on the noise, not the people who made the noise.

- When you want to hide something or when tact is important.

  Example: *An unfortunate mistake was made.*

10 Compose CLEAR communications

Finally, when writing any message ask yourself whether it meets these CLEAR objectives. Your message should be:

Clear   Leave no doubt in your reader's mind. Help yourself by being specific, avoiding vague expressions, using familiar words and using simple English. Remember also to use straightforward language that your reader can understand, written in a friendly, natural, conversational style.

Logical   Structure your messages logically, remembering to use the 4 point plan. Start with an introduction, develop your points logically in the central section, and come to a natural conclusion in which you state the action you need from the reader. Finish with an appropriate one-liner.

Empathetic   Put yourself in your reader's place and ask yourself how the reader will feel when he/she reads your message. If anything is unclear, or if anything is worded badly, then change it before you send it.

Accurate   Make sure all the relevant details are included – times, dates, names, facts and figures.

Right   Proofread carefully (not just spell check!) to make sure everything is 100% right before you send the message.

 One error is too many.

 This letter is full of old-fashioned jargon, standard clichés, passive voice and long-winded writing. Can you identify everything that is wrong with it?

Dear Sirs,

We have received your letter dated 27 March 2003.

We are extremely distressed to learn that an error was made pertaining to your esteemed order. Please be informed that the cause of your complaint has been investigated and it actually appears that the error occurred in our packing section and it was not discerned before this order was despatched to your goodself.

Arrangements have been made for a repeat order to be despatched to you immediately and this should leave our warehouse later today. It is our sincere hope that you will have no cause for further complaint with this replacement order.

Once again we offer our humblest apologies for the unnecessary inconvenience that you have been caused in this instance.

Please find enclosed herewith a copy of our new catalogue for your reference and perusal.

Kindly contact the undersigned if you require any further clarifications.

Very truly yours,

Zachariah Creep & Partners

 When you are writing, ask yourself whether you would say this if you were speaking to the recipient. Eliminate useless jargon by writing as you would speak.

 Here is the same letter written in modern terminology.

Dear Mr Tan

YOUR ORDER NUMBER TH 2457

Thank you for your letter of 27 March.

I am very sorry to hear about the mistake made with your order. I have looked into this and found that the mistake happened in the packing section. Unfortunately it was not discovered before the goods were sent to you.

I have arranged for a repeat order to be sent to you today, and I hope this meets your requirements.

Once again, please accept my apologies for the inconvenience caused.

I enclose a copy of our new catalogue and I hope you find it interesting.

Please give me a call soon on 2358272 if you have any questions.

Yours sincerely

 The key to good business writing is to write in a natural style, as if you were having a conversation.

 To learn more about business writing yesterday and today, check out the Links to Learning section of my website.

www.shirleytaylor.com/learninglinks.html

CHECKLIST

Before signing or sending any written message, ask yourself the following questions:

- [ ] Do you believe what you are saying? Does it sound like you believe it? Will the reader understand it?

- [ ] Have you used simple words and simple expressions?

- [ ] Have you avoided wordiness while remembering the need for courtesy?

- [ ] Is your tone conversational and natural, as if you were speaking?

- [ ] Have you used the right tone for the issue you are writing about and for the person you are addressing?

- [ ] Have you used any old-fashioned language or jargon that should be removed?

- [ ] Is your document structured logically in accordance with the 4 point plan?

- [ ] Is everything consistent? This means style (I, we, etc) as well as layout (fully blocked style with open punctuation). Does it look attractive and well-displayed?

- [ ] Are the spelling, punctuation and grammar correct?

- [ ] Have you included all the essential information? Have you double checked all the facts and figures? Is everything clear and unambiguous?

For a fabulous site about how to write in plain English without lots of jargon and gobbledegook, check out the Plain English Campaign:

www.plainenglish.co.uk

E-mail

The explosive growth of e-mail

7 deadly sins of working with e-mail

The good, the bad and the ugly of e-mail

The weakest link in your e-mails

How can you make e-mail work for you? 4.1–5

Customer care and e-mail

Creating electronic rapport 4.6–8

E-mail @ work 4.9–12

Netiquette

Checklist

THE EXPLOSIVE GROWTH OF E-MAIL

Electronic mail is possibly the greatest invention of my lifetime. It is having a phenomenal effect on the way we communicate. E-mail is not just a quick, easy and relatively cheap way to keep in touch with family and friends, it has also become an essential tool in business, a fundamental part of the way in which we work.

However, the explosive growth of e-mail has created some problems, mainly because there have never been any strict standards or guidelines on how to use it. Hundreds of new users sign on every day without being exposed to the informal online culture that has evolved over the years. There has never been one definitive guide to common standards and expectations among e-mail users. Consequently systems have been overloaded, miscommunication has been rampant, reputations have been damaged, feelings have been hurt and time has been wasted.

Another consideration is that because of the apparent informality of e-mail, things are often written in an e-mail message that would not be written in a business letter. This can have serious implications for some businesses, which may find themselves facing legal action.

Businesses are now realising the importance of protecting themselves against the dangers of e-mail. However, this is not enough. They must also take steps to ensure that e-mail works effectively for them. This section will take you through the good, the bad and the ugly of e-mail, and will help you to make e-mail work for you. You will learn how to enhance your online communication skills and create a good electronic rapport with your customers and colleagues.

7 DEADLY SINS OF WORKING WITH E-MAIL

Before we start, read these statements and tick the boxes that apply to you. If you tick more than a couple of these items, you need help with your e-mail!

1 Your e-mail messages often bounce back because of an error in the address. ☐

2 You sometimes wish you could backtrack after sending a message, but it's too late. ☐

3 You are frequently interrupted throughout the day with a constant flow of e-mails. ☐

4 You have sometimes sent messages via e-mail when you know a telephone call would have been better. ☐

5 You haven't done any housekeeping or deleted any messages for a long time. ☐

6 You have sent private or confidential messages via e-mail, which you have later regretted. ☐

7 You sometimes send messages off quickly without a greeting or a sign-off, and without checking through for good grammar, spelling and punctuation. ☐

 TIP **If you have written a message in anger, leave it in your outbox for at least an hour. Then go back and look at it again. If you still feel the same way and want to send it, do so.**

THE GOOD, THE BAD AND THE UGLY OF E-MAIL

There are many reasons to love (and to hate) e-mail.

Why do we love it?	Why do we hate it?
It's informal	Has it become too informal?
Messages can be sent to many people at the click of a button	Do we receive too many e-mails just because it is so easy?
You can attach a file and send it very easily	If we aren't careful we may download a file that contains a virus; also large files take a longer download time
It's instant – messages are delivered in seconds	It can be too instant (have you ever clicked 'send' and then wished you could retrieve it?)
It's relatively cheap	We receive lots of junk mail (spam)
It's time-zone friendly	Lots of people send ccs and bccs just because they can – not because we need to see them
It can be prioritised. You decide which e-mail to read first when you open your mail	There's a pressure to reply quickly to e-mails
	It means constant interruptions to your working day, so it interferes with your planned work
	There is no confidentiality
	It causes an increase in stress levels. One of the main causes of workplace stress is the pressure of keeping up with e-mail messages
	It spells the death of conversation – workers are sending e-mails to people sitting at the next desk instead of walking over and speaking to them

 Once your message is sent, it may be read by the recipient within seconds. You cannot call it back for second thoughts. So proofread it carefully before you click 'send'.

THE WEAKEST LINK IN YOUR E-MAILS

When I talk to my workshop participants I often ask them what annoys them most about e-mail. Here is my compilation of the top 10 weakest links that I would like to eliminate from e-mail writing.

1 Wrong time and date

It can be very confusing if your computer doesn't have the correct time and date set. Help to keep a track of your messages, and help everyone else too, by setting the time and date correctly.

2 Vague subject line

Readers with huge inboxes will not open your 'Urgent' or 'Enquiry'. Compose a SMART subject line:

S pecific

M eaningful

A ppropriate

R elevant

T houghtful

 What you put in your subject line can often mean the difference between whether your message is read right now, today, tomorrow, next week or never!

3 No greeting and no sign off

Many people dislike receiving messages without these courtesies. There are 2 main reasons for a greeting (Hello Sally, Hi Sally, Dear Mr Lim). Firstly it is just plain courteous, and secondly it's confirmation to the reader that the message is for them and not just a cc or bcc. Two good reasons for a sign off are firstly again for courtesy, and secondly it is confirmation that the message is finished. Simple!

4 Poor formatting

Readers get confused when a message is very long but there are no paragraphs. Messages can become garbled if you don't think and format in paragraphs. Help your reader and help yourself by formatting your messages attractively and putting a blank space between paragraphs.

5 Vague messages

Probably connected with number 4, people complain that many of the messages they receive are vague so that they don't know the reason for the message or what, if anything, they are required to do. Take some time to compose your message carefully, then check through to make sure it is reader-friendly, then check it again before you click 'send'.

6 Hunting for the response

Again linked with 4 and 5, if a message becomes garbled and poorly structured, the reader is left reading the message over and over again and wondering what response is required. Remember the 3 Rs – you must guide your Reader towards the Response expected, otherwise you can never be sure of achieving the right Results.

7 Unfriendly tone

Emotions are hard to convey in e-mails, and some people type out exactly what they would say without thinking of the tone of voice that would be used to signal their emotions. With e-mail all we have are words. Without the right tone, misunderstandings could easily happen, or you could offend and perhaps lose an important business contact – or even a friend! Good writers learn to choose their words carefully and get the tone just right.

8 CC to the whole world

It's become too easy to cc anyone and everyone, so that's what many people do. This results in overflowing inboxes and a lot of time wasted. So send a cc only to people who need to know, not to everyone you know.

9 Bad grammar, spelling and punctuation

As more people use e-mail, sloppy work is becoming a major annoyance. People are receiving poorly formatted messages in one continuous paragraph, poorly structured messages that are not specific in the response required, messages written all in capitals (equivalent to SHOUTING) or all in lower case, and of course messages with poor grammar, spelling and punctuation.

10 Just plain SLOPPY

When I did some research into e-mail I found that most people complained of the need to reply immediately to e-mails just because they are e-mails. Because of this urgency, many writers are not taking as much care. Rushed messages often become garbled, spelling errors creep in, the structure doesn't flow right. Readers don't understand the messages, or are offended by them, and quite simply they are not effective. The messages are just plain sloppy. One friend said to me: 'When I receive a message with lots of errors, poor spelling, poor formatting, etc, I think the writer has no RESPECT for me because he/she couldn't take just one minute to check it through before clicking "SEND"!' Have some respect for YOUR reader in future please! It only takes a minute.

The Internet has made it possible for us to communicate with people from all over the world. The only way those people can form an opinion of us is by looking at the way we write. Your credibility could be ruined with one swift click of the 'send' button.

HOW CAN YOU MAKE E-MAIL WORK FOR YOU?

4.1 Turn off the instant messaging system

Someone once told me that every time they receive a new e-mail, their instant messager shouts 'Yabadabadoo!' just like in the Flintstones! Whether you have a ping, a bing, a bong or a Yabadabadoo, for goodness sake turn it off occasionally. Don't let e-mail take over your life. When you have an important project to work on, switch off your instant messaging system.

4.2 Don't feel obliged to give a detailed reply

If you are pushed for time and cannot reply immediately, don't feel compelled to do so. This will only result in a rushed message, perhaps mistakes, and perhaps it will not be as detailed or effective as it could be. Instead send a quick note saying you will get back to the writer soon with a more considered response. This way the writer knows you have received the message and are dealing with it.

4.3 Send a cc to those who need to know, not to everyone you know

If we are suffering from overflowing inboxes, how much of it is self-inflicted? Has it become too easy to send messages to lots of people just because you can? We must learn to use e-mail more thoughtfully by recognising when we should and should not send messages. Do you really need to send all those cc, bcc and fwd copies? If you receive lots of messages that you don't really need to see, tell the authors so that it doesn't happen again.

4.4 Set up filters on your e-mail system

Filters help you by sending your messages to different folders according to the sender and the subject matter. They will also delete unwanted messages. Some filters will highlight key messages with priority codes or colours.

Don't panic – you can always pick up the phone

Have you ever been involved in a prolonged e-mail exchange that lasts for days? Wouldn't it be better to pick up the phone? E-mail overload is contributing to a decline in oral communication skills – people send e-mails to the person in the next office rather than walk a few steps! So please remember that it's good to talk and don't let e-mail result in the death of conversation.

TIP **If you become involved in a prolonged e-mail exchange, wouldn't it be better to pick up the phone?**

CUSTOMER CARE AND E-MAIL

Everyone today is in the business of providing customer service. If you don't pay good attention to customer care skills in everything that you do, you can be sure your customers will take their business somewhere else. And everything you do involves e-mail.

Studies show that it takes just 15 seconds for your customer to judge you when you first meet and greet him or her. During those 15 seconds your customer will decide whether they will listen to you, believe you and trust you. More important, those 15 seconds will determine whether they will buy from you.

The first impression a customer receives is influenced by three things: body language, tone of voice and words. It may surprise you to know what impact these three areas have on a customer when you meet or talk for the first time. Figure 4.1 shows clearly that it's your body language that is most important – it's how we say things that people pay more attention to. But in e-mail you don't have the benefit of body language. All you have are words and tone. You have to learn how to use only these two aspects to create your own e-mail body language. When you learn to do this you will be making a real connection – and that's what good customer care is all about.

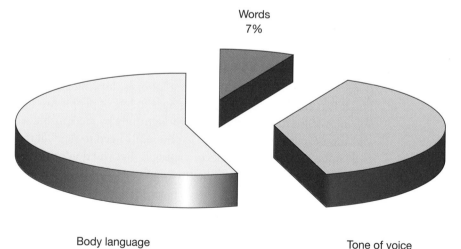

Figure 4.1 Impact of first impressions

TIP **Try to create a special bond with all your customers as well as with your colleagues.**

 For an interesting site on e-mail, check out Mary Houton-Kemp's Everything E-mail.
www.everythingemail.net

Compare these two e-mail messages and decide which one you think is going to help to give a better impression and create a better bond.

Dear John
Thanks for your e-mail. I'm glad your complaint has been sorted out. Please let me know if you need further assistance.
Regards
Mary Tan

Hi John

Thanks for your e-mail.

I'm really pleased that we have been able to find a solution to this problem. Good luck with future progress.

I'll be here when you decide on how we can help you again.

Mary

CREATING ELECTRONIC RAPPORT

Putting into practice the principles of good customer care is easier in person than on the telephone because a real person can be seen and heard. It's easier on the telephone than on e-mail because even without seeing the person you can hear them and the tone of voice used – and yes, you can hear a smile in a voice. On e-mail you haven't got either of these advantages, so you have to take other steps to try to create electronic rapport with customers as well as colleagues. Here are some techniques you can use.

4.6 **Lead the reader into the message**

Try not to just dive into a message blindly. Ease the reader into the message by backtracking or giving some basic background information. Be warm and friendly in your opening where appropriate:

- Thanks for lunch last week. It gave us a good opportunity to learn more about your new project, which sounds very interesting.
- I am glad we were able to speak on the telephone this morning. It was good to clarify this issue.
- Thanks for calling me today. It made a nice change to speak to a real person for once instead of always using e-mail.
- Your news today is interesting – it sounds like you've been working really hard to ensure the success of this project.

4.7 Show emotions

Some people give just the mere facts and only the facts. We are so keen to get straight to the point that we forget to include any emotions, any feelings. Try to remember that emotive and sensory words add texture and dimension to the general message of what you are writing. You owe it to your customers and colleagues to show empathy through your e-mail, using language that will help you to form a better bond. For example:

- I'll be pleased to help you sort out this problem.
- I appreciate your understanding in trying to resolve this issue.
- I hope I can shed some light on this problem very soon.
- I see what you mean and can appreciate your concern.
- This has shown me a clearer perspective and I can see a true picture now.
- I am happy to offer you an extra discount of 5% in the circumstances.

 Don't add so much that you come over as too gushy. You need only a few words to really add something extra to your message and show some extra warmth.

4.8 Use a visual language

Try to paint a picture of what you are communicating. The reader will then be able to see the image that you are trying to create. Use phrases like:

- I can see what you mean.
- This is all quite clear to me now.
- This will now enable us to focus on our mutual goals.
- Your suggestions look good.

 Identify with your reader, appreciate their feelings, and use words they will understand, written in an appropriate tone.

E-MAIL @ WORK

Let's take a look at some e-mails and comment on the good and the bad points.

This is a poor subject line. Be specific

Hi is OK, but use a capital letter

Abbreviations like these are only suitable for mobile phone text messages, not for your e-mails

Use capital letters

Don't abbreviate, and do use initial capitals

Capitals is like shouting, and considered rude

Check your spelling – I think the writer means 'signing'!

Avoid abbreviations like this at the close

From	Harry.Lim@presto.co.my
Date	25:7:03 16:06:29
To	shirley@shirleytaylor.com
CC	
Subject	HELLO!!!!

hi Shirley

Hope things r well with u its good 2 know that u will be back in malaysia again

in nov to hold your seminar on effective biz writing. PLS LET ME HAVE SOME FREE DATE while u r over here. some bookstores r interested ina talk cum singing event, I hope u will agree to take part.

tnks & rgs
Harry

TIP Don't use capitals in e-mail messages. They imply SHOUTING AND AGGRESSION and they are not polite.

From	Harry.Lim@presto.co.my
Date	25:7:03 16:06:29
To	shirley@shirleytaylor.com
CC	
Subject	Book signing in Malaysia

Here is a SMART subject line

A nice opening paragraph, and clear line spaces between paragraphs

No abbreviations and no code

The message is structured in accordance with the 4 point plan

A nice close finishes off the message nicely

Hello Shirley

I hope things are well with you.

I was pleased to hear that you will be back in Malaysia again in November to hold your seminar on Effective Business Writing.

Some bookstores are interested in asking you to do a talk and signing event. I hope you will agree to take part. If so, please let me have some free dates while you are over here.

See you soon.

Harry

TIP Effective communication gives a professional impression of you and of your organisation. Effective communication helps to get things done.

To learn more about how you can e-mail your way to the top, check out the Links to Learnning section of my website:

www.shirleytaylor.com/learninglinks.html

4.9 A simple, informal e-mail

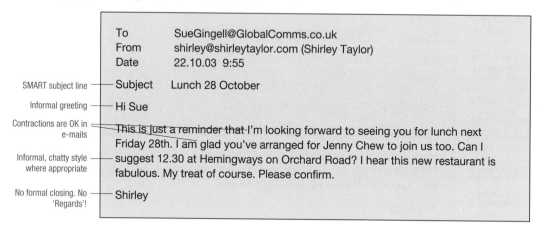

To	SueGingell@GlobalComms.co.uk
From	shirley@shirleytaylor.com (Shirley Taylor)
Date	22.10.03 9:55

SMART subject line — Subject   Lunch 28 October

Informal greeting — Hi Sue

Contractions are OK in e-mails — This is just a reminder that I'm looking forward to seeing you for lunch next Friday 28th. I am glad you've arranged for Jenny Chew to join us too. Can I suggest 12.30 at Hemingways on Orchard Road? I hear this new restaurant is fabulous. My treat of course. Please confirm.

Informal, chatty style where appropriate

No formal closing. No 'Regards'! — Shirley

4.10 A slightly more formal e-mail

To	RosehannahWethern@Pioneer.co.sg
From	shirley@shirleytaylor.com (Shirley Taylor)
Date	14.8.04 14:30
Subject	Customer Services Training

This style is slightly less informal — Dear Rosehannah

We are considering sending some of our staff on a training course on Customer Services. Do you have a suitable course available within the next few months? If so please let me have the dates and times plus costs.

Short sentences, no 'padding'

Short paragraphs, with a space between each — If there isn't a regular Pioneer course scheduled, can you tailor-make a course specially for our staff? We could hold it in our conference room.

Write in a casual style, as if you were speaking — Perhaps we can arrange to meet to discuss this – are you free next Friday 20 August at 11 am? I could come over to you, or you could come over to my office. Please let me know.

Shirley Taylor
Project Manager
Shirley Taylor Training and Consultancy
A standard 'signature block' — Tel: +65 64726076 Fax: +65 63392710
Mobile: +65 96355907
http://www.shirleytaylor.com

4.11 E-mail following up a meeting

Look at how this e-mail message meets the requirements of the:

- SMART subject line
- 4 point plan.

From	georgiathomas@aurorasuperstores.co.uk
Date	10:7:04 11:35:14
To	lilymcbeal@healthylife.com
CC	richardcage@aurorasuperstores.co.uk
A SMART subject line — Subject	Eating for Health Campaign

Dear Lily

Introduction — It was good to meet you again last week. As discussed, I would like to invite you to give the opening speech at the launch of our Healthy Eating Campaign. This will be held at our Leeds superstore on Monday 8 August.

Details — Richard and I are very excited about this campaign. We are hoping it will make the public more aware of the importance of choosing a variety of fresh fruit and vegetables as part of their daily diet.

Action — I am attaching a provisional programme, from which you will see that 10 minutes has been allocated for the opening speech at 9.30 am. We will be happy to arrange your transport to and from our superstore on launch day.

Close — I know that your high profile in this industry would bring the crowds flocking to this launch. We hope you will decide to join us.

Best wishes

Georgia Thomas
Marketing Manager
Aurora Superstores Ltd
Telephone +44 114 2888724
Mobile +44 7770 2342342
www.aurora.com

TIP **When you send an e-mail, it's your responsibility to make sure it is opened, read and acted upon. Composing a clear and specific subject line will help you to achieve this aim.**

TIP In today's fast-paced business world, there is no room for yesterday's old-fashioned jargon.

E-mail where tone is important

 E-mails are often typed and sent very quickly, without paying much thought to appropriate tone. The following e-mail is from an Administration Executive in the Accounts Department to the Manager of the Sales Department.

Read the e-mail and consider how you would feel if you were the recipient.

From	sallyturner@rightway.com
Date	25:7:03 16:06:29
To	johnwong@rightway.com
Subject	REMINDER!!!

John

Appreciate if you would consider and bear in mind that I am no longer responsible for dealing with petty cash. Some of your staffs keep bringing their vouchers to me, but this responsibility has been taken over by Martin in Accounts, he is the one who should be contacted henceforth for all petty cash matters.

Your co-operation is appreciated in making sure all your staffs know about this.

BRgs/Sally

Annotations (left margin):
- This subject line is sure to irritate the reader
- The wording is very abrupt and harsh
- This comma should be a full stop
- 'Henceforth' is very old fashioned
- This statement is sure to cause aggravation
- This close is very abrupt, and staff does not have an 's'
- Don't be lazy with your closings

 Here is the same e-mail written in a more appropriate tone.

From	sallyturner@rightway.com
Date	25:7:03 16:06:29
To	johnwong@rightway.com
Subject	Petty Cash Vouchers

Hi John

Some of the staff from your department are still bringing their petty cash vouchers to me. However this responsibility was taken over by Martin in Accounts last month.

Please inform your staff that they should deal with Martin in future.

Thanks for your help John.

Sally

NETIQUETTE

In personal relationships the conventions of behaviour are called etiquette. In e-mail we have netiquette – a set of rules for e-mail that have evolved from experience. Here are my top tips for better netiquette:

Never think you're talking to a computer!

There's a real live person at the other end. Remember that when you consider the wording, style and tone of your message.

Ensure you follow the rules of good writing.

Just as a business letter is an ambassador for your company, so is your e-mail. Don't allow the speed and ease of e-mail to make your messages abrupt, abbreviated and error-filled. Write your messages with care, considering all the rules of modern business writing.

Take off the caps lock. DON'T SHOUT!

Even though you want to get noticed, please do not use capitals in e-mail messages – this is like shouting, it is rude and will usually be counter-productive. And also ... NEVER RESORT TO EXCESSIVE PUNCTUA-TION*@!!**?!!!!

Informality is OK in e-mails.

Replace formal salutations like 'Dear Leslie' with 'Hi Leslie' or even just 'Leslie'. Similarly, replace 'Yours sincerely' with 'Best wishes' or some other informal closing.

Question your subject heading.

People are most likely to read important-looking e-mails first. Give your messages a clear and specific subject heading.

Use short sentences and short paragraphs.

The shorter your messages, the more likely it is that they will be read and understood. But do not make them so short that they are abrupt or unclear. Use full sentences and explain clearly. Remember to paragraph just the same as in other business documents.

Enumerate with numbers or bullets.

Present your messages attractively. Use numbers, bullets or sub-headings if possible – this will add to the clarity of your message.

Tidy up long sentences.

Tapping away at the keyboard as you think, it is easy to allow sentences to become too long. Read through your message carefully and improve clarity and understanding.

Take a pride in your finished message.

Make sure your message is accurate, brief and clear as well as attractively presented. In this way it will be understood and will achieve the desired results.

Ensure everything is right before you hit 'send'.

You cannot call an e-mail back for second thoughts, so get it right first time!

 TIP If you want to improve your electronic rapport with customers and colleagues, if you want to enhance your credibility and your reputation as well as your productivity, remember – it's not a computer you're talking to. it's a real live human being.

CHECKLIST

☐ Write a SMART subject line after you've written your message.

☐ Include an appropriate greeting and closing section.

☐ Use modern business language and simple sentences instead of old-fashioned, long-winded writing.

☐ Never use ALL CAPITALS for any part of your message.

☐ Learn the importance of structuring your messages logically.

☐ Write as if you are having a conversation with the recipient.

☐ Consider the other person's feelings and make sure you use appropriate tone.

☐ Format messages attractively, using full words, full sentences, and with a space between each paragraph.

☐ Use e-mail as a tool to enhance communication – not as a replacement for communication.

☐ If an e-mail exchange is getting rather long or complicated, it may be more effective to pick up the phone.

Unit 2

Routine business documents

Enquiries and replies

Enquiries for information about goods or services are sent and received in business all the time. In a routine letter of enquiry follow these guidelines:

1 State clearly and concisely what you want – general information, a catalogue, price list, sample, quotation, etc.

2 If there is a limit to the price at which you are prepared to buy, do not mention this otherwise the supplier may raise the quotation to the limit you state.

3 Most suppliers state their terms of payment when replying so there is no need for you to ask for them unless you are hoping for special rates.

4 Keep your enquiry brief and concise.

Enquiries mean potential business, so they must be acknowledged promptly. If it is from an established customer, say how much you appreciate it; if it is from a prospective customer, say you are glad to receive it and express the hope of a lasting and friendly business relationship.

REQUESTS FOR CATALOGUES AND PRICE LISTS

5.1 Routine requests where formal reply is unnecessary

Suppliers receive many *routine requests*[1] for catalogues and price lists. Unless the writer requests information not already included, a written reply is often not necessary, and a *'with compliments' slip*[2] may be sent instead. In the following enquiries, written replies are not necessary. The items requested may be sent under cover of a 'with compliments' slip.

Example 1

> Dear Sir/Madam
>
> Please send me a copy of your catalogue and price list of fax machines, together with copies of any descriptive leaflets that I could pass to prospective customers[3].
>
> Yours faithfully

---

[1] **routine requests** requests of an everyday nature
[2] **with compliments slip** a small printed note containing the company's name, address, contact numbers and the wording 'With compliments'
[3] **prospective customers** people who may be expected to buy

Example 2

Dear Sir/Madam

I have seen one of your safes in the office of a local firm and they passed on your address to me.

Please send me a copy of your current catalogue. I am particularly interested in safes suitable for a small office.

Yours faithfully

5.2 Potentially large business

Where an enquiry suggests that large or regular orders are possible, a 'with compliments' slip is not enough. Instead write a letter and take the opportunity to promote your products.

(a) Enquiry

Dear Sir/Madam

I have a large hardware store in Southampton and am interested in the electric heaters you are advertising in the West Country Gazette.

Please send me your illustrated catalogue and a price list.

Yours faithfully

(b) Reply

Dear Mrs Johnson

Thank you — Thank you for your letter enquiring about electric heaters. I am pleased to enclose a copy of our latest illustrated catalogue.

Provide further information about specific goods and refer to information in catalogue — You may be particularly interested in our newest heater, the FX21 model. Without any increase in fuel consumption, it gives out 15% more heat than earlier models. You will find details of our terms in the price list printed on the inside front cover of the catalogue.

Suggest action for recipient to take — Perhaps you would consider placing a trial order to provide you with an opportunity to test its efficiency. At the same time this would enable you to see for yourself the high quality of material and finish put into this model.

Appropriate close — If you have any questions please contact me on 6234917.

Yours sincerely

5.3 Requests for advice

A written reply is necessary when the enquiry suggests that the writer would welcome advice or guidance.

(a) Enquiry

> Dear Sir/Madam
>
> Please send me a copy of your current typewriter catalogue and price list. I am particularly interested in purchasing an electronic typewriter with a memory and single-line display.
>
> Yours faithfully

(b) Reply

Thank you —

Enclose the requested catalogue —

Provide further details regarding the specific enquiry —

Close by suggesting a demonstration —

> Dear Mr Freeman
>
> Thank you for your enquiry dated 8 February.
>
> I have pleasure in enclosing the catalogue of typewriters as you requested. This includes details of a number of electronic typewriters by various manufacturers.
>
> As you mention your requirement for a memory, have you considered a dedicated word processor? You will find details on pages 15–25, and will see from the price list that prices of the smaller models compare very reasonably with electronic typewriters.
>
> If you would like demonstrations of any of the models in the catalogue, I would be happy to arrange for our representative to call on you whenever convenient.
>
> Yours sincerely

 TIP A clear style projects an efficient image, so choose your words carefully.

5.4 Enquiries through recommendations

When writing to a supplier who has been recommended, it may be to your advantage to mention the fact.

(a) Enquiry

Dear Sir/Madam

My neighbour, Mr W Stevens of 29 High Street, Derby, recently bought an electric lawnmower from you. He is delighted with the machine and has recommended that I contact you.

I need a similar machine, but smaller, and should be glad if you would send me a copy of your catalogue and any other information that will help me to make the best choice for my purpose.

Yours faithfully

(b) Reply

Dear Mrs Garson

I enclose a catalogue and price list of our lawnmowers, as requested in your letter of 18 May.

The machine bought by your friend was a 38 cm RANSOME' which is an excellent machine. You will find details of the smaller size of 30 cm shown on page 15 of the catalogue. Alternatively, smaller than this is the PANTHER JUNIOR shown on page 17.

We have both these models in stock and should be glad to show them to you if you would care to call at our showroom.

Please contact me on 2314679 if I can provide any further help.

Yours sincerely

5.5 Requests for samples

A request for a sample of goods provides the supplier with an excellent opportunity to present products to advantage. A reply should be convincing, giving confidence in the products.

(a) Enquiry

Dear Sirs

We have received a number of enquiries for floor coverings suitable for use on the rough floors which seem to be a feature of much of the new building taking place in this region.

It would be helpful if you could send us samples showing your range of suitable coverings. A pattern-card of the designs in which they are supplied would also be very useful.

Yours faithfully

(b) Reply

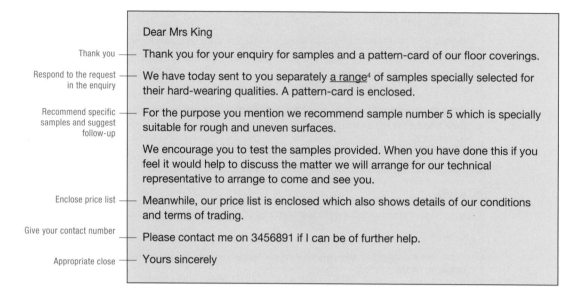

Thank you — Dear Mrs King

Thank you — Thank you for your enquiry for samples and a pattern-card of our floor coverings.

Respond to the request in the enquiry — We have today sent to you separately a range[4] of samples specially selected for their hard-wearing qualities. A pattern-card is enclosed.

Recommend specific samples and suggest follow-up — For the purpose you mention we recommend sample number 5 which is specially suitable for rough and uneven surfaces.

We encourage you to test the samples provided. When you have done this if you feel it would help to discuss the matter we will arrange for our technical representative to arrange to come and see you.

Enclose price list — Meanwhile, our price list is enclosed which also shows details of our conditions and terms of trading.

Give your contact number — Please contact me on 3456891 if I can be of further help.

Appropriate close — Yours sincerely

GENERAL ENQUIRIES AND REPLIES

When writing a general letter of enquiry be sure to be specific in the details required, e.g. prices, delivery details, terms of payment. When replying to an enquiry, be sure you have answered every query in the letter of enquiry.

5.6 An enquiry for office equipment

(a) Enquiry

Dear Sir/Madam

Please send me details of fax machines which you supply, together with prices.

We need a model suitable for sending complex diagrams and printed messages, mostly within the UK.

Yours faithfully

---

[4] **a range** a representative collection

(b) Reply

Dear Mrs Rawson

In reply to your enquiry I have pleasure in enclosing a leaflet showing our latest fax machines.

All the models illustrated can be supplied from stock at competitive prices as shown on the price list inside the catalogue.

May I suggest a visit to our showrooms where you could see demonstrations of the various machines and at the same time view our wide range of office equipment.

Yours sincerely

(c) Request for demonstration

Dear Mr Jenkinson

I have studied with interest the literature you sent me with your letter of 28 April.

Our Administration Manager, Mr Gordon Tan, would like to visit your showrooms to see a demonstration and report on which machine would be most suitable for our purposes. Can we arrange this for next Friday 6 May at 3.30 pm? If this is inconvenient please call me on 2916347.

Yours sincerely

5.7 An enquiry with numbered points

When you have many points on which information is required, it may be useful to number the various points.

(a) Enquiry

Dear Sir/Madam

Background information regarding the enquiry

During a recent visit to the Ideal Home Exhibition I saw a sample of your plastic tile flooring. I think this type of flooring would be suitable for the ground floor of my house, but I have not been able to find anyone who is familiar with such tiling.

Would you please give me the following information:

Numbered points are used for specific questions

1   What special preparation would be necessary for the underflooring?

2   In what colours and designs can the tiles be supplied?

3   Are the tiles likely to be affected by rising damp?

4   Would it be necessary to employ a specialist to lay the floor? If so, can you recommend one in my area?

I should appreciate your advice on these matters.

Close with action required

Yours faithfully

(b) Reply

Dear Mr Wilson

Thank you
Enclose brochure — Thank you for your enquiry of 18 August regarding our plastic tile flooring. A copy of our brochure is enclosed showing the designs and range of colours in which the tiles are supplied.

Give details of local — Bottomline, 22 The Square, Rugby, is a very reliable firm which carries out all our
specialist work in your area. I have asked the company to get in touch with you to inspect your floors. Their consultant will be able to advise you on what preparation is necessary and whether dampness is likely to cause a problem.

Assurance of high — Our plastic tile flooring is hard-wearing and if the tiles are <u>laid professionally</u>,[5] I
quality goods am sure the work will give you lasting satisfaction.

Please let me know if I can provide any further help.

Yours sincerely

5.8 First enquiries

When your enquiry is to a supplier whom you have not dealt with previously, mention how you obtained their name and give some details about your own business.

A reply to a first enquiry should be given special attention in order to create goodwill.

(a) Enquiry

Dear Sir/Madam

Background information — Dekkers of Sheffield inform us that you are manufacturers of polyester cotton
about enquiry bedsheets and pillow cases.

We are dealers in textiles and believe there is a promising market in our area for moderately priced goods of this kind.

Request for details — Please let me have details of your various ranges including sizes, colours and prices, together with samples of the different qualities of material used.

Further queries — Please state your terms of payment and discounts allowed on purchases of
regarding prices for quantities of not less than 500 of specific items. Prices quoted should include
specific quantities of delivery to our address shown above.
goods

Your prompt reply would be appreciated.

Yours faithfully

---

[5] **laid professionally** put down by an expert

(b) Reply

A personal salutation — Dear Mrs Harrison

Thank you —
Enclose relevant publications

I was very pleased to receive your enquiry of 15 January and enclose our illustrated catalogue and price list giving the details requested.

Give further details regarding samples — A full range of samples has also been sent by separate post. When you have had an opportunity to examine them, I feel confident you will agree that the goods are excellent in quality and very reasonably priced.

Reply to specific questions regarding quantities — On regular purchases of quantities of not less than 500 individual items, we would allow a trade discount of 33%. For payment within 10 days from receipt of invoice, an extra discount of 5% of net price would be allowed.

Assurance of quality, demand and delivery — Polyester cotton products are rapidly becoming popular because they are strong, warm and light. After studying our prices you will not be surprised to learn that we are finding it difficult to meet the demand. However, if you place your order not later than the end of this month, we guarantee delivery within 14 days of receipt.

Refer to other products — I am sure you will also be interested to see information on our other products which are shown in our catalogue; if you need further details on any of these please contact me.

I look forward to hearing from you.

Yours sincerely

5.9 First enquiry from foreign importers

This letter is from a foreign importer so a friendly and helpful reply is necessary in order to create a good impression.

(a) Enquiry

Dear Sir/Madam

We learn from Spett, Mancienne of Rome that you are producing for export handmade gloves in a variety of natural leathers. There is a steady demand in this country for gloves of high quality, and although sales are not particularly high, good prices are obtained.

Please send me a copy of your catalogue with details of your prices and payment terms. It would also be helpful if you could supply samples of the various skins in which the gloves are supplied.

I look forward to hearing from you soon.

Yours faithfully

(b) Reply

Dear Mr Fratelli

Thank you for the interest shown in our products in your letter of 22 August.

A copy of our illustrated catalogue is enclosed, together with samples of some of the skins we regularly use in our manufactures. Unfortunately we cannot send you immediately a full range of samples, but you may rest assured that such leathers as chamois and doeskin, which are not represented in the parcel, are of the same high quality.

Mr Frank North, our Overseas Director, will be visiting Rome early next month. He will be pleased to visit you and bring with him a wide range of our goods. When you see them I think you will agree that the quality of materials used and the high standard of the craftsmanship[6] will appeal to the most selective buyer.

We also manufacture a wide range of handmade leather handbags in which you may be interested. They are fully illustrated in the catalogue and are of the same high quality as our gloves. Mr North will be able to show you samples when he calls.

Please let me know if you have any further questions.

Yours sincerely

REQUESTS FOR GOODS ON APPROVAL

Customers often ask for goods to be sent *on approval*.[7] They must be returned within the time stated, otherwise the customer is presumed to have bought them and cannot return them afterwards.

5.10 Customer requests goods on approval

(a) Request

Dear Sir/Madam

Several of my customers have recently expressed an interest in your waterproof garments, and have enquired about their quality.

If quality and price are satisfactory there are prospects of good sales here. However before placing a firm order I should be glad if you would send me on 14 days' approval a selection of men's and children's waterproof raincoats and leggings. Any of the items unsold at the end of this period and which I decide not to keep as stock would be returned at my expense.

I hope to hear from you soon.

Yours faithfully

---

[6] **craftsmanship** expert skill in making something
[7] **on approval** for inspection, and return if not wanted

(b) Reply

> Dear Mrs Turner
>
> I was very pleased to receive your request of 12 March for waterproof garments on approval.
>
> As we have not previously done business together, you will appreciate that I must request either the usual trade references,[8] or the name of a bank to which we may refer. As soon as these enquiries are satisfactorily settled we shall be happy to send you a good selection of the items mentioned in your letter.
>
> I sincerely hope that our first transaction together will be the beginning of a long and pleasant business association.
>
> Yours sincerely

In this reply the supplier seeks protection by asking for references. Some suppliers request a returnable deposit or a third-party guarantee. While safeguarding oneself, it is important not to offend customers by implying lack of trust.

(c) Despatch of goods

Having received satisfactory references, the supplier sends a confident, direct and helpful letter. The reason for the low prices is given in order to *dispel any suspicion*[9] the customer may have that the goods are poor quality.

> Dear Mrs Turner
>
> I have now received satisfactory references and am pleased to be able to send you a generous selection of our waterproof garments as requested in your letter of 12 March.
>
> This selection includes several new and attractive models in which the water-resistant qualities have been improved by a special process. Due to economies in our methods of manufacture, it has also been possible to reduce our prices which are now lower than those for imported waterproof garments of similar quality.
>
> When you have had an opportunity to inspect the garments, please let us know which you have decided to keep and arrange to return the remainder as early as possible.
>
> I hope this first selection will meet your requirements. If you would like a further selection, please do not hesitate to let me know.
>
> Yours sincerely

---

[8] **trade references** names of traders who may be referred to
[9] **dispel any suspicion** remove doubt

(d) Customer returns surplus

In this letter the customer informs the supplier of the goods to be kept and encloses payment.

> Dear Mrs Robinson
>
> A few weeks ago you were good enough to send me a selection of waterproof garments on approval.
>
> Quality and prices are both satisfactory and I have arranged to keep the items shown on the attached statement. My cheque for £1209.55 is enclosed in settlement.
>
> Thank you for the prompt and considerate way in which you have handled this transaction.
>
> Yours sincerely

VISITS BY REPRESENTATIVES

Customers often form their opinions of a company from the impressions created by its representatives. This stresses the need for careful selection and proper training of sales staff. Apart from being specialists in the art of persuasion, such representatives must also fulfil the following requirements:

- They should have an excellent knowledge of the goods to be sold and the uses to which they can be put.
- They should be able to anticipate the customer's needs.
- They should be able to give sound advice and guidance to customers.

5.11 Request for representative to call

(a) Enquiry

> Dear Sir/Madam
>
> I read with interest your advertisement for plastic kitchenware in the current issue of the House Furnishing Review.
>
> I hope you can arrange for your representative to call when next in this district. It would be helpful if he could bring with him a good selection of items from your product range.
>
> This is a rapidly developing district and if prices are right your goods should find a ready sale.
>
> I look forward to hearing from you soon.
>
> Yours faithfully

(b) Supplier's offer of visit

In this reply the supplier uses a friendly and conversational style.

It has a personal tone and does not sound like a routine reply.

It presents the case from the buyer's viewpoint.

It generates interest by referring to successes.

It gives reasons why an order should be placed without delay.

It is helpful and friendly.

Dear Mr Kennings

Thank you for your enquiry dated 1 November.

Our representative, Ms Jane Whitelaw, will be in your area next week and she will be calling on you. Meanwhile I am enclosing an illustrated catalogue of our plastic goods and details of our terms and conditions of sale.

Plastic kitchenware has long been a popular feature of the modern kitchen. Its bright and attractive colours have strong appeal, and wherever dealers have arranged them in special window displays good sales are reported.

When you have inspected the samples Ms Whitelaw will bring with her, you will understand why we have a large demand for these products. Therefore if you wish to have a stock of these goods before Christmas we advise you to place your order by the end of this month.

We look forward to working with you.

Yours sincerely

REQUESTS FOR CONCESSIONS

Customers sometimes ask for goods that are no longer available, or special terms which cannot be granted. Such requests need to be handled carefully to avoid giving offence or losing business.

5.12 Request for <u>sole distribution rights</u>[10]

(a) Enquiry

Dear Sir/Madam

Background information and specific details — We have recently extended our radio and television department and are thinking of adding new ranges to our present stocks. We are particularly interested in your BELLTONE radio and television models and should be glad if you would send us your trade catalogue and terms of sale and payment.

Request for sole distribution rights — Your products are not yet offered by any other dealer in this town, and if we decide to introduce them we should like to request <u>sole distribution rights</u>[10] in this area.

Suitable close — I hope to hear from you soon.

Yours faithfully

(b) Request declined

In this reply the supplier tactfully refuses the request. The refusal is not stated in so many words but is implied in the third paragraph.

Dear Mr Sanderson

Thank you — Thank you for your letter of 8 April enquiring about our BELLTONE radio and television products.

Enclose catalogue and give further details — This range has been discontinued and replaced by the CLAIRTONE. You will see from the enclosed catalogue that the new models are attractively designed and include the latest technical improvements. Although rather more expensive than their predecessors, the CLAIRTONE models have already been well received and good sales are being reported regularly from many areas.

A tactful response to request for sole distribution rights — As part of our efforts to keep down manufacturing costs, I am sure you will understand that we must increase sales by distributing through as many outlets as possible. Dealers in other areas appear to be well satisfied with their sales under this arrangement, and it appears to be working very well.

Express a hope for the future — I hope we can look forward to receiving your orders soon, and will be glad to include your name in our list of approved dealers, with your permission.

I look forward to your early reply.

Yours sincerely

[10] **sole distribution rights** the right to be the only distributor in a given area for certain products

5.13 Request for special terms

(a) Enquiry

Note the excellent use of the 4 point plan in this letter.

Dear Sir or Madam

Introduction — Please send us your current catalogue and price list for bicycles. We are interested in models for both men and women, and also for children.

Give details — We are the leading bicycle dealers in this city where cycling is popular, and have branches in five neighbouring towns. If the quality of your products is satisfactory and the prices are reasonable, we expect to place regular orders for fairly large numbers.

What action is required — In the circumstances please indicate whether you will allow us a special discount. This would enable us to maintain the low selling prices which have been an important reason for the growth of our business. In return we would be prepared to place orders for a guaranteed annual minimum number of bicycles, the figure to be mutually agreed.

Close (include contact number) — If you wish to discuss this please contact me on 6921671.

Yours faithfully

(b) Reply

In this reply the manufacturer is cautious, offering allowances on a *sliding scale basis*.[11]

Dear Ms Denning

I was glad to learn from your letter of 18 July of your interest in our products. As requested our catalogue and price list are enclosed, together with details of our conditions of sale and terms of payment.

We have considered your proposal to place orders for a guaranteed minimum number of machines in return for a special allowance. However after careful consideration we feel it would be better to offer you a special allowance on the following sliding scale basis.

On purchases exceeding an annual total of:

£1,000 but not exceeding £3,000	3%
£3,000 but not exceeding £7,500	4%
£7,500 and above	5%

No special allowance could be given on annual total purchases below £1,000.

I feel that an arrangement on these lines would be more satisfactory to both our companies.

Orders will be subject to the usual trade references.

I look forward to working with you and hope to hear from you soon.

Yours sincerely

[11] **sliding scale basis** varying with the quantity bought

5.14 Letter declining special terms

In this letter a supplier tactfully refuses a request to reduce prices. Instead a counter-suggestion is made.

Dear Mr Ellis

We have carefully considered your letter of 18 December.

As our companies have done business with each other for many years, we would like to grant your request to lower the prices of our sportswear. However our own overheads[12] have risen sharply in the past 12 months, and to reduce prices by the 15% you mention could not be done without considerably lowering our standards of quality. This is something we are not prepared to do.

Instead of a 15% reduction on sportswear, we suggest a reduction of 5% on all our products for orders of £800 or more. On orders of this size we could make such a reduction without lowering our standards.

I hope that you will agree to this suggestion and look forward to continuing to receive regular orders from you.

Yours sincerely

 To develop a diplomatic writing style, imagine the person is standing in front of you and you are speaking to him/her.

[12] **overheads** regular standing charges such as rent, lighting, administration costs, etc

USEFUL EXPRESSIONS

Requests

Openings

1 We are interested in … as advertised recently in …
2 We have received an enquiry for your …
3 I was interested to see your advertisement for …
4 I understand you are manufacturers of (dealers in) … and should like to receive your current catalogue.

Main section and closes

1 When replying please also include delivery details.
2 Please also state whether you can supply the goods from stock as we need them urgently.
3 If you can supply suitable goods, we may place regular orders for large quantities.

Replies to requests

Openings

1 Thank you for your letter of … As requested we enclose …
2 I was pleased to learn … that you are interested in our …
3 Thank you for your enquiry dated … regarding …

Closes

1 We look forward to receiving a trial order from you soon.
2 We shall be pleased to send you any further information you may need.
3 Any orders you place with us will have our prompt attention.
4 Please let me know if you need any further details.

Quotations, estimates and tenders

A quotation is a promise to supply goods on the terms stated. The prospective buyer is under no obligation to buy the goods for which a quotation is requested, and suppliers will not normally risk their reputations by quoting for goods they cannot or do not intend to supply. A satisfactory quotation will include the following:

- an expression of thanks for the enquiry
- details of prices, discounts and terms of payment
- a clear indication of what the prices cover, eg packing, carriage, insurance
- an undertaking regarding date of delivery
- the period for which the quotation is *valid*[1]
- an expression of hope that the quotation will be accepted.

TERMINOLOGY

When requesting a quotation the buyer must be careful to establish clearly whether the prices are to include such additional charges as carriage and insurance. Failure to do this may, if not specified in the supplier's quotation, lead to serious disagreement, especially where such charges are heavy as in foreign trade dealings. Some terminology associated with quotations is shown here:

- **Carriage paid.** The quoted price includes delivery to the buyer's premises.
- **Carriage forward.** The buyer pays the delivery charges.
- **Loco, ex works, ex factory, ex warehouse.** The buyer pays all expenses of handling from the time the goods leave the factory or warehouse.
- **For (free on rail).** The quotation covers the cost of transport to the nearest railway station and of loading on to truck.
- **Fas (free alongside ship).** The quotation covers the cost of using lighters or barges to bring the goods to the ship, but not the expense of lifting the goods on board.
- **Fob (free on board).** The quotation covers the cost of loading the goods on to the ship, after which the buyer becomes responsible for all charges.
- **Ex ship.** The quoted price includes delivery over the side of the ship, either into lighters or barges or, if the ship is near enough, on to the quay.

ROUTINE QUOTATIONS

6.1 Request for quotations for printing paper

(a) Request

This request complies with the requirements of a satisfactory letter of enquiry.

---

[1] **valid** hold good

- It states clearly and concisely what is required.
- It explains what the paper is for, and thus helps the supplier to quote for paper of the right quality.
- It states the quantity required, which is important because of the effect of quantity upon price.
- It states when delivery is required – an important condition in any contract for the purchase of goods.
- It states what the price is to cover – in this case 'delivery at our works'.

Dear Sir,

We will soon be requiring 200 reams of good quality white poster paper suitable for auction bills and poster work generally. We require paper which will retain its white appearance after pasting on walls and hoardings.

Please let us have some samples and a quotation, including delivery at our works within 4 weeks of our order.

Yours faithfully

(b) Quotation

The supplier's reply should be sent promptly and it should be equally businesslike, ensuring that all the points from the enquiry are answered.

Dear Mr Keenan

Thank you for your enquiry dated 21 June.

As requested we enclose samples of different qualities of paper suitable for poster work.

We are pleased to quote as follows:

A1 quality Printing Paper white £2.21 per kg
A2 quality Printing Paper white £2.15 per kg
A3 quality Printing Paper white £2.10 per kg

These prices include delivery at your works.

All these papers are of good quality and quite suitable for poster work. We guarantee that they will not discolour when pasted.

We can promise delivery within one week from receiving your order, and hope you will find both samples and prices satisfactory.

Please give me a call on 2634917 if you have any questions.

Yours sincerely

6.2 Request for quotation for crockery

Here is another example of a satisfactory request for a quotation. It states exactly what is wanted and covers the important points of discounts, packing, delivery and terms of payment.

(a) Request

Dear Sir

You have previously supplied us with crockery and we should be glad if you would now quote for the items named below, manufactured by Ridgeway Pottery Company of Hanley. The pattern we require is 'number 59 Conway Spot (Green)'.

300 Teacups and Saucers
300 Tea Plates
 40 1-litre Teapots

When quoting prices please include packing and delivery to the above address. Please also state discounts allowable, terms of payment and earliest possible date of delivery.

I hope to hear from you soon.

Yours faithfully

(b) Quotation

Dear Mr Clarke

CONWAY SPOT (GREEN) GILT RIMS

Thank you for your enquiry of 18 April for a further supply of our crockery. We are pleased to quote as follows:

Teacups	£83.75 per hundred
Tea Saucers	£76.00 per hundred
Tea Plates	£76.00 per hundred
Teapots, 1-litre	£4.20 each

These prices include packing and delivery, but a charge is made for crates, with an allowance for their return in good condition.

Delivery can be made from stock and we will allow you a 5% discount on items ordered in quantities of 100 or more. There would be an additional cash discount of 2% on total cost of payment within one month from date of invoice.

We hope that you will find these terms satisfactory. Please give me a call on 3614917 if you have any questions.

Yours sincerely

QUOTATIONS SUBJECT TO CONDITIONS OF ACCEPTANCE

Very often a quotation is made subject to certain conditions of acceptance. These conditions vary according to the circumstances and the type of business.

They may relate to a stated time within which the quotation must be accepted, or to goods of which supplies are limited and cannot be repeated. The supplier must make it clear when quoting for goods in limited supply or subject to their being available when the order is received. Examples of qualifying statements are:

- This offer is made subject to the goods being available when the order is received.
- This offer is subject to acceptance within 7 days.
- The prices quoted will apply only to orders received on or before 31 March.
- Goods ordered from our 2004 catalogue can be supplied only while stocks last.
- For acceptance within 14 days.

6.3   Foreign buyer's request for quotation

(a) Enquiry

> Dear Sirs
>
> We have recently received a number of requests for your lightweight raincoats and believe that we could place regular orders with you, as long as your prices are competitive.
>
> From the description in your catalogue we feel that your AQUATITE range would be most suitable for this region. Please let me have a quotation for men's and women's coats in both small and medium sizes, delivered *cif Alexandria*.[2]
>
> If your prices are right, we will place a first order for 400 raincoats, namely 100 of each of the 4 qualities. Shipment would be required within 4 weeks of order.
>
> I look forward to a prompt reply.
>
> Yours faithfully

(b) Quotation

The reply by the English manufacturer is a good example of the modern style in business letter writing. The tone is friendly and the language is simple and clear. The writer shows an awareness of the problems of the tropical resident (eg the reference to condensation) and gives information that is likely to bring about a sale (eg mention of 'repeat orders' and 'specially treated').

Another point of interest here is the statement of freight and insurance charges separate from the cost of the goods. This is convenient for calculating the trade

---

[2] **cif Alexandria** price covers charges for insurance and transport to the port named

discount and also tells the buyer exactly what is to be paid for the goods themselves. Note also the statement 'For acceptance within one month'. Here the supplier promises to sell goods at the quoted price within a given period of time.

The supplier's attempt to interest the customer in other products is very good business technique.

Dear Mrs Barden

AQUATITE RAINWEAR

Thank you — Thank you for your letter of 15 June. I was pleased to learn about the enquiries you have received for our raincoats.

Discuss popularity of product with particular reference to tropical climates — Our AQUATITE range is particularly suitable for warm climates. During the past year we have supplied this range to dealers in several tropical countries. We have already received repeat orders[3] from many of those dealers. This range is popular *Mention of 'repeat orders' gives assurance of quality* — not only because of its light weight but also because the material used has been specially treated to prevent excessive condensation on the inside surface.

We are pleased to quote as follows:

Specific details regarding prices —

100 AQUATITE coats	men's	medium	£17.50 ea	1750.00
100 AQUATITE coats	men's	small	£16.80 ea	1680.00
100 AQUATITE coats	women's	medium	£16.00 ea	1600.00
100 AQUATITE coats	women's	small	£15.40 ea	1540.00
				6570.00
less 33⅓% trade discount				2187.81
Net price				4382.19
Freight (London to Alexandria)				186.00
Insurance				122.50
TOTAL				4690.69

Details regarding terms, shipment and acceptance — Terms: 2½% one month from date of invoice

Shipment: Within 3–4 weeks of receiving order

For acceptance within one month.

Refer to other products and enclose literature — We feel you may be interested in some of our other products, and enclose descriptive booklets and a supply of sales literature for issue to your customers.

We hope to receive your order soon.

Yours sincerely

TABULATED QUOTATIONS

Many quotations are either tabulated or prepared on special forms. Such tabulated quotations are:

---

[3] **repeat orders** successive orders for similar goods

- clear, since information is presented in a form which is readily understood
- complete, since essential information is unlikely to be omitted.

Tabulated quotations are particularly suitable where there are many items. Like quotations on specially prepared forms, they should be sent with a *covering letter*[4] which:

- expresses thanks for the enquiry
- makes favourable comments about the goods themselves
- draws attention to other products likely to interest the buyer
- expresses hope of receiving an order.

Such treatment creates a favourable impression and helps to build goodwill.

6.4 Covering letter with quotation on specially prepared form

(a) Covering letter

Dear Mrs Greenway

Thank you for your enquiry of 15 August. Our quotation for leather shoes and handbags is enclosed. All items can be delivered from stock.

These items are made from very best quality leather and can be supplied in a range of designs and colours wide enough to meet the requirements of a fashionable trade such as yours.

Also enclosed is a copy of our catalogue in which you will find details of our other products. These include leather purses and gloves, described and illustrated on pages 18–25.

The catalogue gives all the essential facts about our goods, but if you have any queries please do not hesitate to give me a call on 9635117.

Yours sincerely

(b) Quotation

In this quotation, note the following points:

- It is given a serial number to assist future reference.
- Use of catalogue numbers identifies items with precision and avoids misunderstandings. Individual shapes and sizes are also given their own serial numbers.
- 'For acceptance within 21 days' protects the supplier should the buyer order goods at a later date when prices may have risen.
- '4% one month' indicates that a discount of 4% will be allowed on quoted prices if payment is made within one month; for payment made after one month but within two months, the discount is reduced to 2%.

---

[4] **covering letter** a brief letter enclosing other documents

CENTRAL LEATHERCRAFT LTD
85–87 Cheapside, London EC2V 6AA
Telephone 020-7242-2177/8

Quotation no JBS/234

Date 20 August 200—

Smith Jenkins & Co
15 Holme Avenue
SHEFFIELD
S6 2LW

Catalogue Number	Item	Quantity	Unit Price
S 25	Men's Box Calf Shoes (brown)	12 pairs	65.75
	Men's Box Calf Shoes (black)	36 pairs	65.50
S 27	Ladies' Glace Kid Tie Shoes (various colours)	48 pairs	64.80
S 42	Ladies' Calf Colt Court Shoes	24 pairs	64.35
H 212	Ladies' Handbags – Emperor	36	66.50
H 221	Ladies' Handbags – Paladin	36	78.75
H 229	Ladies' Handbags – Aristocrat	12	80.00
	FOR ACCEPTANCE WITHIN 21 DAYS		

Delivery   ex works

Terms   4% one month 2½% two months

(signed)
for Central Leathercraft Ltd

6.5   A covering letter enclosing a quotation

Dear Miss Richardson

Thank you for your interest in StarWay.

I am pleased to enclose our quotation for the StarWay laptop system that you require. This gives details of a standard specification and also outlines the cost of configuring the system to meet your needs.

As one of the world's leading direct marketers of personal computers, we believe our success is primarily due to putting our clients first. We want to custom-build the right personal computer for you as well as ensure that you get the ongoing service and support that you need.

Please call me on 0800 345234 to finalise your purchase. If you have any questions at all, please do not hesitate to give me a call.

Yours sincerely

 Good writers learn to present the positives rather than the negatives.

ESTIMATES AND SPECIFICATIONS

Whereas a quotation is an offer to sell goods at a price and under stated conditions, an estimate is an offer to do certain work for a stated price, usually on the basis of a specification. Like a quotation, an estimate is not legally binding so the person making it is not bound to accept any order that may be placed against it.

6.6 Estimate for installation of central heating

(a) Enquiry

In this enquiry the writer encloses a specification giving a detailed description of the work to be done and materials to be used. This will provide the basis for the contractor's estimate. The plan would consist of a rough sketch (drawn to scale) showing the required positions of the radiators.

> Dear Sirs
>
> Please let me have an estimate for installing central heating in my bungalow at 1 Margate Road, St Annes-on-Sea. A plan of the bungalow is attached showing required positions and sizes of radiators, together with a specification showing further details and materials to be used.
>
> As you will note from the specification, I am interested only in first-class workmanship and in the use of best quality materials. However cost is, of course, a matter of some importance. It is essential that this work is completed by 31 August at the latest.
>
> In your reply please include a firm completion date.
>
> Your prompt reply will be appreciated.
>
> Yours faithfully

(b) Specification

SPECIFICATION FOR INSTALLING CENTRAL HEATING at 1 MARGATE ROAD, ST ANNES-ON-SEA

1 Installation[5] of the latest small-bored central heating, to be carried out with best quality copper piping of 15 mm bore, fitted with 'Ryajand' electric pump of fully adequate power and lagged under floor to prevent loss of heat.

2 Existing boiler to be replaced by a Glow-worm No 52 automatic gas-fired boiler, rated at 15.2 kW and complete with gas governor, flame failure safety device and boiler water thermostat.

3 Installation of a Randall No 103 clock controller to give automatic operation of the central heating system at predetermined times.

4 Existing hot-water cylinder to be replaced by a *calorifier-type cylinder*[6] suitable for supplying domestic hot water separately from the central heating system.

5 Seven 'Dimplex' or similar flat-type radiators to be fitted under windows of five rooms, and in hall and kitchen, according to plan enclosed; also a towel rail in bathroom. Sizes of radiators and towel rail to be as specified in plan attached to my letter dated 5 July 200— addressed to yourselves.

6 Each radiator to be separately controlled, swivelled for cleaning and painted pale cream with red-lead undercoating.

7 The system to be provided with the necessary fall for emptying and to prevent air-locks.

8 All work to be carried out from under floor to avoid cutting or lifting floor boards, which are tongued and grooved.

9 Insulation[7] of roof with 80 mm fibreglass.

J HARRIS

5 July 200—

(c) Contractor's estimate

The contractor can calculate costs from the information provided, and will send an estimate with a covering letter. The letter should provide the following information:

- a reference regarding satisfactory work carried out elsewhere which will give the customer confidence

---

[5] **installation** the act of putting equipment in position
[6] **calorifier-type cylinder** a cylinder which keeps water hot
[7] **insulation** a covering used to retain heat

- a promised completion date
- a market prices and wages adjustment clause to protect the contractor from unforeseen increases that may raise costs and reduce profits
- a hope that the estimate will be accepted.

In this letter note that the contractor aims to inspire confidence by referring to work done elsewhere and the promise to arrange an inspection if required.

Dear Mr Harris

INSTALLATION OF CENTRAL HEATING AT 1 MARGATE ROAD, ST ANNES-ON-SEA

Thank you — Thank you for your letter of 6 July enclosing specification and plan for a gas-fired central heating system at the above address.

Mention price and discount — We should be glad to carry out the work for a total of £2,062.50 with a 2½% discount for settlement within one month of the date of our account. We can *Promised completion date* — promise to complete all work by 31 August if we receive your instructions by the end of this month. Please note that the price quoted is based on present costs of *This clause protects the contractor from unforeseen increases* — materials and labour. Should these costs rise we should have to add the increased costs to our price.

Mention of satisfactory work carried out elsewhere will give confidence — We have installed many similar heating systems in your area. Our reputation for high class work is well known. If you would like to inspect one of our recent installations before making a firm decision, this can be arranged.

We hope you will be satisfied with the price quoted, and look forward to receiving your instructions soon.

Yours sincerely

TENDERS

A tender is usually made in response to a published advertisement. It is an offer for the supply of specified goods or the performance of specified work at prices and under conditions set out in the tender. A tender becomes legally binding only when it is accepted; up to that time it may be withdrawn. It is usual for tenders to be made on the advertisers' own forms which include a specification where necessary and set out the terms in full detail.

6.7 A public invitation to tender

THE COUNTY COUNCIL OF LANCASHIRE
COUNTY HALL, PRESTON PR1 2RL

Tenders are invited for the supply to the Council's power station at Bamford, during the year 200—, of approximately 2,000 tonnes of best quality furnace coke, delivered in quantities as required. Tenders must be submitted on the official form obtainable from County Hall to reach the Clerk of the Council not later than 12.00 noon on Friday 30 June.

The Council does not bind itself to accept the lowest, or any, of the tenders submitted.

B BRADEN

Clerk to the Council

6.8 Contractor's letter enclosing tender

After obtaining the official form and completing it accordingly, it should be returned with a formal covering letter.

CONFIDENTIAL

Clerk to the Council
County Hall
PRESTON
PR1 2RL

Dear Mr Braden

TENDER FOR FURNACE COKE

Having read the terms and conditions in the official form supplied by you, I enclose my tender for the supply of coke to the Bamford power station during 200—. I hope to learn that it has been accepted.

Yours sincerely

6.9 A closed invitation to tender

An invitation to tender restricted to members of a particular organisation or group is called a 'closed tender'. This example is taken from the *Baghdad Observer*.

STATE ORGANISATION FOR ENGINEERING INDUSTRIES
P O BOX 3093 BAGHDAD IRAQ

TENDER NO 1977
FOR THE SUPPLY OF 16,145 TONNES
OF
ALUMINIUM AND ALUMINIUM ALLOY INGOTS,
BILLETS AND SLABS

1 The SOEI invites tenderers who are registered in the Chamber of Commerce and hold a Certificate of Income Tax of this year, as well as a certificate issued by the Registrar of Commercial Agencies confirming that he is licensed by the Director General of Registration and Supervision of Companies, to participate in the above tender. General terms and conditions together with specifications and quantities sheets can be obtained from the Planning and Financial Control Department at the 3rd floor of this Organisation against payment of one Iraqi Dinar for each copy.

2 All offers are to be put in the tender box of this Organisation, Commercial Affairs Department, 4th floor, marked with the name and number of the tender at or before 1200 hours on Saturday 31 January 200—.

3 Offers should be accompanied by preliminary guarantee issued by the Rafidain Bank, equal to not less than 5 per cent of the C & F value of the offer.

4 Any offer submitted after the closing date of the tender, or which does not comply with the above terms, will not be accepted.

5 This Organisation does not bind itself to accept the lowest or any other offer.

6 Foreign companies who have no local agents in Iraq shall be exempted from the conditions stated in item number 1 above.

ALI AL-HAMDANI (ENGINEER)
PRESIDENT

QUOTATIONS NOT ACCEPTED OR AMENDED

When a buyer rejects a quotation or other offer, it is courteous to write and thank the supplier for their trouble and explain the reason for rejection. The letter of rejection should:

- thank the supplier for their offer
- express regret at inability to accept
- state reasons for non-acceptance
- if appropriate, make a *counter-offer*[8]
- suggest that there may be other opportunities to do business together.

---

[8] **counter-offer** an alternative to another offer

6.10 Buyer rejects supplier's quotation

Dear Mr Walton

Thank you for your quotation dated 19 February for strawboards.

I appreciate your trouble in this matter but as your prices are very much higher than those I have been quoted by other dealers, I regret I cannot give you an immediate order.

I shall bear your company in mind when I require other products in the future.

Yours sincerely

6.11 Supplier grants request for better terms

(a) Enquiry

Dear Ms Hansen

Thank you — Thank you for your letter of 18 August and for the samples of cotton underwear you very kindly sent to me.

Mention good quality but express concern at high prices leaving small profit — I appreciate the good quality of these garments, but unfortunately your prices appear to be on the high side even for garments of this quality. To accept the prices you quote would leave me with only a small profit on my sales since this is an area in which the principal demand is for articles in the medium price range.

Repeat feelings regarding quality and desire to do business. Request special allowance — I like the quality of your goods and would welcome the opportunity to do business with you. May I suggest that perhaps you could make some allowance on your quoted prices which would help to introduce your goods to my customers. If you cannot do so, then I must regretfully decline your offer as it stands.

I hope to hear from you soon.

Yours sincerely

(b) Reply

Acknowledge letter ——
Respond to query regarding high prices ——

Give assurance that prices are reasonable ——

Special discount on first order will be appreciated by new customer ——

Dear Mr Daniels

I am sorry to learn from your letter of 23 August that you find our prices too high. We do our best to keep prices as low as possible without sacrificing quality. To this end we are constantly investigating new methods of manufacture.

Considering the quality of the goods offered we do not feel that the prices we quoted are at all excessive. However, bearing in mind the special character of your trade, we are prepared to offer you a discount of 4% on a first order for £1000. This allowance is made because we should like to do business with you if possible, but I must stress that it is the furthest we can go to help you.

I hope this revised offer will enable you to place an order, and I look forward to hearing from you soon.

Yours sincerely

FOLLOW-UP LETTERS

When a buyer has asked for a quotation but does not place an order or even acknowledge the quotation, it is natural for the supplier to wonder why. A keen supplier will arrange for a representative to call, or send a follow-up letter if the enquiry is from a distance.

6.12 Supplier's follow-up letter

Here is an effective follow-up letter written in a tone which shows the supplier genuinely wants to help and in a style which is direct and straight to the point. It considers the buyer's convenience by offering a choice of action and closes with a reassuring promise of service.

Dear Mrs Larkin

As we have not heard from you since we sent you our catalogue of filing systems, we wonder whether you require further information before deciding to place an order.

The modern system of lateral filing has important space-saving advantages wherever economy of space is important. However if space is not one of your problems, our flat-top suspended system may suit you better. The neat and tidy appearance it gives to the filing drawers and the ease and speed with which files are located are just two of its features which many users find attractive.

Would you like us to send our representative to call and discuss your needs with you? John Robinson has advised on equipment for many large, modern offices and would be able to recommend the system most suited to your own requirements. There would of course be no obligation of any kind. Perhaps you would prefer to pay a visit to our showroom and see for yourself how the different filing systems work.

You may be sure that whichever of these opportunities you decide to accept, you would receive personal attention and the best possible advice.

If you have any further questions please call me on 2356123.

Yours sincerely

6.13 Letter to save a lost customer

No successful business can afford to lose its regular customers. Periodical checks must be carried out to identify those customers whose orders have tended to fall off, and suitable follow-up letters must be sent.

Dear Sirs

We notice with regret that it is some considerable time since we last received an order from you. We hope this is in no way due to dissatisfaction with our service or with the quality of goods we have supplied. In either of these situations we should be grateful to hear from you. We are most anxious to ensure that customers obtain maximum satisfaction from their dealings with us. If the lack of orders from you is due to changes in the type of goods you handle, we may still be able to meet your needs if you will let us know in what directions your policy has changed.

As we have not heard otherwise, we assume that you are still selling the same range of sports goods, so a copy of our latest illustrated catalogue is enclosed. We feel this compares favourably in range, quality and price with the catalogues of other manufacturers. At the same time we take the opportunity to mention that our terms are now much easier than previously, following the withdrawal of exchange control[9] and other official measures since we last did business together.

I hope to hear from you soon.

Yours faithfully

[9] **exchange control** official control in the foreign exchange market

USEFUL EXPRESSIONS

Requests for quotations, estimates, etc

Openings

1 Please quote for the supply of ...

2 Please send me a quotation for the supply of ...

3 We wish to have the following work carried out and should be glad if you would submit an estimate.

Closes

1 As the matter is urgent we should like this information by the end of this week.

2 If you can give us a competitive quotation, we expect to place a large order.

3 If your prices compare favourably with those of other suppliers, we shall send you an early order.

Replies to requests for quotations, etc

Openings

1 Thank you for your letter of ...

2 We thank you for your enquiry of ... and are pleased to quote as follows:

3 With reference to your enquiry of ..., we shall be glad to supply ... at the price of ...

4 We are sorry to learn that you find our quotation of ... too high.

Closes

1 We trust you will find our quotation satisfactory and look forward to receiving your order.

2 We shall be pleased to receive your order, which will have our prompt and careful attention.

3 As the prices quoted are exceptionally low and likely to rise, we would advise you to place your order without delay.

4 As our stocks of these goods are limited, we suggest you place an order immediately.

Orders and their fulfilment

PLACING ORDERS

Printed order forms

Most companies have official printed order forms (see Fig. 7.1). The advantages are:

(a) such forms are pre-numbered and therefore reference is easy

(b) printed headings ensure that no information will be omitted.

Printed on the back of some forms are general conditions under which orders are placed. It is usual to refer on the front to these conditions, otherwise the supplier is not legally bound by them.

Letter orders

Smaller companies may not have printed forms but instead place orders in the form of a letter. When sending an order by letter, always ensure accuracy and clarity by including:

(a) an accurate and full description of goods required

(b) catalogue numbers

(c) quantities

(d) prices

(e) delivery requirements (place, date, mode of transport, whether the order will be carriage paid or *carriage forward*,[1] etc) and

(f) terms of payment agreed in *preliminary negotiations*.[2]

Legal position of the parties

According to English law the buyer's order is only an offer to buy. The arrangement is not legally binding until the supplier has accepted the offer. After that both parties are legally bound to honour their agreement.

(a) The buyer's obligations

When a binding agreement comes into force, the buyer is required by law to:

- accept the goods supplied as long as they comply with the terms of the order
- pay for the goods at the time of delivery or within the period specified by the supplier
- check the goods as soon as possible (failure to give prompt notice of faults to the supplier will be taken as acceptance of the goods).

---

[1] **carriage forward** transportation costs paid by the buyer
[2] **preliminary negotiations** earlier discussions regarding terms

```
                    J B SIMPSON & CO LTD
               18 Deansgate, Sheffield S11 2BR
                    Telephone 0114 234234
                       Fax: 0114 234235


Order no 237                                    Date 7 July 200—


Nylon Fabrics Ltd
18 Brazenose Street
MANCHESTER
M60 8AS


Please supply:
```

Quantity	Item(s)	Catalogue Number	Price
25	Bed Sheets (106 cm) blue	75	£10.50 each
25	Bed Sheets (120 cm) primrose	82	£10.00 each
50	Pillow Cases blue	117	£6.90 each
50	Pillow Cases primrose	121	£6.90 each

```
                                            _____
                                                (signed)
                                          for J B Simpson & Co Ltd
```

Figure 7.1 An order form

(b) The supplier's obligations

The supplier is required by law to:

- deliver the goods exactly as ordered at the agreed time
- guarantee the goods to be free from faults of which the buyer could not be aware at the time of purchase.

If faulty goods are delivered, the buyer can demand either a reduction in price, a replacement of the goods or cancellation of the order. Damages may possibly be claimed.

ROUTINE ORDERS

Routine orders may be short and formal but they must include essential details describing the goods, as well as delivery and terms of payment. Where two or more items are included on an order, they should be listed separately for ease of reference.

7.1 Confirmation of telephone order

Dear

We confirm the order which was placed with you by telephone this morning for the following:

3   'Excelda Studio' electronic typewriters
    each with 12 pitch daisy wheel

Price: £895 each, less 40% trade discount
                carriage forward

These machines are urgently required. We understand that you are arranging for immediate delivery from stock.

Yours sincerely

7.2 Tabulated order

Dear Sirs

Please accept our order for the following books on our usual discount terms of 25% off published prices:

NUMBER OF COPIES	TITLE	AUTHOR	PUBLISHED PRICE
50	Communication for Business	Shirley Taylor	£8.99
40	Essential Communication Skills	Shirley Taylor	£7.99

We look forward to prompt delivery.

Yours faithfully

7.3 Order based on quotation

> Dear
>
> Thank you for your quotation of 4 June. Please supply:
>
> 100 reams of A2 quality Printing Paper, white, at £2.16 per kg, including delivery.
>
> Delivery is required not later than the end of this month.
>
> Yours sincerely

7.4 Covering letter with order form

When a covering letter is sent with an order form (as shown in Fig. 7.1), all essential details will be shown on the form and any additional explanations in the covering letter.

> Dear
>
> Thank you for your quotation of 5 July. Our order number 237 for four of the items is enclosed.
>
> All these items are urgently required by our customer so we hope you will send them immediately.
>
> Yours sincerely

ACKNOWLEDGING ORDERS

An order should be acknowledged immediately if it cannot be fulfilled straight away. For small routine orders a printed acknowledgement or an e-mail may be enough, but a short letter stating when delivery may be expected also helps to create goodwill. If the goods cannot be supplied at all, you should write explaining why and offer suitable substitutes if they are available.

7.5 Formal acknowledgement of routine order (by fax)

> Thank you for your order number 237 for bed coverings.
>
> As all items were in stock, they will be delivered to you tomorrow by our own transport.
>
> We hope you will find these goods satisfactory and that we may have the pleasure of receiving further orders from you.

7.6 ▮ Acknowledgement of a first order

First orders, ie orders from new customers, should most certainly be acknowledged by letter.

Dear

Thank you — We were very pleased to receive your order of 18 June for cotton prints, and welcome you as one of our customers.

Confirm prices and delivery information Give assurance of satisfaction — We confirm supply of the prints at the prices stated in your letter. Delivery should be made by our own vehicles early next week. We feel confident that you will be completely satisfied with these goods and that you will find them of exceptional value for money.

Mention other goods and enclose catalogue — As you may not be aware of the wide range of goods we have available, we are enclosing a copy of our catalogue.

Close with a wish for future business dealings — We hope that our handling of your first order with us will lead to further business between us and mark the beginning of a happy working relationship.

Yours sincerely

7.7 ▮ Acknowledgement of order pointing out delayed delivery

When goods ordered cannot be delivered immediately, a letter should apologise for the delay and give an explanation. A delivery date should also be given, if possible, and express the hope that the customer is not inconvenienced unduly.

(a) Reason for delay: breakdown in production

Dear

Thank you for your order of 15 March for electric shavers. We regret that we cannot supply them immediately owing to a fire in our factory.

Every effort is being made to resume production and we fully expect to be able to deliver the shavers by the end of this month.

We apologise for the delay and trust it will not cause you serious inconvenience.

Yours sincerely

(b) Reason for delay: stocks not available

> Dear
>
> We were pleased to receive your order of 20 January.
>
> Unfortunately we are out of stock of the model you ordered. This is due to the prolonged cold weather which has increased demand considerably. The manufacturers have, however, promised us a further supply by the end of this month and if you can wait until then we will fulfil your order promptly.
>
> We are sorry not to be able to meet your present order immediately, but hope to hear from you soon that delivery at the beginning of next month will not inconvenience you unduly.
>
> Yours sincerely

DECLINING ORDERS

There may be times when a supplier will not accept a buyer's order:

- He is not satisfied with the buyer's terms and conditions.
- The buyer's credit is suspect.
- The goods are not available.

Utmost care should be taken when writing to reject an order so that goodwill and future business are not affected.

7.8 Supplier refuses price reduction

When a supplier cannot grant a request for a lower price, reasons should be given.

> Dear
>
> We have carefully considered your counter-proposal[3] of 15 August to our offer of woollen underwear, but regret that we cannot accept it.
>
> The prices quoted in our letter of 13 August leave us with only the smallest of margins. They are in fact lower than those of our competitors for goods of similar quality.
>
> The wool used in the manufacture of our THERMALINE range undergoes a special patented process which prevents shrinkage and increases durability. The fact that we are the largest suppliers of woollen underwear in this country is in itself evidence of the good value of our products.
>
> We hope you will give further thought to this matter, but if you then still feel you cannot accept our offer we hope it will not prevent you from contacting us on some future occasion.
>
> We will always be happy to consider carefully any proposals likely to lead to business between us.
>
> Yours sincerely

---

[3] **counter-proposal** an alternative to an earlier proposal

7.9 ## Supplier rejects buyer's delivery terms

When delivery terms cannot be met, the supplier should show a genuine desire to help customers in difficulty.

> Dear Mr Johnson
>
> YOUR ORDER NUMBER R345
>
> We were pleased to receive your order of 2 November for 24 ATLANTIS television sets. However since you state the firm condition of delivery before Christmas, we regret that we cannot supply you on this occasion.
>
> The manufacturers of these goods are finding it impossible to meet current demand for this popular television set. We placed an order for 100 sets one month ago but were informed that all orders were being met in strict rotation.[4] Our own order will not be met before the end of January.
>
> I understand from our telephone conversation this morning that your customers are unwilling to consider other models. In the circumstances I hope you will be able to meet your requirements from some other source. May I suggest that you try Television Services Ltd of Leicester. They usually carry large stocks and may be able to help you.
>
> Yours sincerely

Thank you. Mention that delivery date cannot be met

Further details regarding demand for the goods and how orders are being dealt with

This suggestion that the customer should try another supplier is sure to be appreciated and will help to build goodwill

7.10 ## Supplier refuses to extend credit

If a previous account remains unpaid, the utmost tact is necessary when rejecting another order. Nothing is more likely to offend a customer than the suggestion that they may not be trustworthy. In this letter, the writer tactfully avoids suggestion of mistrust and instead gives internal difficulties as the reason for refusing further credit.

> Dear Mr Richardson
>
> We were pleased to receive your order of 15 April for a further supply of CD players.
>
> However, owing to current difficult conditions we have had to try to ensure that our many customers keep their accounts within reasonable limits. Only in this way can we meet our own commitments.[5]
>
> At present the balance of your account stands at over £1800. We hope that you will be able to reduce it before we grant credit for further supplies.
>
> In the circumstances we should be grateful if you would send us your cheque for, say, half the amount owed. We could then arrange to supply the goods now requested and charge them to your account.
>
> Yours sincerely

[4] **in strict rotation** in turn, as received
[5] **commitments** obligations to be fulfilled

COUNTER-OFFERS FROM SUPPLIERS

When a supplier receives an order which cannot be met for some reason, any of the following options are available:

1 Send a *substitute*.[6] Careful judgement will be required, however, since there is the risk that the customer may be annoyed to receive something different from what was ordered. It is advisable to send a substitute only if a customer is well known or if there is a clear need for urgency. Such substitutes should be sent 'on approval', with the supplier accepting responsibility for carriage charges both ways.

2 Make a counter-offer.

3 Decline the order.

7.11 Supplier sends a substitute article

Dear

We were pleased to receive your letter of 10 April together with your order for a number of items included in our quotation reference RS980.

All the items ordered are in stock except for the 25 cushion covers in strawberry pink. Stocks of these have been sold out since our quotation, and the manufacturers inform us that it will be another 4 weeks before they can send replacements.

As you state that delivery of all items is a matter of urgency, we have substituted cushion covers in a fuschia pink, identical in design and quality to those ordered. They are attractive and rich-looking, and very popular with our other customers. We hope you will find them satisfactory. If not, please return them at our expense. We shall be glad either to exchange them or to arrange credit.

All items will be on our delivery schedule tomorrow. We hope you will be pleased with them.

Yours sincerely

7.12 Supplier makes a counter-offer

In making a counter-offer the supplier must exercise a great deal of skill to bring about a sale. The buyer is, after all, being offered something that has not been asked for. Therefore it is important that the suggested substitute is at least as good as the one ordered.

---

[6] **substitute** goods which take the place of others

Thank you	Dear
	Thank you for your letter of 12 May ordering 800 metres of 100 cm wide watered silk.
Respond to the enquiry with regret that the material is no longer available	We regret to say that we can no longer supply this silk. Fashions constantly change and in recent years the demand for watered silks has fallen to such an extent that we no longer produce them.
Mention a replacement material and give assurance of quality and reliability	In their place we can offer our new GOSSAMER brand of rayon.[7] This is a finely woven, hard-wearing, non-creasable material with a most attractive lustre.[8] The large number of repeat orders we regularly receive from leading distributors and dress manufacturers is clear evidence of the widespread popularity of this brand.
Include price information	At the low price of only £3.20 per metre, this rayon is much cheaper than silk and its appearance is just as attractive.
Mention other products/ samples sent separately Give delivery details	We also manufacture other cloths in which you may be interested and are sending a complete range of patterns by separate post. All these cloths are selling very well in many countries and can be supplied from stock. If you decide to place an order we can meet it within one week.
	Please contact me if you have any queries.
	Yours sincerely

PACKING AND DESPATCH

When goods are despatched the buyer should be notified either by an advice note or by letter stating what has been sent, when it was sent, and the means of transport used. The customer then knows that the goods are on the way and can make the necessary arrangements to receive them.

7.13 Request for forwarding instructions

Dear

We are pleased to confirm that the 12 Olivetti KX R193 word processors which you ordered on 15 October are now ready for despatch.

When placing your order you stressed the importance of prompt delivery, and I am glad to say that by making a special effort we have been able to improve by a few days on the delivery date agreed.

We await your shipping instructions, and immediately we hear from you we will send you our advice of despatch.

Yours sincerely

---

[7] **rayon** artificial silk
[8] **lustre** a shiny surface

7.14 Advice of goods ready for despatch

Dear

We are pleased to confirm that all the books which you ordered on 3 April are packed and ready for despatch.

The consignment awaits collection at our warehouse and consists of two cases, each weighing about 100 kg.

Arrangements for shipment, cif Singapore, have already been made with W Watson & Co Ltd, our forwarding agents.[9] As soon as we receive their statement of charges, we will arrange for shipping documents to be sent to you through Barclays Bank against our draft for acceptance, as agreed.

We look forward to further business with you.

Yours sincerely

7.15 Notification of goods despatched

Dear

ORDER NUMBER S 524

The mohair rugs you ordered on 5 January have been packed in four special waterproof-lined cases. They will be collected tomorrow for consignment by passenger train and should reach you by Friday.

We feel sure you will find the consignment supports our claim to sell the best rugs of their kind and hope we may look forward to further orders from you.

Yours sincerely

7.16 Report of damage in transit

It is the legal duty of the buyer to collect any purchases from the supplier. Unless the terms of the sale include delivery, the railway or other carrier is considered the agent of the buyer. The buyer is, therefore, responsible for any loss, damage or delay which may affect the goods after the carrier has taken over.

---

[9] **forwarding agents** agents who arrange for transportation of goods

> Dear
>
> ORDER NUMBER S 524
>
> We regret to inform you that of the four cases of mohair rugs which were sent on 28 January, one was delivered damaged. The waterproof lining was badly torn and it will be necessary to send seven of the rugs for cleaning before we can offer them for sale.
>
> Will you therefore please arrange to send replacements immediately and charge them to our account.
>
> We realise that the responsibility for damage is ours and have already taken up the matter of compensation[10] with the railway authorities.
>
> Yours sincerely

7.17 Report of non-delivery of goods

When goods do not arrive as promised, avoid the tendency to blame the supplier as it may not be their fault. Your letter should be restricted to a statement of the facts and a request for information.

> Dear
>
> ORDER NUMBER S 524
>
> You wrote to us on 28 January informing us that the mohair rugs supplied to the above order were being despatched.
>
> We expected these goods a week ago and on the faith of your notification of despatch promised immediate delivery to a number of our customers. As the goods have not yet reached us, we naturally feel our customers have been let down.
>
> Delivery of the rugs is now a matter of urgency. Please find out what has happened to the consignment and let us know when we may expect delivery.
>
> We are of course making our own enquiries at this end.
>
> Yours sincerely

[10] **compensation** payment for loss

7.18 Complaint to carrier concerning non-delivery

Upon receiving the report of non-delivery the supplier should at once take up the matter with the carriers. The message must contain no suggestion of the annoyance that is naturally felt, but should be confined to the facts and ask for an immediate enquiry into the circumstances.

Dear

We regret to report that a consignment of mohair rugs addressed to W Hart & Co, 25–27 Gordon Avenue, Warrington, has not yet reached them.

These cases were collected by your carrier on 28 January for consignment by passenger train and should have been delivered by 1 February. We hold your carrier's receipt number 3542.

As our customer is urgently in need of these goods, we must ask you to make enquiries and let us know the cause of the delay and when delivery will be made.

Please treat this matter as one of extreme urgency.

Yours sincerely

USEFUL EXPRESSIONS

Placing orders

Openings

1 Thank you for your quotation of ...

2 We have received your quotation of ... and enclose our official order form.

3 Please supply the following items as quickly as possible and charge to our account:

Closes

1 Prompt delivery would be appreciated as the goods are needed urgently.

2 Please acknowledge receipt of this order and confirm that you will be able to deliver by ...

3 We hope to receive your advice of delivery by return of post.

Acknowledging orders

Openings

1 Thank you for your order dated …
2 We thank you for your order number … and will despatch the goods by …
3 We are sorry to inform you that the goods ordered on … cannot be supplied.

Closes

1 We hope the goods reach you safely and that you will be pleased with them.
2 We hope you will find the goods satisfactory and look forward to receiving your further orders.
3 We are pleased to say that these goods have been despatched today (will be despatched in …/are now awaiting collection at …).

Invoicing and settlement of accounts

Payment of the amount owing for goods supplied or services rendered is the final stage in a business transaction. In the retail trade transactions are usually for cash whereas in wholesale and foreign trade it is customary to allow credit.

INVOICES AND ADJUSTMENTS

When goods are supplied on credit the supplier sends an invoice to the buyer to:

- inform the buyer of the amount due
- enable the buyer to check the goods delivered
- enable entry in the buyer's purchases day book.

When an invoice is received it should be checked carefully, not only against the goods supplied but also for the accuracy of both prices and calculations.

Invoices are sometimes sent with the goods but they are more usually posted separately. Any buyer who is not a regular customer will be expected to settle the account at once; regular customers will be given credit, with invoices being charged to their accounts. Payment will then be made later on the basis of a statement of account sent by the supplier monthly or at other periodic intervals.

An example of an invoice is shown in Fig. 8.1.

PRO FORMA INVOICES

'Pro forma' means 'for form's sake'. A pro forma invoice is used:

- to cover goods sent 'on approval' or 'on consignment'
- to serve as a formal quotation
- to serve as a request for payment in advance for goods ordered by an unknown customer or a doubtful payer
- where the value of goods exported is required for customs purposes.

Pro forma invoices are not entered in the books of account and are not charged to the accounts of the persons to whom they are sent.

8.1 Covering letter with invoice

It is not normally necessary to send a covering letter with an invoice, particularly when the invoice is sent with the goods. If the invoice is sent separately a short but polite covering letter may be sent with it.

JOHN G GARTSIDE & CO LTD
Albion Works, Thomas Street
Manchester M60 2QA
Telephone 0161-980-2132

INVOICE

Johnson Tools & Co Ltd
112 Kingsway
LIVERPOOL
L20 6HJ

Your order no: AW 25

Date: 18 August 200—

Invoice no: B 832

Quantity	Item(s)	Unit Price	Total £
10	Polyester shirts, small	25.00	250.00
21	Polyester shirts, medium	26.00	546.00
12	Polyester shirts, large	27.25	327.00
			1123.00
	VAT (@ 17.5%)		196.53
	One case (returnable)		23.25
			1342.78
	Terms 2½% one month		

E & OE

Registered in England No 523807

Figure 8.1 Invoice

The invoice informs the buyer of the amount due for goods supplied on credit.

VAT: Value Added Tax. A tax on goods and services, payable to HM Customs and Excise.

E & OE: Errors and omissions excepted. This statement reserves the supplier's right to correct any errors which the document may contain.

(a) Non-regular customer

Dear Sir/Madam

YOUR ORDER NUMBER AW25

We are pleased to enclose our invoice number B 832 for the polyester shirts ordered on 13 August.

The goods are available from stock and will be sent to you immediately we receive the amount due, namely £1342.78.

Yours faithfully

(b) Regular customer

Dear Sir or Madam

YOUR ORDER NUMBER AW 25

Our invoice number B 832 is enclosed covering the polyester shirts ordered on 13 August.

These shirts have been packed ready for despatch and are being sent to you, carriage paid,[1] by rail. They should reach you within a few days.

Yours faithfully

DEBIT AND CREDIT NOTES

If the supplier has undercharged the buyer a debit note may be sent for the amount of the undercharge. A debit note is in the nature of a supplementary invoice.

If the supplier has overcharged the buyer then a credit note is sent. Credit notes are also issued to buyers when they return either goods (as where they are unsuitable) or packing materials on which there is a *rebate*.[2] Credit notes are usually printed in red to distinguish them from invoices and debit notes. Examples of credit and debit notes are shown in Figs 8.2 and 8.3.

[1] **carriage paid** sender pays for transport
[2] **rebate** a refund or allowance

JOHN G GARTSIDE & CO LTD
Albion Works, Thomas Street
Manchester M60 2QA
Telephone 0161-980-2132

DEBIT NOTE

Johnson Tools & Co Ltd
112 Kingsway
LIVERPOOL
L20 6HJ

Date 22 August 200—

Debit Note No. D.75

Date	Details	Price
		£
18.8.—	To 21 Polyester Shirts, medium charged on invoice number B 832 @ £26.00 each	
	Should be £26.70 each	
	Difference	14.70

Registered in England No 523807

Figure 8.2 **Debit note** A debit note is sent by the supplier to a buyer who has been undercharged in the original invoice

JOHN G GARTSIDE & CO LTD
Albion Works, Thomas Street
Manchester M60 2QA
Telephone 0161-980-2132

CREDIT NOTE

Johnson Tools & Co Ltd
112 Kingsway
LIVERPOOL
L20 6HJ

Date 25 August 200—

Credit Note No. C.521

Date	Details	Price
		£
18.8.—	By One case returned charged to you on invoice number B 832	23.25

Registered in England No 523807

Figure 8.3 **Credit note** A credit note is sent by the supplier to a buyer who has been overcharged in the original invoice, or to acknowledge and allow credit for goods returned by the buyer. It is usually printed in red.

8.2 Supplier sends debit note

Dear Sir/Madam

I regret to inform you that an error was made on our invoice number B 832 of 18 August.

The correct charge for polyester shirts, medium, is £26.70 and not £26.00 as stated. We are therefore enclosing a debit note for the amount undercharged, namely £14.70.

This mistake was due to an input error and we are sorry it was not noticed before the invoice was sent.

Yours faithfully

8.3 Buyer requests credit note

When notifying of an overcharge some customers send a debit note to the supplier as a claim for the amount overcharged. If the supplier agrees to the claim, he will then issue a credit note to the customer.

(a) Returned packing case

Dear Sirs

We have today returned to you by rail one empty packing case, charged on your invoice number B 832 of 18 August at £23.25.

A debit note for this amount is enclosed and we shall be glad to receive your credit note in return.

Yours faithfully

(b) Incorrect trade discount

Dear Sirs

Your invoice number 2370 dated 10 September allows a trade discount of only 33⅓% instead of the 40% to which you agreed in your letter of 5 August because of the unusually large order.

Calculated on the invoice gross total of £1,500 the difference in discount is exactly £100. If you will please adjust your charge we shall be glad to pass the invoice for immediate payment.

Yours faithfully

8.4 Supplier refuses request for credit note

(a) Retailer's request

> Dear Sir or Madam
>
> On 1 September we returned to you by parcel post one cassette tape recorder, Model EK76, Serial Number 048617, one of a consignment of 12 delivered on 5 August and charged on your invoice number 5624 dated 2 August.
>
> The customer who bought this recorder complained about its performance. It was for this reason that we returned it to you after satisfying ourselves that the complaint was justified.
>
> We have received no acknowledgement of the returned recorder or of the letter we sent to you on 1 September. It may be that you are trying to obtain a replacement for us. If this is the case and a replacement is not immediately available, please send us a credit note for the invoiced cost of the returned recorder, namely £175.
>
> We hope to hear from you soon.
>
> Yours faithfully

(b) Wholesaler's reply

> Dear
>
> We are sorry to learn from your letter of 16 September of the need to return one of the recorders supplied to you and charged on our invoice number 5624.
>
> We received your letter of 1 September but regret that we have no trace of the returned recorder. It would help if you could describe the kind of container in which it was packed and state exactly how it was addressed and the method of delivery used. As soon as we receive this information we will make a thorough investigation.[3]
>
> Meanwhile I am sure you will understand that we cannot either provide a free replacement or grant the credit you request. If you could wait for about 10 days, we could replace the tape recorder but would have to charge it to your account if our further enquiries should prove unsuccessful.
>
> Yours sincerely

[3] **investigation** a detailed enquiry

STATEMENTS OF ACCOUNT

A statement (see Fig. 8.4) is a demand for payment. It is a summary of the transactions between buyer and supplier during the period it covers, usually one month. It starts with the balance owing at the beginning of the period, if any. Thereafter amounts of invoices and debit notes issued are listed, and amounts of any credit notes issued and payments made by the buyer are deducted. The closing balance shows the amount owing at the date of the statement.

Statements, like invoices, are generally sent without a covering letter. If a covering letter is sent, it need only be very short and formal.

JOHN G GARTSIDE & CO LTD
Albion Works, Thomas Street
Manchester M60 2QA
Telephone 0161-980-2132

STATEMENT

Johnson Tools & Co Ltd
112 Kingsway
LIVERPOOL
L20 6HJ

Date 31 August 200—

Date	Details	Debit	Credit	Balance
		£	£	£
1.8.—	Account rendered			115.53
18.8.—	Invoice B 832	1342.78		1458.31
20.8.—	Cheque received		500.00	958.31
22.8.—	Debit Note D 75	35.70		994.01
25.8.—	Credit Note C 52		23.25	970.76

E & OE

Registered in England No 523807

Figure 8.4 **Statement** A statement is a demand for payment sent at regular periods by the supplier to buyers. It summarises all transactions over the period it covers and enables the buyer to check against the particulars given. Any errors discovered and agreed will be adjusted either by debit or credit note.

8.5 Covering letter with statement

Dear Sirs

We enclose our statement of account for all transactions during August. If payment is made within 14 days you may deduct the customary cash discount of 2½%.

Yours faithfully

8.6 Supplier reports underpaid statement

(a) Supplier's letter

Dear Sirs

We are enclosing our September statement totalling £820.57.

The opening balance brought forward is the amount left uncovered by the cheque received from you against our August statement which totalled £560.27. The cheque received from you, however, was drawn for £500.27 only, leaving the unpaid balance of £60 brought forward.

We should appreciate early settlement of the total amount now due.

Yours faithfully

(b) Buyer's reply

Dear Sirs

We have received your letter of 15 October enclosing September's statement.

We apologise for the underpayment of £60 on your August statement. This was due to a misreading of the amount due. The final figure was not very clearly printed and we mistakenly read it as £500.27 instead of £560.27.

Our cheque for £820.57, the total amount on the September statement, is enclosed.

Yours faithfully

8.7 Buyer reports errors in statement

(a) Buyer's notification

Dear Sirs

On checking your statement for July we notice the following errors:

1   The sum of £14.10 for the return of empty packing cases, covered by your credit note number 621 dated 5 July, has not been entered.

2   Invoice Number W825 for £127.32 has been debited twice – once on 11 July and again on 21 July.

Therefore we are deducting the sum of £141.42 from the balance shown on your statement, and enclose our cheque for £354.50 in full settlement.

Yours faithfully

(b) Supplier's acknowledgement

Dear Sirs

Thank you for your letter of 10 August enclosing your cheque for £354.50 in full settlement of the amount due against our July statement.

We confirm your deduction of £141.42 and apologise for the errors in the statement. Please accept our apologies for the inconvenience caused.

Yours faithfully

VARYING THE TERMS OF PAYMENT

When a customer is required to pay for goods when, or before, they are delivered, he is said to pay 'on invoice'. Customers known to be *creditworthy*[4] may be granted 'open account' terms, under which invoices arc charged to their accounts. Settlement is then made on the basis of statements of account sent by the supplier.

When a customer finds it necessary to ask for time to pay, the reasons given must be strong enough to convince the supplier that the difficulties are purely temporary and that payment will be made later.

[4]   **creditworthy** believed to be financially sound

8.8 Customer requests time to pay (granted)

(a) Customer's request

> Dear Sirs
>
> We have received your letter of 6 August reminding us that payment of the amount owing on your June statement is overdue.
>
> We were under the impression that payment was not due until the end of August when we would have had no difficulty in settling your account. However it seems that we misunderstood your terms of payment.
>
> In the circumstances we should be grateful if you could allow us to defer payment[5] for a further 3 weeks. Our present difficulty is purely temporary. Before the end of the month payments are due to us from a number of our regular customers who are notably prompt payers.
>
> We very much regret having to make this request and hope you will be able to grant it.
>
> Yours faithfully

Acknowledge supplier's letter
Explain why payment has not been made
Request deferred payment and give assurance
Express regret

(b) Supplier's reply

> Dear Mr Jensen
>
> Having carefully considered your letter of 8 August, we have decided to allow you to defer payment of your account to the end of August.
>
> This request is granted as an exceptional measure only because of the promptness with which you have settled your accounts in the past. We hope that in future dealings you will be able to keep to our terms of payment. We take this opportunity to remind you that they are as follows:
>
> 2½% discount for payment within 10 days
> Net cash for payment within one month
>
> We look forward to continuing to work with you.
>
> Yours sincerely

Respond to request for deferred payment
Explain reason for granting request
Reminder about future terms

[5] **defer payment** pay at a later date

8.9 Customer requests time to pay (not granted)

(a) Customer's request

> Dear Mr Wilson
>
> Thank you for your letter of 23 July asking for immediate payment of the £687 due on your invoice number AV54.
>
> When we wrote promising to pay you in full by 16 July, we fully expected to be able to do so. However we were unfortunately called upon to meet an unforeseen and unusually heavy demand earlier this month.
>
> We are therefore enclosing a cheque for £200 on account,[6] and ask you to be good enough to allow us a further few weeks in which to settle the balance. We fully expect to be able to settle your account in full by the end of August. If you would grant this deferment, we should be most grateful.
>
> I hope to hear from you soon.
>
> Yours sincerely

(b) Supplier's reply

In refusing requests of this kind it is better for suppliers to stress the benefits the customer is likely to gain from making payments promptly rather than to stress their own difficulties in seeking prompt payment. The customer is, after all, more interested in problems closer to home.

> Dear Mrs Billingham
>
> *Thank you* — Thank you for your letter of 25 July sending us a cheque for £200 on account and asking for an extension of time in which to pay the balance.
>
> *Tactfully state that payment is insufficient and delay quite unreasonable* — As your account is now more than 2 months overdue we find your present cheque quite insufficient. It is hardly reasonable to expect us to wait a further month for the balance, particularly as we invoiced the goods at a specially low price which was mentioned to you at the time.
>
> *Tone is important in this letter which is firm but expressed in a style which would not offend*
>
> *Express sympathy but explain why prompt payment is desirable* — We sympathise with your difficulties but need hardly remind you that it is in our customers' long-term interests to pay their accounts promptly so as to qualify for discounts and at the same time build a reputation for financial reliability.
>
> *The request for immediate payment is worded appropriately* — In the circumstances we hope that in your own interests you will make arrangements to clear your account without further delay. We look forward to receiving your cheque for the balance on your account within the next few days.
>
> Yours sincerely

---

[6] **on account** in part payment

8.10 Supplier questions partial payment

When making payment on a statement, the debtor should always state whether the payment is 'on account' or 'in full settlement' otherwise it may give rise to letters such as the following.

Dear

We thank you for your letter of 10 October enclosing your cheque for £58.67. Our official receipt is enclosed as requested.

As you do not say that the cheque is on account, we are wondering whether the amount of £58.67 was intended to be £88.67 – the balance on your account as shown in our September statement.

In any case we look forward to receiving the uncleared balance of £30 within the next few days.

Yours sincerely

8.11 Supplier rejects discount deduction

Dear

Thank you for your letter of 15 October enclosing your cheque for £292.50 in full settlement of our May statement.

We regret that we cannot accept this payment as a full discharge of the £300 due on our statement. The terms of payment allow the 2½% cash discount only on accounts paid within 10 days of statement whereas your present payment is more than a month overdue.

The balance still owing is £7.50 and to save you the trouble of making a separate payment we will include this amount in your next payment and will prepare our July statement accordingly.

Yours sincerely

METHODS OF PAYMENT

Various methods of payment may be used in settling accounts. The form of payment to be used is a matter for arrangement between the parties concerned.

1 Cash (coins and notes).

2 Payments through the Post Office.

(a) *Postal orders and money orders* (the latter for foreign payments only). British postal orders and money orders are issued and paid in many countries abroad. Payment is made in the currency of the country of payment at the current rate of exchange. Postal orders are used for small sums (up to £20 in the United Kingdom).

Money orders (other than telegraph money orders) are no longer issued for payment in the United Kingdom but are issued for amounts up to £50 for payment abroad. This method is used by senders who have no bank or giro (postal cheque) account. A person sending a money order should ask the payee for a receipt since there is no other evidence of payment.

(b) *Giro transfers.* 'Giro' is a term commonly applied to the postal cheque system run by post offices in most Western European countries and Japan. Apart from cash transactions, giro transfer or postal cheque is the chief means of payment. Anyone can make a deposit or receive a payment, whether or not a giro account is held.

(c) *The COD system.* In the COD (cash on delivery) system the buyer pays for the goods at the time they are handed over by the carrier (this includes the postal system). In this way the supplier makes certain of receiving payment for goods supplied to unknown customers.

3 Payments through banks

(a) Home trade relies on online banking, cheques, credit transfers (bank giro), banker's drafts and letters of credit.

- *Online banking:* More and more people are paying bills using Internet digital banking services. After setting up your unique passwords, you can pay bills, transfer money, do virtually anything with your accounts at the click of a mouse.

- *Cheques:* A bank cheque is always payable on demand. It is by far the most common form of payment used to settle credit transactions in the home trade of countries where the bank cheque system has been developed. It may also be used to pay debts abroad. A receipt is the best, but not the only, evidence of payment and cheques which have been paid by a banker and later returned to customers may be produced as receipts. When payment is made by cheque a separate receipt is therefore unnecessary but the payer may legally demand a receipt if required.

- *Credit transfers:* The system of credit transfers operated by banks is in many ways similar to the postal cheque (giro) system and is now commonly referred to as a bank giro. The payer completes a credit transfer or giro transfer slip for each separate payment and enters it on a list, which is passed (in duplicate) to the banker together with the slips and a cheque for the total amount. The banker then distributes the slips to the banks of the payees concerned and their accounts are then credited. Payees receive the transfer slips from their bankers. A separate advice of payment by the payer is therefore unnecessary but some payers make it their practice to send one.

- *Banker's drafts:* A banker's draft is a document bought from a bank. It orders the branch bank, or the agent on whom it is drawn, to pay the stated sum of money on demand to the person named in the draft (the payee). In foreign transactions the payee receives payment in the local currency at the current rate of exchange. Banker's drafts are convenient for paying large sums of money in circumstances where a creditor would hesitate to take a cheque in payment. Like cheques, they may be crossed for added safety.

(b) Foreign trade may use bank transfers (mail, telegraphic and telex); bills of exchange and promissory notes; bank commercial credits (documentary credits if a documentary bill is used); banker's drafts; and letters of credit.

8.12 Supplier asks customer to select terms of payment

> Dear
>
> Thank you for your letter of 3 April, but you do not say whether you wish this transaction to be for cash or on credit.
>
> When we wrote to you on 20 March we explained our willingness to offer easy credit terms to customers who do not wish to pay cash, and also that we allow generous discounts to cash customers.
>
> We may not have made it clear that when placing orders customers should state whether cash or credit terms are required.
>
> Please let me know which you prefer so that we can arrange your account accordingly.
>
> Yours sincerely

8.13 Form letter enclosing payment (and acknowledgement)

Every business has a good deal of purely routine correspondence. Letters enclosing or acknowledging payments are of this kind. They often take a standard form suitable for all occasions and are therefore known as 'form letters'. In such cases a supply of preprinted letters is prepared with blank spaces for the insertion of variable types of information (reference numbers, names and addresses, dates, sums of money, etc).

Of course the personal touch which personalised letters provide is lost with such form letters. However many companies now use mail merge facilities on word processors to produce personalised form letters which look like originals.

(a) Sender's form letter

> Dear Sir or Madam
>
> We have pleasure in enclosing our cheque (bill/draft/etc) for £... in full settlement (part settlement) of your statement (invoice) dated ...
>
> Please send us your official receipt.
>
> Yours faithfully

(b) Form letter acknowledging payment

> Dear
>
> Thank you for your letter of ... enclosing cheque (bill/draft/etc) for £... in full settlement (part payment) of our statement of account (invoice) dated ...
>
> We enclose our official receipt.
>
> Yours sincerely

8.14 Letter informing supplier of payment by credit transfer (bank giro)

> Dear Sirs
>
> A credit transfer has been made to your account at the Barminster Bank, Church Street, Dover, in payment of the amount due for the goods supplied on 2 May and charged on your invoice number 1524.
>
> Yours faithfully

8.15 Letter informing supplier of payment by banker's draft

> Dear Sirs
>
> Our banker's draft is enclosed, drawn on the Midminster Bank, Benghazi, for £672.72 and crossed 'Account Payee only'.
>
> The draft is sent in full settlement of your account dated 31 May.
>
> Please acknowledge its safe receipt.
>
> Yours faithfully

8.16 Supplier sends goods COD (cash on delivery)

> Dear Sir or Madam
>
> Thank you for your order for one of our Model X50 cameras. This model is an improved version of our famous Model X40, which has already established itself firmly in public favour. We feel sure you will be delighted with it. At the price of £89.25 we believe it represents the best value on the market for cameras of this type.
>
> Your camera will be sent to you today by compensation-fee parcel post, for delivery against payment of our trade charge of £90. This charge includes packing and postal registration and COD charges.
>
> Under our guarantee you are entitled to a refund of your payment in full if you are not completely satisfied, but you must return the camera by compensation-fee parcel post within 7 days.
>
> Yours faithfully

USEFUL EXPRESSIONS

Payments due

Openings

1 Enclosed is our statement for the quarter ended ...

2 We enclose our statement to 31... showing a balance of £...

3 We are sorry it was necessary to return our invoice number ... for correction.

4 We very much regret having to ask for an extension of credit on your January statement.

Closes

1 Please let us have your credit note for the amount of this overcharge.

2 Please make the necessary adjustment and we will settle the account immediately.

3 We apologise again for this error and enclose our credit note for the overcharge.

Payments made

Openings

1 We enclose our cheque for £... in payment for goods supplied on ...

2 We enclose our cheque for £... in payment of your invoice number ...

3 We acknowledge with thanks your cheque for £...

4 We thank you for your cheque for £... in part payment of your account.

Closes

1 We hope to receive the amount due by the end of this month.

2 We should be obliged if you would send us your cheque immediately.

3 As the amount owing is considerably overdue, we must ask you to send us your cheque by return.

Letters requesting payment

Tone

Checklist

Useful expressions

TONE

When a customer fails to pay promptly it is always annoying to the supplier, but no suggestion of annoyance must be allowed to creep into the correspondence. It may be better not to write at all and instead call on the customer if possible, or telephone tactfully to persuade at least part payment to be made on account. In difficult cases it may even be good policy to accept a part payment rather than resort to legal action which would be both expensive and time-consuming.

There may be several good reasons why a customer fails to pay on time, some of them deserving sympathy. There is, however, always the customer who is only too ready to invent excuses and who needs to be watched. Each case must be treated on its merits.

The style and tone of any letters should depend on such factors as the age of the debt, whether later payment is *habitual*,[1] and how important the customer is. However no letter must ever be less than polite, and even the final letter threatening legal action must be written 'with regret'.

 For more on tone see page 36.

LATE PAYMENTS

When there is a need to write explaining difficulties in paying an account by the due date and to ask to defer payment, the following plan is useful:

1 Refer to the account that cannot be paid immediately.

2 Apologise for inability to pay and give reasons.

3 Suggest an extension of period for payment.

4 Hope that the suggestion will be accepted.

9.1 **Customer explains inability to pay**

This letter is from a regular and reliable customer. It makes a reasonable request and a supplier refusing it would run the risk of driving away that customer. If the supplier refuses, the customer might pay the outstanding amount, but could then start buying from a competitor. In the process the supplier could lose many valuable future orders.

[1] **habitual** customary, usual

Dear Sirs

Your invoice number 527 dated 20 July for £1516 is due for payment at the end of this month.

Unfortunately a fire broke out in our Despatch Department last week and destroyed a large part of a valuable consignment due for delivery to a cash customer. Our claim is now with the insurance company but it is unlikely to be met for another 3 or 4 weeks. Until then we are faced with a difficult financial problem.

I am therefore writing for permission to <u>defer payment</u>[2] of your invoice until the end of September.

As you are aware, my accounts with you have always been settled promptly, and it is with regret that I am now forced to make this request. I hope that you will find it possible to grant it.

Yours faithfully

9.2 Customer explains late payment

Dear

Further to your letter of 4 July, I enclose a cheque for £1182.57 in full settlement of your invoice number W 563. Many apologies for late payment.

This is due to my absence from the office through illness and my failure to leave instructions for your account to be paid. I did not discover the <u>oversight</u>[3] until I returned to the office yesterday.

I would not like you to think that failure to settle your account on time was in any way intentional. My apologies once again for this delay.

Yours sincerely

COLLECTION LETTERS

The preliminary steps in debt collection are as follows:

1 A first end-of-month statement of account.

2 A second end-of-month statement of account with added comment.

3 A first letter worded formally.

4 Second and third letters.

5 A final letter notifying that legal action will be taken unless the amount is paid within a stipulated period of time.

[2] **defer payment** pay later
[3] **oversight** unintentional omission

A customer whose account is only slightly *overdue*[4] would understandably be offended to receive a personal letter concerning this. This is why the first 2 reminders usually take the form of end-of-the-month statements of account. Even where the second of these statements is marked with such comments as 'Second application', 'Account overdue – please pay' or 'Immediate attention is requested', this is unlikely to give offence.

1 FIRST APPLICATIONS FOR PAYMENT

It is not wise to write a letter until a customer has been given the opportunity to pay on these impersonal statements. Letters requesting payment of overdue accounts are termed 'collection letters'. They aim to:

(a) persuade the customer to settle the account

(b) retain custom and goodwill.

It would be easy to give offence so any letters must be written with tact and restraint. It may also be the case that the supplier is at fault, as in the case where a payment received has not been recorded, or goods sent or service given are not satisfactory.

9.3 A printed collection letter

A first collection letter may be printed as a 'form letter' as in this example where the individual details are keyed in appropriately. Alternatively the details may be stored on a word processor so that the letter may be personalised.

Dear Sir/Madam

ACCOUNT NUMBER ...

According to our records the above account dated ... has not been settled.

The enclosed statement shows the amount owing to be £...

We hope to receive an early settlement[5] of this account.

Yours faithfully

9.4 Personalised collection letters

There may be circumstances when an individual letter rather than a form letter is more appropriate. It should then be addressed to a named senior official and marked 'Confidential'.

---

[4] **overdue** remaining unpaid
[5] **settlement** completion by payment

(a) To a regular payee

Dear

ACCOUNT NUMBER 6251

As you are usually very prompt in settling your accounts, we wonder whether there is any special reason why we have not received payment of this account, which is already a month overdue.

In case you may not have received the statement of account sent on 31 May showing a balance owing of £105.67, a copy is enclosed. We hope this will receive your early attention.

Yours sincerely

(b) To a new customer

Dear Sir/Madam

ACCOUNT NUMBER 5768

We regret having to remind you that we have not received payment of the balance of £105.67 due on our statement for December. This was sent to you on 2 January and a copy is enclosed.

We must remind you that unusually low prices were quoted to you on the understanding of an early settlement.

It may well be that non-payment is due to an oversight, and so we ask you to be good enough to send us your cheque within the next few days.

Yours faithfully

(c) To a customer who has sent a part payment

Dear

Thank you for your letter of 8 March enclosing a cheque for £500 in part payment of the balance due on our February statement.

Your payment leaves an unpaid balance of £825.62. As our policy is to work on small profit margins, we regret that we cannot grant long-term credit facilities.

We are sure that you will not think it is unreasonable for us to ask for immediate payment of this balance.

Yours sincerely

9.5 Reminder to customer who has already paid

The need for a cautious approach is always necessary since the customer may not be at fault, as where the payment has *gone astray*,[6] or where the supplier has received it but failed to record it.

---

[6] **gone astray** been lost in transit

(a) Request for payment

Dear Sir/Madam

ACCOUNT NUMBER S542

According to our records our account for cutlery supplied to you on 21 October has not been paid.

We enclose a detailed statement showing the amount owing to be £310.62 and hope you will make an early settlement.

Yours faithfully

(b) Customer's reply

Dear

YOUR ACCOUNT NUMBER S542

I was surprised to receive your letter of 8 December stating that you had not received payment of the above account.

In fact our cheque (number 065821, drawn on Barclays Bank, Blackpool) for £310.62 was posted to you on 3 November. As this cheque appears to have gone astray, I have instructed the bank not to pay on it. A replacement cheque for the same amount is enclosed.

Yours sincerely

2 SECOND APPLICATION LETTERS

If a reply to the first application is not received, a second application should be sent after about 10 days. This should be firmer in tone but still polite. Nothing must be said to cause annoyance or ill will. Co-operation is required and this will not be achieved by annoying the customer.

Such letters should be addressed to a senior official under 'Confidential' cover and planned as follows:

1 Refer to previous application.
2 Assume that something unusual accounts for the delay in payment.
3 Suggest tactfully that an explanation would be welcome.
4 Ask for payment to be sent.

9.6 Specimen second application letters

(a) Second letter, following 9.4(a)

Dear

ACCOUNT NUMBER 6251

As we have not received a reply to our letter of 5 July requesting settlement of the above account, we are writing again to remind you that the amount still owing is £105.67.

No doubt there is some special reason for the delay in payment, and we should welcome an explanation together with your remittance.

Yours sincerely

(b) Second letter, following 9.4(b)

Dear Sir/Madam

On 18 February we wrote to remind you that our December statement sent on 2 January showed a balance of £105.67 outstanding and due for payment by 31 January.

Settlement of this account is now more than a month overdue. Therefore we must ask you either to send us your remittance within the next few days or at least to offer an explanation for the delay in payment.

Your prompt reply will be appreciated.

Yours faithfully

(c) Second letter, following 9.4(c)

Dear

We have not heard from you since we wrote on 10 March about the unpaid balance of £825.62 on your account. In view of your past good record we have not previously pressed for a settlement.

To regular customers such as yourself our terms of payment are 3% one month,[7] and we hope you will not withhold payment any longer, otherwise it will be necessary for us to revise these terms.

In the circumstances we look forward to receiving your cheque for the outstanding amount within the next few days.

Yours sincerely

---

[7] **3% one month** subject to a discount if paid within one month

3 THIRD APPLICATION LETTERS

If payment is still not made and if no explanation has been received, a third letter becomes necessary. Such a letter should show that steps will be taken to enforce payment if necessary, such steps depending on individual circumstances. Third letters should follow this plan:

1 Review earlier efforts to collect payment.
2 Give a final opportunity to pay by stating a reasonable *deadline date*.[8]
3 State that you wish to be fair and reasonable.
4 State action to be taken if this third request is ignored.
5 Regret the necessity for the letter.

9.7 **Specimen third application letters**

(a) Third letter, following 9.6(a)

> Dear
>
> ACCOUNT NUMBER 6251
>
> We do not appear to have received replies to our two previous requests of 5 and 16 July for payment of the sum of £105.67 still owing on this account.
>
> It is with the utmost regret that we have reached the stage when we must press for immediate payment. We have no wish to be unreasonable, but failing payment by 7 August you will leave us no choice but to place the matter in other hands.
>
> We sincerely hope this will not become necessary.
>
> Yours sincerely

(b) Third letter, following 9.6(b)

> Dear Sir/Madam
>
> It is very difficult to understand why we have not heard from you in reply to our two letters of 18 February and 2 March about the sum of £105.67 due on our December statement. We had hoped that you would at least explain why the account continues to remain unpaid.
>
> I am sure you will agree that we have shown every consideration in the circumstances. Failing any reply to our earlier requests for payment, I am afraid we shall have no choice but to take other steps to recover the amount due.
>
> We are most anxious to avoid doing anything through which your credit and reputation might suffer. Therefore even at this late stage we are prepared to give you a further opportunity to put matters right.
>
> In the circumstances, we propose to give you until the end of this month to clear your account.[9]
>
> Yours faithfully

Margin notes: Even in this third letter restraint is shown in the wording rather than directly attacking the customer · Terms like 'every consideration' and 'no choice...' somewhat soften the blow · This paragraph gives the customer a final chance to clear the account · A specific timeframe is given

[8] **deadline date** final date for payment
[9] **clear your account** pay the total balance owing

(c) Third letter, following 9.6(c)

Dear

We are surprised and disappointed not to have heard from you in response to our two letters of 10 and 23 March reminding you of the balance of £825.62 still owing on our February statement.

This failure either to clear your account or even to offer an explanation is all the more disappointing because of our past satisfactory dealings over many years.

In the circumstances we must say that unless we hear from you within 10 days we shall have to consider seriously the further steps we should take to obtain payment.

Yours sincerely

4 FINAL COLLECTION LETTERS

If all three applications are ignored, it is reasonable to assume that the customer either cannot, or will not, settle the account. A brief notification of the action that is to be taken must then be sent as a final warning.

9.8 Specimen final collection letters

(a) Final letter, following 9.7(a)

Dear

We are surprised that we have received no reply to the further letter we sent to you on 28 July regarding the long overdue payment of £105.67 on your account.

Our relations in the past have always been good. Even so we cannot allow the amount to remain unpaid indefinitely. Unless the amount due is paid or a satisfactory explanation received by the end of this month, we shall be reluctantly compelled to put this matter in the hands of our solicitors.

Yours sincerely

(b) Final letter, following 9.7(b)

Dear Sir/Madam

We are disappointed not to have received any response from you in answer to our letter of 16 March concerning non-payment of the balance of £105.67 outstanding on our December statement.

We are now making a final request for payment in the hope that it will not be necessary to hand the matter over to an agent for collection.

We have decided to defer this step for 7 days to give you the opportunity either to pay or at least to send us an explanation.

Yours faithfully

(c) Final letter, following 9.7(c)

Dear

We are quite unable to understand why we have received no reply to our letter of 7 April, our third attempt to secure payment of the balance of £825.62 still owing on your account with us.

We feel that we have shown reasonable patience and treated you with every consideration. However we must now regretfully take steps to recover payment at law, and the matter will be placed in the hands of our solicitors.

Yours sincerely

CHECKLIST

- ☐ Use a tone that is firm but understanding.
- ☐ Mention when the payment was originally due.
- ☐ State the amount owed.
- ☐ State the penalties if any.
- ☐ Mention the grace period.
- ☐ Give a new deadline.
- ☐ Indicate the consequences.

USEFUL EXPRESSIONS

First applications

Openings

1 We notice that your account which was due for payment on ... is still outstanding.

2 We wish to draw your attention to our invoice number ... for £... which remains unpaid.

3 We must remind you that we have not yet received the balance of our ... statement amounting to £..., payment of which is now more than a month overdue.

Closes

1 We hope to receive your cheque by return.

2 We look forward to your payment within the next few days.

3 As our statement may have gone astray, we enclose a copy and shall be glad if you will pass it for payment immediately.

Second applications

Openings

1 We do not appear to have had any reply to our request of ... for settlement of £... due on our invoice ... dated ...

2 We regret not having received a reply to our letter of ...

3 We are at a loss to understand why we have received no reply to our letter of ... requesting settlement of our ... statement in the sum of £...

Closes

1 We trust you will attend to this matter without further delay.

2 We must ask you to settle this account by return.

3 We regret that we must ask for immediate payment of the amount outstanding.

Third applications

Openings

1 We wrote to you on ... and again on ... concerning the amount owing on our invoice number ...

2 We have had no reply to our previous requests for payment of our ... statement ...

3 We note with surprise and disappointment that we have had no replies to our two previous applications for payment of your outstanding account.

Closes

1 Unless we receive your cheque in full settlement by ... we shall have no option but to instruct our solicitors to recover the amount due.

2 Unless we receive your cheque in full settlement by the end of this month, we shall be compelled to take further steps to enforce payment.

3 We still hope you will settle this account without further delay and thus save yourself the inconvenience and considerable costs of legal action.

Credit and status enquiries

REASONS FOR CREDIT

The main reason for buying on credit is for convenience. Basically it allows us to 'buy now, pay later'.

1 Credit enables a retailer to hold stocks and to pay for them out of the proceeds of later sales. This increases the working capital and thus helps to finance the business.

2 Credit enables the buying public to enjoy the use of goods before they have saved the money needed to buy them.

3 Credit avoids the inconvenience of separate payments each time a purchase is made.

The main reason for selling on credit is to increase profits. Credit sales not only attract new customers but also keep old customers, since people who run accounts tend to shop at the place where the account is kept, whereas cash customers are free to shop anywhere.

DISADVANTAGES OF CREDIT

There are a number of disadvantages in dealing on credit both for the supplier and for the customer:

1 It increases the cost of doing business since it involves extra work in keeping records and collecting payments.

2 It exposes the supplier to the risk of bad debts.

3 The buyer pays more for the goods since the supplier must raise prices to cover the higher costs.

REQUESTS FOR CREDIT

A buyer who makes regular purchases from the same supplier will usually wish to avoid the inconvenience of paying for each transaction separately, and will ask for '*open account*'[1] terms under which purchases will be paid for monthly or quarterly or at some other agreed period. In other words the goods are to be supplied on credit.

[1] **open account** credit terms with periodic settlements

10.1   Customer requests open-account terms

(a) Request

> Dear
>
> We have been very satisfied with your handling of our past orders, and as our business is growing expect to place even larger orders with you in the future.
>
> As our dealings have extended over a period of nearly 2 years, we hope you will agree to allow us open-account facilities with, say, quarterly settlements. This arrangement would save us the inconvenience of making separate <u>payments on invoice</u>.[2]
>
> Banker's and trade references can be provided if required.
>
> We hope to receive your favourable reply soon.
>
> Yours sincerely

(b) Reply

> Dear
>
> Thank you for your letter of 18 November requesting the transfer of your business from payment on invoice to open-account terms.
>
> As our business relations with you over the past 2 years have been entirely satisfactory, we are quite willing to make the transfer, based on a 90-day settlement period. In your case it will not be necessary to supply references.
>
> We are pleased that you have been satisfied with our past service and that expansion of your business is likely to lead to increased orders. We can assure you of our continued efforts to give you the same high standard of service as in the past.
>
> Yours sincerely

10.2   Customer requests extension of credit

(a) Cash flow problem

> Dear
>
> We regret you have had to remind us that we have not settled your account due for payment on 30 October.
>
> We had intended to settle this account before now, but because of the present depressed state of business our own customers have not been meeting their obligations as promptly as usual. This has <u>adversely affected</u>[3] our cash flow.
>
> Investment income due in less than a month's time will enable us to clear your account by the end of next month. We should therefore be grateful if you would accept the enclosed cheque for £200 as a <u>payment on account</u>.[4] The balance will be cleared as soon as possible.
>
> Yours sincerely

[2] **payments on invoice** payment due on presentation of invoice
[3] **adversely affected** made worse
[4] **payment on account** part payment

(b) Lending restrictions and bad trade

Dear

STATEMENT OF ACCOUNT FOR AUGUST 200—

We have just received your letter of 8 October requesting settlement of our outstanding balance of £1686.00.

We are sorry not to have been able to clear this balance with our usual promptness. However, the present depressed state of business and the current restrictions on bank lending have created difficulties for us. These difficulties are purely temporary as payments from customers are due to us early in the New Year on a number of recently completed contracts.

Our resources[5] are quite sufficient to meet all our obligations, but as you will appreciate we have no wish to realise on our assets[6] at the moment. We hope you will therefore grant us a 3-month extension of credit, when we will be able to settle your account in full.

Yours sincerely

10.3 Customer requests credit extension due to bankruptcy

(a) Letter to supplier

Dear

Introduction gives background details

We have received and checked your statement for the quarter ended 30 September and agree with the balance of £785.72 shown to be due.

History of prompt payment is explained and details of current situation mentioned

Until now we have had no difficulty in meeting our commitments and have always settled our accounts with you promptly. We could have done so at this time but for the bankruptcy[7] of an important customer whose affairs are not likely to be settled for some time.

Tactful request to defer payment

We should be most grateful if you would allow us to defer payment of your present account to the end of next month. This would enable us to meet a temporarily difficult situation forced upon us by events that could not be foreseen.

Final assurance of early settlement

During the next few weeks we will be receiving payments under a number of large contracts. If you grant our request we shall have no difficulty in settling with you in full in due course.

If you wish to discuss this please give me a call on 2468742.

Yours sincerely

[5] **resources** financial position
[6] **realise on our assets** sell assets in order to raise cash
[7] **bankruptcy** inability to pay one's debts

(b) Request granted

Dear

Refer to customer's letter and request — Thank you for your letter of 10 October requesting an extension of time for payment of the amount due on our 30 September statement.

State reason for agreeing to extension — In view of the promptness with which you have always settled with us in the past, we are willing to grant this extension in these special circumstances.

Give a final date for full settlement — Please let us have your cheque in full settlement by 30 November.

Yours sincerely

(c) Request refused

Dear

Refer to customer's letter and request — I am sorry to learn from your letter of 10 October of the difficulty in which the bankruptcy of an important customer has placed you.

Tactful wording is necessary when a request is refused — I should like to say at once that we fully understand your wish for an extension of time and would like to be able to help you. Unfortunately this is impossible because of commitments which we must meet by the end of this month.

Explain regret at requesting immediate payment — Your request is not at all unreasonable and if it had been possible we would have been pleased to grant it. In the circumstances, however, we must ask you to settle with us on the terms of payment originally agreed.

Yours sincerely

BUSINESS REFERENCES

When goods are sold for cash there is no need for the supplier to enquire into the financial standing of the buyer. Where they are sold on credit, however, the ability to pay will be important.

For credit to be allowed the supplier will want to know what the buyer's reputation is like, the extent of their business, and in particular whether accounts are paid promptly. It is on this information that the supplier will decide whether to allow credit and, if so, how much.

This information can be obtained from:

- trade references supplied by the customer
- the customer's banker
- various trade associations
- credit enquiry agencies.

When a customer places an order with a new supplier it is customary to supply trade references, that is the names of persons or firms to whom the supplier may refer for information. Alternatively or additionally the customer may give the name and address of the banker. References of this kind, supplied as they are by customers themselves, must be accepted with caution since naturally only those who are likely to report favourably will be named as referees. Even a bank reference can be misleading – a customer may have a satisfactory banking account and yet have business dealings which would not bear looking into.

10.4 Supplier requests references

When a new customer places an order but fails to provide references the supplier will naturally want some evidence of the customer's creditworthiness, especially if the order is a large one. The supplier's letter asking for references must avoid any suggestion that the customer is not to be trusted.

Dear

We were pleased to receive your first order with us dated 19 May.

When opening new accounts it is our practice to ask customers for trade references. Please be good enough to send us the names and addresses of two other suppliers with whom you have dealings.

We hope to receive this information by return, and meanwhile your order has been put in hand for despatch immediately we hear further from you.

Yours sincerely

10.5 Supplier asks for completion of credit application form

(a) Letter from supplier

Dear

Thank you for your order number 526 of 15 June for polyester bedspreads and pillow cases.

As your name does not appear on our books and as we should like you to take advantage of our usual credit terms, we enclose our credit application form for your completion and return as soon as possible.

We should be able to deliver your present order in about 2 weeks, and look forward to receiving your further orders.

We hope that this first transaction will mark the beginning of a pleasant business connection.

Yours sincerely

(b) Customer returns completed credit application form

Dear

Thank you for your letter of 18 June. As we fully expect to place further orders, we should obviously like to take advantage of your offer of credit facilities.

We quite understand the need for references and have completed your credit application form giving the relevant information. This is enclosed.

We look forward to receiving delivery of our first order by the end of this month and to our future business dealings with you.

Yours sincerely

10.6 Customer supplies trade references

Dear Sirs

Thank you for the catalogue and price list received earlier this month.

We have pleasure in sending you our first order, number ST6868, for 6 Olivetti portable electronic typewriters, elite type, at your list price of £255 less 25% on your usual monthly terms.

These machines are needed for early delivery to customers and as we understand you have the machines in stock we should be glad if you would arrange for them to reach us by the end of next week. We hope this will leave enough time for you to take up references with the following firms with which we have had dealings over many years:

B Kisby & Co Ltd, 28–30 Lythan Square, Liverpool
The Atlas Manufacturing Co Ltd, Century House, Bristol

We look forward to doing further business with you in the future.

Yours faithfully

10.7 Customer supplies a banker's reference

Dear Sirs

Our cheque for £2513 is enclosed in full settlement of your invoice number 826 for the stereo tape recorders supplied earlier this month.

My directors have good reason to believe that these particular products will be a popular selling line in this part of the country. As we expect to place further orders with you from time to time, we should be glad if you would arrange to provide open-account facilities on a quarterly basis.

For information concerning our credit standing[8] we refer you to Barclays Bank Ltd, 25–27 The Arcade, Southampton.

Yours faithfully

---

[8] **credit standing** financial position

STATUS ENQUIRIES

Letters taking up trade references are written in formal, polite terms. They usually conform to the following 4 point plan:

- Give background information about the customer's situation.
- Request information about the prospective customer's *standing*[9] and an opinion on the wisdom of granting credit within a stated limit.
- Give an assurance that the information will be treated confidentially.
- Enclose a stamped addressed envelope or an international postal reply coupon if the correspondent lives abroad.

Some large firms make their enquiries on a specially printed form containing the questions they would like answered. Use of such forms makes it easier for the companies approached, and helps to ensure prompt replies.

When the supplier receives the information requested, it is courteous to send a suitable letter of acknowledgement and thanks.

Letters taking up references should be addressed to a senior official and marked 'Confidential'.

10.8 Supplier takes up trade references

(a) Example 1

Dear Sirs

Watson & Jones of Newcastle wish to open an account with us and have given your name as a reference.

We should be grateful for your view about the firm's general standing and your opinion on whether they are likely to be reliable for credit up to £1000 and to settle their accounts promptly.

Any information provided will of course be treated in strict confidence.

We enclose a stamped, addressed envelope for your reply.

Yours faithfully

---

[9] **standing** status, reputation

(b) Example 2

Dear Sirs

We have received a request from Shamlan & Shamlan & Co of Bahrain for supplies of our products on open-account terms. They state that they have regularly traded with you over the past 2 years and have given your name as a reference.

We should be obliged if you would tell us in confidence whether you have found this company to be thoroughly reliable in their dealings with you and prompt in settling their accounts.

We understand their requirements with us may amount to approximately £2000 a quarter, and should be glad to know whether you feel they will be able to meet commitments of this size. Any other information you can provide would be very welcome.

Your reply, for which we enclose an international postal reply coupon, will of course be treated in strict confidence.

Yours faithfully

10.9 Supplier requests his banker to take up bank reference

In view of the highly confidential relationship between bankers and their customers, a banker will not normally reply direct to private enquiries about the standing of a client. This information is usually given willingly to fellow bankers. When taking up a bank reference, the supplier must do so through their own banker.

Dear Sir/Madam

The Colston Engineering Co Ltd in Mumbai has asked for a standing credit of £5000 but as our knowledge of this company is limited to a few months trading on a cash-on-invoice basis, we should like some information about their financial standing before dealing with their request.

The only reference they give us is that of their bankers – the National Bank of Nigeria, Ibadan. We would appreciate any information you can let us have.

Yours faithfully

10.10 Supplier refers to credit enquiry agency

A supplier who wants an independent reference concerning a customer's business standing may refer either to a trade association or to one of the numerous credit enquiry agencies. These agencies make it their business to supply information on the financial standing of both trading firms and professional and private individuals. They have a remarkable store of information which is kept up to date from a variety of sources including their own local agents. If the information requested is not immediately available from their records, they will set up enquiries and can usually supply it within a few days.

Dear Sirs

We have been asked by A Griffiths & Co, Cardiff to supply goods to the value of £1750 on open-account terms against their first order.

We have no information about this company but as there are prospects of further large orders from them, we should like to meet the present order on the terms requested if it is safe to do so.

Please let us have a report on the reputation and financial standing of the company and in particular your advice on whether it would be advisable to grant credit for this first order. Your advice on the maximum amount for which it would be safe to grant credit on a quarterly account would also be appreciated.

Yours faithfully

REPLIES TO STATUS ENQUIRIES

Where a company's credit has been found to be satisfactory, the reply to the enquiry presents no problem. However, if the firm's credit is uncertain, the reply calls for the utmost care. It is usual to phrase such replies in a manner that leaves the enquirer to 'read between the lines', ie to gather for themselves the true meaning, rather than bluntly state disparaging facts.

Replies to letters taking up references should be marked 'Confidential' and follow the following 4 point plan:

- Acknowledge the request and give background information.
- State the facts and offer an honest expression of opinion.
- Hope that the information supplied will be useful.
- Tactfully remind that the information is confidential and that no responsibility for it can be accepted.

10.11 **Trader's replies to credit information enquiry**

(a) **Favourable reply to 10.8(a)**

Dear

Thank you for your letter of 25 May.

We are pleased to inform you that this company is a small but well-known and highly respectable firm that has been established in this town for more than 25 years.

We have been doing business with this company for over 7 years on quarterly-account terms. Although they have not usually taken advantage of cash discounts they have always paid their account promptly on the net dates. The credit we have allowed this company has at times been well over the £1000 you mention.

We hope this information will be helpful and that it will be treated as confidential.

Yours sincerely

(b) **Discouraging reply to 10.8(b)**

Dear

The company mentioned in your letter of 25 May has placed regular orders with us for several years. We believe the company to be trustworthy and reliable, but we have to say that they have not always settled their accounts by the due date.

Their account with us is on quarterly settlement terms but we have never allowed it to reach the sum mentioned in your letter. This to us seems to be a case in which caution is necessary.

We are glad to be of help but ask you to ensure that the information provided is treated as strictly confidential.

Yours sincerely

 TIP **Take pride in composing effective messages that are structured logically.**

10.12 Banker's replies to credit information enquiry

(a) Favourable reply to 10.9

Dear

We have received from the National Bank of Nigeria the information requested in your letter of 18 September.

The company you mention is a private company that was founded 15 years ago and is run as a family concern by three brothers. It enjoys a good reputation. Our information shows that the company punctually meets its commitments and a credit in the sum you mention would seem to be safe.

This information is strictly confidential and is given without any responsibility on our part.

Yours sincerely

(b) Unfavourable reply to 10.9

Dear

We have received information from the National Bank of Nigeria concerning the company mentioned in your letter of 18 September.

This is a private company run as a family concern and operating on a small scale.

More detailed information we have received suggests that this is a case in which we would advise caution. You will of course treat this advice as strictly confidential.

Yours sincerely

10.13 Agency's replies to credit information enquiry

(a) Favourable reply to 10.10

Dear

Introduction acknowledges letter and gives initial details — Thank you for your letter of 10 February.

We have completed our enquiries relating to A Griffiths & Co and are pleased to report favourably.

Details regarding the firm's standing are given with a personal opinion — This is a well-founded and highly reputable firm. There are four partners and their capital is estimated to be at least £100,000. They do an excellent trade and are regarded as one of the safest accounts in Cardiff.

Recommendation about credit which could be allowed — From the information we have obtained we believe that you need not hesitate to allow the initial credit of £1750 requested. On a quarterly account you could safely allow at least £5000.

Yours sincerely

(b) Unfavourable reply to 10.10

Dear

Introduction acknowledges letter and advises caution

We have completed our enquiries concerning A Griffiths & Co following your letter of 10 February. I am sorry to advise caution in their request for credit.

Details are given regarding knowledge of the firm in question

About a year ago an action was brought against this company by one of its suppliers for recovery of sums due, though payment was later recovered in full.

The facts as known are stated

Our enquiries reveal nothing to suggest that the firm is not straightforward. On the contrary the firm's difficulties would seem to be due to bad management and in particular to overtrading.[10] Consequently most of the firm's suppliers either give only very short credit for limited sums or make deliveries on a cash basis.

A reminder that the information should be kept confidential

This information is of course supplied in the strictest confidence.

Yours sincerely

[10] **overtrading** trading beyond one's means

USEFUL EXPRESSIONS

Suppliers' requests for references

Openings

1 Thank you for your letter of ... Subject to satisfactory references we shall be glad to provide the open-account facilities requested.

2 We were pleased to receive your order dated ... If you will kindly supply the usual trade references, we will be glad to consider open-account terms.

Closes

1 We will be in touch with you as soon as references are received.

2 It is our usual practice to request references from new customers, and we hope to receive these soon.

Customers supply references

Openings

1 Thank you for your letter of ... in reply to our request for open-account terms.

2 We have completed and return your credit application form.

Closes

1 The following firms will be pleased to answer your enquiries ...

2 For the information required please refer to our bankers, who are ...

Suppliers take up references

Openings

1 ... of ... has supplied your name as a reference in connection with his (her, their) application for open-account terms.

2 We have received a large order from ... and should be grateful for any information you can provide regarding their reliability.

3 We should be grateful if you would obtain reliable information for us concerning ...

Closes

1 Any information you can provide will be appreciated.

2 Any information provided will be treated in strictest confidence.

3 Please accept our thanks in advance for any help you can give us.

Replies to references taken up

Openings

1 We welcome the opportunity to report favourably on ...

2 Thank you for your letter requesting a reference for ...

3 The firm mentioned in your letter of ... is not well known to us.

Closes

1 This information is given on the clear understanding that it will be treated confidentially.

2 We would not hesitate to grant this company credit up to £...

3 This information is given to you in confidence and without any responsibility on our part.

A typical business transaction
(correspondence and documents)

Letters of the kind considered in this unit are handled in business every day. This chapter illustrates their use in a typical transaction in the home trade.

G Wood & Sons have recently opened an electrical goods store in Bristol and place an order with Electrical Supplies Ltd, Birmingham, for the supply of goods on credit. The transaction opens with a request by G Wood & Sons for information regarding prices and terms for credit.

11.1 Request for quotation

G WOOD & SONS
36 Castle Street
Bristol BS1 2BQ
Telephone 0117 954967

GW/ST

15 November 200—

Mr Henry Thomas
Electrical Supplies Ltd
29–31 Broad Street
Birmingham
B1 2HE

Dear Mr Thomas

We have recently opened an electrical goods store at the above address and have received a number of enquiries for the following domestic appliances of which at present we do not hold stocks:

Swanson Electric Kettles, 2 litre
Cosiwarm Electric Blankets, single-bed size
Regency Electric Toasters
Marlborough Kitchen Wall Clocks

When I phoned you this morning you informed me that all these items are available in stock for immediate delivery.

Please let me have your prices and terms for payment 2 months from date of invoicing. If prices and terms are satisfactory, we would place with you a first order for 10 of each of these items.

The matter is of some urgency and I would appreciate an early reply.

Yours sincerely

GORDON WOOD
Manager

11.2 **Supplier's quotation**

ELECTRICAL SUPPLIES LTD
29–31 Broad Street
Birmingham B1 2HE
Tel: 0121–542 6614

HT/JH

17 November 200—

Mr Gordon Wood
Messrs G Wood & Sons
36 Castle Street
Bristol
BS1 2BQ

Dear Mr Wood

QUOTATION NUMBER E542

Thank you for your enquiry of 15 November. I am pleased to quote as follows:

	£
Swanson Electric Kettles, 2 litre	25.00 each
Cosiwarm Electric Blankets, single-bed size	24.50 each
Regency Electric Toasters	25.50 each
Marlborough Kitchen Wall Clocks	27.50 each

The above are current catalogue prices from which we would allow you a trade discount of 33⅓%. Prices include packing and delivery to your premises.

It is our usual practice to ask all new customers for trade references. Please let us have the names and addresses of two suppliers with whom you have had regular dealings. Subject to satisfactory replies, we shall be glad to supply the goods and to allow you the 2 months' credit requested.

As there may be other items in which you are interested, I enclose copies of our current catalogue and price list.

I look forward to the opportunity of doing business with you.

Yours sincerely

HENRY THOMAS
Sales Manager

Enc

11.3 Request for permission to quote company as reference

A buyer should obtain permission from the suppliers whose names are to be submitted as references. Consent may be obtained verbally if there is urgency, but otherwise the buyer should make this request in writing. In this case, a letter was sent to J Williamson & Co, Southey House, Coventry, CV1 5RU, as well as the addressee of the following letter.

G WOOD & SONS
36 Castle Street
Bristol BS1 2BQ
Telephone 0117 954967

GW/ST

19 November 200—

Mr Robert Johnson
Johnson Traders Ltd
The Hayes
Cardiff
CF1 IJW

Dear Robert

I wish to place an order with Electrical Supplies Ltd, Birmingham, with facilities on credit. As this will be a first order they have asked me to supply trade references.

I have been a regular customer of yours for the past 4 years and should be grateful if you would allow me to submit your company's name as one of my references.

I shall very much appreciate your consent to stand as referee and hope to hear from you soon.

Yours sincerely

GORDON WOOD
Manager

11.4 Permission granted

JOHNSON TRADERS LTD
The Hayes
Cardiff CF1 1JW
Telephone 01222 572382

RH/KI

22 November 200—

Mr Gordon Wood
G Wood & Sons
36 Castle Street
Bristol
BS1 2BQ

Dear Mr Wood

Thank you for your letter of 19 November requesting permission to use our name as a reference in your transaction with Electrical Supplies Ltd.

During the time we have done business together you have been a very reliable customer. If your suppliers decide to approach us for a reference we shall be very happy to support your request for credit facilities.

Yours sincerely

ROBERT JOHNSON
Financial Controller

11.5 Order

(a) Covering letter

G WOOD & SONS
36 Castle Street
Bristol BS1 2BQ
Telephone 0117 954967

GW/ST

24 November 200—

Mr Henry Thomas
Electrical Supplies Ltd
29–31 Broad Street
Birmingham
B1 2HE

Dear Mr Thomas

ORDER NUMBER 3241

Thank you for your letter of 17 November quoting for domestic appliances and enclosing copies of your current catalogue and price list.

We have had regular dealings with the following suppliers for the past 4 or 5 years. They will be happy to provide the necessary references.

Johnson Traders Ltd, The Hayes, Cardiff CF1 1JW
J Williamson & Co, Southey House, Coventry CV1 5RU

Our order number 3241 is enclosed for the goods mentioned in our original enquiry. They are urgently needed and as they are available from stock we hope you will arrange prompt delivery.

I appreciate your agreement to allow 2 months' credit on receipt of satisfactory references.

Yours sincerely

GORDON WOOD
Manager

Enc

(b) Order form

G WOOD & SONS
36 Castle Street
Bristol BS1 2BQ
Telephone 0117 954967

ORDER NO 3241   Date 24 November 200—

Electrical Supplies Ltd
29–31 Broad Street
BIRMINGHAM
B1 2HE

Please supply

Quantity	Item(s)	Price
		£
10	Swanson Electric Kettles (2 litre)	25.00 each
10	Cosiwarm Electric Blankets (single-bed size)	24.50 each
10	Regency Electric Toasters	25.50 each
10	Marlborough Kitchen Wall Clocks	27.50 each

Terms   33⅓% trade discount

_____
for G Wood & Sons

11.6 Supplier's acknowledgement

It is good business practice to acknowledge and thank buyers particularly for a first order and trade reference information. The supplier will then take up the references and put the order in hand when favourable replies are received.

ELECTRICAL SUPPLIES LTD
29–31 Broad Street
Birmingham B1 2HE
Telephone 0121–542–6614

HT/JH

1 December 200—

Mr G Wood
G Wood & Sons
36 Castle Street
Bristol
BS1 2BQ

Dear Mr Wood

YOUR ORDER NUMBER 3241

Thank you for your letter of 24 November. We were very pleased to receive your order and confirm that the goods will be supplied at the prices and on the terms stated.

Your order has been passed to our warehouse for immediate despatch of the goods from stock. We hope you will be pleased with them.

Please do not hesitate to contact me if I can be of any further help.

Yours sincerely

HENRY THOMAS
Sales Manager

11.7 Advice note

Documents dealing with the despatch and delivery of goods include packing notes, advice of despatch notes, consignment notes and delivery notes. These documents are really copies of the invoice and are often prepared in sets, with the use of NCR (no carbon required) paper, at the same time as the invoice. The copy which acts as the advice note will not contain information regarding pricing.

The advice or despatch note informs the buyer that the goods are on the way and enables a check to be made when they arrive. Very often, however, an advice note is replaced either by an invoice sent on or before the day the goods are despatched or sometimes by a letter notifying despatch.

For small items sent by post a packing note, which is simply a copy of the advice note, would be the only document used. Some suppliers, especially those using their own transport, dispense with the advice note and instead use either a packing note or a delivery note.

11.8 Consignment note

When goods are sent by rail the supplier is required to complete a consignment note which represents the contract of carriage with the railway. It gives particulars of the quantity, weight, type and destination of the goods and states whether they are being sent carriage paid (ie paid by the sender) or carriage forward (ie paid by the buyer). In most cases the printed forms supplied by the railway are used but a trader will sometimes prefer to use their own.

The completed consignment note is handed to the carrier when the goods are collected and it travels with them. When the goods are delivered to the buyer the note must be signed as proof of delivery.

11.9 Delivery note

Sometimes two copies of the delivery note are prepared, one to be retained by the buyer, the other to be given back to the carrier signed as evidence that the goods have been delivered. Alternatively the carrier may ask the buyer to sign a Delivery Book or a Delivery Sheet recording the calls a carrier has made.

Where it is not possible for the buyer to inspect the goods before signing for them, the signature should be qualified with some comment such as 'not examined' or 'goods unexamined' as a precaution.

11.10 Invoice

Invoice practice varies. Sometimes the invoice is enclosed with the goods and sometimes it is sent separately, either in advance of the goods (in which case it also serves as an advice note) or after the goods. The invoice will be sent separately where the goods are baled or supplied loose or in bulk.

(a) Covering letter

It is not always necessary to send a covering letter with an invoice, but if a letter is sent it need only be very short and formal.

ELECTRICAL SUPPLIES LTD
29–31 Broad Street
Birmingham B1 2HE
Telephone 0121–542–6614

HT/JH

3 December 200—

G Wood & Sons
36 Castle Street
Bristol
BS1 2BQ

Dear Sirs

YOUR ORDER NUMBER 3241

We enclose our invoice number 6740 for the domestic electrical appliances supplied to your order dated 24 November.

The goods have been packed in three cases, numbers 78, 79 and 80, and sent to you today by rail, carriage paid. We hope they will reach you promptly and in good condition.

If you settle the account within 2 months we will allow you to deduct from the amount due a special cash discount of 1½%.

Yours faithfully

SALLY YAP (Mrs)
Credit Control Manager

Enc

(b) Invoice

When G Wood & Sons receive the invoice they will check it with the packing note or delivery note received with the goods to ensure all goods invoiced have been received. They will check the invoice for trade discounts and arithmetical accuracy before recording it in their books of account.

As a rule the invoice is not used as a demand for payment but as a record of the transaction and statement of the indebtedness to which it gives rise. The supplier will then later send a statement of account to the buyer.

ELECTRICAL SUPPLIES LTD
29–31 Broad Street
Birmingham B1 2HE
Telephone 0121–542–6614

INVOICE

G Wood & Sons
36 Castle Street
BRISTOL
BS1 2BQ

Date 3 December 200 —

Your order no 3241

Invoice No 6740

For reference purposes the invoice is given a serial number. The order number is also quoted

Quantity	Item(s)	Unit Price	Total Price
		£	£
10	Swanson Electric Kettles (2 litre)	25.00	250.00
10	Cosiwarm Electric Blankets (single-bed size)	24.50	245.00
10	Regency Electric Toasters	25.50	255.00
10	Marlborough Kitchen Wall Clocks	27.50	275.00
			1025.00
	Less 33⅓% trade discount		341.33
			683.67
	VAT @ 17.5%		119.64
			803.31
	3 packing cases (returnable)		15.00
			817.92
	Terms: 1½% two months		

The agreed 33⅓% trade discount has been given

The terms of payment indicate an allowable cash discount for payment within 2 months from date of invoice. This discount is deducted at the time of payment

'E & O E' means 'errors and omissions excepted'. It reserves the right for the seller to correct any error in or omissions from the invoice

E & OE

Registered in England No 726549

11.11 Debit and credit notes

For the purposes served by these two documents, refer to pages 116–118.

(a) Buyer requests credit note

In our specimen transaction, G Wood & Sons will return the three packing cases charged on the invoice. They will then write to the suppliers asking for a credit note for the invoiced value of the cases. Depending on their usual practice G Wood & Sons may or may not prepare and send a debit note when making the request.

G WOOD & SONS
36 Castle Street, Bristol BS1 2BQ
Telephone 0117 954967

GW/ST

10 December 200—

Mrs Sally Yap
Credit Control Manager
Electrical Supplies Ltd
29–31 Broad Street
Birmingham
B1 2HE

Dear Mrs Yap

INVOICE NUMBER 6740

We have today returned to you by rail the three packing cases charged on this invoice at a cost of £15.00.

We enclose a debit note for this amount and shall be glad to receive your credit note by return.

All the goods supplied and invoiced reached us in good condition. Thank you for your promptness in dealing with our first order.

Yours sincerely

GORDON WOOD
Manager

Enc

```
                        G WOOD & SONS
                        36 Castle Street
                        Bristol BS1 2BQ
                    Telephone 0117 954967

                          DEBIT NOTE

Electrical Supplies Ltd                    Date 10 December 200—
29–31 Broad Street
BIRMINGHAM
B1 2HE                                     Debit Note No D 841
```

Date	Details	Total
		£
10.12.—	To 3 packing cases charged on your invoice number 6740 and returned	15.00

Debit note

(b) Seller issues credit note

When Electrical Supplies Ltd receive the debit note they will check return of the cases. They will then prepare the credit note requested and send it to G Wood & Sons, with or without a covering letter. Any letter sent need only be short and formal, but as this is the buyer's first transaction the supplier would be wise to add a short note to encourage future business.

ELECTRICAL SUPPLIES LTD
29–31 Broad Street
Birmingham B1 2HE
Telephone 0121–542–6614

HT/JH

14 December 200—

Mr Gordon Wood
Manager
G Wood & Sons
36 Castle Street
Bristol
BS1 2BQ

Dear Mr Wood

Thank you for your letter of 10 December enclosing debit note number D841. I confirm receipt of the three packing cases returned. Our credit note number C672 for the sum of £15.00 is enclosed.

Yours sincerely

SALLY YAP (Mrs)
Credit Control Manager

Enc

ELECTRICAL SUPPLIES LTD
29–31 Broad Street
Birmingham B1 2HE
Telephone 0121–524–6614

CREDIT NOTE

G Wood & Sons   Date 14 December 200—
36 Castle Street
BRISTOL
BS1 2BQ   Credit Note No C 672

Date	Details	Total
		£
10.12.—	To 3 packing cases charged on your invoice number 6740 and returned	15.00

Credit note

11.12 Statement of account

Statements of account are sent to customers at periodic intervals, normally monthly. As well as serving as a request for payment the statement enables the buyer to compare the account kept by the supplier with that kept in the buyer's own books. Statements are usually sent without a covering letter (see page 120).

ELECTRICAL SUPPLIES LTD
29–31 Broad Street
Birmingham B1 2HE
Telephone 0121–524–6614

STATEMENT

G Wood & Sons   Date 31 January 200—
36 Castle Street
BRISTOL
BS1 2BQ

Date	Details	Debit	Credit	Balance
		£	£	£
3.12.—	Invoice 6740	818.31		818.31
14.12.—	Credit note C 672		15.00	803.31
	(2½% seven days)			

E & OE   Registered in England No 726549

Statement

11.13 Payment

Invoices and statements usually indicate the terms of payment. For example:

Prompt cash: A somewhat elastic term but generally taken to mean payment within 15 days from date of invoice or statement.

2½% 30 days: This means that the debtor is entitled to deduct 2½% from the amount due if payment is made within 30 days of the invoice or statement, otherwise the full amount becomes payable.

Net 30 days: This means that the debtor must pay in full within 30 days.

Payments in business are usually made by cheque or, if they are numerous, by credit transfer (bank giro). In this transaction the buyer settles the account by sending a cheque to the supplier.

G WOOD & SONS
36 Castle Street, Bristol BS1 2BQ
Telephone 0117 954967

GW/ST

4 February 200—

Mrs Sally Yap
Credit Control Manager
Electrical Supplies Ltd
29–31 Broad Street
Birmingham
B1 2HE

Dear Mrs Yap

We have received your statement of account dated 31 January 200— showing a balance due of £803.31.

From the total amount due on the statement I have deducted the allowable cash discount of 2½% and enclose a cheque for £783.23 in full settlement.

Yours sincerely

GORDON WOOD
Manager

Enc

11.14 Receipt

A cheque usually supplies all the evidence of payment necessary. Consequently it is not usual practice for formal receipts to be issued. This does not affect the payer's legal right to request a receipt if one is required.

In this transaction evidence of payment could be obtained by the supplier's formal receipt or the buyer's cheque after being paid by the bank.

Unit 3

Creative and persuasive documents

Complaints and adjustments

HANDLING COMPLAINTS

No matter how good our intentions and efforts, there are bound to be occasions when it is necessary to deal with a complaint, or even to make one. Complaints may be necessary for several reasons, such as:

- wrong goods received
- poor service
- unsatisfactory quality of goods
- late delivery
- damaged goods
- prices not as agreed.

Complaining about goods

Be sure to keep your receipt for all goods you buy, and go back to the shop as soon as possible. Explain what the problem is (be assertive, not aggressive) and say what you expect to be done about it. Hopefully the person in charge will deal with your complaint satisfactorily, but if you are still not satisfied you will need to put your complaint in writing. Address your letter to the Customer Service Manager, and if possible find out his/her name so that you can address the letter personally.

Complaining about a service

Give the supplier a chance to put matters right. If it is necessary to put your complaint in writing, say what you expect to be done and set a deadline. You may wish to consider withholding any further money until the problem has been sorted out satisfactorily, but do check the small print of any contract or credit agreement that you have signed.

Making a written complaint

When you have a genuine complaint you will feel angry, but you must show restraint in your letter, if only because the supplier may not be to blame. The following points need to be remembered:

(a) Do not delay as this will weaken your position, and the supplier may have difficulty investigating the cause.

(b) Do not assume that the supplier is automatically to blame. They may have a perfectly good defence.

(c) Avoid rudeness. This would create ill-feeling and cause the supplier to be unwilling to resolve matters.

(d) In your letter:
  - describe the item or service you bought
  - say where and when you bought the item (or when the service was carried out) and how much it cost
  - explain what is wrong, any action you have already taken, to whom you spoke and what happened
  - explain what you expect to be done to rectify the situation, for example a refund or repair, or the job done again without charge.

(e) Use recorded/special delivery so that you have a check that your letter has been received.

(f) Keep copies of your letters, and never send original documents or receipts.

Dealing with a complaint

Most suppliers naturally wish to hear if customers have cause to complain. This is better than losing custom or trade being taken elsewhere. It also provides an opportunity to investigate, to explain, and to put things right. In this way goodwill may be preserved. Receiving such complaints may also suggest ways in which the supplier's products or services could be improved. When dealing with dissatisfied and unhappy customers, remember the following guidelines:

(a) It is often said that the customer is always right. This may not always be the case, but it is sound practice to assume that the customer may be right.

(b) Acknowledge a complaint promptly. If you are unable to reply fully, explain that it is being investigated and a full reply will be sent later.

 Good writers learn to choose their words very carefully and get the tone just right.

COMPLAINTS CONCERNING GOODS

12.1 Complaint concerning wrong goods

If goods are received which are not of the kind or quality ordered then you are entitled to return them at the supplier's expense.

(a) Complaint

Order number and date —

Reasons for dissatisfaction —

Action requested —

> Dear Sirs
>
> On 12 August I ordered 12 copies of <u>Background Music</u> by H Lowery under my order number FT567.
>
> On opening the parcel received this morning I found that it contained 12 copies of <u>History of Music</u> by the same author. I regret that I cannot keep these books as I have an adequate stock already. I am therefore returning the books by parcel post for immediate replacement, as I have several customers waiting for them.
>
> Please credit my account with the invoiced value of the returned copies including reimbursement[1] for the postage cost of £17.90.
>
> Yours faithfully

(b) Reply

Express regret —

Explain how the mistake occurred —

Action taken to rectify the matter —

A closing apology —

> Dear Mr Ramsay
>
> I was sorry to learn from your letter of 18 August that a mistake was made in dealing with your order.
>
> This mistake is entirely our own and we apologise for the inconvenience it is causing you. This occurred because of staff shortage during this unusually busy season and also the fact that these 2 books by Lowery have identical bindings.
>
> 12 copies of the correct title have been sent to you today.
>
> Your account will be credited with the invoiced value of the books and cost of return postage. Our credit note is enclosed.
>
> Our apologies again for this mistake.
>
> Yours sincerely

[1] **reimbursement** a refund of money

12.2 Complaint concerning quality

A buyer is entitled to *reject*[2] goods that are not of the quality or description ordered. However, later deliveries may also not be accepted, even if the goods are correct.

(a) Complaint

Dear Sirs

Reasons for complaint — We have recently received several complaints from customers about your fountain pens. The pens are clearly not giving satisfaction and in some cases we have had to refund the purchase price.

Further details — The pens are part of the batch of 500 supplied against our order number 8562 dated 28 March. This order was placed on the basis of a sample pen left by your representative. We have ourselves compared the performance of this sample with that of a number of the pens from this batch, and there is little doubt that many of them are faulty – some of them leak and others blot when writing.

The complaints we have received relate only to pens from the batch mentioned. Pens supplied before these have always been satisfactory.

Action required — We therefore wish to return the unsold balance, amounting to 377 pens. Please replace them with pens of the quality which our earlier dealings with you have led us to expect.

Close — Please let us know what arrangements you wish us to make for the return of these unsuitable pens.

Yours faithfully

(b) Reply (accepting complaint)

Dear

Thank you for your letter dated 10 May pointing out faults in the pens supplied to your order number 8562. This has caused us a good deal of concern and we are glad that you brought this matter to our notice.

We have tested a number of pens from the production batch you mention, and agree that they are not perfect. The defects have been traced to a fault in one of the machines, which has now been rectified.

Please arrange to return to us your unsold balance of 377 pens; the cost of postage will be reimbursed in due course. We have already arranged for 400 pens to be sent to replace this unsold balance. The extra 23 pens are sent without charge, and will enable you to provide free replacement of any further pens about which you may receive complaints.

We apologise for the inconvenience this has caused you.

Yours sincerely

---

[2] **reject** refuse

(c) Alternative reply (rejecting complaint)

If circumstances show that a complaint needs to be rejected, you must show an understanding of the customer's position and carefully explain why a rejection is necessary.

	Dear
A tactful opening	We are sorry to learn from your letter of 10 May of the difficulties you are having with the pens supplied to your order number 8562.
Explanation of quality control	All our pens are manufactured to be identical in design and performance and we cannot understand why some of them should have given trouble to your customers. It is normal practice for each pen to be individually examined by our Inspection Department before being passed into store. However, from what you say, it would seem that a number of the pens included in the latest batch escaped the usual examination.
Reject the request, but very diplomatically	We sympathise with your problem but regret that we cannot accept your suggestion to take back all the unsold stock from the batch concerned. Indeed there should be no need for this since it is unlikely that the number of faulty pens can be very large. We will gladly replace any pen found to be unsatisfactory, and on this particular batch are prepared to allow you a special discount of 5% to compensate for your inconvenience.
The offer of a discount adds a 'softener'	We trust you will accept this as being a fair and reasonable solution of this matter.
	Please give me a call on 4626123 if you have any further questions.
	Yours sincerely

12.3 Complaint concerning quantity

(a) Surplus goods delivered

When a supplier delivers more than the quantity ordered, the buyer is legally entitled to reject either all the goods or only the excess quantity. Alternatively all the goods may be accepted and the excess paid for at the same rate. In this letter the buyer rejects the surplus goods but is not obliged to return them; it is the supplier's responsibility to arrange for their collection.

> Dear Sirs
>
> Thank you for your promptness in delivering the coffee we ordered on 30 July. However 160 bags were delivered this morning instead of 120 as stated on our order.
>
> Our present needs are completely covered and we cannot make use of the 40 bags sent in excess of our order. These bags will therefore be held in our warehouse until we receive your instructions.
>
> Yours faithfully

(b) Shortage in delivery

When a supplier delivers less than the quantity ordered the customer cannot be compelled to accept delivery by instalments. Immediate delivery of the balance may be requested.

Dear Sir/Madam

OUR ORDER NUMBER 861

We thank you for so promptly delivering the gas coke ordered on 20 March. Although we ordered 5 tonnes in 50-kg bags, only 80 bags were delivered. Your carrier was unable to explain the shortage and we have not received any explanation from you.

We still need the full quantity ordered, so please arrange to deliver the remaining 20 bags as soon as possible.

Yours faithfully

12.4 Complaint to manufacturer

(a) Customer's complaint

In this letter the buyer was advised by the supplier to write directly to the manufacturer regarding faulty goods.

Dear Sirs

On 15 September I bought one of your 'Big Ben' alarm clocks (mains operated) from Stansfield Jewellers in Leeds. Unfortunately I have been unable to get the alarm system to work and am very disappointed with my purchase.

The manager of Stansfield's has advised me to return the clock to you for correction of the fault. This is enclosed.

Please arrange for the clock to be put in full working order and return it to me as soon as possible.

Yours faithfully

(b) Manufacturer's reply

In this reply the manufacturer shows genuine interest in the complaint and does everything possible to ensure customer satisfaction. The considerate manner in which the complaint is treated helps to build a reputation for reliability and fair dealing.

Dear Mrs Wood

Thank you for your letter of 20 September enclosing the defective 'Big Ben' alarm clock.

Your comments on the performance of the clock are very interesting and I have passed it to our engineers for inspection.

Meanwhile we are arranging to replace your clock with a new one that has been tested thoroughly to ensure that it is in perfect working order. This will be sent to you within the next few days.

I am sorry for the trouble and inconvenience this matter has caused you, but am confident that the replacement clock will prove satisfactory and give you the service you are entitled to expect from our products.

Yours sincerely

COMPLAINTS CONCERNING DELIVERY

No supplier likes to be accused of negligence or carelessness, which is often what a complaint about packaging amounts to. Such complaints must be carefully worded so as not to give offence. Nothing is to be gained by being sarcastic or insulting – you are much more likely to get what you want by being courteous. Show that you regret having to complain, but explain that the trouble is too serious not to be reported.

12.5 Complaint concerning damaged goods

(a) Complaint

The writer of this letter points out damage which was discovered after checking the consignment. Any suggestion that the damage to the goods is due to faulty packing is tactfully avoided.

Dear Sirs

OUR ORDER NUMBER R569

Introduction and background details — We ordered 160 compact discs on 3 January and they were delivered yesterday. I regret that 18 of them were badly scratched.

Explain details which evolved after receipt of goods — The package containing these goods appeared to be in perfect condition and I accepted and signed for it <u>without question</u>.[3] It was on unpacking the compact discs the damage was discovered; I can only assume that this was due to careless handling at some stage prior to packing.

Enclose full list of damaged goods and request replacement — I am enclosing a list of the damaged goods and shall be glad if you will replace them. They have been kept aside in case you need them to support a claim on your suppliers for compensation.

Yours faithfully

[3] **without question** without raising any objection

(b) Reply

The supplier's reply promptly complies with the customer's request and shows a desire to improve the service to customers.

Dear

YOUR ORDER NUMBER R569

Acknowledge letter and show regret about damages — I was sorry to learn from your letter of 10 January that some of the compact discs supplied to this order were damaged when they reached you.

Give details about replacements — Replacements for the damaged goods have been sent by parcel post this morning. It will not be necessary for you to return the damaged goods; they may be destroyed.

Give further information about follow-up action — Despite the care we take in packing goods there have recently been several reports of damage. To avoid further inconvenience and annoyance to customers, as well as expense to ourselves, we are now seeking the advice of a packaging consultant in the hope of improving our methods of handling.

Assurance about future orders — We apologise once again for this, and hope the steps we are taking will ensure the safe arrival of all your orders in future.

Yours sincerely

12.6 Complaint regarding bad packing

(a) Complaint

Dear Sirs

Introduction about reason for writing — The carpet supplied to our order number C395 of 3 July was delivered by your carriers this morning.

Details about complaint — We noticed that one of the outer edges of the wrapping had been worn through, presumably as a result of friction in transit. When we took off the wrapping it was not surprising to find that the carpet itself was soiled and slightly frayed at the edge.

Further details and questions about precautions — This is the second time in 3 weeks that we have had cause to write to you about the same matter. We find it hard to understand why precautions could not be taken to prevent a repetition of the earlier damage.

Suggestions about future handling of orders — Although other carpets have been delivered in good condition, this second experience within such a short time suggests the need for special precautions against friction when carpets are packed onto your delivery vehicles. We hope that you will bear this in mind in handling our future orders.

Requests for special concession — In view of the condition of the present carpet we cannot offer it for sale at the normal price and propose to reduce our selling price by 10%. We suggest that you make us an allowance of 10% on the invoice cost. If you cannot do this, we shall have to return the carpet for replacement.

I hope to hear from you soon.

Yours faithfully

(b) Reply

Express regret at customer's dissatisfaction

Dear

I was very sorry to learn from your letter of 15 August that the carpet supplied to your order number C395 was damaged on delivery.

Explain circumstances surrounding the complaint

Our head packer informs us that the carpet was first wrapped in heavy oiled waterproof paper and then in a double thickness of jute canvas. Under normal conditions this should have been enough protection. However on this occasion our delivery van contained a full load of carpets for delivery to other customers on the same day, and it is obvious that special packing precautions are necessary in such cases.

Follow-up action taken

In all future consignments, we are arranging for specially reinforced end-packings which should prevent any future damage.

Confirm special discount to customer

We realise the need to reduce your selling price for the damaged carpet and readily agree to the special allowance of 10% which you suggest.

Yours sincerely

12.7 Complaint regarding non-delivery

(a) Complaint

Dear Sirs

On 25 September we placed our order number RT56 for printed headed notepaper and invoice forms. You acknowledged the order on 30 September. As that is some 3 weeks ago and we have not yet received advice of delivery, we are wondering whether the order has since been overlooked.

Your representative promised an early delivery and this was an important factor in persuading us to place this order with you.

The delay in delivery is causing considerable inconvenience. We must ask you to complete the order immediately, otherwise we shall have no option but to cancel it and obtain the stationery elsewhere.

Yours faithfully

(b) Reply

Only a very *diplomatic*[4] reply can keep the goodwill of this customer, who is obviously feeling very let down. With an understanding and helpful reply from the printer as shown here, the customer cannot continue to feel annoyed.

---

[4] **diplomatic** tactful and considerate

Dear Mr Sargeant

Thank you for your letter of 18 October. I quite understand your annoyance at not yet having received the stationery ordered on 25 September.

Orders for printed stationery are at present taking from 3 to 4 weeks for delivery, and our representatives have been instructed to make this clear to customers. Apparently you were not told that it would take so long, and I apologise for this oversight.

On receiving your letter we put your order in hand at once. The stationery will be sent from here tomorrow by express parcel post, and it should reach you within 24 hours of your receiving this letter.

It is very unfortunate that there should have been this misunderstanding but we hope you will forgive the delay that has been caused.

Yours sincerely

12.8 Complaint regarding frequent late deliveries

This correspondence shows how important it is when sending letters of complaint to write with restraint and not to assume that the supplier is at fault.

(a) Complaint

Dear Sirs

We ordered 6 filing cabinets from you on 2 July on the understanding that they would be delivered within one week. However these were not received until this morning.

Unfortunately there have been similar delays on several previous occasions, and their increasing frequency in recent months compels us to say that business between us cannot continue in such conditions.

We have felt it necessary to make our feelings known since we cannot give reliable delivery dates to our customers unless we can count on undertakings given by our suppliers.

We hope you will understand our position in this matter, and trust that from now on we can rely on punctual delivery of our orders.

I look forward to receiving your comments on this matter.

Yours faithfully

(b) Reply

In this reply the supplier carefully explains that the fault is not on their part, and goodwill with the customer should be retained.

Dear

Your letter of 18 July regarding delays in delivery came as a surprise as the absence of any earlier complaints led us to believe that goods supplied to your orders were reaching you promptly.

It is our usual practice to deliver goods well in advance of the promised delivery dates; the filing cabinets to which you refer left here on 5 July. We are very concerned that our efforts to ensure punctual delivery should be frustrated by delays in transit. It is possible that other customers are also affected and we are taking up this whole question with our carriers.

We thank you for drawing our attention to a situation of which we had been quite unaware until you wrote to us. Please accept our apologies for the inconvenience you have been caused.

Yours sincerely

12.9 Complaint regarding uncompleted work

This correspondence relates to a builder's failure to complete work on a new bungalow within the agreed contract time. The buyer's letter is firm but reasonably worded. The builder's reply shows understanding and is convincing, businesslike and helpful.

(a) Complaint

Dear Sirs

BUNGALOW AT 1 CRESCENT ROAD, CHINGFORD

When I signed the contract for the building of this property you estimated that the work would be completed and the bungalow ready for occupation 'in about 6 months'. That was 8 months ago and the work is still only half finished.

The delay is causing inconvenience not only to me but also to the buyer of my present home which I cannot transfer until this bungalow is finished.

I urge you to press forward with this work without any further delay. Please let me know when you expect it to be completed.

Yours faithfully

(b) Reply

Dear Mr Watson

BUNGALOW AT 1 CRESCENT ROAD, CHINGFORD

Thank you for your letter of 18 June. We are of course aware that the estimated period for completion of your bungalow has already been exceeded and wish to say at once that we realise what inconvenience the delay must be causing you.

We would ask you, however, to remember first that we have had an exceptionally severe winter – work on the site has been quite impossible during several prolonged periods of heavy snow. Secondly, there has been a nationwide shortage of building materials, especially bricks and timber, from which the trade is only just recovering. Without these 2 difficulties, which could not be foreseen, the estimated completion period of 6 months would have been observed.

In the improved weather conditions work on the bungalow is now proceeding satisfactorily. Unless we have other unforeseen hold-ups[5] we can safely promise that the bungalow will be ready for you by the end of August.

Yours sincerely

 TIP **If you wouldn't say it, don't write it.**

12.10 Complaint regarding delivery charges

Some customers are only too ready to complain if things do not suit them. Others who are dissatisfied do not complain, but instead they quietly withdraw their custom and transfer it to some other supplier. This correspondence relates to such a case.

(a) Supplier's enquiry

Dear Sirs

We are sorry to notice that we have had no orders from you since last April. As you have at no time notified us of defects in our products or about the quality of our service, we can only assume that we have given you no cause to be dissatisfied. If we have, then we should be glad to know of it.

If the cause of your discontinued orders is the present depressed state of the market, you may be interested in our latest price list showing a reduction of 7½% on all grocery items. A copy of this is enclosed.

Should there be any matter in which we have given you cause to be dissatisfied, we hope you will give us the opportunity to put it right so that our custom can be renewed.

Yours faithfully

---

[5] **hold-ups** delays

(b) Customer's reply (complaint)

Dear

Thank you for your letter of 5 July. As you wish to know why we have placed no orders with you recently, I will point out a matter which caused us some annoyance.

On 21 April last year we sent you two orders, one for £274 and one for £142. Your terms at the time provided for free delivery of all orders for £300 or more, but although you delivered these two orders together we were charged with the cost of carriage.

As the orders were submitted on different forms, we grant that you had a perfect right to treat them as separate orders. However for all practical purposes they could very well have been treated as one, as they were placed on the same day and delivered at the same time. The fact that you did not do this seemed to us to be a particularly ungenerous[6] way of treating a regular long-standing customer.

I would welcome your comments on this matter.

Yours sincerely

(c) Supplier's reply

Dear

Suitable introduction — Thank you for your letter of 8 July. Your explanation gives us the opportunity to explain a most regrettable misunderstanding.

Circumstances surrounding the situation are explained in detail — Our charge for carriage on your last two orders arose because they were for goods dealt with by two separate departments, neither of which was aware that a separate order was being handled by another.

Further details given to assure the customer that this situation will not be repeated — At that time these departments were each responsible for their own packing and despatch arrangements. Since then this work has been taken over by a centralised packing and despatch department so a repetition of the same kind of misunderstanding is now unlikely.

This tactful close expresses a hope for renewed business dealings — I hope you will understand that the charge we made was quite unintentional.[7] In the circumstances I hope you will feel able to renew your former custom.

Yours sincerely

12.11 Complaint regarding poor service

This correspondence relates to circumstances where a customer does not receive proper attention. In answer to their telephone enquiry regarding a damaged tape recorder the supplier suggests that the goods be sent for inspection in order to obtain a quotation for repair. The customer does so but then hears no more.

[6] **ungenerous** mean, selfish
[7] **unintentional** not done purposely

(a) Customer's initial letter

The customer writes to the supplier on 28 June after a telephone conversation with Mr Jackson.

Introduction refers to telephone conversation and details discussed

Dear Mr Jackson

STEREO CASSETTE RECORDER, MODEL NUMBER 660

Further to our telephone conversation this morning, I am sending my faulty tape recorder. I understand that arrangements can be made for it to be inspected and also a quotation given for its repair.

The following faults will be found:

The faults are listed and numbered for clarity

1   The recorder does not reproduce clearly on the right-hand speaker.
2   Distortion suggests that the recording head may need replacing.
3   The winding mechanism appears to be faulty.

It is possible that an inspection may reveal other faults.

Closing section requests an immediate quotation

It would help to speed matters if you would let me have the quotation by telephone as I want this work to be carried out and the recorder returned as quickly as possible.

Yours sincerely

(b) Supplier's acknowledgement

On 5 July the supplier sent a printed form number WE69376 acknowledging receipt of both the recorder and the customer's letter of 28 June, but did not quote as promised. Two weeks later, on 18 July, the customer wrote to the supplier again. Note that rather than suggest that the quotation has not been sent, the letter states more tactfully that it has not yet been received.

Dear Mr Jackson

STEREO CASSETTE RECORDER, MODEL NUMBER 660

On 28 June I sent the above recorder to you for inspection and a quotation for servicing. As the matter was of some urgency I requested a quotation by telephone.

On 5 July your form number WE69376 acknowledged receipt of the recorder and my letter, but to date I have not received a quotation.

If a quotation has not already been sent I should be grateful if you would send it immediately to enable work on the recorder to be put in hand without further delay.

A prompt reply will be appreciated.

Yours sincerely

(c) Quotation is received and customer sends remittance

On 25 July a service card headed 'Job Reference WE69376' was received by the customer requesting payment of £60.85 before the service could be carried out. On 28 July the customer sends a cheque for this amount with a covering letter.

Dear Mr Jackson

STEREO CASSETTE RECORDER, MODEL NUMBER 660

I am returning your service card WE69376 with a cheque for £60.85 to cover the cost of servicing the above recorder.

This recorder has been with you for over 4 weeks and I am greatly inconvenienced without it. I hope you can arrange for its immediate repair and that it can be returned within the next few days.

Yours sincerely

(d) Customer receives a further payment request

No acknowledgement of receipt of the customer's cheque was received. On 14 August the customer received a printed note stating that work on the recorder had been completed and requesting payment of the amount due.

(e) Customer writes to the Manager

Delay in returning the recorder and a request for payment of an amount already paid understandably angered the customer. The immediate reaction was to write a strong letter to the Manager. Instead the result was in terms more likely to gain co-operation in rectifying what was probably quite an innocent mistake.

Dear Mrs Stansfield

STEREO CASSETTE RECORDER, MODEL NUMBER 660

The letter opens tactfully — I am sorry to have to write to you personally regarding delay in the return of the above recorder sent in for repair on 28 June. The facts are as follows:

A list is given of all the stages of the complaint —

1   On 28 June I spoke to your Mr Keith Jackson regarding my faulty tape recorder. As a result I sent my letter dated 28 June with the recorder requesting a quotation.

2   On 5 July your Service Department acknowledged receipt of the recorder and my letter.

3   Not having received the quotation I sent a reminder on 18 July, and on 25 July I received a service card (reference WE69376) quoting a charge of £60.85 for servicing.

Only the facts are stated, no emotions —

4   This card was returned on 28 July with my cheque for that amount and my letter asking for the service to be carried out and the recorder returned as a matter of urgency.

> I heard nothing more until this morning when I was surprised to receive a printed form stating that the work had been completed and asking for payment of the amount due.
>
> I am sure you will appreciate my concern at the length of time involved in this matter. As it is 2 full months since I sent the recorder to you, I hope you will arrange to return it immediately.
>
> Yours sincerely

The writer closes tactfully

(f) Manager's apology

In the reply the Manager admits fault. Sincerity in this matter will help to restore customer confidence and goodwill.

> Dear Mr Richards
>
> STEREO CASSETTE RECORDER, MODEL NUMBER 660
>
> I was very sorry to learn from your letter of 14 August of the problems experienced in the repair and return of your tape recorder.
>
> I have investigated this matter personally, and regret that the delay is due to the absence through illness of the assistant who was dealing with your order initially.
>
> Please accept my apologies for the inconvenience caused. The recorder has been sent to you today by express parcel post, and I hope it will reach you quickly and in good condition.
>
> Please do not hesitate to contact me on 4962123 if I can be of further help.
>
> Yours sincerely

(g) Customer thanks Manager

The correspondence could have ended with the Manager's letter, but the customer rightly felt that it would be a matter of courtesy to thank the Manager for such prompt intervention.

> Dear Mrs Stansfield
>
> STEREO CASSETTE RECORDER, MODEL NUMBER 660
>
> Thank you for your letter of 3 September and for dealing so promptly with this matter. I can appreciate the circumstances that led to the delay which was experienced.
>
> My tape recorder has been delivered and appears to be in good working order.
>
> Yours sincerely

CANCELLING ORDERS

A buyer is legally entitled to cancel his/her order at any time before it has been accepted by the supplier, or if:

- the goods delivered are of the wrong type or quality (if they do not conform to sample)
- the goods are not delivered by the stated time (or within a reasonable time if no delivery date has been fixed)
- more or less than the quantity ordered is delivered
- the goods arrive damaged (but only where transportation is the supplier's responsibility).

Unless the contract provides otherwise, it is the buyer's legal duty to collect and transport the goods from the supplier's premises. This would be so where the goods are sold *loco*, ex works or similar terms. The buyer is then liable for any loss or damage occurring during transport. Similarly under an fob or a cif contract, the customer is liable from the time the goods are loaded onto the ship.

12.12 Buyer seeks to cancel order due to adequate stocks

(a) Customer's letter

> Dear Sirs
>
> On 2 March I ordered 100 tennis rackets to be delivered at the end of this month.
>
> Persistent bad weather has seriously affected sales so I find that my present stock will probably satisfy demand in the present season. I am therefore writing to ask you to cancel part of my order and to deliver only 50 of these rackets instead of the 100 ordered.
>
> I am sorry to make this request so late but hope that you will be able to agree to it in view of our long-standing business association. Should sales improve I will get in touch with you again and take a further delivery.
>
> Yours faithfully

(b) Supplier agrees to cancel order

A supplier will often agree to cancel or modify the buyer's order for a number of reasons:

- a wish to oblige a good customer
- the loss of profit involved may be minimal
- it helps to create customer goodwill
- there may be a ready market for the goods elsewhere

- the customer's financial position may be doubtful
- legal proceedings are costly.

Dear

We have received your letter of 2 May asking us to cancel part of the order you placed on 2 March for tennis rackets.

We are naturally disappointed that there should be any need for this request. However we always like to oblige our regular customers and in the circumstances we are prepared to reduce the number of rackets from 100 to 50 as requested.

We do hope that your sales will improve sufficiently to enable you to take up the balance of your order at a later date.

In this respect we hope to hear from you again soon.

Yours sincerely

(c) Supplier refuses to cancel order

The supplier will sometimes refuse to cancel an order for various reasons:

- a wish to retain a sale
- the manufacture of goods that cannot easily be sold elsewhere may have begun
- a keen entrepreneur may be unwilling to forgo their legal rights.

The letter refusing a request for cancellation must be worded carefully and considerately if it is not to cause offence and drive a customer away for good. Such a letter must show that you understand the buyer's problems, and tactfully explain the difficulties that cancellation would create for the supplier. The reasons given must be convincing, otherwise the supplier is liable to lose the customer's goodwill.

Dear

We have received your letter of 2 May asking us to cancel part of your order of 2 March for tennis rackets.

We are sorry you find it necessary to make this request, especially at this late stage. To be able to meet our customers' needs promptly we have to place our orders with manufacturers well in advance of the season. In estimating quantities we rely very largely upon the orders we have received.

We do not like to refuse requests of any kind from regular customers. However on this occasion we have no choice but to do so. All orders, including your own, have already been made up and are awaiting delivery.

I hope you will understand why we must hold you to your order. If we had received your request earlier we should have been glad to help you.

Yours sincerely

12.13 Cancellation of order through delay in delivery

Dear

In our order number 8546 dated 18 August we stressed the importance of delivery by 4 October at the very latest.

We have already written to you twice reminding you of the importance of prompt delivery. However as you have failed to make delivery on time we are left with no choice but to cancel the order.

We take this action with regret but as the goods were required for shipment abroad, and as the boat by which they were to be sent sails tomorrow, we have no means of getting them to our client in time for the exhibition for which they were required.

We have informed our client of the action we have taken and should be glad if you would acknowledge the cancellation.

Yours sincerely

PERSONAL COMPLAINTS

There may be many reasons why it is necessary for you to write a letter of complaint. Although you will probably feel angry, you must remember that the other party might have a good explanation or may not be to blame. Confine your letter to a statement of the facts and stress your disappointment, then ask what the company intends to do.

12.14 Complaint regarding soup quality

(a) Customer's letter

Dear Mr Turner

CHUNKY ROASTED VEGETABLE SOUP

I was recently in your High Street, Sheffield branch and I bought 3 tins of Chunky Roasted Vegetable Soup because I thought the description sounded excellent – Mediterranean flavours of roasted peppers, courgettes and olives with fusilli pasta.

However I was very disappointed when I opened the first tin to find that there was no pasta in the soup at all. This made the soup quite weak and watery, and not very substantial at all.

I am enclosing the label from this tin of soup, and also noted the details on the foot of the can as follows:

BB <0827> MRVI   31.10.2003

I felt you would wish to know about this because you will want to address the issue and find out why this happened. I am used to good quality food products from Manson and Spindlers, so I was very disappointed that this soup fell far short of my expectations.

I look forward to your early reply.

Yours sincerely

(b) Reply from store manager

Address the customer by name —— Dear Miss Taylor

Companies want to know when you are dissatisfied —— Thank you for letting us know that a recent purchase of our Chunky Roasted Vegetable Soup did not contain the stated pasta. Please accept my apologies.

Tell the customer what you are currently doing to ensure quality —— We try very hard to make sure that all our products are of the highest quality and they should be correctly prepared. It is obvious from your comments that on this occasion a mistake was made.

Explain what has been done —— I have passed the details of this issue to the department concerned. They will investigate the error and will contact the supplier to prevent it from happening again.

Go the extra mile when appropriate —— I am pleased to enclose a voucher for £10 as a gesture of our goodwill, and I hope you will continue to be a valued customer of Manson and Spindlers.

Yours sincerely

 TIP When writing or replying to a letter of complaint, do not use the word 'complaint'.

12.15 Missing mileage request to airline

(a) Customer's letter

Dear Sirs

MISSING MILEAGE REQUEST

I attach my missing mileage request form for missing mileage from my Harrisons Car Rental in July this year.

Also attached is a copy of the missing mileage request form faxed to you last week by my travel agent (Travel Shop) who booked this flight for me.

I hope you are able to credit me with the missing miles. This flight back to the UK was arranged very quickly because I received a phone call to say that my mother was ill and was being taken into hospital. I arranged the flight and flew home very quickly – I remember my travel agent telling me that if I paid a few hundred dollars extra, my flight would be eligible for air miles, so I chose to do this. However, when I got to the check-in desk at the airport, I was very upset and anxious, and I don't recall reminding the check-in clerk that I was a Content Club member. Perhaps this is why my account has not been credited with the extra miles?

As you will see from my Harrisons Car Rental receipt, I did mention that I was a Content Club member when I picked up my hire car at Manchester airport. However, again these miles have not been credited to me.

I hope that you can look into this and that I will be credited with the air miles that are due from both my air travel and my hire car rental.

Yours faithfully

(b) Reply from the airline

Dear Mr Green

Thank the customer for the letter and apologise up front — Thank you for your letter dated 21 August and many apologies for the printing mistake on your recent Content Club statement.

Explain what has been done about the situation — Our Information Management team has isolated the error and the problem happened at the printing stage. However I can assure you that your personal data has not been affected and the information stored on the Content Club database is correct, provided your membership number has been recorded in your booking in the usual way.

Give additional information to reassure the customer — I am pleased to enclose a corrected version of your Content Club statement. If you have any further questions about your statement please feel free to contact me. Alternatively your most recent travel history is available on our website www.contentclub.com.sg.

Go the extra mile — In the circumstances I feel we should make amends for the inconvenience caused, and we will credit your account with 100 bonus air miles.

Thank you for your patience and understanding.

Yours sincerely

12.16 Complaint about insurance claim

(a) Customer's letter

Dear Mr Watson

CLAIM AL54323432 – STORM DAMAGE TO ROOF

I received a cheque for £623 dated 26 January in payment of my recent claim. However I wish to place on record how much upset has been caused by the way your Claims Assessor, Mr Michael Tan, handled this claim.

When Mr Tan first called me he specifically told me that he believed I had been overcharged for this work, and said he would expect to pay that price for work on a double garage rather than a single garage like mine. Mr Tan said that in his opinion I should neither use nor recommend this contractor again. He proceeded to tell me that as such it was unlikely that I would receive payment for the full cost which I had paid out. Never during this conversation did he mention that the reason for not receiving full payment was because of the nature of my insurance policy.

Consequently I wrote to the contractor, Mr Lance Ashe, to complain about his pricing, stating that I was very upset thinking that he could have knowingly taken advantage by overcharging a 73-year-old woman. Mr Ashe telephoned me immediately and explained his charges in detail, as he was very upset that he had caused me some distress. I believe Mr Ashe then called Mr Tan, because he later reported back to me that Mr Tan had told him that the reason I would not receive full payment in regard to my claim was because of the type of policy that I hold, which does not cover wear and tear. This was the first time this issue had been brought to my attention, so you can imagine my surprise.

When I received Mr Tan's letter of 2 February this situation was explained. If this had been explained to me in this way in the first place I would have been able to accept it and would certainly not have questioned Mr Ashe's charges. Instead, by telling me initially that I had been overcharged for this work, it caused a great deal of upset not only for me but also for Lance Ashe who was naturally most upset that anyone should think his work was unfairly priced.

I believe this claim was handled badly by Mr Tan from the beginning in that I was led to believe that I would not be reimbursed in full because I had been overcharged – not because of the nature of my policy, which I now know to be the case. I have been caused a great deal of embarrassment and upset over this issue, and this has caused a lot of upset between me and Mr Ashe.

I felt you should know how disappointed and upset I am. I trust you will look into this and ensure that such claims are handled more appropriately in the future.

Yours sincerely

(b) Acknowledgement from insurance company

The insurance company cannot reply immediately as they need to investigate. However it is good business practice to send a brief note explaining what is happening.

Dear Mrs Richardson

Thank you for your letter of 4 February. I am sorry to learn of the problems you have experienced recently with your claim.

I am looking into the matter you have raised and I, or one of my colleagues, will write to you again as soon as possible, definitely within the next 7 working days. However, if you would like to discuss this matter further in the meantime, please do not hesitate to call me on 0114 2347827.

Yours sincerely

(c) Detailed reply from insurance company

Dear Mrs Richardson

Following my letter of 6 February, I have reviewed our file on your recent claim.

I am sorry that you feel you were given the impression by our claims assessor that there was a problem with the work carried out by your chosen contractor and the price that he charged. It was not the assessor's intention to cause any distress to you by his initial thoughts, and I am sorry about the distress this caused you. However, after discussion with Mr Ashe, the assessor was satisfied that the cost was reasonable and that the work had been completed satisfactorily.

We are always interested in any feedback from our customers on the service that we provide, and are continually looking for ways to improve this. However, on this occasion, I do not feel that it is necessary to adjust our procedure. Our assessors are highly trained to investigate claims and ensure that claims settlements are fair and reasonable. They have a responsibility to ensure that all relevant enquiries are made before settling a claim and I am happy that the assessor has acted properly in this respect. However, it is unfortunate that in the first place he gave you the wrong impression, and I do apologise for this.

Thank you again for writing to us. If I can be of any further help, please let me know.

Yours sincerely

This letter has obviously been written in anger and in haste. The tone is very disrespectful, the contents are not structured logically, important details have been omitted, and the letter would not achieve results.

Don't write a general letter to the store – call up and ask for the name of the Customer Service Manager

The Manager
Robinsons Departmental Store
High Street
Manchester
M20 4HT

Use a personalised salutation

Dear Sir/Madam

Don't say 'I am writing' or use the word 'complain'! 'A few days ago' is useless.

I am writing to complain about how I was treated when I visited your store a few days ago.

When I asked the sales clerk for help she ignored me and continued gossiping with a colleague. When I interrupted them they both 'tutted' loudly and stared at me. When I persisted, one sales clerk offered some assistance very begrudgingly and when I requested specific help she said, 'You'll have to be quick – I'm due for my break soon.'

Give the name of the sales clerks concerned

This information is misplaced – it should be in the introduction

One assistant's bad manners does not mean the whole store's customer service policy is bad

I have been a customer of this store for 10 years now but it is obvious that your customer service policy leaves a lot to be desired, otherwise the assistant would not have dared to be so rude. In the circumstances I shall be taking my business elsewhere in future.

Yours faithfully

It is unlikely that the writer would never visit the department store ever again

 When replying to a letter of complaint, do not be rude or sarcastic. This will cause ill-feeling, which will be counter-productive.

This letter is more structured, the tone is respectful, and the writer remains courteous while giving a clear indication of the reason for her dissatisfaction. All the details are provided so that the Manager will have no problem in investigating the matter.

Use a personalised salutation	Dear Mrs Williams
It is always good to begin with a compliment when writing a complaint	I have been a customer of Robinsons for the last 10 years and have always been very happy with the service.
Give all the details – where, when, who, what time, what happened	However when I visited the Ladies' Department around noon on Monday 12 June one of your assistants, Sandra Wong, was very unprofessional. When I asked for help she continued talking to her colleague. Eventually she said abruptly, 'You'll have to be quick – I'm due for my break soon!'
Don't tell the Manager what you expect – just ask him to investigate	This is not the sort of service that I have come to expect from staff of Robinsons, and I hope you will investigate this matter.
Finish with a simple close stating that you expect an early reply	I look forward to your prompt reply.
	Yours sincerely

Here is a reply to a complaint that has been written quickly and in a tone that is far from courteous.

From	grace.peng@global.co.cn
Date	25.10.03 15.29.45
To	robinzhang@midway.co.cn
CC	
Subject	Your Complaint

Your complaint about your fax machine that you bought from us last year has been past to me for my attn. Please be informed that your policy document shows that you only have a one year guarantee for this product and it ran out on 2nd Sept. So if you want it fixing you will have to pay for it.

Let me know what you want to do.

Here is the same reply written in a more courteous tone.

From	grace.peng@global.co.cn
Date	25.10.03 15.29.45
To	robinzhang@midway.co.cn
CC	
Subject	ST101 Fax Machine

Dear Robin

Thank you for your message. I am sorry to hear about the problems you have experienced with this fax machine.

I have checked your policy document and unfortunately our one-year guarantee for this machine ended on 2 September. I am sorry to say that you must pay for any repairs.

We will be pleased to repair the machine for you and can promise immediate attention and reasonable terms.

Please give me a call soon on 2874722 to discuss this.

Grace Peng
Global Communications
www.global.co.cn

CHECKLIST

Making a complaint

- ☐ Act promptly.
- ☐ Show restraint in your wording – the supplier may have a good defence.
- ☐ State the facts briefly, exactly and clearly.
- ☐ Avoid rudeness.
- ☐ Suggest desired results/action.

Responding to a complaint

- ☐ Investigate the matter promptly.
- ☐ Show understanding and empathy.
- ☐ If unreasonable, be firm but polite, and try not to offend.
- ☐ If you are at fault, express regret and admit it.
- ☐ Explain how the matter will be put right or has been rectified.
- ☐ Never blame staff.
- ☐ Provide extra effort, information or compensation if appropriate.
- ☐ Give personalised attention.
- ☐ Thank the person again for writing.
- ☐ Reassure the customer of future good service, to build loyalty.

USEFUL EXPRESSIONS

Letters of complaint

Openings

1 The goods we ordered from you on ... have not yet been delivered.

2 Delivery of the goods ordered on ... is now considerably overdue.

3 We regret having to report that we have not yet received the goods ordered on ...

4 We regret to report that one of the cases of your consignment was badly damaged when delivered on ...

5 When we examined the goods despatched by you on ... we found that ...

6 We have received a number of complaints from several customers regarding the ... supplied by you on ...

Useful central phrases

1 I am very unhappy with ...

2 This situation is causing us a great deal of inconvenience.

3 This standard of workmanship is not what I have come to expect from you.

4 This service is well below the standard expected.

5 I felt you would wish to know about this.

6 I am sure you will wish to look into this and find out what happened.

7 I am used to good quality from ...

Closes

1 Please look into this matter at once and let us know the reason for this delay.

2 We hope to hear from you soon that the goods will be sent immediately.

3 We feel there must be some explanation for this delay and await your prompt reply.

4 We hope to learn that you are prepared to make some allowance in these circumstances.

5 I hope to receive a complete refund soon.

Replies to complaints

Openings

1 We are concerned to learn from your letter of ... that the goods sent under your order number ... did not reach you until ...

2 I am sorry that you have experienced delays in the delivery of ...

3 I am very sorry to hear about ... in your letter of ...

4 Thank you for your letter of ..., which has given us the opportunity to rectify a most unfortunate mistake.

5 We wish to apologise for the unfortunate mistake pointed out in your letter of ...

Useful central phrases

1 We appreciate the opportunity to clarify this issue.

2 From your comments it is obvious that on this occasion a mistake was made.

3 You have rightly pointed out that ...

4 In the circuumstances I feel we should make amends for the inconvenience caused.

5 Due to an oversight ...

6 It is unfortunate that ...

7 I am sorry about the distress this caused you.

Closes

1 We assure you that we are doing all we can to speed delivery and offer our apologies for the inconvenience this delay is causing you.

2 We hope you will be satisfied with the arrangements we have made.

3 We trust these arrangements will be satisfactory and look forward to receiving your future orders.

4 We regret the inconvenience which has been caused in this matter.

5 We apologise once again for the unfortunate mistake and can assure you that a similar incident will not occur again.

6 As a gesture of goodwill I am pleased to enclose ...

7 Thank you once again for taking the time to write to us.

Goodwill messages

One of the most important functions of all communications is to create good business relations. Many managers and executives take the opportunity to send goodwill letters on many different occasions such as:

apologies	unwelcome news	sympathy	welcome
promotion	congratulations	death	special award
thanks	condolence	appreciation	wedding

Every opportunity should be taken to write goodwill letters. They are appreciated by customers and colleagues and are very good for business. For very little cost and effort they not only strengthen existing relationships but may also create new business opportunities.

Goodwill letters should be written and sent promptly. They should be brief and to the point, always sincere and informal. Handwritten notes will give an added touch of sincerity and intimacy where appropriate.

GENERAL GOODWILL MESSAGES

The following letters are examples of ways in which goodwill can be built into the everyday business letter. The tone of the letters is courteous and friendly, and the added touches of personal interest are certain to make a good impression.

 Your writing reflects an impression of you – make sure it's a good one.

13.1 Letter with short personal greeting

A personal touch may sometimes take the form of a short final paragraph conveying a personal greeting.

Dear Mr Ellis

I am sorry not to have replied sooner to your letter of 25 October regarding the book <u>English and Commercial Correspondence</u>. My Export Director is in Lebanon and Syria on business; as I am dealing with his work as well as my own I am afraid my correspondence has fallen behind.

Whether this book should be published in hardback or paperback is a decision I must leave to my Editorial Director, Tracie James, to whom I have passed on your letter. No doubt she will be writing to you very soon.

I hope you are keeping well.

With best wishes

Yours sincerely

13.2 Letter with extended personal greeting

An even more personal note may be introduced in the final paragraph.

> Dear Mrs Jenner
>
> Importing Made Easy
>
> I have had an opportunity to review the book you sent to me recently.
>
> This book presents a concise and clear account of the new import regulations with good examples of how they are likely to be applied.
>
> More detailed comments are made on my written review which is attached.
>
> I remember you mentioned that you will be spending your summer holiday in the south of France. I hope you have good weather and an enjoyable time.
>
> Yours sincerely

13.3 Letter explaining delayed reply

A favourable impression is created when a letter is answered on the day it is received. If this is not possible the letter should be acknowledged as soon as possible with an explanation of the delay.

> Dear Mrs Jones
>
> I am sorry we cannot send you immediately the catalogue and price list requested in your letter of 13 March as we are presently out of stock.
>
> Supplies are expected from our printers in 2 weeks' time; as soon as they are received, we will send a copy to you.
>
> Yours sincerely

13.4 Supplier's letter with friendly tone

Customers always look for a spirit of friendliness in those with whom they seek to do business. In this letter the writer is both helpful and friendly. The aim is to interest the prospective customer, to create a feeling of confidence and to win their consideration, friendship – and ultimately their custom.

Dear Mr Jackson

I am pleased to enclose our catalogue and price list as requested in your letter of 12 October.

In this latest catalogue we have taken trouble to ensure it is both attractive and informative; particulars of our trade discounts are shown inside the front cover.

May I suggest that next time you are in Bristol you allow us to show you our factory where you could see for yourself the high quality of materials and workmanship put into our products. This would also enable you to see at first hand the latest fancy leather goods, and to return home with interesting and useful information for your customers.

If I can be of service in any way please do not hesitate to let me know.

Yours sincerely

13.5 Letter welcoming a visitor from abroad

When customers from overseas visit your country it is sound business practice to extend hospitality and to give any help and advice you can. The tone of such letters must be sincere and friendly, giving the impression that the writer is genuinely anxious to be of service.

Dear Mr Brandon

I was pleased to receive your letter of 24 April and to learn that your colleague, Mr John Gelling, is making plans to visit England in July. We shall be very pleased to welcome him and to do all we can to make his visit enjoyable and successful.

I understand this will be Mr Gelling's first visit to England, and am sure he will wish to see some of our principal places of interest. A suitable programme is something we can discuss when he arrives. I would be pleased to introduce him to several firms with which he may like to do business.

When the date of Mr Gelling's visit is settled please let me know his arrival details. I will arrange to meet him at the airport and drive him to his hotel. He may be assured of a warm welcome.

Yours sincerely

LETTERS OF APOLOGY

When it is necessary to apologise for something, it is important to get the tone right. Sometimes you may have to swallow your pride and say you are sorry even if you're not. Legal pressure may mean an apology is necessary if you have caused injury or offence to someone.

13.6   Apology for poor service

Background details regarding complaint —

State action taken and express regret —

Follow-up action —

Apologise again —

> Dear Mrs Taylor
>
> Thank you for your letter of 12 June regarding the poor service you received when you visited our store recently.
>
> The incident was most unlike our usual high standards of service and courtesy. The member of staff who was rude to you has been reprimanded; he also expresses his regret.
>
> I am enclosing a gift voucher for £20 which you may use at any Omega store. If I can be of any further assistance to you please do not hesitate to contact me.
>
> With my apologies once again.
>
> Yours sincerely

13.7   Apology for cancelling an appointment

> Dear Mr James
>
> I am so sorry that I had to cancel our meeting yesterday at such short notice. As my secretary explained to you I am afraid an urgent matter came up which I had to deal with immediately.
>
> I understand our appointment has been rearranged for next Tuesday 12 May at 11.30.
>
> Perhaps we can extend our meeting over lunch.
>
> Yours sincerely

 Remember, how you say something is much more important than what you say. Consider tone carefully.

LETTERS IN WHICH TONE IS PARTICULARLY IMPORTANT

In business it is sometimes necessary to refuse requests, increase prices, explain an unfortunate oversight, apologise for mistakes, etc. In such letters tone has to be the writer's main concern. Without due consideration, offence could be caused, bad feeling could be created and business may be lost.

13.8 Letter conveying unwelcome news

It is sometimes necessary to refuse a request or to convey unwelcome news. When this is necessary, think of the reader – prepare the way for their disappointment by a suitable opening paragraph, and use an appropriate tone.

Dear Mr Foster

It was good of you to let me see your manuscript on <u>English for Business Studies</u>. I read it with interest and was impressed by the careful and thorough way in which you have treated the subject. I particularly like the clear and concise style of writing.

Had we not recently published <u>Practical English</u> by Freda Leonard, a book that covers very similar ground, I would have been happy to accept your manuscript for publication. In the circumstances, I am unable to do so and am returning your manuscript with this letter.

I am sorry to have to disappoint you.

Yours sincerely

13.9 Letter disclaiming liability for loss

Here is another letter in which the opening paragraph is used to prepare the recipient for the rejection of his insurance claim.

Dear Mr Burn

When we received your letter of 23 November we sent a representative to inspect and report on the damage caused by the recent fire in your warehouse.

This report has now been submitted and it confirms your claim that the damage is extensive. However, it states that a large proportion of the stock damaged or destroyed was very old and some of it obsolete.

Unfortunately, therefore, we cannot accept your figure of £45,000 as a fair estimate of the loss as it appears to be based on the original cost of the goods.

Yours sincerely

13.10 Letter refusing a request for credit

A letter refusing a request for credit without causing offence is one of the most difficult to write. Refusal will be prompted by doubts about the would-be creditor's standing but the letter must contain no suggestion of this. Other reasons for the refusal must be given and tactfully explained.

This letter is a wholesaler's reply to a trader who has started a new business which appears to be doing well. However, the business has not been established long enough to inspire confidence in the owner's financial standing.

Dear Miss Wardle

We were glad you approached us with a view to placing an order, and to learn of the good start of your new business.

The question of granting credit for newly established businesses is never an easy one. Many owners get into difficulties because they overcommit themselves before they are thoroughly established. Although we believe that your own business promises very well, we feel it would be better for you to make your purchases on a cash basis at present. If this is not possible for the full amount, we suggest that you cut the size of your order, say by half.

If you are willing to do this we will allow you a special cash discount of 4% in addition to our usual trade terms. If this suggestion is acceptable to you, the goods could be delivered to you within 3 days.

We hope that you will look upon this letter as a mark of our genuine wish to enter into business with you on terms that will bring lasting satisfaction to us both. When your business is firmly established we will be very happy to welcome you as one of our credit customers.

Yours sincerely

13.11 Letter regretting an oversight

If you have made a mistake or are in any way at fault, it should be admitted freely and without excuses. A letter written in an apologetic tone is likely to create goodwill, and it will be difficult for the recipient to continue to feel a grudge against you.

Dear Mrs Wright

I was very concerned when I received your letter of yesterday stating that the central heating system in your home has not been completed by the date promised.

On referring to our earlier correspondence I find that I had mistaken the date for completion. The fault is entirely mine and I deeply regret that it should have occurred.

I realise the inconvenience which my oversight must be causing you and will do everything possible to avoid any further delay.

I have already given instructions for this work to take first priority; our engineers will be placed on overtime to complete the work. These arrangements should ensure that the work is completed by next weekend.

My apologies once again for the inconvenience caused.

Yours sincerely

13.12 Letter regretting price increase

Customers will naturally resent increases in prices of goods, especially if they feel the increases are not justified. Goodwill can be preserved by explaining clearly and convincingly the reasons for the increases.

Dear

Many businesses have been experiencing steadily rising prices over the past few years and it will come as no surprise to you that our own costs have continued to rise with this general trend.

Increasing world demand has been an important factor in raising the prices of our imported raw materials. A recent national wage award has added to our labour costs which have been increased still further by constantly increasing overheads.

Until now we have been able to absorb rising costs by economies in other areas. We find that we can no longer do so, and therefore increases in our prices are unavoidable. The new prices will take effect from 1 October, and revised price lists are being prepared. These should be ready within the next 2 weeks and copies will be sent to you.

We are sorry that these increases have been necessary but can assure you that they will not amount to an average of more than about 5%. As general prices have risen by nearly 10% since our previous price list, we hope you will not feel that our own increases are unreasonable.

Yours sincerely

LETTERS OF THANKS

Business executives have many opportunities for writing letters expressing appreciation and creating goodwill. Such letters of thanks can be as brief and as simple as you like, but they must express your appreciation with warmth and sincerity, making the reader feel that you really mean what you say – and that you enjoy saying it.

In letters of appreciation do not include specific sales matters or the reader may think that your thanks are merely an excuse for promoting business.

13.13 Letter of thanks for a first order

Dear Mr Martin

You will have already received our formal acknowledgement of your order number 456 dated 12 July. However as this is your first order with us I felt I must write to say how pleased we were to receive it and to thank you for the opportunity given to us to supply the goods you need.

I hope our handling of your order will lead to further business between us, and to a happy and mutually beneficial association.

Yours sincerely

13.14 Letter of thanks for a large order

Dear Mrs Usher

I understand that you placed an unusually large order with us yesterday, and I want to say how very much your continued confidence in us is appreciated.

The happy working relationship between us for many years has always been valued and we shall do our best to maintain it.

Yours sincerely

13.15 Letter of thanks for prompt settlement of accounts

Dear Mr Watts

I am writing to say how much we appreciate the promptness with which you have settled your accounts with us during the past year, especially as a number of them have been for very large amounts.

This has been of great help to us at a time when we have been faced with heavy commitments connected with the expansion of our business.

I hope our business relationship will continue in the future.

Yours sincerely

13.16 Letter of thanks for a service performed

Dear Miss Armstrong

Thank you for your letter of 30 March returning the draft of the catalogue we propose to send to our customers.

I am very grateful for the trouble you have taken to examine the draft and comment on it in such detail. Your suggestions will be very helpful.

I realise the value of time to a busy person like you and this makes me all the more appreciative of the time you have so generously given.

Yours sincerely

13.17 Letter of thanks for information received

Dear Mrs Webster

Thank you for your letter enclosing an article explaining the organisation and work of your local trade association.

I am very grateful for the interest you have shown in our proposal to include details of your association in the next issue of the <u>Trade Association Year Book</u>, and for your trouble in providing such an interesting account of your activities. This feature is sure to inspire and encourage associations in other areas.

Yours sincerely

LETTERS OF CONGRATULATION

One of the best ways to promote goodwill is to write a letter of congratulation. The occasion may be a promotion, a new appointment, the award of an honour, the establishment of a new business, success in an examination, even a marriage or a birthday. Your letter may be short and formal, or conversational and informal, depending on the circumstances and the relationship between you and the recipient.

13.18 Formal letter of congratulation on the award of a public honour

Letters of congratulation sent to mark the award of a public honour need only be short and formal. To show a sign of personal interest the salutation and complimentary close should be handwritten.

> I was delighted to learn that your work at the South Down College of Commerce has been recognised in the New Year Honours List.
>
> At a time when commercial education is so much in the public eye, it gives us all at the Ministry great pleasure to learn of your OBE.

13.19 Informal letter of congratulation on the award of a public honour

> On looking through the <u>Camford Times</u> this morning I came across your name in the New Years Honours List. I would like to add my congratulations to the many you will be receiving.
>
> The award will give much pleasure to a wide circle of people who know you and your work. Your services to local industry and commerce over many years have been quite outstanding and it is very gratifying to know that they have been so suitably rewarded.
>
> With very best wishes

13.20 Formal letter of congratulation on a promotion

> Dear Dr Roberts
>
> I would like to convey my warm congratulations on your appointment to the Board of Electrical Industries Ltd.
>
> My fellow directors and I are delighted that the many years of service you have given to your company should at last have been rewarded in this way.
>
> We all join in sending you our very best wishes for the future.
>
> Yours sincerely

13.21 Letter of congratulation on employee's 10th anniversary

> This month marks your tenth anniversary as a member of staff of SingComm Pte Ltd. We would like to take this opportunity to thank you for these past 10 years of fine workmanship and company loyalty.
>
> We know that the growth and success of our company is largely dependent on having strong and capable staff members such as yourself. We also recognise the contributions you make in helping us maintain the position we enjoy in the industry.
>
> We are hoping that you will remain with us for many years to come and would like to offer our congratulations on this special anniversary.

 TIP **Avoid waffle. Read through your message and tidy up anything that is repetitive or out of logical flow.**

13.22 Letter acknowledging congratulations

Courtesy requires that letters of congratulation should be acknowledged. In most cases a short formal acknowledgement is all that is necessary.

This letter would be a suitable reply to the letter of congratulation in 13.18. The writer very properly takes the opportunity to acknowledge her debt to colleagues who have supported her in her work.

Dear Mrs Fleming

Thank you for your letter conveying congratulations on the award of my OBE.

I am very happy that anything I may have been able to do for commercial education in my limited field should have been rewarded by a public honour. At the same time I regard the award as being less of a tribute to me personally than to the work of my college as a whole – work in which I have always enjoyed the willing help and support of many colleagues.

Thank you again for your good wishes.

Yours sincerely

LETTERS OF CONDOLENCE AND SYMPATHY

Letters of condolence are not easy to write. There can be no set pattern to such letters since a lot depends on what kind of relationship the writer has with the recipient. As a general rule such letters should usually be short and written with sincerity. To show special consideration letters of this kind should be handwritten.

Your letter should be written as soon as you learn the news. Express your sympathy in simple words which are warm and convincing and say what you feel sincerely.

13.23 Letter of condolence to a neighbour

Dear Mrs McDermott

It was not until late last night that my wife and I learned of your husband's tragic death. Coming as it did without warning, it must have been a great shock to you. I want you to know how very sorry we both are, and to send our sincere sympathy.

If there is any way in which we can be of any help, either now or later, do please let us know. We shall be only too glad to do anything we can.

Yours sincerely

Peter Brand

13.24 Letter of condolence to a customer

Dear Mr Kerr

I have just learned with deep regret of the death of your wife.

There is not much one can say at a time like this, but all of us at Simpsons who have dealt with you would like to extend our sincere sympathy at your loss.

Please include us among those who share your sorrow at this sad time.

Yours sincerely

13.25 Letter of condolence to a business associate

Dear Mrs Anderson

We were distressed to read in <u>The Times</u> this morning that your Chairman has died and I am writing at once to express our deep sympathy.

I had the privilege of knowing Sir James for many years and always regarded him as a personal friend. By his untimely passing our industry has lost one of its best leaders. He will be greatly missed by all who knew him.

Please convey our sympathy to Lady Langley and her family.

Yours sincerely

13.26 Letter of condolence to an employee

Dear Maxine

I was very sorry to learn of your father's death. I remember your father very well from the years he served in our company's Accounts Department until his retirement 2 years ago. I well recall his love for his family and the great sense of pride with which he always spoke of his daughters. He has been greatly missed at Wilson's since his retirement. We all join in expressing our sympathy to you and your family at this very sad time.

Yours sincerely

13.27 Letter of condolence to a friend

Dear Henry

I felt I must write to say how deeply sorry we were at the news of Margaret's passing.

She was a very dear friend and we shall greatly miss her cheerful outlook on life, her generous nature and her warmth of feeling for anyone in need of help. Above all we will miss her for her wonderful sense of fun.

Tom and I send you our love and our assurance of continued friendship, now and always. If there is any help we can provide at any time, just let us know.

Yours

Alice

13.28 Letter of sympathy to a business associate

Dear Bill

When I called at your office yesterday I was very sorry to learn that you had been in a car accident on your way home from work recently. However I was equally relieved to learn that you are making good progress and are likely to be back at work again in a few weeks.

I had a long talk with Susan Carson and was glad to learn of your rising export orders. I expect to be in Leicester again at the end of next month and shall take the opportunity to call on you.

Meanwhile I wish you a speedy recovery.

Yours sincerely

13.29 Acknowledgements of sympathy or condolence

You will naturally wish to acknowledge letters of the kind illustrated in this section. Such acknowledgements need only be short but they show that you are genuinely moved by the warm expressions of sympathy you have received.

(a) Personal acknowledgement

Individual personalised acknowledgements should be made to relatives and close friends.

Dear Mrs Hughes

My mother and family join me in thanking you for your very kind letter on the occasion of my father's death.

We have all been greatly comforted by the kindness and sympathy of our relatives and friends. Both at home and in the hospital, where my father spent 2 weeks prior to his passing, the kindness and sympathy shown by everyone has been almost overwhelming.

Yours sincerely

Laura Darabi

(b) Printed acknowledgement

When many letters of condolence have been received it will be sufficient to prepare a printed general acknowledgement.

Mr and Mrs Ashton and family thank you most sincerely for your kind expression of sympathy at their sad loss.

The kindness of so many friends and the many expressions of affection and esteem in which Margaret was held will always remain a proud and cherished memory.

97 Lake Rise
Romford
Essex
RM1 4EF

CHECKLIST

- [ ] Write and send letters promptly.
- [ ] Use an appropriate tone.
- [ ] Be sincere.
- [ ] Use an informal style.
- [ ] Use a personalised approach (handwritten if appropriate).
- [ ] Keep them short and to the point.
- [ ] Ask yourself how you would feel on receiving such a letter.

Reports and proposals

1
2
3
4
5
6
7
8
9
10
11
12
13
14
15
16
17
18
19
20
21
22
23
24
25
26
27
28
29
30

INTRODUCTION TO REPORTS AND PROPOSALS

Many different types of report are used in business – some quite short and informal, others fairly lengthy and formal. The ultimate purpose of any report is to provide the foundation for decisions to be made and action taken.

Some reports contain no more than a simple statement recording an event, a visit or some circumstances, with a note of action taken. Other reports include detailed explanations of facts, conclusions, and perhaps recommendations for action.

More detailed reports require a lot of research. This may involve interviews, visits, questionnaires and investigations. The information may be presented in written, tabular or graphic form, and the writer needs to produce clear conclusions and recommendations.

The skills in writing a proposal are the same as in writing a report. However, there are certain differences between these two documents:

Reports
- contain information about what has happened in the past
- aim mainly to provide information

- record objective facts.

Proposals
- examine what may happen in the future
- aim mainly to persuade the reader to make a specific decision
- express opinions – albeit supported by objective facts.

I would like to thank the Plain English Campaign for granting me permission to reproduce its *Plain English Guide to Writing Reports* here. This is an excellent guide going through all the principles of report writing – in plain English of course. If you want to find out more about the Plain English Campaign please visit www.plainenglish.co.uk.

 A well-presented title page on your report will create a good impression.

THE PLAIN ENGLISH GUIDE TO WRITING REPORTS

When writing reports, make your audience's job as easy as possible. Use active verbs and short sentences and keep to the point, just as you would in any other kind of writing.

This guide covers the main stages of writing a report:

- defining the purpose
- investigating the topic
- organising the report into sections
- order of presentation
- order of writing

- numbering sections and paragraphs
- planning the writing
- revision.

We finish with a memo from Sir Winston Churchill and a summary of this guide.

Defining the purpose

This helps you to be clear about:

- why you are writing
- what to include
- what to leave out and
- who your readers are.

If you can express the purpose in a single sentence, so much the better.

Investigating the topic

How you do this depends on the topic and purpose. You may need to read, interview, experiment and observe. Get advice from someone more experienced if you need to.

Organising the report into sections

Your job is to make it easy for the readers to find the information they want. In reports that are one or two pages long, readers should have no trouble finding their way around. With a 'long' report (more than four or five pages), you need to take great care in how you organise the information.

Reports can be set out in eight parts, but you won't always need them all.

- title or title page
- contents list
- abstract
- introduction
- discussion
- summary and conclusions
- recommendations
- appendix.

A short report won't need a title page, but should have a title.

The contents list is only needed in long reports.

The abstract is only needed in formal reports, such as reports of scientific research. It is a summary of the report. The abstract appears in library files and journals of abstracts. It won't usually be printed with the report so it needs to be able to stand alone.

Keep it between 80 and 120 words. Don't confuse this with an 'executive summary' which we will talk about later.

The introduction should be brief and answer any of the following questions that seem relevant.

- What is the topic?
- Who asked for the report and why?
- What is the background?
- What was your method of working? If the method is long and detailed, put it in an appendix.
- What were the sources? If there are many, put them in an appendix.

The discussion is the main body of the report. It is likely to be the longest section, containing all the details of the work organised under headings and sub-headings.

Few readers will read every word of this section. So start with the most important, follow it with the next most important, and so on.

You should follow the same rule with each paragraph. Begin with the main points of the paragraph, then write further details or an explanation.

The summary and conclusion section is sometimes placed before the discussion section. It describes the purpose of the report, your conclusions and how you reached them.

The conclusions are your main findings. Keep them brief. They should say what options or actions you consider to be best and what can be learned from what has happened before. So they may include or may lead to your recommendations: what should be done in the future to improve the situation?

Often, writers will put the summary and conclusions and the recommendations together and circulate them as a separate document. This is often called an executive summary because people can get the information they need without having to read the whole report.

It may be better (and cheaper) to send everyone an executive summary, and only provide a copy of the full report if someone asks for it. You may save a few trees, and you will certainly save your organisation plenty of time and money.

The appendix is for material which readers only need to know if they are studying the report in depth. Relevant charts and tables should go in the discussion where readers can use them. Only put them in an appendix if they would disrupt the flow of the report.

Order of presentation

We recommend the following order of presentation. You won't always need all these sections, especially those in brackets.

Long reports
- Title or title page
- (Contents list)

- (Abstract)
- Introduction
- Summary and conclusions
- Recommendations
- Discussion
- (Appendix)

Short reports

- Title
- Introduction
- Discussion
- Summary and conclusions
- Recommendations
- (Appendix)

Order of writing

The order in which you write needn't follow the order of presentation.

We recommend the following order of writing, because each section you finish helps you write the next one.

- Introduction
- Discussion
- Summary and conclusions
- Recommendations
- (Abstract)
- Title or title page
- (Contents list)
- (Appendix)

After writing all the sections, read and revise them. Rewrite sections if necessary.

Numbering sections and paragraphs

If you use plenty of clear headings and have a full contents list at the start of the report, you should find this is enough to show where each part begins and ends, and to cross-refer if necessary.

If you do have to label sections and paragraphs, keep it as simple as possible. Use capital letters to label sections and numbers to label paragraphs (A1, A2 and so on). If necessary, use small letters on their own for parts of paragraphs.

Planning the writing

Usually you will have collected such a mass of information that you cannot decide where to plunge in and begin. So, before you start to write you must make some kind of plan.

This will save you hours of writing and will help to produce a better organised report.

Here are two different ways of planning.

An outline begins as a large, blank sheet of paper onto which your pour out all your facts, ideas, observations and so on, completely at random. Write in note form, and try to get everything down as fast as possible.

When you have got all your points on paper, start to organise them, group them, and assess them for strength, relevance and their place in the report.

You can then number the points in order or put headings next to them such as 'Intro', 'Discussion', 'Conclusion' and so on. Use lines and arrows to link up related points.

Gradually you will create a network of ideas grouped under headings – this is the structure of your report. Leave it for a day or two if you can. Return with fresh ideas, add points you'd forgotten, and cross out anything you don't need.

Mind mapping is a different way of planning that suits some writing better. The idea is the same: by pouring out ideas at random, you can concentrate on the content, and organise the material at leisure when the ideas are set down.

There is no special magic to a mind map. Start by putting the topic in a box in the middle of the page, then draw lines to branch out from it with your main ideas.

It is easy to add new information and to make links between the main ideas. Order and organisation will often take care of themselves.

Revision

Always read critically what you have written. If possible, leave it alone for a few days and then re-read it. Or ask someone else to read it for you. Ask: 'Is this clear, concise and persuasive?' Be prepared to revise your language and structure. You may even have to rewrite parts that don't work.

14.1 'Brevity' – memo to the War Cabinet from Sir Winston Churchill

Even in 1940 Sir Winston Churchill could see the benefits of cutting out padding and overuse of passive writing.

 TIP Don't use too many different fonts or sizes, as it will not be attractive and could confuse the reader

"To do our work, we all have to read a mass of papers. Nearly all of them are far too long. This wastes time, while energy has to be spent in looking for the essential points.

I ask my colleagues and their staff to see to it that their reports are shorter.

The aim should be reports which set out the main points in a series of short, crisp paragraphs.

If a report relies on detailed analysts of some complicated factors, or on statistics, these should be set out in an appendix.

Often the occasion is best met by submitting not a full-dress report, but an aide-memoire consisting of headings only, which can be expanded orally if needed.

Let us have an end of such phrases as these:

'It is also of importance to bear in mind the following considerations', or 'Consideration should be given to the possibility of carrying into effect'. Most of these woolly phrases are mere padding, which can be left out altogether, or replaced by a single word. Let us not shrink from using the short expressive phrase, even if it is conversational.

Reports drawn up on the lines I propose may first seem rough as compared with the flat surface of officialese jargon. but the saving in time will be great, while the discipline of setting out the real points concisely will provide an aid to clearer thinking."

Sir Winston Churchill, 9 August 1940

 TIP Ask yourself whether the report can be read and understood by someone who knows nothing about the situation, without that person having to ask questions to clarify anything.

14.2 Memorandum

MEMORANDUM

To   Jean Lee, Manager

From   Sally Turner, Administration Assistant

Ref   JL/ST

Date   20 April 200–

VISIT OF MR HO CHWEE LEONG, WANCHAI IMPORTING COMPANY, HONG KONG

Mr Ho Chwee Leong is to visit us on (date). As we can expect a large order from his company, Wanchai Importing Company of Hong Kong, it is important that he receives a good impression of our company. The following are the arrangements for the visit.

ARRANGEMENTS MADE

1   Accommodation has been arranged for Mr Ho at Hotel Moderne and I have arranged for a taxi to collect him from the hotel at 9.30 am to bring him to Shazini Shoes factory.

2   When Mr Ho arrives at Shazini Shoes at 10.00 am he will be met by Mr Lee and senior staff who will take him on a visit of the factory.

3   A buffet lunch has been arranged in the guest room at 12.30 am. Vegetarian food has been provided.

4   The board room has been booked for a conference for the whole afternoon for Mr Ho, Mr Lee and senior staff. Refreshments have been laid on during the afternoon.

5   A taxi has been booked to take Mr Lee to the airport at 5.30 pm, so he can check in for his flight before 6.00 pm.

ARRANGEMENTS STILL TO BE MADE

1   Up to date price lists, catalogues and samples of shoes will be provided in the boardroom.

2   Staff will be informed that Mr Lee and senior staff will not be available next Friday.

14.3 Report

MARUMAN STORES, NOTTING HILL BRANCH
REPORT ON POSSIBILITY OF OPENING A CRÈCHE

INTRODUCTION

State who asked for the report and what you were asked to do.

I was asked to investigate the opening of a crèche at the Notting Hill branch by Mrs Lillian Cheng. In order to do this the following steps were taken.

List the steps taken to gather the information.

1   I obtained a breakdown of figures showing the number of customers with young children.

2   I discussed this issue with several customers who brought children to the store.

3   The accommodation, staffing and insurance issues were considered.

4   I investigated the experience of other shops that already have a crèche.

DISCUSSION

State the findings in a logical order. Use reported speech.

1   7.3% of Maruman customers have at least one child under the age of 3.

2   The majority of customers interviewed said they would use a crèche if the cost was reasonable. Some of these customers also commented that other friends who are not presently customers might also consider using the shop if there was a crèche.

3   There are strict laws and regulations concerning accommodation and staffing of a crèche. The site would have to be approved to run a crèche before we could start one.

4   Staff appointed to run the crèche would have to be fully qualified.

5   A suitable space would have to be found. This would require running water as well as toilets. The crèche would have to be close to the store entrance but due to noise levels it should be kept separate from the main store.

6   The company would be required to ensure adequate insurance.

7   Many rival stores in the neighbourhood are offering crèche facilities.

CONCLUSIONS

Make a logical conclusion from the findings.

A crèche would be popular and well-used if we decided to go ahead with this.

RECOMMENDATIONS

Make a logical conclusion from the findings.

I suggest that the company should give further consideration to offering a crèche and investigate the financial aspects that would be involved.

Suggest action that should be taken.

Sally Turner

Sign the document and state your name and title. Include a reference and date.

Customer Services Executive
LC/ST
20 April 200—

Make sure all the information in your report is well-researched and substantiated.

14.4 A longer proposal

This proposal is reproduced with permission from 'How to Write Proposals and Reports that get Results' written by Ros Jay and published by Prentice Hall.

FLEXIBLE WORKING HOURS
An initial study for ABC Ltd

by
Jane Smith

An initial study

Objective

To identify the factors involved in introducing flexible working hours, to examine their benefits and disadvantages and to recommend the best approach to take.

Summary

At present, almost all employees of ABC Ltd work from 9.00 to 5.00. A handful work from 9.30 to 5.30.

Many, though not all, staff are unhappy with this and would prefer a more flexible arrangement. Some are working mothers and would like to be able to take their children to and from school. Some, particularly the older employees, have sick or elderly relatives who make demands on their time which do not fit comfortably with their working hours.

For the company itself, this dissatisfaction among staff leads to low morale and reduced productivity. It also makes it harder to attract and retain good staff.

There are three basic options for the future:

1   *Leave things as they are*. This is obviously less demanding on resources that implementing a new system. At least we know it works even if it isn't perfect.

2   *Highly flexible system*. Employees would clock on and clock off anytime with a 12½ hour working day until they have 'clocked up' 35 hours a week. This would be the hardest system to implement.

3   *Limited flexibility*. Staff could start work any time between 8.00 to 10.00 am and work through for eight hours. This would not solve all employees' problems but it would solve most of them.

Proposal

Introduce a system of limited flexibility for now, retaining the option of increasing flexibility later if this seems appropriate.

Position

The current working hours at ABC Ltd are 9.00 to 5.00 for most employees, with a few working from 9.30 to 5.30.

Problem

Although this works up to a point, it does have certain disadvantages, both for the organisation and for some of the employees.

The organisation: The chief disadvantage of the current system is that many of the staff are dissatisfied with it. This has become such a serious problem that it is becoming harder to attract and retain good staff. Those staff who do join the company and stay with it feel less motivated: this, as research has shown, means they are less productive than they could be.

The employees: Some employees are satisfied with their current working hours, but many of them find the present system restrictive. There are several reasons for this but the employees most strongly in favour of greater flexibility are, in particular:

- parents, especially mothers, who would prefer to be able to take their children to and from school, and to work around this commitment
- employees, many of them in the older age range, who have elderly or sick relatives who they would like to be more available for.

A more flexible approach would make it easier for many staff to fulfil these kinds of demands on their time.

An initial study questioned nearly 140 employees in a cross-section of ages. A large majority were in favour of a more flexible approach, in particular the women and the younger members of the company. It is worth noting that a minority of staff were against the introduction of flexible working hours. Appendix I gives the full results of this study.

Possibilities

Since this report is looking at the principle and not the detail of a more flexible approach, the options available fall broadly into three categories: retaining the present system, introducing limited flexibility of working hours, and implementing a highly flexible system.

Although the system is not perfect, at least we know it works. The staff all signed their contracts on the understanding that the company worked to standard hours of business, and while it may not be ideal for them it is at least manageable. Better the devil you know.

Implementing any new system is bound to incur problems and expense, consequently retaining the present working hours is the least expensive option in terms of direct cost.

Highly flexible system. A highly flexible system would mean keeping the site open from, say, 7.30 am to 8.00 pm. All staff are contracted to work a certain number of hours a week and time clocks are installed. Employees simply clock on and off whenever they enter or leave the building, until they have reached their full number of hours each week.

This system has the obvious benefit that it can accommodate a huge degree of flexibility which should suit the various demands of all employees. They could even elect to work 35 hours a week spread over only three days. A further benefit to the company would be that doctors' appointments and so on would no longer happen 'on company time' as they do at present. This system does have several disadvantages, however:

- Many staff regard occasional time off for such things as doctors' appointments or serious family crises as a natural 'perk' of the job. With this system they would have to make up the hours elsewhere. Not only would they lose the time off, but many would also feel that the company did not trust them. This would obviously be bad for company morale.

- It would be difficult to implement this system fairly. The sales office, for example, must be staffed at least from 9.00 to 5.30 every day. What if all the sales staff want to take Friday off? How do you decide who can and who can't? What if the computer goes down at 4 o'clock in the afternoon and there are no computer staff in until 7.30 the following morning?

Limited flexibility: This would make asking employees to continue to work an eight hour day, but give them a range of, say, ten hours to fit it into. They could start any time between 8.00 and 10.00 in the morning, so they would finish eight hours later – between 4.00 and 6.00.

On the plus side, this would give the employees the co-operation and recognition of their problems that many of them look for, and would therefore increase staff motivation. For some it would provide a way around their other commitments.

Proposal

Given the number of staff in favour of more flexible working hours, and the importance of staff motivation, it seems sensible to adopt some kind of flexible approach. But it is probably advisable to find a system that allows the significant minority who prefer to stay as they are to do so.

So which is the best system to choose? It is harder to go backwards than forwards in developing new systems: if the highly flexible approach failed it would be difficult to pull back to a less flexible system (in terms of keeping the staff happy). On the other hand, a limited degree of flexibility could easily be extended later if this seemed appropriate.

So at this stage it seems that the most workable system, which contains most of the benefits required by the employees, is the limited flexibility of working hours.

Appendix I

Table of employee responses to the proposal for flexible working hours.

AGE GROUP	MEN Total number consulted	MEN Positive response	MEN Negative response	WOMEN Total number	WOMEN Positive response	WOMEN Negative response
18–30	20	19	1	18	18	0
30–40	23	19	4	29	27	2
40–50	15	8	7	12	8	4
50–60	12	2	10	8	7	1
	70	48	22	67	60	7

CHECKLIST

☐ Plan reports and proposals very carefully before you start writing.

☐ Use sub-headings to organise your document into sections.

☐ Use everyday, straightforward English.

☐ Avoid jargon, and explain any technical terms that you must use.

☐ Keep your sentences to 15–20 words, with one main idea in each sentence.

☐ Use active verbs wherever possible.

☐ Be clear and concise.

☐ Write sincerely and personally, as if you are talking to the reader.

☐ Draft your report first. Some reports will need strict editing, rearranging, rewording, etc.

☐ Ask someone else to read it through to check that your report meets all these objectives, and that it is readable and accurate.

Notices, advertisements and information sheets

NOTICES

Most organisations have notice boards at prominent places throughout the offices. These are used to bring special items to the attention of all staff. The information must be displayed attractively so that it gains attention and co-operation.

Notices may be posted about:

- new procedures
- social events
- advertisements for internal appointments
- reports on matters of interest
- reminders of company procedures.

15.1 Notice

Headline to draw attention	**CAN YOU ACT?** **(OR WOULD YOU LIKE TO TRY?)**
Make it sound interesting	This year Global Communications celebrates its 10th year of providing quality telecommunications equipment. To mark this special occasion we are holding a 10th Anniversary Celebration at the Regal Prince Hotel in July. Special guests, directors and staff are to be invited.
Give full details	A special 20-minute sketch has been written and we are now looking for aspiring actors and actresses to perform the sketch.
Use another heading if relevant	**INTERESTED?**
Use attractive layout to draw attention to special points	If you would like to attend an audition for a part in this sketch please come along and find out more. When? Monday 15 March Where? Training Room, Global House Time? 6.00–8.00 pm If you will be coming along to the auditions please call Mandy Jones, Marketing Department, to put your name down.
Include name/title at foot of notices	James Porter Marketing Manager
Always date notices	JP/ST 2 March 200–

ADVERTISEMENTS

Most organisations advertise in newspapers, magazines or trade journals to reach out to a wide and sometimes specific market. Advertisements may be placed to:

- advertise vacant posts
- promote products or services
- announce special events or functions
- publicise changes in the organisation.

15.2 Job advertisement

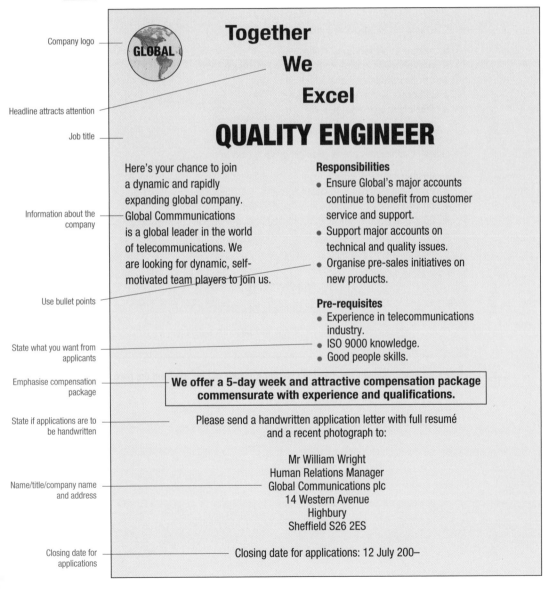

Company logo

Headline attracts attention

Job title

Information about the company

Use bullet points

State what you want from applicants

Emphasise compensation package

State if applications are to be handwritten

Name/title/company name and address

Closing date for applications

GLOBAL

Together
We
Excel

QUALITY ENGINEER

Here's your chance to join a dynamic and rapidly expanding global company. Global Commmunications is a global leader in the world of telecommunications. We are looking for dynamic, self-motivated team players to join us.

Responsibilities
- Ensure Global's major accounts continue to benefit from customer service and support.
- Support major accounts on technical and quality issues.
- Organise pre-sales initiatives on new products.

Pre-requisites
- Experience in telecommunications industry.
- ISO 9000 knowledge.
- Good people skills.

We offer a 5-day week and attractive compensation package commensurate with experience and qualifications.

Please send a handwritten application letter with full resumé and a recent photograph to:

Mr William Wright
Human Relations Manager
Global Communications plc
14 Western Avenue
Highbury
Sheffield S26 2ES

Closing date for applications: 12 July 200–

15.3 Notice or advertisement announcing a job

GLOBAL COMMUNICATIONS

require a

TEAM LEADER – CUSTOMER SERVICES

Do you have what it takes to build a successful team?
We are looking for someone who can coach, support and develop
individuals to improve team performance.

The successful applicant will have:

- excellent supervisory skills
- proven skills in directing and controlling projects
- good organisational skills
- effective decision-making skills
- first-class leadership skills

Global Communications provide great working conditions:

- flexible working hours
- excellent training and development
- private medical insurance (after one year)
- 20 days' holiday allowance, increasing with length of service
- incentive schemes
- career opportunities.

IF YOU THINK YOU HAVE WHAT IT TAKES

please apply ONLINE ONLY at

www.global.com.sg

 Make your advertisement eye-catching so that it stands out clearly from the rest.

LEAFLETS AND INFORMATION SHEETS

Many types of leaflets and information sheets are produced in business today. They are useful to convey information to a large number of people. Leaflets and information sheets may be handed out in the street or at the entrance to shopping centres, left in public areas for people to pick up, at museums and exhibitions, at department stores and shops, or even delivered to your home inside newspapers and magazines. Information sheets are also given out by teachers in the form of student handouts.

WOW! WHAT A GREAT OFFER !...

15.4 Leaflet

Most infections get better without antibiotics

In cases where patients will get better without antibiotics,
it makes sense for your doctor not to prescribe them.
Your body's defence system can often protect against
infection without the need for antibiotics.

Listen to your doctor
Your doctor will be able to recognise whether you have an infection that needs antibiotics, so you should not always expect to be given a prescription. Doctors need to prescribe antibiotics with care: This is because inappropriate use of antibiotics can be dangerous for individual patients and for the whole population.

Overuse of antibiotics can also cause resistance and result in them not working in the future. This is a very worrying trend, especially for patients with serious life-threatening infections.

Harmful side-effects
Potential side-effects are another reason why doctors are cautious about prescribing antibiotics. Some antibiotic treatment can cause side-effects such as stomach upset and thrush. For women on the pill, antibiotics can reduce contraceptive protection.

Antibiotic facts
- Antibiotics have no effect on viral infections (*eg. colds, flu and most sore throats*). Viral infections are much more common than bacterial infections.
- Inappropriate use of antibiotics can encourage the development of resistant bacteria. This could mean that the antibiotic may not work when you really need it.
- Some antibiotics have harmful side-effects such as diarrhoea and allergic reactions.
- Antibiotics do not just attack the infection they are prescribed for – they can also kill useful bacteria which normally protect you against other infections such as thrush.

- There are effective alternative remedies for managing the symptoms of many infections.

> **If you are prescribed antibiotics ensure you take the medication according to instructions.**
> - Although you may begin to feel better, you must take the full course of antibiotics to prevent your illness coming back.
> - Not taking the full course of antibiotics can lead to future antibiotic resistance.

If you have an infection such as a cold, flu or sore throat
- Take paracetamol according to the instructions to help reduce fever and relieve aches and pains.
- Drink plenty of water to avoid dehydration.
- Ask your pharmacist (*chemist*) for advice. Many infections can be managed effectively with over-the-counter medications. The pharmacist will refer you to your doctor or practice nurse if they think it is necessary.

When to contact your GP
Call your GP's surgery for advice if, after taking over-the-counter medications as directed, you or your child are experiencing any of the following:
- symptoms which are severe or unusually prolonged.
- extreme shortness of breath.
- coughing up of blood or large amounts of yellow or green phlegm.

DEVELOPING PATIENT PARTNERSHIP

*Promoting a healthy partnership between
patients and health professionals*

BMA House   Tavistock Square   London   WC1H 9JP
Fax: 0171 383 6403   Internet:www.doctorpatient.org.uk

Reproduced courtesy of Developing Patient Partnership

15.5 Handout

Use a clear heading ——

PASSIVE vs ACTIVE VOICE

Which is more effective?

#1 Your order was received by us today. The goods you requested have been despatched by courier. You should receive them within 48 hours. Should they not have been received by you tomorrow our despatch department should be contacted as soon as possible.

Why?

#2 Thank you for your order number HT121 dated 21 June. Our special courier service will deliver these goods within 48 hours. If you have not received them by Friday morning please contact me on 254 8777.

Why NOT passive voice?

Leave some blanks so that you can elicit details from students

☺ It makes your writing vague
☺ It denies responsibility
☺ It creates a distance between you and your reader

Why USE active voice?

☺
☺
☺

✍ YOUR TURN

Rewrite these sentences using ACTIVE voice.

Allow some practice ——

1 The seminar will be conducted by Robert Sim.

2 The leak was fixed by the plumber.

3 Your thoughtful suggestions are accepted graciously.

4 Arrangements have been made for the conference to be held at the Hilton Hotel.

5 The investigation has been concluded by our client, and the paperwork has been signed.

6 The design of our new systems was simplified by the use of hydraulics.

Use sub-headings ——

Is passive voice ever appropriate?

✓ **In minutes of meetings**   Mrs Jones reported that the photocopier had broken down for the third time in a month.

✓ **When tact is important**   A serious mistake was made.

To learn more about using active and passive voice, check out:

www.shirleytaylor.com/learninglinks.html

Information sheets may give details about:

- goods or services
- special promotions
- special events or functions
- guidelines and information.

DESIGN SKILLS

The design skills for all these documents are very similar. These AIDA principles are very useful guidelines:

A   Attention   You must attract the reader's attention:
– use company logo?
– compose specific heading
– put special information in boxes/shaded section
– use sub-headings/numbered points/bullets.

I   Interest   Get the reader's interest by mentioning something that will appeal to them:
– be persuasive
– use simple language, short sentences.

D   Desire   Arouse the reader's desire to buy, to attend, to find out more or to contact the writer:
– make everything sound interesting
– point out the benefits.

A   Action   Make the audience want to do something after reading the notice or advertisement.

TIP   **The Chinese would say that good design and good presentation is good feng shui!**

CHECKLIST

- ☐ Include a company logo, prominently displayed, if appropriate.
- ☐ Compose a catchy headline to give the gist of the contents.
- ☐ Use spacing carefully to give prominence to special items.
- ☐ Use sub-headings and shaded sections to attract attention.
- ☐ Use numbered points and bullets to categorise information.
- ☐ Ensure your display is eye-catching, attractive and effective.
- ☐ Use straightforward, simple language and short sentences.
- ☐ Use persuasive and convincing writing skills to make everything sound useful, exciting, interesting or beneficial.
- ☐ Aim for your document to stand out when alongside many others.
- ☐ State the action that you want the reader to take and if necessary include name, telephone number, e-mail address, etc.

Circulars

1
2
3
4
5
6
7
8
9
10
11
12
13
14
15
16
17
18
19
20
21
22
23
24
25
26
27
28
29
30

Circular letters are used to send the same information to a number of people. They are extensively used in sales campaigns (see Chapter 17) and for announcing important developments in business, such as extensions, reorganisations, changes of address, etc.

A circular letter is prepared once only and it may then be duplicated for distribution to the various recipients. Names, addresses and individual salutations may be inserted after duplication in order to personalise the letter.

Word processing with its mail-merge facilities makes it possible for each letter to be an original, with the 'variable' details (eg inside address, salutation, etc) being merged with the letter during printing.

Although circulars are being sent to many people, it is important to suggest an interest in the recipient by giving them a personal touch. Remember the following rules:

1 Be brief – people will not read a long-winded circular.

2 Make the letter as personal as possible by addressing each letter to a particular person, by name if you know it. Use *Dear Mr Smith* instead of *Dear Reader*, *Dear Subscriber* or *Dear Customer* instead of *Dear Sir or Madam*. Never use the plural form for the salutation – remember, one recipient will read each individual letter.

3 Create the impression of personal interest by using *you*, never *our customers*, *all customers*, *our clients*, *everyone*.

Instead of	Say
Our customers will appreciate …	You will appreciate …
We are pleased to inform all our clients …	We are pleased to inform you …
Everyone will be interested to learn …	You will be interested to learn …
Anyone visiting our new showroom will see …	If you visit our new showroom you will see …

CIRCULARS ANNOUNCING CHANGES IN BUSINESS ORGANISATION

Changes in a firm's business arrangements may be announced by circular letters such as those which follow. Where the salutation has been left blank, it has been presumed that the letter would be word processed and individual names, addresses and salutations would be merged to add a personal touch.

16.1 Change of company name

Dear Customer

Change of Company Name/Transfer of Business

In November 2001 Merlion Communications was acquired by SingComm Pte Ltd. As a result of this acquisition and renaming the company, we are amending the registered name for direct debit processing.

This change will not affect the service you receive in any way, except that future direct debits will be collected by SingComm Pte Ltd instead of Merlion Communications with immediate effect. The only change you will notice is the different name on your bank/building society statement for this direct debit.

You need not take any action. Details of the change have been sent to your bank/building society. Your rights under the direct debit guarantee are not affected, as detailed on the attached guarantee.

Yours sincerely

In direct mail letters or e-mails, address the reader directly by using 'you' to get their attention and make it more personal.

16.2 Opening of a new store

Dear

BEST SUPERSTORE OPENS AT BEDFORD – 12 JULY 2004

Have you seen the great news in the national newspapers recently? Best International are opening a chain of furniture superstores throughout the UK. The first one will be open at Bedford on Monday 12 July 2004.

Special discounts will be given to the first 50 customers who come through our doors from 0900 on our opening day.

Open times are   0900–2000 Monday to Saturday
                               0900–1700 Sunday

A variety of kitchens, bathrooms, dining rooms and lounges will be on display. A full planning service is available so you can leave it to the experts to design just what you want. Each department in the Superstore is supervised by friendly, qualified staff.

The store will be of particular interest to the DIY enthusiast. You will find everything you may need – paints, wall coverings, tiles, carpets, and so much more. We will deliver free of change any orders over £100 – for smaller orders there will be a minimal charge. Credit facilities are available at low interest rates.

Our car park has spaces for 400 cars but if you prefer to take the bus, number 214 stops right outside the Best Superstore. Do don't miss our grand opening on Monday 12 July – **remember there's a special discount waiting for you if you are among the first 50 customers.**

See you at the superstore!

16.3 Expansion of existing business

Dear Customer

To meet the growing demand for a hardware and general store in this area we have decided to extend our business by opening a new department.

Our new department will carry an extensive range of hardware and other domestic goods at prices which compare very favourably with those charged by other suppliers.

We would like the opportunity to demonstrate our new merchandise to you so we are arranging a special window display during the week beginning 24 June. The official opening of our new department will take place on the following Monday 1 July.

We hope you will visit our new department during opening week and give us the opportunity to show you that the reputation enjoyed by our other departments for giving sound value for money will apply equally to this new department.

Yours sincerely

16.4 Opening of a new business

Dear Householder

We are pleased to announce the opening of our new retail grocery store on Monday 1 September.

Mrs Victoria Chadwick has been appointed Manager. She has 15 years' experience of the trade and we are sure that the goods supplied will be of sound[1] quality and reasonably priced.

Our new store will open at 0800 hours on Monday 1 September. As a special celebration offer a discount of 10% will be allowed on all purchases made by the first 50 customers. We hope we can look forward to your being one of them.

Yours sincerely

---

[1] **sound** reliable

16.5 Establishment of a new branch

Dear

Owing to the large increase in the volume of our trade with the Kingdom of Jordan, we have decided to open a branch in Amman. Mr Faisal Shamlan has been appointed as Manager.

Although we hope we have provided you with an efficient service in the past, this new branch in your country will result in your orders and enquiries being dealt with more promptly.

This new branch will open on 1 May and from that date all orders and enquiries should be sent to

Mr Faisal Shamlan
Manager
Tyler & Co Ltd
18 Hussein Avenue
Amman
Tel: (00962)6–212421
Fax: (00962)6–212422

We take this opportunity to express our thanks for your custom in the past. We hope these new arrangements will lead to even higher standards in the service we provide.

Yours sincerely

16.6 Removal to new premises

Dear

The steady growth of our business has made necessary an early move to new and larger premises. We have been fortunate in acquiring[2] a particularly good site on the new industrial estate at Chorley, and from 1 July our new address will be as follows:

Unit 15
Chorley Industrial Estate
Grange Road
Chorley
Lincs CH2 4TH
Telephone 456453 Fax 456324

This new site is served by excellent transport facilities, both road and rail, enabling deliveries to be made promptly. It also provides scope[3] for better methods of production which will increase output and also improve the quality of our goods even further.

We have very much appreciated your custom in the past and confidently expect to be able to offer you improvements in service when the new factory moves into full production.

Yours sincerely

[2] **acquiring** obtaining
[3] **scope** opportunity

16.7 Reorganisation of a store's departments

Dear

In order to provide you with even better service, we have recently extended and relocated[4] a number of departments in our store.

- On the ground floor we have a wide selection of greetings cards, including both boxed and single Christmas cards.

- In the Children's and Babywear Department on the first floor there is a new 'Ladybird' section.

- Our Fashion Fabrics and Soft Furnishings Departments are together on the second floor. Light Fittings and Electrical Goods are relocated on the third floor.

- The basement displays a good collection of wallpapers, most of which we are able to supply within 24 hours.

We thank you for your past custom and hope we may continue to be of service to you.

Yours sincerely

16.8 Death of a colleague

Dear

It is with much sadness that I have to tell you of the sudden death of our Marketing Director, Michael Spencer. Michael had been with this company for 10 years and he made an enormous contribution to the development of the business. He will be greatly missed by all his colleagues.

I am anxious to ensure continuing service to you. Please contact me directly with any matters which Michael would normally deal with.

Yours sincerely

CIRCULARS ANNOUNCING CHANGES IN BUSINESS PARTNERSHIPS

When a change takes place in the membership of a partnership, suppliers and customers should be informed by letter. For retiring partners this is particularly important since they remain liable not only for debts contracted by the firm during membership but also for debts contracted with old creditors in retirement.

[4] **relocated** moved to a different place

The correct signature on such letters is that of the name of the firm without the addition of any partner's name.

16.9 Retirement of a partner

Dear

We regret to inform you that our senior partner, Mr Harold West, has decided to retire on 31 May due to recent extended ill-health.

The withdrawal of Mr West's capital will be made good by contributions from the remaining partners, and the value of the firm's capital will therefore remain unchanged. We will continue to trade under the name of West, Webb & Co, and there will be no change in policy.

We hope that the confidence you have shown in our company in the past will continue and that we may rely on your custom in the future.

Yours sincerely

16.10 Appointment of a new partner

Dear

A large increase in the volume of our business has made necessary an increase in the membership of this company. It is with pleasure that we announce the appointment of Mrs Briony Kisby as partner.

Mrs Kisby has been our Head Buyer for the past 10 years and is well acquainted with every aspect of our policy. Her expertise and experience will continue to be of great value to the company.

There will be no change to our firm's name of Taylor, Hyde & Co.

We look forward to continuing our mutually beneficial business relationship with you.

Yours sincerely

16.11 Conversion of partnership to private company

Dear

The need for additional capital to finance the considerable growth in the volume of our trade has made it necessary to reorganise our business as a private company. The new company has been registered with limited liability in the name Barlow & Hoole Limited.

We wish to stress that this change is in name only and that the nature of our business will remain exactly as before. There will be no change in business policy.

The personal relationship which has been built up with all customers in the past will be maintained; we shall continue to do our utmost to ensure that you are completely satisfied with the way in which we handle your future orders.

Yours sincerely

LETTERS ANNOUNCING CHANGE OF REPRESENTATIVES

16.12 Dismissal of firm's representative

Dear

We wish to inform you that Miss Rona Smart who has been our representative in North-West England for the past 7 years has left our service. Therefore she no longer has authority to take orders or to collect accounts on our behalf.

In her place we have appointed Mrs Tracie Coole. Mrs Coole has for many years had control of our sales section and is thoroughly familiar with the needs of customers in your area. She intends to call on you some time this month to introduce herself and to bring samples of our new spring fabrics.

We look forward to continuing our business relationship with you.

Yours sincerely

NB If the representative left of her own free will and was a valued member of staff, the first paragraph of the above letter would be more suitably expressed as follows:

It is with regret that we inform you that Miss Rona Smart, who has been our representative for the past 7 years, has decided to leave us to take up another appointment.

16.13 Appointment of new representative

Dear

Mr Samuel Goodier, who has been calling on you regularly for the past 6 years, has now joined our firm as junior partner. His many friends will doubtless be sorry that they will see him much less frequently and we can assure you that he shares their regret.

Mr Goodier hopes to keep in touch with you and other customers by occasional visits to his former territory.

Mr Lionel Tufnell has been appointed to represent us in the South West and Mr Goodier will introduce him to you when he makes his last regular call on you next week. Mr Tufnell has worked closely with Mr Goodier in the past and he will continue to do so in the future. Mr Goodier will continue to offer help and advice in matters affecting you and other customers in the South West, and his intimate knowledge of your requirements will be of great benefit to Mr Tufnell in his new responsibilities.

Our business relations with you have always been very good, and we believe we have succeeded in serving you well. It is therefore with confidence that we ask you to extend to our new representative the courtesy and friendliness you have always shown to Mr Goodier.

Yours sincerely

INTERNAL CIRCULARS TO STAFF

Many circulars are written to staff regarding various matters concerning the general running of the business, safety and security, administrative matters and many other things. A memo is sometimes used for more day-to-day matters, but in some cases a formal letter may be printed on the company' s letterheaded paper.

16.14 Announcement about new working hours

NEW WORKING HOURS

With effect from 1 September 200— working hours will be amended to 0930 to 1730 Monday to Friday instead of the present working hours of 0900 to 1700.

I hope you will find these new hours convenient. If you anticipate experiencing any difficulties please let me know before 14 August.

16.15 Notice about new car park

NEW CAR PARK

You may be aware that some old buildings on our site have been demolished. A piece of land in this area has been cleared so that it may be used as a car park.

The new car park should be ready for use by 28 October. It will be available between 0730 and 1830 hours Monday to Friday. The company takes no responsibility for loss or damage to vehicles or contents while in the car park.

If you wish to use the car park please obtain an agreement form from Mr John Smithson, Security Officer. This form must be completed and returned to him before using the car park.

Copy   John Smithson, Security Officer

16.16 Information about store discount

DISCOUNT AT QUANTUM STORES

An agreement has been reached which will allow all our employees to take advantage of the special discount scheme operated by Quantum Stores.

As an employee of Omega International you will receive 10% discount on any goods which are not already reduced in price. A discount of 2½% will be given on reduced price or sale goods. If you wish to claim the discount you must show your Omega identification badge.

These discounts will take effect from 1 September 200—.

16.17 Security information to Heads of Department

SECURITY

Reason for writing — In view of recent bomb threats received by several competitors, please brief your staff on the following points of security.

1 All employees must wear a name badge at all times.
Number points for ease of reference — 2 All areas must be kept as clean and tidy as possible. This will reduce potential areas where bombs may be hidden.
3 Do not tamper with or move any suspicious object. The Manager should be informed and the police notified.
4 Evacuation should follow established fire drills.

Follow-up action — All incidents must be taken seriously and a detailed report must be submitted to me.

Final emphasis — Please stress to all your staff that they have an important part to play in maintaining a high level of security in all areas at all times.

16.18 Letter regarding outstanding holiday entitlement

In the past it has been a policy of the company that all staff must take their holiday entitlement within one calendar year. Any holiday entitlement not taken before 31 December each year has been forfeited.

It has now been decided to amend this rule to provide staff with more flexibility regarding holidays.

With immediate effect anyone who has up to 5 days' holiday entitlement outstanding at 31 December may carry this over to 31 March the following year. Any days that have not been used by 31 March will be forfeited. Unused holiday entitlement may not be converted to pay in lieu.

The approval of staff leave is still subject to agreement with your manager/ supervisor. This will take into account the business and operational needs of the department and especially clashes with other staff.

If you have any questions about this new policy, please telephone the Human Resource Department on extension 456.

16.19 Reminder about health and safety policy

In view of the recent unfortunate accident involving a visitor to our premises, I would like to remind you about our health and safety policy.

Whenever you have a visitor to the building, you are responsible for their health and safety at all times. For his/her own safety, a visitor should not be allowed to wander freely around the building. If, for example, a visitor needs to use the washroom, you should accompany them and escort them back.

For security reasons, if you see someone you do not recognise wandering around the building unaccompanied, do not be afraid to ask questions. Ask politely why he or she is here, which member of staff they are visiting, and if that person knows the visitor has arrived.

All SingComm employees have a responsibility to take reasonable care of themselves and others and to ensure a healthy and safe workplace. If you notice any hazard or potential hazard, please bring it to the attention of the Health and Safety Manager, Michael Wilson, who will investigate the issue.

A copy of the company's health and safety policy is attached. Please take a few minutes to read it through to remind yourself of the main points.

Thank you for your help in ensuring the health and safety of all employees and visitors to SingComm.

CIRCULARS WITH REPLY FORMS

A tear-off slip is often used when a reply is required from people to whom a circular is sent. Alternatively a separate reply form may be used. The important points to remember with such reply sections are:

- always begin with 'Please return by ... to ...' . This is a safeguard in case someone separates the tear-off portion or reply form from the main letter
- use double spacing for the portion which will be completed
- leave sufficient space for completion after each question/heading
- use continuous dots where answers are required.

16.20 Invitation to function (with tear-off slip)

10TH ANNIVERSARY CELEBRATION

Omega International is celebrating its 10th year of providing quality communications equipment. Approximately 50 representatives from Omega clients are expected to attend a special 10th Anniversary Celebration on Friday 29 October 200—.

The directors have decided to invite all employees who have been with Omega for at least 5 years to attend this special function. I am pleased to extend to you an invitation to join us at Omega's 10th Anniversary Celebration. Cocktails and a buffet supper will be provided.

This special function will take place from 1800 to 2300 hours at The Mandarin Suite, Oriental Hotel, West Street, London.

Please let me know whether you will be attending by returning the tear-off portion before 31 August.

I hope you will be able to join us.

....

For use internally, just include name/title; the full address is not required

Please return to Mrs Judy Brown, Administration Manager, before 31 August.

I shall/shall not* be attending the 10th Anniversary Celebration on Friday 29 October.

Keep it simple and precise

Name ....

Use double spacing

Designation/Department ....

Signature .... Date ....

Remember footnote where appropriate

* Please delete as applicable.

16.21 Reply form

(reproduced with permission from *Communication for Business* by Shirley Taylor)

Here is a reply form to accompany a letter sent to clients of a training organisation. Clients were asked to specify whether or not they would like to attend a one-day management conference, when accommodation would be required, and enclose a cheque to cover the cost.

REPLY FORM

Give full address when used externally; don't forget reply date

Please complete and return by 15 February 200— to

Mr Edward Teoh
Personnel Manager
Professional Training Pte Ltd
126 Buona Vista Boulevard
KUALA LUMPUR
Malaysia

Use same heading as on covering document

ONE-DAY MANAGEMENT CONFERENCE
SATURDAY 3 APRIL 200—

Use numbered points if appropriate

1   I wish/do not wish* to attend this conference.

Use the personal term 'I wish…, require…', etc

2   I require accommodation on

Use option/boxes where appropriate

☐ Friday 2 April

☐ Saturday 3 April   (Please tick)

3   My cheque for M$400 is attached (made payable to Professional Training Pte Ltd)

Signature... Date..

Name (in caps) ....

Choose appropriate details at the foot

Title ....

Company ....

Address ....

Leave sufficient space

....

.... Post code...............................

Telephone .... Fax ....

Don't forget footnote

* Please delete as necessary.

CHECKLIST FOR CIRCULAR LETTERS

☐ Personalise circular letters by merging individual inside address.

☐ Address the recipient by name if you know it, otherwise use singular form 'Dear Customer', 'Dear Reader' – NOT 'Customers', 'Readers'.

☐ Insert a handwritten salutation if appropriate.

☐ Show a personal interest – use 'you' instead of 'all customers', 'everyone'.

CHECKLIST FOR TEAR-OFF SLIP/REPLY FORM

☐ State reply date.

☐ Mention to whom the form should be returned:

Internal forms – name/title only.

External forms – name/title/company name and address.

☐ Use same heading as covering document.

☐ Use double spacing.

☐ Use personal terms – I wish, I shall/shall not.

☐ Use options/boxes where appropriate.

☐ Leave sufficient space for completion.

☐ Ensure the form contains everything you need to know.

Sales letters and voluntary offers

SALES LETTERS

A sales letter is the most selective of all forms of advertising. Unlike press and poster advertising, a sales letter aims to sell particular kinds of goods or services to selected types of customers. The purpose of a sales letter is to persuade readers that they need what you are trying to sell, and persuade them to buy it.

You take something attractive and make it seem necessary, or you take something necessary and make it seem attractive.

 Remember when writing sales letters that although they will be circulated to many people, they must be written with a personal touch. Use 'you' rather than 'all of you'.

THE WEAKEST LINK IN YOUR SALES LETTERS

Here is my compilation of some of the weakest links that need attention in your sales letters.

1 Weak headline

The headline is probably the most important part of your sales letter. It is your first opportunity to capture your reader's attention and make him/her interested in what you have to offer. Powerful headlines in your sales letters can increase your profits substantially.

2 Weak copy

If your customers fall asleep while reading your sales letters, something is wrong. Your letters should hold the reader's attention from start to finish. They should be worded in a way that sounds interesting and exciting, with a sharp and snappy writing style.

3 Weak range of purchasing options

An easy way to attract sales is by offering customers more ways to pay. Most customers will want to use credit cards for convenience. However you also want to attract customers who prefer other payment methods, such as cheque, debit card, online purchasing, etc.

4 Weak selling proposition

What makes your product or service different from your competitors'? Lower prices, higher quality, faster delivery, a wider selection of products? Customers want to see a logical, realistic reason for doing business with you. You need to hone in on a unique selling proposition – something you can deliver that your competition cannot. Be sure to mention this in all your advertisements and sales letters.

5 Weak or no endorsements

Endorsements can really boost your sales. A good endorsement is equal to a positive word-of-mouth referral. Potential customers trust what satisfied customers say about your products or services. When you receive favourable comments from customers, always ask them for permission to quote them and use their comments as endorsements in your sales letters.

6 Weak guarantee

Short guarantees are not popular with customers because they don't offer much time to find out whether your product or service works for them. Longer guarantees generally boost sales and reduce the number of returns.

7 Weak follow-up plan

The majority of visitors to your website will probably not buy anything from you the first time around. You must design an effective follow-up plan so that you maximise on potential sales. One suggestion here is to offer a free sample of something in exchange for contact information.

SUCCESSFUL SALES LETTERS

A good sales letter must be structured to follow a general 4 point plan as follows:

- arouse interest
- create desire
- carry conviction
- induce action.

Each of these elements will now be considered in detail.

Arouse interest

Your opening paragraph must arouse interest and encourage the reader to take notice of what you have to say. If care is not taken in this opening paragraph your letter could end up in the waste-paper bin without being read. Your letter may begin with a question, an instruction or a quotation. Here are some examples:

(a) An appeal to self-esteem

Are you nervous when asked to propose a vote of thanks, to take the Chair at a meeting, or to make a speech? If so this letter has been written specially for you!

(b) An appeal to economy

Would you like to cut your domestic fuel costs by 20 per cent? If your answer is 'yes', read on …

(c) An appeal to health

'The common cold,' says Dr James Carter, 'probably causes more lost time at work in a year than all other illnesses put together.'

(d) An appeal to fear

More than 50 per cent of people have eye trouble and in the past year no fewer than 16,000 people in Britain have lost their sight. Are your eyes in danger?

Create desire

Having aroused interest in the opening paragraph, you must now create a desire for the product or service you are selling. To do this it must point out the benefits to the readers and how it will affect them.

If the letter is sent to a person who knows nothing about the product, you must describe it and give a clear picture of what it is and what it can do. Study the product and then select those features which make it superior to others of its kind. Stress the features from the reader's point of view.

To claim that a particular hi-fi system is 'the best on the market' or 'the latest in electronic technology' is of little use. Instead stress such points as quality of the materials used and the special features that make the equipment more convenient or efficient than its rivals. The following description stresses such points:

In this description, note the final statement 'as finished as a Rolls-Royce' equates the product with one which is well known and recognised as a high-level product. This creates a picture of a reasonably priced yet superb product

This hi-fi system is carefully designed and incorporates the latest technological developments to give high-quality sound including full stereo recording and playback on the twin-cassette deck. Its clearly arranged controls make for very simple operation. It is supplied with two detachable loudspeakers separately mounted in solid, polished teak cabinets, as finely finished as a Rolls-Royce.

Carry conviction

You must somehow convince your reader that the product is what you claim it to be. You must support your claims by evidence – facts, opinions. You can do this in a number of ways, eg:

- invite the reader to your factory or showroom
- offer to send goods on approval
- provide a guarantee
- quote your 100 years of experience in the field.

In this extract from a letter from a cotton-shirt manufacturer, note how convincing it sounds. No manufacturer would dare to make such an offer without the firm belief in what is claimed. All the proof is supplied to give the reader complete confidence and to persuade them to buy

> Remember, we have manufactured cotton shirts for 50 years and are quite confident that you will be more than satisfied with their quality.
>
> This offer is made on the clear understanding that if the goods are not completely to your satisfaction you can return them to us without any obligation whatever and at our own expense. The full amount you paid will be refunded immediately.

As a caution, however, remember that it is against the law to make false or exaggerated claims. Remember also that the good name and standing of your business – as well as its success – depends upon honest dealing.

Induce action

Your closing paragraph must persuade the reader to take the action that you want – to visit your showrooms, to receive your representative, to send for a sample or to place an order.

The final paragraph must also provide readers with a sound reason why they should reply

> If you will return the enclosed request card we will show you how you can have all the advantages of cold storage and at the same time save money.

Sometimes the closing paragraph will give special reasons why the reader should act immediately

> The special discount now offered can be allowed only on orders placed by 30 June. So hurry and take advantage of this limited offer while there is still time.

You must make it easy for the reader to do these things, such as providing a tear-off slip to complete and return or enclosing a prepaid card.

When composing sales letters remember: your readers will not be anywhere near as interested in the product, service or idea you have to sell as they are in how it will benefit them. You must persuade your readers of the benefits of what you are selling and tell them what it can do for them.

 TIP **Avoid 'hype' (hyperbole), eg totally fantastic, truly awesome, extraordinary, incredible, astounding.**

SPECIMEN SALES LETTERS

Here are some examples of effective sales letters which follow the 4 point plan of *interest*, *desire*, *conviction* and *action*.

17.1 Sales appeal to economy

Dear Mr Reading

Interest — Have you ever thought how much time your typist wastes in taking down your dictation? It can be as much as a third of the time spent on correspondence. Why not record your dictation – on our Stenogram – and she can be doing other jobs while you dictate?

Desire — You will be surprised at how little it costs. For 52 weeks in the year your Stenogram works hard for you, and you can never give it too much to do – all for less than an average month's salary for a secretary! It will take dictation anywhere at any time – during lunch-hour, in the evening, at home – you can even dictate while you are travelling or away on business. Simply post the recorded messages back to your secretary for typing.

Conviction — The Stenogram is efficient, reliable, time-saving and economical. Backed by our international reputation for reliability, it is in regular use in thousands of offices all over the country. It gives superb reproduction quality with every syllable as clear as a bell. It is unbelievably simple to use – just slip in a preloaded cassette, press a button, and it is ready to record your dictation, interviews, telephone conversations, reports, instructions or whatever. Nothing could be simpler! And with our unique after-sales service contract you are assured lasting operation at the peak of efficiency.

Action — Some of your business friends are sure to be using our Stenogram. Ask them about it before you place an order and we are sure they will back up our claims. If you prefer, return the enclosed prepaid card and we will arrange for our representative to call and arrange a demonstration for you. Just state the day and time that will be most convenient for you.

Yours sincerely

17.2 Sales appeal to efficiency

Dear Mr Wood

Interest — Reports from all over the world confirm what we have always known – that the RELIANCE solid tyre is the fulfilment of every car owner's dream.

Desire — You will naturally be well aware of the weaknesses of the ordinary air-filled tyre – punctures, outer covers which split under sudden stress, and a tendency to skid on wet road surfaces, to mention only a few of motorists' main complaints. Our RELIANCE tyre enables you to offer your customers a tyre which is beyond criticism in those vital[1] qualities of road-holding and reliability.

Conviction — We could tell you a lot more about RELIANCE tyres but would prefer you to read the enclosed copies of reports from racing car drivers, test drivers, motor dealers and manufacturers. These reports really speak for themselves.

Action — To encourage you to hold a stock of the new solid RELIANCE, we are pleased to offer you a special discount of 3% on any order received by 31 July.

Yours sincerely

17.3 Sales appeal to security

Dear Mr Goodwin

Interest — A client of mine is happier today than he has been for a long time – and with good reason. For the first time since he married 10 years ago he says he feels really comfortable about the future. Should he die within the next 20 years, his wife and family will now be provided for. For less than £2 a week paid now, his wife would receive £50 per month for a full 20 years, and then a lump sum of £10,000.

Desire — Such protection would have been beyond his reach a short time ago, but a new and novel scheme has enabled him to ensure this security for his family. The scheme does not have to be for 20 years. It can be for 15 or 10 or any other number of years. And it need not be for £10,000. It could be for much more or much less so that you arrange the protection you want.

Conviction — For just a few pounds each month you can buy peace of mind for your wife, your children and for yourself. You cannot – you dare not – leave them unprotected.

Action — I would appreciate an opportunity to call on you to tell you more about this scheme which so many families are finding so attractive. I shall not press you to join; I shall just give you all the details and leave the rest to you. Please return the enclosed prepaid reply card and I will call at any time convenient to you.

Yours sincerely

[1] **vital** essential

17.4 • Sales appeal to comfort

Dear Mrs Walker

Interest — What would you say to a gift that gave you a warmer and more comfortable home, free from draughts, and a saving of over 20% in fuel costs?

Desire — You can enjoy these advantages, not just this year but every year, simply by installing our SEALTITE panel system of <u>double glazing</u>.[2] Can you think of a better gift for your entire family? The enclosed brochure will outline some of the benefits which make SEALTITE the most completely satisfactory double-glazing system on the market thanks to a number of features not provided in any other system.

Conviction — Remember that the panels are <u>precision-made</u>[3] by experienced craftsmen to fit your own particular windows. Remember too that you will be dealing with a well-established company which owes its success to the satisfaction given to scores of thousands of customers.

Action — There is no need for you to make up your mind right now. First why not let us give you a free demonstration in your own home without any obligation whatsoever? If you are looking for an investment with an annual average return of over 20%, then here is your opportunity. If you post the enclosed card to reach us by the end of August, we can complete the installation for you in good time before winter sets in.

Secure your home with SEALTITE!

Yours sincerely

17.5 • Sales appeal to leisure

Dear Mrs Hudson

Interest — 'Modern scientific invention is a curse to the human race and will one day destroy it,' said one of my customers recently. Rather a <u>rash statement</u>,[4] and quite untrue for there are modern inventions which, far from being a curse, are real blessings.

Desire — Our new AQUAMASTER washer is just one of them. It takes all the hard work out of the weekly wash and makes washing a pleasure. All you have to do is put your soiled clothes in, press a button and sit back while the machine does the work. It does everything – washing, rinsing and drying – and we feel it does it quicker and better than any washing machine on the market today.

Conviction — Come along and see the AQUAMASTER at work in our showroom. A demonstration will take up only a few minutes of your time, but it may rid you of your dread of washing day and make life much more pleasant.

Action — I hope you will accept this invitation and come along soon to see what this latest of domestic time-savers can do for you.

Yours sincerely

---

[2] **double glazing** double-glass window panels
[3] **precision-made** manufactured to a high degree of accuracy
[4] **rash statement** a statement made recklessly, without thought

17.6 Sales appeal to sympathy

This letter was sent together with a leaflet containing a form for readers to return with a donation.

Dear Reader

You can walk about the house, at work, in the streets, in the country. You take this ability for granted, yet it is denied to thousands of others – those who are born crippled, or crippled in childhood by accident or illness.

It is estimated that every 5 minutes in Britain a deformed child is born or a child is crippled by accident or illness. This means that every day there could be 288 more crippled children.

Does this not strike you as unfair? Most of what is unfair in life is something we can do little about but here is one very important inequality which everyone can help with. The enclosed leaflet explains how you can help. Please read it carefully while remembering again just how lucky you are.

Yours faithfully

17.7 Sales appeal to comfort

Dear Home-owner

At half the actual cost you can now have SOLAR HEATING installed in your home.

As part of our research and development scheme introduced two years ago we are about to make our selection of a number of properties throughout the country as 'Research Homes' – yours could be one of them.

The information received from selected 'Research Homes' in the past 2 years has proved that SOLAR HEATING is successful even in the most northern parts of the United Kingdom. This information has also enabled us to modify[5] and improve our designs, which we will continue to do.

If your home is selected as one of the properties to be included in our research scheme, we will bear half the actual cost of installation.

If you are interested in helping our research programme in return for a half-price solar heating system, please complete the enclosed form and return it by the end of May. Within three weeks we will inform you if your home has been selected for the scheme.

Yours sincerely

---

[5] **modify** alter, rearrange

17.8 Sales appeal to heat

Dear Madam

Thousands of people who normally suffer from the miseries of cold, damp, changeable weather wear THERMOTEX. Why? The answer is simple – tests conducted at the leading Textile Industries Department at Leeds University have shown that of all the traditional underwear fabrics THERMOTEX has the highest warmth insulating properties.

THERMOTEX has been relieving aches and pains for many years, particularly those caused by rheumatism. It not only brings extra warmth but also soothes those aches caused by icy winds cutting into your bones and chilling you to the marrow. THERMOTEX absorbs much less moisture than conventional underwear fabrics, so perspiration passes straight through the material. It leaves your skin dry but very, very warm.

Don't just take our word for it – take a good look at some of the testimonials shown in the enclosed catalogue. The demand for THERMOTEX garments has grown so much in recent years that we often have to deal with over 20,000 garments in a single day.

The enclosed catalogue is packed with lots of ways in which THERMOTEX can keep you warm and healthy this winter. Just browse through it, choose the garment you would like, and send us your completed order form – our FREEPOST address means there is even no need for a postage stamp!

Warmth and health will soon be on their way to you. If you are not completely satisfied with your purchase, return it to us within 14 days and we will refund your money without question and with the least possible delay.

Let THERMOTEX keep you warm this winter!

Yours faithfully

VOLUNTARY OFFERS

An offer which is not asked for and which is sent to an individual or a small number of individuals is a form of sales letter. It serves the same purpose and follows the same general principles.

Such offers take a variety of forms. They may be:

- offers of free samples
- goods on approval
- special discounts on orders received within a stated period
- offers to send brochures, catalogues, price lists, patterns, etc, upon return of a form or card which is usually prepaid.

17.9 Offer to a newly established trader

Dear Sir

We would like to send our best wishes for the success of your new shop specialising in the sale of toys. Naturally you will wish to offer your customers the latest toys – toys that are attractive, hard wearing and reasonably priced. Your stock will not be complete without the mechanical toys for which we have a national reputation.

We are sole importers of VALIFACT toys and as you will see from the enclosed price list our terms are very generous. In addition to the trade discount stated, we would allow you a special first-order discount of 5%.

We hope that these terms will encourage you to place an order with us and feel sure you would be well satisfied with your first transaction.

We will be happy to arrange for one of our representatives to call on you to ensure that you are fully briefed on the wide assortment of toys we can offer. Please complete and return the enclosed card to say when it would be convenient.

Yours faithfully

17.10 Offer to a regular customer

Dear Mr Welling

We have just bought a large quantity of high quality rugs and carpets from the bankrupt stock of one of our competitors.

As you are one of our most regular and long-standing customers, we would like you to share in the excellent opportunities which our purchase provides. We can offer you mohair rugs in a variety of colours at prices ranging from £55 to £1500; also premier quality Wilton and Axminster carpeting in a wide range of patterns at 20% below current wholesale prices.

This is an exceptional opportunity for you to buy a stock of high-quality products at prices we cannot repeat. We hope you will take full advantage of it.

If you are interested please call at our warehouse to see the stock for yourself not later than next Friday 14 October. Or alternatively call our Sales Department on 0114-453 2567 to place an immediate order.

Yours sincerely

17.11 Offer to new home owners

Dear Newcomers

Welcome to your new home! We have no wish to disturb you as you settle in but we would like to tell you why people in this town and the surrounding areas are very familiar with the name BAXENDALE.

Our store is situated at the corner of Grafton Street and Dorset Road and we invite you to visit us to see for yourself the exciting range of goods which have made us a household name.

Our well-known shopping guide is enclosed for you to browse through at your leisure. You will see practically everything you need to add to the comfort and beauty of your home.

As a special attraction to newcomers into the area we are offering a free gift worth £2 for every £20 spent in our store. The enclosed card is valid for one calendar month and it will entitle you to select goods of your own choice as your free gift.

We sincerely hope that you enjoy living in your new home.

Yours faithfully

17.12 Offer of a demonstration

Dear Mrs Thornton

The Ideal Home Exhibition opens at Earls Court on Monday 21 June and you are certain to find attractive new designs in furniture as well as many new ideas.

The exhibition has much to offer which you will find useful, but we would like to extend our special invitation to our own display on Stand 26 where we shall be revealing our new WINDSOR range of unit furniture.[6]

WINDSOR represents an entirely new concept in luxury unit furniture at very modest prices and we hope you will not miss the opportunity to see it for yourself. The inbuilt charm of this range comes from the use of solid elm and beech, combined with expert craftsmanship to give a perfect finish to each piece of furniture.

I enclose two admission tickets to the Ideal Home Exhibition. I am sure you will not want to miss this opportunity to see the variety of ways in which WINDSOR unit furniture can be arranged to suit any requirements.

I look forward to seeing you there.

Yours sincerely

---

[6] **unit furniture** furniture made in standard sections

The reader of this letter would not be at all inspired or motivated to find out more about Global Mobile. The letter meets none of the AIDA principles.

This introduction is flat and boring, and it does not attract Attention.

It is written in a very uninteresting style, so it does not create Interest.

It does not arouse any kind of Desire in the reader.

This close does not make the audience want to take Action and buy.

> Dear Customers
>
> Staying in touch is easy with Global Mobile.
>
> We would like to tell you all about new Connect Cards. With the Connect Card you can enjoy the benefit of our network without worrying about monthly bills. This month's issue of *In Touch* magazine explains how it works. In *In Touch* you can also read about our improved international roaming services. Roam-a-round allows you to roam anywhere – take Global Mobile with you all over the world.
>
> *In Touch* also explains how you can make savings when you call another GM customer, also details of our website and you can see and read about our performance at a recent Communications Exhibition. I'm sure you'll be very impressed.
>
> Inside *In Touch* we have also included a contest for you to win things like a free subscription to our services, a free Connect Card and also some restaurant privileges.
>
> Enjoy the magazine and we look forward to your custom continuing in the future.
>
> Yours faithfully
>
>
> Maxine Pearson
> Customer Services

Now look at the revised letter on the next page.

C* Aurora Mobile

it's important
to stay ... in touch

Dear Valued Customer

With the introduction of our new **Connect Card**, Aurora Mobile has brought a new era of convenience in mobile communications. With the **Connect Card** you can enjoy all the benefits of Aurora Mobile's leading-edge network without worrying about monthly bills. Find out how in this month's issue of **In Touch**.

In Touch also introduces you to our vastly expanded international roaming services – Roam-a-round – which allows you to roam to all corners of the globe. Inside **In Touch** you will find out why no one covers the world better than Aurora Mobile.

Many more features can be found inside **In Touch** ...

℃ generous savings when you call another Aurora Mobile customer
℃ what's new at our website
℃ see and read about our performance at a recent Communications Exhibition.

Inside **In Touch** we have also included an exciting contest for you to win fabulous prizes such as a free subscription to our value-added services, a free **Connect Card** worth £20 and restaurant privileges in leading restaurants.

With your continued support we have become the UK's leading network service provider. Thank you for staying with us.

Yours sincerely

Lesley Bolan (Ms)
Senior Director
Marketing, Sales and Customer Service

C Aurora Mobile, Aurora House, Temple Street, London SE1 4LL
Tel: +44(0)181 542 4444 Fax: +44(0)181 555 4444 Email: auroramobile@cfb.co.uk

CHECKLIST

- ☐ Arouse interest in first paragraph.
- ☐ Create a desire for the product or service.
- ☐ Describe the product if appropriate.
- ☐ Point out the benefits.
- ☐ Stress quality and special features.
- ☐ Convince the reader that what you claim is correct.
- ☐ Give evidence to support your claim.
- ☐ Persuade the reader to take appropriate action.

USEFUL EXPRESSIONS

Openings

1 We are enclosing a copy of our latest catalogue and price list.
2 As you have placed many orders with us in the past, we would like to extend our special offer to you.
3 We are able to offer you very favourable prices on some goods we have recently been able to purchase.
4 We are pleased to introduce our new ... and feel sure that you will find it very interesting.
5 I am sorry to note that we have not received an order from you for over ...

Closes

1 We hope you will take full advantage of this exceptional offer.
2 We feel sure you will find a ready sale for this excellent material and that your customers will be well satisfied with it.
3 We would be pleased to provide a demonstration if you would let us know when this would be convenient.
4 We feel sure you will agree that this product is not only of the highest quality but also very reasonably priced.

Publicity material

PRESS RELEASES

Very often it is necessary to write an article or feature for publication in the press or other media. In this case it is necessary to compose a press release. This is a good way of publicising many things such as:

- relocation of offices
- expansion of business
- introduction of new products/services
- changes in top personnel
- human interest stories.

For a release to be considered newsworthy it must have a broad general interest or a special angle. It must be written objectively as though someone else is writing the story for you. Most importantly, you need to bear in mind that you are giving information, not just selling something.

18.1 Press release announcing new store

© Turner Communications
Mobile Phone specialists

21 Ashton Drive
Sheffield
S26 2ES

Tel   +44 114 2871122
Fax   +44 114 2871123
Email   TurnerComm@intl.uk

ST/BT

Include reference and date — 15 June 200—

The embargo date is the date before which the information cannot be published — PUBLICATION DATE: Immediate

NEW JOBS IN TURNER SUPERSTORE

Introduction: state the main message quickly — Mobile phone specialists, Turner Communications, have today announced the opening of their new store Turner's Office Supplies. More than 50 new jobs have been created.

Use short, self-contained paragraphs – include all essential details — Turner Communications have established themselves as leaders in the field of mobile communications in the UK. Roaming agreements have been set up with many countries throughout the world.

Use double spacing for the press release — The company has now announced that it is diversifying. Their new Office Supplies superstore will sell everything from stationery and office sundries to computers and other office equipment. It will be situated in a prime location at Meadowhall Retail Park on the outskirts of Sheffield, very close to the M1 motorway.

A grand opening ceremony is planned to take place on Monday 1 July with special offers to the first 100 customers and a grand draw at 5.00 pm.

Round it off with a conclusion or quotation — Sally Turner, Managing Director, said, 'We are very excited about this new office superstore and feel confident that it will prove to be an overwhelming success.'

State contact details (for further information/ photographs) — Contact: Susan Gingeu, Marketing Manager, Turner Communications

Telephone: 0114 2871122

18.2 Press release announcing new hotel wing

FK/ST
14 September 2003
EMBARGO DATE: Immediate

NEW SERVICE CONCEPTS AT PAGODA SINGAPORE

Service, the magic word in today's hotel industry, gains a new perspective when the new Regency Suites wing of the Pagoda Hotel Singapore opens in early 2004.

The hotel's new upmarket product is targeted at the corporate traveller. In line with this, a range of personalised services in major areas can now be expected by the discerning traveller.

The Business Centre, a vital facility for businessmen on the move, will operate 24 hours 7 days a week. With this extension of operating hours, busy executives will enjoy the convenience of conducing business at any time of the day. Whether it is an urgent fax required at 1 am or an e-mail, fax or letter by send in the middle of the night, time is no longer an issue. The Business Centre is well equipped with a complete range of secretarial services including a comprehensive reference library, personal computer, access to the Internet, private offices and conference room with lounge.

Housekeeping and laundry services will also be available 24 hours daily. Guests arriving late at night will no longer worry about getting a suit pressed for the next morning. Requests for extra pillows, shampoo or stationery, or any other item, will be met regardless of the hour.

A professional concierge team will answer queries and provide the wealth of information often required, from dinner reservations to theatre shows, or even finding the best shoe-maker in town.

The hotel's airport representatives will not only greet guests upon arrival at the airport but also meet them during departure too. In addition to its 2 limousines, a fleet of 14 other cars are available at all times for a city tour or business trips.

With 148 Pagoda Hotels and resorts around the world, the Pagoda Singapore is positioning itself as a top deluxe hotel, making it the perfect choice for any traveller.

-end-

Contact: Florence Cheung, Public Relations Manager
            Telephone 3432343 Extension 145.

 A flat, dull, boring, long-winded press release will end up in the editor's waste-paper bin!

NEWSLETTERS

Staff newsletters are a good way of keeping employees informed about matters of interest, and they often improve company/staff relations. Some companies produce separate newsletters for customers.

These newsletters may contain such information as:

- promotions
- births/marriages/deaths
- retirements
- sports and social news
- contributions from employees
- updates on products/services
- developments in certain industries
- news from branches/departments.

18.3 Article in staff newsletter

Catchy headline

SUPERSTARS TEAM GAIN SECOND PLACE

Give main message quickly in the first paragraph

The stamina and strength of 3 Global employees were put to the test when they competed in the European finals of the Tech-stars competition held in Rotterdam, Holland.

Use short, self-contained paragraphs

Global Holdings was invited to the European finals after winning the regional heat at Leeds and being runners-up in the British final.

Use double spacing in case of editing

All entrants must work with information technology in some way, and Global has entered a team every year since 1985 when they won the European final. This year's competition consisted of 8 strenuous, athletic-based events in one day, in which 3 of the 5 team members had to compete.

Make it a human-interest story

Unfortunately due to holiday commitments, this year's Global team entered without 2 of their top athletes, leaving John Holmes, Martin Wilson and Andrew Johnson to compete in this event. After a long day's work the team then had to face the final event, which was a 2000 metre steeplechase, and all team members performed extremely well in this.

Finish with a snappy conclusion

The final result was that Global put in a very creditable performance and achieved second place. Well done to the team!

WRITING SKILLS

The same writing skills are needed for press releases and articles:

Headline   Compose an interesting, snappy headline that tells the whole story in a line.

Opening   Write a good opening paragraph to grab the editor's or reader's attention. Give the main gist of the message here.

Middle   Use short, self-contained paragraphs and write in the third person as if the editor is 'speaking'. Remember the 5 Ws:
What is happening?
Who is involved?
Where is it happening?
When is it happening?
Why is it newsworthy?

Closing   A quotation from a key person is very useful to close, otherwise a summary or conclusion.

18.4 Article announcing dinner and dance

ARE YOU READY FOR THE GLOBAL DINNER AND DANCE?

The year has flown and it's time once again to get ready for the Global Annual Dinner and Dance. Put these details in your diary now:

Where?   Dynasty Suite, Shangri La Hotel
When?   Saturday 17 December 200–
What time?   7.30 pm until late

As usual there will be a 10-course Chinese dinner (we can of course cater for any special requirements). Carmen Fashions will be entertaining us with a fashion show as we eat. With lucky draws, spot prizes and after-dinner entertainment and dancing, it's sure to be a great evening that you will not want to miss.

This company-sponsored dinner dance will cost you only S$50 each. Partners pay the same price too. If it's anything like previous years' functions, you can be assured of a fabulous time. Get your registration forms from Reception or the Human Resource Department – and book early.

If you have any queries please contact:

Caroline Marshall
Human Resource Department
Extension 216
E-mail: carolinemarshall@global.com.my

Always look critically at everything you write.

CHECKLIST

- [ ] Use an embargo (publication date) on a press release – a date before which the newspaper or magazine cannot publish your article.

- [ ] Compose a snappy headline, and limit this to no more than one line – it should really grab the editor's attention and provide an interesting snapshot of what the release is all about.

- [ ] Grasp the editor's attention with a good opening paragraph, including all the key details. Get to the point quickly.

- [ ] Keep central paragraphs short and self-contained, so that the editor may cut them out if necessary. Make sure the details flow in a logical sequence.

- [ ] Make sure you include all the details like who, what, when, where, why and how.

- [ ] Use an interesting, snappy, punchy style for your writing. Even a seemingly uninteresting event can be made into an effective, appealing story by clever wording.

- [ ] Write in an objective style, as if the writer has no affiliation with your company, as if the newspaper or magazine is actually 'speaking'.

- [ ] Use double line spacing for the central section.

- [ ] Close the release by saying something exciting about the main message again. A quotation from a key person is very useful in this final section.

- [ ] Remember to include a contact name, website URL and telephone number.

Marketing matters

Business success depends on customers. Since the advent of the Internet and other exciting new technologies, communications with customers have never been more important. Four or five decades ago most people were happy if their products simply worked. It really was a sellers' market, and buying was more often made on the basis of needs rather than wants. However, as organisations have expanded and become global, all this has changed. As competition has increased, customers' expectations have also increased, and as a result companies are now realising that good communication with customers is essential if business is to survive.

IDENTIFYING YOUR AUDIENCES

When planning an external communications strategy it is important first of all to identify all your audiences. Not all audiences will need the same information, so this step is important so that you can think more clearly about what it is that you wish to communicate with them. Figure 19.1 identifies some of the external audiences with whom a company may communicate.

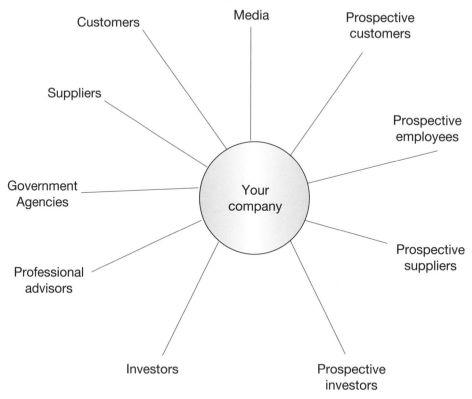

Figure 19.1 External audiences

WHY IS CUSTOMER CARE SO IMPORTANT?

More and more companies are realising that positive action is needed to make customer satisfaction their prime aim. If companies are to fight the competitive battle taking place in the marketplace it is essential to make sure that the quality of the product or service is not only satisfactory but exceptional.

Today's companies need to place great emphasis on marketing communications as well as providing quality customer care and aftercare so that they retain their customers in the long term. There are many more reasons why quality customer care is important today:

- increased competition
- product similarity
- better informed customers
- customers' willingness to pay for value
- rising expectations for improved support
- everyone wants everything yesterday!

The ultimate goal of successful customer care is to increase your company's market share by increasing your customers' satisfaction. All members of staff have a responsibility to help achieve this aim.

Yesterday's customer care was:	*Today's customer care is:*
Best price	Best quality
Satisfaction	Exceed expectations
Getting the job done	Get the job done promptly
Competence	A real bond, real caring

 If your company is to survive in business today, your aim should be to endeavour to exceed customers' expectations ... even when their expectations continue to rise.

19.1 Change of company name

Dear

CHANGE OF COMPANY NAME

We are pleased to announce that further to the 100% acquisition by FGB Insurance (Asia Pacific) Holdings Limited, Ruben Insurance Pte Ltd has been renamed FGB Insurance (Singapore) Pte Ltd. General insurance operations will start using this new name from 2 August 2004.

You will continue to enjoy the same high level of service that you have previously received from Ruben Insurance Pte Ltd. You will also see additional benefits arising from the wide-ranging expertise, products and services of the FGB Group, as well as the strong financial standing that FGB brings to our 34 million customers all over the world.

With effect from 2 August 2004 we will be relocating to this new address:

45 Robinson Road, #02-04-06 Wisma Supreme, Singapore 234381

Our new telephone number will be +65 63453456

Please visit our website at www.fgbins.com.sg for the latest information.

Your current insurance policy remains legally valid and we will honour all our obligations and liabilities under documents bearing our former corporate name.

If you have any questions at any time please call us on 63453456.

We thank you for your support and look forward to being of great service to you.

Yours sincerely

19.2 Notification about new association

Dear Client

It gives us great pleasure to announce that on 1 April we have entered into a close association with Garner Accountancy Co Ltd of 22 High Street, Cheltenham.

We have formed a new company that will practise as Garner and Barret Accounting Co Ltd, and as a result we will be moving to bigger premises at:

21 Hillington Rise
Sheffield
S24 5EJ

Telephone: 0114 2874722
Fax: 0114 2874768
Website: **www.garnerbarret.co.uk**

This association provides us with a much bigger base that will enable us to offer improved services to our customers. We will of course ensure that we retain the close personal contact and interest in our clients' affairs.

We also take this opportunity to announce that Mr Robin Wilson, who is already known to many clients, will become a partner in the new company with effect from the same date.

Yours sincerely

19.3 Appointment of new Managing Director

Dear

NEW MANAGING DIRECTOR

We are pleased to announce the appointment of Richard Wilson as Managing Director with effect from 2 September 2004. His appointment follows the early retirement in July of Francis Billington due to ill health.

Richard is already known to many of you through his position as Marketing Director. He has 12 years' experience with Yangon Electrics, and he is looking forward to taking over this more challenging role in the company.

We are happy to assure you that we shall continue to provide the high-quality service for which we are proud to enjoy such a good reputation.

If you have any urgent queries please do not hesitate to contact me personally.

Yours sincerely

19.4 Survey of customer attitudes

Dear

Mansor Communications are committed to providing quality service, and as such we like to keep in touch with customer needs and views on the products that we sell.

To maintain our high standard of quality products and services to you, I hope you will take a few moments to complete the enclosed questionnaire. In appreciation of your trouble, I shall be pleased to send you one of our superb Mansor Pens on receipt of your completed questionnaire.

I look forward to receiving your reply, and can assure you of our continued good service to you in the future.

Yours sincerely

19.5 Notification of price increase

Dear

I am sorry to inform you that, due to an unexpected price increase from our manufacturers in Europe, we have no option but to raise the prices of all our imported shoes by 4% from 6 October 2004.

Orders received before this date will be invoices at the old price levels.

We sincerely regret the need for these increased prices. However we know you will understand that this increase is beyond our control.

We look forward to a continuing association with you, and can assure you of our continued commitment to good-quality products and service.

Yours sincerely

19.6 Invitation to special function

Dear

10TH ANNIVERSARY CELEBRATION

Omega International is commemorating its 10th year of providing quality communications equipment. We are planning to hold a special celebration in August.

As one of our major clients, we are pleased to invite you to join over 100 of our management and staff to attend this celebration. Details of the function are:

Where?   Orchid Suite, Merlion Hotel, Orchard Road
When?   Friday 27 August 2004
What time?   Cocktails 6.30 pm
              Dinner 7.30 pm

There will be many highlights during this special evening, including speeches and special awards to clients and employees, plus lucky draw prizes and a cabaret act.

Please let us know whether you will be able to attend by returning the enclosed reply form before 31 July or by telephoning Suzanne Sutcliffe on 64545432.

We do hope you will join us to help make this evening a success.

Yours sincerely

CUSTOMER CARE THROUGH THE INTERNET AND E-MAIL

Internet use is increasing constantly. There has never been a more singular and spectacular opportunity for you to use the Internet to enhance your sales and service to your customers.

The phenomenal growth of the World Wide Web has brought about a totally new environment as far as customer relations are concerned. When a customer goes looking on the Web for a specific product or service, there are literally hundreds of options to choose from. Quite simply, customer will go to the companies that have websites that clearly offer the best service, the most integrated e-commerce package and exceptional after-sales service.

This book is primarily about writing and not really about how to use your website to enhance your company's business. However I thought it would be relevant here to take a brief look at what your customers expect from you in this electronic world, and how you can make the most of the Internet to maximise its potential.

Here are some general principles to follow to ensure your online sales and services are customer-friendly and web-wise:

1 Be easy to find online

Visibility is essential on the Internet, so make sure people can find you. The following are a few essentials.

- Get listings in search engines. Web marketing experts can help you here.
- Link up with other sites. Create online relationships with other sites that may have a similar audience to yours.
- Send out a press release announcing your website in the local and national press, as well as in any trade-specific publications.

2 Ensure a visual appeal

When choosing packaging for a new product you always make sure it looks attractive and appealing. Similarly you must ensure you present your company appropriately online. Give browsers a good first impression so that they keep coming back for more.

3 Ensure simple site navigation

People are generally impatient – they want to find things quickly and easily. You will help yourself as well as your customers by making sure site section names are clearly identified, and give clear descriptions of links.

4 Include lots of links

Include an e-mail link on every page so that it's easy for anyone to contact you immediately.

5 Offer something extra

You can provide a great online experience by considering offering some added extras on your website:

- links to relevant articles providing further information about your company and its products
- Frequently Asked Questions (FAQs) built up from experience and updated regularly
- contact information and comments so that customers can send you a message easily. Include details of telephone, fax and mail address too.
- freebies – ask visitors to fill in a form so that they receive something for nothing. This is a good way to collect valuable data.

 Put some zip into your presentation by getting rid of clutter.

MARKETING THROUGH THE WEB

Using advertising and direct marketing will make it easy for potential customers to find you. Some methods are:

- Give all your customers your e-mail address and offer to answer any queries by e-mail. Customers will appreciate this as it will avoid them making long, and sometimes expensive, phone calls.
- Advertise your website and e-mail addresses on company business cards, stationery, business directories and yellow pages, advertisements, posters, circular mailings and all promotional materials.
- Build an online community of potential customers. One of the first challenges of any e-mail marketer is to build up a roster of recipients who choose to receive e-mail about specific topics, such as your products and services. This is called an 'opt-in' list, and it can be created by asking potential customers for their e-mail addresses, or by including a button on your website for users to indicate their interest.
- Market, market, market! Once you have your electronic customer list up and running, use e-mail as a marketing tool. Use e-mail to send out regular information about new products, promotions, new offices, internal appointments, special announcements and newsletters. You could also consider customising the content of such mailings for each recipient by matching a user's preferences with the information you deliver.
- Send out a regular e-mail newsletter. See 19.7.

E-mail marketing is probably the most measurable, most effective direct marketing ever. There are many software programs available that will help you set up a database, create a message template and then work with you to craft an effective e-mail campaign. All you have to do is consider the content, and the software does the rest, including providing results of how many people read your message, how many people clicked on links, and much more. E-mail campaigns are known to be about 10 to 20 times more effective than standard direct mail, and results vary according to the strategy, frequency and professional level of the campaign, not to mention the origination of the database.

TIP **Successful e-marketing is not just about creating a website. It is about using the power of the Internet and the wonders of e-mail to create, build and maintain prosperous and profitable customer relationships online.**

19.7 Extract from an e-newsletter

SHIRLEY TAYLOR
Training and Consultancy

bringing out the best in you

Shirley Says

E-Newsletter Issue 2
December 2002

Greetings!

First of all, a huge **thank you** to all who wrote to me after receiving my first e-newsletter. It was fantastic to receive such a great response, and to know you enjoyed the first issue.

Special thanks to all those who wrote in with suggestions for a name for my e-newsletter. There were so many suggestions – including Wise Words from the Wise One (thanks for that!), Cool Shirley, Shirley's Tete-a-Tete and Shirl's Whirl'd (very clever, that one!) I chose **Shirley Says** because it seemed simple, brief and straight to the point – rather like our business writing should be these days.

This month I'm pleased to introduce the new Links to Learning channel on my website. Every month I will be adding new pages so that you can learn more about good business writing skills.

I hope you enjoy this month's e-newsletter, and don't forget to write to me at news@shirleytaylor.com with your comments.

Shirley

Shirley Says

It's official!
My e-newsletter now has a name. Here I am raising a toast to René Patat from ABN AMRO Bank in Sydney, Australia who suggested the name **Shirley Says.** Congratulations, René.

Business plans

Components of a business plan

Checklist

If you are setting up a new business or want people to invest serious money in your business, you need a business plan. A business plan defines your business and identifies your operations and your aims. It provides specific and organised information about your company – it's like a resumé of your company.

A business plan has two main purposes:

1 To provide you with a detailed plan to help you as you make your new venture grow.

2 To convince investors that you are the sort of person and that this is the sort of business in which they should invest.

COMPONENTS OF A BUSINESS PLAN

Before writing your business plan it will help to look at as many examples as possible. This will not be difficult because there are a wealth of sites on the Internet giving sample business plans for all types of companies. Most of them contain similar components.

1 Executive summary

This is the first section of your business plan, and it is exactly what it sounds like – a compact, concise outline of the whole plan. In this section you should state:

- the nature of the company
- the products/services you will offer
- what's special about your products/services
- who the managers are
- how much money you need and what you will use it for.

Most people only read the summary so you need to generate excitement in your executive summary, showing how unique your business and your team are.

2 Table of contents

Try to keep this to one page, listing everything your plan includes along with page numbers.

3 Company description

- How did you get started?
- How has the company grown?
- Provide a history of sales, profits and other important information.

- Where are you now?
- What plans do you have for the future?

4 Products/Services

Put yourself in the investor's shoes and ask yourself what you would want to know before investing money in your business. Questions like these:

- What products or services do you offer?
- What makes them different from others?
- How does it make people's lives better?
- What kind of equipment do you need?

5 Market analysis

This section shows all the research you have done, such as distribution problems, government regulations, technological opportunities, industry characteristics and trends, projected growth, customer behaviour, complementary products/services, etc.

6 Marketing plan

After discussing what the market is like, you have to show how you and your fellow managers intend to capture the market. List the steps you will take to ensure that customers know about your product/service and why they will prefer it over the competition. List all the tactics you will use, from the cheapest to the most expensive.

7 Operations plan

This is the nuts and bolts of your business plan. You have to give precise information about what is involved in running your business – the location, the bricks and mortar, the equipment you will need, the staff requirements, etc.

8 Financial plan

In this section you will need to include details of sales forecasts, profit-and-loss statements, cash flow projections, balance sheets, etc.

9 Management

Include details of the management of your company, who is on the board, who will manage each department and why.

10 Appendices

There will probably be lots of appendices attached to your business plan – managers' resumés, promotional materials, product photographs and descriptions, financial details, etc.

For sample business plans online, check out:

www.bplans.com

TIP **Today's business writing is simple, concise and uncluttered. That means as few commas as possible.**

CHECKLIST

- [ ] Read lots of sample business plans – just put in a search on any search engine and you will find lots of useful sites.

- [ ] Check out the bookshelves too – there are lots of books providing excellent detailed advice on how to write your business plan.

- [ ] Don't wait until the last minute to start writing. If you have ideas for your business, a solid plan will enable you to formulate all your thoughts better.

- [ ] Concentrate on strengths rather than originality. Investors usually pay more attention to the strength of the management team than to looking for a truly original idea.

- [ ] Try to be as concise as possible. Business plans are, of essence, very long documents, probably 40–60 pages.

- [ ] Keep focused. Stick to the essential facts, and cut out any padding.

- [ ] Spruce up your display. Make an effort to jazz up the formatting with headings, shaded sections, tables, charts, bullets and other graphics.

- [ ] Package it appropriately. It's not worth spending a lot of money on expensive leather-bound packaging. Investors want something that is easy to read and that lies flat on the desk.

- [ ] Edit ... edit ... edit. Get it right and you will achieve the results you want.

- [ ] Proofread the executive summary carefully. This is the most important section – make sure it is exciting, interesting and that there are no mistakes. People should read this and want to know more!

Meetings documentation

Many meetings take place in business, and an effective meeting is an efficient tool in the communication process. Meetings provide a useful opportunity for sharing information, making suggestions and proposals, taking decisions and obtaining instant feedback.

NOTICE AND AGENDA

The success of any meeting depends on essential preparatory work. Part of this work involves making sure that all the documentation is in order. The notice and agenda are usually combined in one document. The portion at the top is known as the notice – this gives details of the type, place, day, date and time of the meeting. The agenda is the list of topics to be discussed at the meeting.

It is important to send out the notice and agenda prior to a meeting so that all members have notice of what is to be discussed. They can then make the necessary preparations for each discussion point.

21.1 **Memo requesting agenda items**

M E M O R A N D U M

To   Departmental Heads

From   Steven Broom, Administration Manager

Ref   SB/ST

Date   2 July 200—

OPERATIONS MEETING – 14 JULY

The next Operations Meeting will be held in the Conference Room at 1000 hours on Monday 14 July.

Follow-up items from our last meeting which will be included under Matters Arising are:

- New brochure (Suzanne Sutcliffe)
- Annual Dinner and Dance (Mandy Lim)

If you wish to add any further items to the agenda please let me know before 8 July.

Annotations (left margin):

- Display memo headings in the usual way
- Heading states name and date of meeting
- Clarify meeting, venue, time and date of meeting
- Mention any items already included on the agenda
- Give a deadline for submission of extra items

21.2   Memo including agenda

MEMORANDUM

Display memo headings in the usual way

To   Departmental Managers

From   Steven Broom, Administration Manager

Ref   SB/ST

Date   2 July 200—

OPERATIONS MEETING

Confirm details regarding venue, date and time

The next monthly Operations Meeting will be held in the Conference Room at 1000 hours on Monday 14 July 200—.

State the word AGENDA

AGENDA

These first 3 items of 'ordinary business' should be included on every agenda

1   Apologies for absence

2   Minutes of last meeting

3   Matters arising from the Minutes

      3.1 New brochure (Suzanne Sutcliffe)

      3.2 Annual Dinner and Dance (Mandy Lim)

4   New branches (Suzanne Sutcliffe)

These are items of 'special business', specific to this meeting only

5   Far East Trip (Sally Turner)

6   European Telecommunications Conference (John Stevens)

7   5th Anniversary Celebrations (Suzanne Sutcliffe)

These final 2 items are again 'ordinary business'

8   Any other business

9   Date of next meeting

21.3 ## Notice and agenda

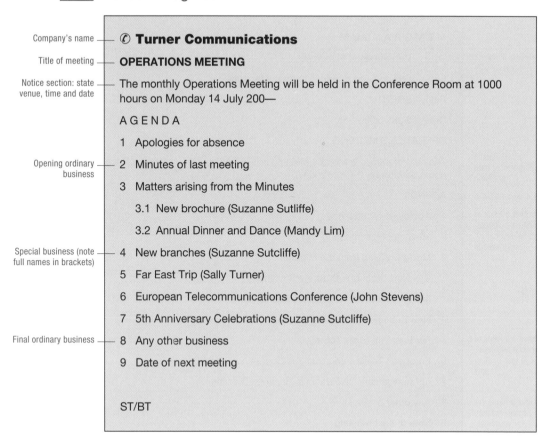

Company's name
Title of meeting
Notice section: state venue, time and date

Opening ordinary business

Special business (note full names in brackets)

Final ordinary business

© **Turner Communications**

OPERATIONS MEETING

The monthly Operations Meeting will be held in the Conference Room at 1000 hours on Monday 14 July 200—

A G E N D A

1 Apologies for absence

2 Minutes of last meeting

3 Matters arising from the Minutes

    3.1 New brochure (Suzanne Sutliffe)

    3.2 Annual Dinner and Dance (Mandy Lim)

4 New branches (Suzanne Sutcliffe)

5 Far East Trip (Sally Turner)

6 European Telecommunications Conference (John Stevens)

7 5th Anniversary Celebrations (Suzanne Sutcliffe)

8 Any other business

9 Date of next meeting

ST/BT

MINUTES OF MEETING

Minutes are a written record of what took place at a meeting. An accurate written record is essential not only for those who attend the meeting but also for those who were absent. Minutes should be written in the past tense using third person and reported speech.

TYPES OF MINUTES

Verbatim minutes

These are used primarily in court reporting, where everything needs to be recorded word for word.

21.4 Minutes of resolution

Only the main conclusions that are reached are recorded, not a note of the discussions that took place. These are usually used for minutes of AGMs and other statutory meetings. It is important to note the exact wording of any resolutions that are passed.

PURCHASE OF PHOTOCOPIER

The Company Secretary submitted a report from the Administration Manager containing full details of the trial of the AEZ photocopier.

IT WAS RESOLVED THAT the AEZ photocopier be purchased at a cost of £11,500.

21.5 Minutes of narration

These minutes are a concise summary of all the discussion that took place, reports received, decisions made and action to be taken.

PURCHASE OF PHOTOCOPIER

The Company Secretary submitted a report from the Administration Manager containing full details of the trial of the AEZ photocopier. The machine had been used for a period of 4 weeks in the Printing Room. Its many benefits were pointed out, including reduction/enlarging features and collating. After discussion it was agreed that such a machine would be extremely valuable to the company.

The Company Secretary was asked to make the necessary arrangements for the photocopier to be purchased at the quoted price of £11,500.

21.6 Minutes of meeting

AURORA HOLDINGS plc

WELFARE COMMITTEE

MINUTES OF A MEETING OF THE WELFARE COMMITTEE HELD IN THE
CHAIRMAN'S OFFICE ON TUESDAY 21 OCTOBER 200– AT 1630.

PRESENT: Eileen Taylor (Chairman)
                 Jim Cage
                 Robert Fish
                 Ellen McBain
                 Wendy Sheppard
                 Georgia Thomas
                 Will Thomas

1 APOLOGIES FOR ABSENCE

Apologies were received from Anthony Long who was attending a business
conference.

2 MINUTES OF LAST MEETING

The minutes had already been circulated and the Chairman signed them as
a correct record.

3 MATTERS ARISING

Will Thomas reported that he and Georgia had visited Reneé Simpson in
hospital on 16 October to deliver the committee's basket of flowers and
good wishes for a speedy recovery. Reneé said she hopes to return to work
on Monday 4 November and will be able to attend the next committee
meeting.

4 STAFF RESTAURANT

Jim Cage distributed copies of the accounts for the half year ending
31 July. He pointed out that a profit of £1300 was made over the first 6
months of the year. He suggested that some of this be used to buy a new
coffee machine as the present one is old and unreliable. It was agreed that
he would obtain some estimates and discuss this further at the next meeting.

5 WASHROOM FACILITIES

Mr Taylor announced that several complaints had been received about the
female toilets on the second floor. He had investigated the complaints and
agreed that the need upgrading. Several locks were reported to be faulty,
plus chipped tiles and poor decoration.

Miss McBain volunteered to arrange for some local workmen to provide an
estimate on the cost of repairs and to report back at the next meeting.

6 STUDY LEAVE FOR YOUNG TRAINEES

Mr Robert Fish reported that examinations would be held in December for
the company's trainees who presently attend evening courses at Cliff

College. He suggested that they should be allowed 2 weeks' study leave prior to their examination.

The Chairman pointed out that it was not within the committee's power to make this decision. She advised Mr Fish to write formally to the Board of Directors asking them to include this item on the agenda of the November Board Meeting. An answer should be obtained before the next meeting.

7 CHRISTMAS DINNER AND DANCE

Miss Wendy Sheppard passed around sample menus which had been obtained from hotels. After discussion it was agreed that arrangements should be made with the Marina Hotel for Saturday 21 December. Miss Sheppard agreed to make all the necessary arrangements.

8 ANY OTHER BUSINESS

There was no other business.

9 DATE OF NEXT MEETING

It was agreed that the next meeting would be held on Wednesday 20 November at 2000.

.... (Chairman)

.... (Date)

ET/ST
30 June 200—

Remember to use past tense and reported speech in minutes:

was	*not*	is
would be	*not*	will be
had been	*not*	has been
were	*not*	are

MEETINGS TERMINOLOGY

(This list is reproduced with permission of Desk Demon, the UK's No 1 spot for secretarial resources, information and community, from their website www.deskdemon.co.uk)

Ad hoc: from Latin, meaning 'for the purpose of', as for example when a sub-committee is set up specially to organise a works outing.

Adjourn: to hold a meeting over until a later date.

Adopt minutes: minutes are 'adopted' when accepted by members and signed up by the Chairman.

Advisory: providing advice or suggestion, not taking action.

Agenda: a schedule of items drawn up for discussion at a meeting.

AGM: Annual General Meeting: all members are usually eligible to attend.

Apologies: excuses given in advance for inability to attend meeting.

Articles of Association: rules required by Company law which govern a company's activities.

Attendance list: in some committees a list is passed round to be signed as a record of attendance.

Bye-laws: rules regulating an organisation's activities.

Casting vote: by convention, some committee chairmen may use a 'casting vote' to reach a decision, if votes are equally divided.

Chairman: leader or person give authority to conduct a meeting.

Chairman's agenda: based upon the committee agenda, but containing explanatory notes.

Collective responsibility: a convention by which all committee members agree to abide by a majority decision.

Committee: a group of people usually elected or appointed who meet to conduct agreed business and report to a senior body.

Consensus: agreement by general consent, no formal vote being taken.

Constitution: set of rules governing activities of voluntary bodies.

Convene: to call a meeting.

Decision: resolution minutes are sometimes called 'decision minutes'.

Eject: remove someone (by force if necessary) from a meeting.

Executive: having the power to act upon taken decisions.

Extraordinary meeting: a meeting called for all members to discuss a serious issue affecting all is called an Extraordinary General Meeting; otherwise a non-routine meeting called for a specific purpose.

Ex officio: given powers or rights by reason of office.

Guillotine: cut short a debate – usually in Parliament.

Honorary post: a duty performed without payment, eg Honorary Secretary.

Information, point of: the drawing of attention in a meeting to a relevant item of fact.

Intra vires: within the power of the committee or meeting to discuss, carry out.

Lie on the table: leave item to be considered instead at the next meeting (see Table).

Lobbying: a practice of seeking members' support before a meeting.

Minutes: the written record of a meeting; resolution minutes record only decision reached, while narrative minutes provide a record of the decision-making process.

Motion: the name given to a 'proposal' when it is being discussed at a meeting.

Mover: one who speaks on behalf of a motion.

Nem con: from Latin, literally, 'no one speaking against'.

Opposer: one who speaks against a motion.

Order, point of: the drawing of attention to a breach of rules or procedures.

Other business: either items left over from a previous meeting, or items discussed after the main business of a meeting.

Point of order: proceedings may be interrupted on a 'point of order' if procedures or rules are not being kept to in a meeting.

Proposal: the name given to a submitted item for discussion (usually written) before a meeting takes place.

Proxy: literally 'on behalf of another person' – proxy vote.

Quorum: the number of people needed to be in attendance for a meeting to be legitimate and so commence.

Refer back: to pass an item back for further consideration.

Resolution: the name given to a motion which has been passed or carried; used after the decision has been reached.

Seconder: one who supports the 'proposer' of a motion or proposal by 'seconding' it.

Secretary: committee official responsible for the internal and external administration of a committee.

Secret ballot: a system of voting in secret.

Shelve: to drop a motion which has no support.

Sine die: from Latin, literally, 'without a day', that is to say indefinitely, eg 'adjourned *sine die*'.

Standing committee: a committee which has an indefinite term of office.

Standing orders: rules of procedure governing public sector meetings.

Table: to introduce a paper or schedule for noting.

Taken as read: to save time, it is assumed the members have already read the minutes.

Treasurer: committee official responsible for its financial records and transactions.

Ultra vires: beyond the authority of the meeting to consider.

Unanimous: all being in favour.

Personnel

LETTERS OF APPLICATION

A letter of application for a job is essentially a sales letter. In such a letter you are trying to sell yourself, so your letter must:

- capture attention by using a good writing style
- arouse interest in your qualifications
- carry conviction by your past record and testimonials
- bring about the action you want the prospective employer to take – to grant an interview and eventually give you the job.

Style of application

Unless an advertisement specifies that you must apply in your own handwriting, or the post is purely clerical or bookkeeping, your application should be typed. A well-displayed, easy-to-read letter will attract attention at once and create a favourable first impression.

Some applicants write a long letter containing lots of information about education, qualifications and experience – this is not advisable as the information is not easy to locate and it can sound rather boastful.

Your curriculum vitae should give full details of your personal background, education, qualifications and experience

Preferably you should write a short letter applying for the post and stating that your curriculum vitae (or resumé) is enclosed.

Do not duplicate such information in your covering letter.

Points of guidance

- Remember the purpose of your application is not to get the job but to get an interview.
- Ensure your application looks attractive and neatly presented; make it stand out from the rest.
- Be brief; give all the relevant information in as few words as possible.
- Write sincerely, in a friendly tone, but without being familiar.
- Do not make exaggerated claims or sound boastful; simply show a proper appreciation of your abilities.
- Do not imply that you are applying for the job because you are bored with your present one.
- If your main interest is the salary, do not state the figure you expect. Instead mention what you are earning now.
- Do not enclose originals of your testimonials; send copies with your application but take your originals along to the interview.

Checklist

A busy employer has little time for long, rambling correspondence. Avoid the temptation to include details in which the recipient is unlikely to be interested, no matter how important they may be to you. You should also avoid generalising, and instead be quite specific in the information provided. For example instead of saying 'I have had several years of relevant experience in a well-known firm of engineers', state the number of years, state the experience and give the name of the firm.

When you have written your letter, read it carefully and ask yourself these questions:

(a) Does it read like a good business letter?

(b) Will the opening paragraph interest the employer enough to prompt him/her to read the rest?

(c) Does it suggest that you are genuinely interested in the post and the kind of work to be done?

(d) Is your letter neatly presented and logically structured?

If your answer to these questions is 'Yes', then you may safely send your letter.

22.1 Application for an advertised post

(a) Application letter

When your application is in response to an advertisement in a newspaper or journal, this should always be mentioned in the opening paragraph or in the subject heading.

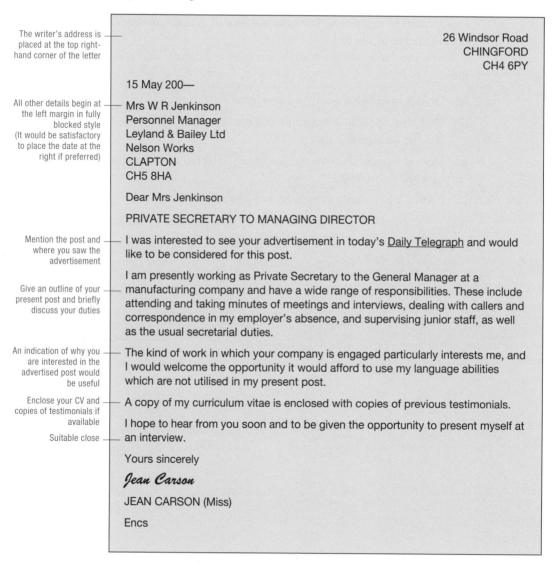

The writer's address is placed at the top right-hand corner of the letter

26 Windsor Road
CHINGFORD
CH4 6PY

15 May 200—

All other details begin at the left margin in fully blocked style (It would be satisfactory to place the date at the right if preferred)

Mrs W R Jenkinson
Personnel Manager
Leyland & Bailey Ltd
Nelson Works
CLAPTON
CH5 8HA

Dear Mrs Jenkinson

PRIVATE SECRETARY TO MANAGING DIRECTOR

Mention the post and where you saw the advertisement

I was interested to see your advertisement in today's <u>Daily Telegraph</u> and would like to be considered for this post.

Give an outline of your present post and briefly discuss your duties

I am presently working as Private Secretary to the General Manager at a manufacturing company and have a wide range of responsibilities. These include attending and taking minutes of meetings and interviews, dealing with callers and correspondence in my employer's absence, and supervising junior staff, as well as the usual secretarial duties.

An indication of why you are interested in the advertised post would be useful

The kind of work in which your company is engaged particularly interests me, and I would welcome the opportunity it would afford to use my language abilities which are not utilised in my present post.

Enclose your CV and copies of testimonials if available

A copy of my curriculum vitae is enclosed with copies of previous testimonials.

Suitable close

I hope to hear from you soon and to be given the opportunity to present myself at an interview.

Yours sincerely

Jean Carson

JEAN CARSON (Miss)

Encs

(b) Curriculum vitae

Your curriculum vitae (sometimes called a résumé) should set out all your personal details, together with your education, qualifications and working experience. It should be displayed attractively so that all the information can be seen at a glance. It should not extend to more than 2 pages. Wherever possible, the information should be categorised under headings and columns.

CURRICULUM VITAE

NAME	Jean Carson
ADDRESS	26 Windsor Road Chingford Essex CH4 6PY
TELEPHONE	020 8529 3456
DATE OF BIRTH	26 May 1965
NATIONALITY	British
MARITAL STATUS	Single

Personal details should be shown at the beginning

EDUCATION

State full- and part-time educational courses

19— to 19—	Woodford High School
19— to 19—	Bedford Secretarial College (Secretarial Course)

QUALIFICATIONS

List qualifications in full (don't just say '4 A levels')

GCE A Level	English Language	19—
	Mathematics	19—
	Spanish	19—
	French	19—
GCE O Level	Biology	19—
	Philosophy	19—
	Commerce	19—
	History	19—
LCCI	Private Secretary's Diploma	19—
LCCI 3rd level	Text Production	19—
	Audio	19—
	Shorthand	19—
	English for Business	19—
RSA	140 wpm Shorthand	19—
PITMAN	160 wpm Shorthand	19—

SPECIAL AWARDS

Mention any special achievements

RSA Silver medal for shorthand 140 wpm
Governors' prize for first place in college examinations

WORKING EXPERIENCE

Mention your present job first and work backwards

April 200— to present	Personal Secretary to General Manager	Reliance Cables Vicarage Road Leyton LONDON E10 5RG
Sept 19— to March 19—	Shorthand Typist	Bains, Hoyle & Co Solicitors 60 Kingsway LONDON WC2B 6AB

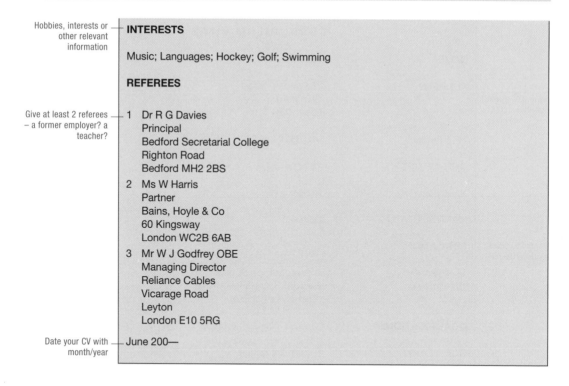

Hobbies, interests or other relevant information —

INTERESTS

Music; Languages; Hockey; Golf; Swimming

REFEREES

Give at least 2 referees – a former employer? a teacher? —

1   Dr R G Davies
    Principal
    Bedford Secretarial College
    Righton Road
    Bedford MH2 2BS

2   Ms W Harris
    Partner
    Bains, Hoyle & Co
    60 Kingsway
    London WC2B 6AB

3   Mr W J Godfrey OBE
    Managing Director
    Reliance Cables
    Vicarage Road
    Leyton
    London E10 5RG

Date your CV with month/year —

June 200—

22.2 Application using an introduction

Sometimes your application will result from an introduction by a friend or colleague. In this case such an introduction should be mentioned in the opening paragraph as a useful way of attracting attention.

> Dear Mr Barker
>
> Mrs Phyllis Naish, your Personnel Officer, has told me that you have a vacancy for a Marketing Assistant. I should like to be considered for this post.
>
> As you will see from my enclosed curriculum vitae I have several A levels as well as secretarial qualifications gained during an intensive one-year course at Walthamstow College of Commerce.
>
> I have been Shorthand Typist in the Marketing Department of Enterprise Cables Ltd for 2 years and have been very happy there, gaining a lot of valuable experience. However the office is quite small and I now wish to widen my experience and hopefully improve my prospects.
>
> My former headmistress has written the enclosed testimonial and has kindly agreed to give further details should they be needed. If you are interested in my application my present employer has agreed to provide further information.
>
> I am able to attend an interview at any time and hope to hear from you soon.
>
> Yours sincerely

22.3 Application for post of Sales Manager

Dear Sir

Mention the post and advertisement — I was very interested to see your advertisement for a Sales Manager in yesterday's Daily Telegraph and should like to be considered for this post.

Enclose CV and briefly discuss working experience — My full particulars are shown on my enclosed curriculum vitae, from which you will see that I have had 10 years' experience in the sales departments of two well-known companies. My special duties at Oral Plastics Ltd include the training of sales personnel, dealing with the company's foreign correspondence and organising market research and sales promotion programmes. I thoroughly enjoy

Mention why you are applying — my work and am very happy here but feel that the time has come when my experience in marketing has prepared me for the responsibility of full sales management.

Refer to referees — Mr James Watkinson, my Managing Director, and Ms Harriet Webb, Sales Manager of my former company, have both agreed to provide references for me: their details can be found on my curriculum vitae.

Suitable close — I shall be pleased to provide any further information you may need and hope I may be given the opportunity of an interview.

Yours faithfully

22.4 Application for a teaching post

This letter of application is sent by a trainee teacher to the Chief Education Officer of her local authority enquiring about suitable teaching posts.

Dear Sir

At the end of the present term I shall complete my one-year teacher training course at Garnett College of Education. For domestic reasons, I would like to obtain a post at a school or college in the area administered by your authority.

From my curriculum vitae which is attached you will see that I have 6 O level and 2 A level passes, as well as advanced qualifications in many secretarial subjects. I have held secretarial positions in the London area for a total of 8 years, during which time I studied for my RSA Shorthand and Typewriting Teachers' Diplomas. Having enjoyed the opportunity to teach these subjects in evening classes at the Chingford Evening Institute for 2 years, I was prompted to take up a full-time Certificate in Education at Garnett.

I like young people and get on well with them, and I am looking forward to helping them in the very practical way which teaching makes possible. If there is a suitable vacancy in your area, I hope you will consider me for it.

Yours faithfully

22.5 Application for post of Data Processing Trainee

In this letter the writer gives details of his education and qualifications in his letter instead of in a separate curriculum vitae. This style is useful when the applicant does not have a lot of previous working experience to warrant a CV.

Dear Sir

I would like to apply for the post of Management Trainee in your Data Processing Department advertised today in <u>The Guardian.</u>

I obtained A level passes in Mathematics, Physics and German at Marlborough College, Wiltshire. The College awarded me an open scholarship to Queens College, Cambridge, where I obtained a first in Mathematics and a second in Physics. After leaving university last year I accepted a temporary post with Firma Hollander & Schmidt in order to improve my German and gain some practical experience in their laboratories at Bremen. This work comes to an end in 6 weeks' time.

My special interest for many years has been computer work and I should like to make it my career. I believe my qualifications in Mathematics and Physics would enable me to do so successfully.

I am unmarried and would be willing to undertake the training courses away from home to which you refer in your advertisement.

My former Housemaster at Marlborough, Mr T Gartside, has consented to act as my referee (telephone 0117 234575), as has Dr W White, Dean of Queens College, Cambridge (telephone 01246 453453). I hope that you will take up these references and grant me the opportunity of an interview.

Yours faithfully

22.6 An unsolicited application

An *unsolicited*[1] application is the most difficult to write since there is no advertisement or introduction to tell you anything about the work or indeed whether there is a vacancy. In such a situation you must try to find out something about the company's activities and then show how your qualifications and experience could be used.

[1] **unsolicited** not asked for

Dear Sir

For the past 8 years I have been a Statistician in the Research Unit of Baron & Smallwood Ltd, Glasgow. I am now looking for a change of employment which would widen my experience and at the same time improve my prospects. It has occurred to me that a large and well-known organisation such as yours might be able to use my services.

I am 31 years of age and in excellent health. At the University of London I specialised in merchandising and advertising, and was awarded a PhD degree for my thesis on 'Statistical Investigation in Research'. I thoroughly enjoy working on investigations, particularly where the work involves statistics.

Although I have had no experience in consumer research, I am familiar with the methods employed and fully understand their importance in the recording of buying habits and trends. I should like to feel that there is an opportunity to use my services in this type of research and that you will invite me to attend an interview. I could then give you further information and bring testimonials.

I am unmarried and would be willing to undertake the training courses away from home to which you refer in your advertisement.

I hope to hear from you soon.

Yours faithfully

 TIP When writing to someone for the first time, remember: there is no second chance to create a first impression!

TESTIMONIALS

As well as sending a copy of your curriculum vitae with an application letter, it is useful to send copies of any testimonials you may have from previous employers. The originals of such open testimonials are addressed TO WHOM IT MAY CONCERN. They are generally given by your previous employers if requested; you should always retain the originals and send photocopies only to prospective employers.

There is no legal obligation for anyone to give a testimonial, but if one is written it must state only what is true otherwise the writer may become legally liable, either to the applicant for *libel*,[2] or to the employer if the testimonial is at all misleading.

Any testimonial should follow the following 4 point plan:

1 State duration of employment and post(s) held.

2 Give details of the duties carried out.

3 Mention work attitude and personal qualities.

4 Finish with a recommendation.

[2] **libel** a statement damaging a person's reputation

22.7 Formal testimonial for Secretary

This testimonial was requested by an employee who worked at a company for a period of 8 years until she took up teacher training.

TO WHOM IT MAY CONCERN

Duration of employment/Position — Miss Sharon Tan was employed as Shorthand Typist in this Company's Sales Department when she left secretarial college in July 19—. She was promoted to my Personal Secretary in 200—.

Duties — Her responsibilities included the usual secretarial duties involved in such a post as well as attending meetings, transcribing minutes and supervising and advising junior secretaries.

Working attitude — Sharon used her best endeavours at all times to perform her work conscientiously and expeditiously. She was an excellent secretary, an extremely quick and accurate shorthand typist and meticulous in the layout, presentation and accuracy of her work. I cannot overstress her exceptional work rate which did not in any way detract from the very high standards she set for herself.

Personal qualities — Sharon enjoyed good health and was a good time-keeper. She was very personable, friendly, sociable and quick to share in a joke. It was a great loss to both myself and the company when Sharon took up teacher training.

Recommendation — In my opinion, Sharon has the necessary character, dedication and approach to be suitable for the position of personal secretary or to enter the teaching profession. I can recommend her highly and may be contacted for further information.

IAN HENLEY
Deputy Chairman

22.8 Testimonial for Head of Department

Here is another very favourable testimonial which was issued to someone who left a private college after completing a 2-year contract as Head of Department.

TO WHOM IT MAY CONCERN

Norman Tyler has been employed by this College as Head of Business Studies from August 200— to 9 March 200—.

As well as capably handling the responsibilities for the overall administration of his department Norman ably taught Economics, Commerce and Management Appreciation to students of a wide range of ability and age groups on courses leading to Advanced LCCI examinations.

Norman is a highly competent and professional teacher whose class preparation is always thorough and meticulous. His committed approach to teaching is matched by his administrative abilities. He has made a substantial contribution to course planning, student counselling, curriculum development and programme marketing.

Norman possesses an outgoing personality and he mixes well. He makes his full contribution to a team and is popular with his students and colleagues alike.

In view of his dedication and ability I am confident that Norman will prove to be a valuable asset to any organisation fortunate enough to employ him. It is with pleasure that I recommend him highly and without hesitation.

FAISAL SHAMLAN
Principal

22.9 Testimonial for colleague

April 2003

TO WHOM IT MAY CONCERN

State how you know the person —— I have known Sonja Bergenstein for several months in her capacity as Business Development Executive of SingaJobs.com, Singapore.

As a freelance Training Consultant, I have worked with SingaJobs.com on many occasions. They have acted as my agent in marketing and promoting my 2-day workshops 'Transform your Business Writing Skills', and Sonja has been one of the team working on this.

Mention some key points about work/responsibilities —— My contact with Sonja has been mainly on the days of the workshops, when Sonja has always been well organised, helpful and friendly. She has a very sociable and pleasant personality, and she always goes the extra mile in making sure that all participants are kept happy during each workshop. She has been an expert in public relations during breaks, when it is important to mix with participants and make sure they are well looked after. When it has been necessary to address groups, Sonja has always been confident and able to express herself clearly and with interest.

Give additional comments on personality and attitude —— Working with many different nationalities in the Singaporean scene has been no problem for Sonja. She had adapted well to the different cultures, and she has been able to mix and get on well with people from all races. From my experience, she has been very well liked and respected, a hard-working member of the team at SingaJobs.com who will be sorely missed.

Close with a recommendation —— I have certainly enjoyed working with Sonja, and wish her every success in her future career, in which I am sure she will do extremely well.

SHIRLEY TAYLOR
Author and Training Consultant

FAVOURABLE REFERENCES

Even if testimonials are provided at the time of sending an application letter, it is usual to state (either on your CV or covering letter) the names of one or two people who have consented to act as referees. Prospective employers may contact such referees either by telephone or letter to obtain further information about an applicant's work performance and character.

22.10 Letter taking up a reference

Dear Mrs Lambert

Mention applicant's name and post applied for — Mr James Harvey, at present employed by you as Foreign Correspondent, has applied to us for a similar post and has given your name as a referee.

Ask for information about his work — I should be grateful if you would state whether his services with you have been entirely satisfactory and whether you consider he would be able to accept full responsibility for the French and German correspondence in a large and busy department.

Include specific details regarding ability — I am aware that Mr Harvey speaks fluent French and German but I am particularly interested in his ability to produce accurate translations into these languages of letters that may be dictated to him in English.

Give an assurance of confidentiality — Any other information you can provide would be appreciated, and of course will be treated as strictly confidential.

Yours sincerely

22.11 Favourable reply

In this reply, the writer recommends the employee very highly and without hesitation, feeling confident that he can carry out the duties required in the post stated.

Dear Mr Brodie

I am pleased to be able to reply favourably to your enquiry of 6 April concerning Mr James Harvey.

Mr Harvey is an excellent linguist and for the past 5 years has been in sole charge of our foreign correspondence, most of which is with European companies, especially in France and Germany.

We have been extremely pleased with the services provided by Mr Harvey. Should you engage him you may rely upon him to produce well-written and accurate transcripts of letters into French and German. He is a very reliable and steady worker and has an excellent character.

We wish him success, but at the same time shall be very sorry to lose him.

Yours sincerely

22.12 Cautious reply

In this reply the writer is very cautious, implying that the applicant lacks the experience needed for control of a department. However the writer is very careful not to come straight out and say this in so many words.

Dear Mr Brodie

Thank you for your letter of 6 April concerning Mr James Harvey.

Mr Harvey is a competent linguist and for the past 5 years has been employed as senior assistant in our foreign correspondence section. He has always been conscientious[3] and hard-working. Whether he would be capable of taking full responsibility for a large and busy department is difficult to say; his work with us has always been carried out under supervision.

Should you require any further information please do not hesitate to contact me.

Yours sincerely

22.13 Enquiry letter requesting a reference

In this letter another prospective employer requests information about the work and character of an applicant.

Dear Mr Jones

Mr Lionel Picton has applied to us for an appointment as Manager of our factory in Nairobi. We are leading manufacturers of engineered components used in the petrochemical industry and are looking for a qualified engineer with works manager's experience in medium or large batch production.

Mr Picton informs us that he is employed by you as Assistant Manager of your factory in Sheffield. We should be grateful for any information you can give us about his competence, reliability and general character.

Any information provided will be treated in strictest confidence.

Yours sincerely

22.14 Favourable reply

Dear Mr Gandah

Acknowledge letter and give background information

Thank you for your letter of 6 August regarding Mr Lionel Picton, who has been employed by this company for the past 10 years.

Give details about the applicant's work, qualifications and attitude

Mr Picton served his apprenticeship with Vickers Tools Ltd in Manchester, followed by a 3 course for the Engineering and Work Study Diploma of the Institution of Production Engineers. He is technically well qualified and for the past 5 years has been our Assistant Works Manager responsible for production and associated activities in our Sheffield factory. In all aspects of his work he has shown himself to be hard-working, conscientious and in every way a very dependable employee.

Finish with a recommendation and personal word about the applicant

I can recommend Mr Picton without the slightest hesitation. I feel sure that if he was appointed to manage your factory in Nairobi he would bring to his work a genuine spirit of service, which would be found stimulating and helpful by all who worked with him.

Yours sincerely

[3] **conscientious** careful to do what is right

22.15 Applicant's thank you letter

Those who have provided references will naturally be pleased to know how the applicant has fared and whether successful or not. Applicants should therefore always inform and thank those who supported them.

Dear Mr Freeman

I would like to thank you for supporting my application for the post as Manager of the Barker Petrochemical Company in Nairobi.

I know that the generous terms in which you wrote about me had much to do with my being offered the post and I am very grateful to you for the reference you provided for me.

Your help and encouragement have always been much appreciated and this will always be remembered.

Yours sincerely

22.16 Enquiry using numbered points

In this enquiry the writer is looking for certain qualities. To make sure that each one is covered in a reply, numbered points are used.

Dear Miss French

Introduction states name of applicant and post applied for — Miss Jean Parker has applied for a post as Administrator in our Sales Department. She states that she is presently employed by you and has given your name as a referee.

Specific questions regarding the applicant are numbered and listed — I should be grateful if you would answer the following questions regarding her abilities and character:

1 Is she conscientious, intelligent and trustworthy?

2 Is she capable of dealing with any difficult situations?

3 Are her keyboarding and administrative skills satisfactory?

4 Is she capable of dealing accurately with figure work?

5 Is her output satisfactory?

6 Does she get on well with her colleagues?

7 Are her health and time-keeping satisfactory?

Give an assurance of confidentiality — Any information you are kind enough to provide will be treated in strict confidence.

Yours sincerely

22.17 Reply

Dear Mr Kingston

In reply to your letter of 15 April I have nothing to say but good about Miss Jean Parker. She has been employed as Assistant Sales Administrator in our general office for the past 2 years and I feel sure that you will find her in every way satisfactory.

In reply to each of the questions in your letter, I have no hesitation in saying that Miss Parker meets all these requirements.

We will be sorry to lose Miss Parker, but realise that her abilities demand wider scope than is possible at this company.

Yours sincerely

22.18 Favourable reference – former student

Dear Mrs Thompson

MISS CAROLINE BRADLEY

In reply to your enquiry of 3 June I welcome the opportunity to support Miss Bradley's application for the post of your Marketing Assistant.

Miss Bradley was a student at this college during the year 200— to 200—. Admission to this intensive one-year course is restricted to students with good school-leaving qualifications. The fact that Miss Bradley was admitted to the course is in itself evidence of excellent academic ability. Upon completing her course she was awarded the title 'Student of the Year', being the student gaining highest qualifications over the one-year course.

In all other respects Miss Bradley's work and attitude were entirely satisfactory, and I can recommend her to you with every confidence. I feel sure that if she was appointed she would perform her duties diligently and reliably.

Yours sincerely

22.19 Favourable reference – Department Manager

Dear Mr Lee

In reply to your letter of yesterday Mr Leonard Burns is both capable and reliable. He came to us 5 years ago to take charge of our Hardware Department.

Leonard knows the trade thoroughly and does all the buying for his department with notable success. I know that for some time he has been looking for a similar post with a larger store. While we would be sorry to lose his services, we would not wish to stand in the way of the advancement which could be offered by a store such as yours.

Yours sincerely

USEFUL SENTENCES FOR REFERENCES AND TESTIMONIALS

- Mr John Smith was employed by this company from . . . to . . .

- I am very glad of this opportunity to support Miss Lim's application for a position in your company.

- Mr Johnson has proven to be an efficient, hard-working, trustworthy and very personable employee.

- Sharon used her best endeavours at all times to perform her work conscientiously.

- In my opinion, Harrison has the necessary character, dedication and approach to be suitable for the position of personal secretary.

- Nigel has an outgoing personality and he mixes well.

- He makes his full contribution to a team and is popular with his colleagues and clients.

- Geetha made a substantial contribution to the work of the Sales Department and always performed her work in a businesslike and reliable manner.

- It was a great loss to both myself and the company when Miss Turner moved abroad.

- We were very sorry to lose Miss Fisher and she will be greatly missed.

- It is with great pleasure that I recommend Martha Tan for this position in your company.

- I can recommend Mr Cheong without hesitation, and know you will find him an excellent addition to your staff.

- We were very sorry to lose Miss Franks and are pleased to recommend her highly and without hesitation.

UNFAVOURABLE REFERENCES

An employer is not likely to give a testimonial to an employee whose services have not been entirely satisfactory. Instead, the employer should tell the employee that their name may be given as a referee. When asked for such a reference, it is always safer to make unfavourable comments either over the telephone or in person rather than in writing. If an unfavourable reference is put in writing, it should be worded with caution and restraint, and with as little detail as possible.

There is always a danger that unfavourable reports may be seen by unauthorised people so it is safer to make such comments either over the telephone or in person instead of in writing. If an unfavourable reference is put in writing, it should be worded with caution and restraint and with as little detail as possible.

22.20 Unfavourable reference

A reference such as this would almost certainly prevent this prospective employee from getting a good post anywhere, but if the writer sincerely believes in what is said then they should not fear to send it

> Dear Ms Samson
>
> Thank you for your letter of 18 January regarding Mr Ian Bell.
>
> Mr Bell was employed as Clerk in this company from February to October last year. We released him because his work fell below the standards we normally require. His punctuality also left a lot to be desired and he had a disturbing influence on other members of our staff.
>
> Mr Bell is an intelligent young man and with the exercise of a little self-discipline he could do well. However, from my personal experience I am afraid that I cannot conscientiously recommend him.
>
> Yours sincerely

22.21 Alternative unfavourable reference

The letter in 22.20 is quite specific about the applicant's unsuitability. Perhaps a safer and wiser course would be to write in more general terms and to be less specific in criticism, as in this letter

> Dear Ms Samson
>
> I am replying to your letter of 18 January in which you enquire about Mr Ian Bell.
>
> This young man was a member of our clerical staff from February to October last year but I am sorry to say that we did not find him suitable. It is quite possible that he may do better in another office.
>
> Yours sincerely

INTERVIEW LETTERS

If a lot of applications are received for a post it is unlikely that all applicants can be interviewed. In such cases a shortlist will be drawn up of those applicants thought to be most suitable for interview. Letters should also be sent to the unsuccessful applicants.

22.22 Invitation to attend for interview

A letter inviting an applicant for interview should first acknowledge receipt of the application, and then go on to give a day, date and time for the interview. The name of the person the applicant should ask for should also be stated. Confirmation is often requested.

Dear Miss Wildman

SENIOR SECRETARY TO TRAINING MANAGER

Thank you for your application for this post.

You are invited to attend for an interview with me and Mrs Angela Howard, Training Manager, on Friday 29 May at 3.30 pm.

Please let me know either by letter or telephone whether this appointment will be convenient for you.

Yours sincerely

22.23 Confirmation of attendance

Dear Mrs Graham

SENIOR SECRETARY TO TRAINING MANAGER

Thank you for your letter inviting me to attend for interview on Friday 29 May at 3.30 pm.

I shall be pleased to attend and look forward to meeting you and Mrs Howard.

Yours sincerely

22.24 Letter of rejection before interview

It is courteous to write to the applicants who have not been included on the shortlist. The letter can be worded in such a way that it does not cause offence or negative feelings.

Dear

Thank you for your application for the post of Senior Secretary to the Training Manager.

We have received many applications for this post. I am afraid that your experience and qualifications do not match all our requirements closely enough so we cannot include you on our shortlist for this post.

I realise you will be disappointed but would like to thank you for the considerable time and effort you put into preparing your application. You have a lot of useful experience and I am sure that you will soon find suitable employment.

Yours sincerely

JOB DESCRIPTION

22.25 Job description for Senior Secretary

A job description gives details of the duties and responsibilities involved in a post, including any supervisory duties, specific authority and any special features of the post.

If plain paper is used include the company's name. Sometimes letterheaded paper is used

© Turner Communications

JOB DESCRIPTION

Use appropriate headings relevant to the post

JOB TITLE	Senior Secretary
REPORTS TO	Training Manager
LOCATION	Head Office, Sheffield
MAIN PURPOSE	To provide a confidential secretarial and support service to the Training Manager

REQUIREMENTS

Sometimes specific requirements of the post holder are included

1 Abilities: use initiative, decide priorities, work without supervision

2 Previous experience at senior level

3 Skills: Microsoft Office, notetaking skills, minute-taking skills, good organiser, good interpersonal skills

4 High standard of education with appropriate secretarial/administration qualifications

MAIN DUTIES AND RESPONSIBILITIES

List the main duties and responsibilities

1 To provide secretarial support to the Training Manager.

2 To deal with mail, answer telephone enquiries, take messages and compose correspondence.

3 To take shorthand dictation and deal with instructions from manuscript, audio or disk and to transcribe documents accurately and consistently.

Make sure all points are expressed in a consistent style (eg 'To…')

4 To maintain the diary of the Training Manager.

5 To arrange meetings and produce accurate minutes.

6 To arrange training courses and seminars.

7 To make travel and accommodation arrangements as may be required.

8 To ensure the security of the office and confidential documents.

Finish with this standard clause

9 To carry out any other duties as may be expected in a post of this level.

ST/BT

June 200—

22.26 Job description for Telephone Execuive

JOB DESCRIPTION

Job Title	Telephone Executive (Marketing)
Location	Marketing Department, Head Office
Responsible to	Marketing Manager
Main Purpose of Job	To telephone customers with the objective of identifying opportunities where business can be increased

MAIN DUTIES AND RESPONSIBILITIES

1 To achieve daily call rate targets and any target set for sales campaigns.

2 To have a good telephone manner and be courteous to customers at all times.

3 To carry out any administrative requirements generated by the telephone calls in an accurate and efficient manner. This may include sending letters, fax messages, e-mails, reports, product literature, etc.

4 To undertake training courses to make good use of telephone selling techniques.

5 To undertake training on the company's products and services and to promote associated products where appropriate.

6 To carry out competitor market research by contracting their branches to gather information on pricing, product availability, etc, as directed by your supervisor.

7 To carry out any other tasks as requested by your supervisor.

OFFERS OF APPOINTMENT

Letters appointing staff should state clearly the salary and any other conditions of appointment. If the duties of the post are described in detail on a Job Description and enclosed with the letter, it will not be necessary to duplicate such details in the letter itself.

22.27 Letter confirming offer of employment

If an appointment is made verbally at the interview, it should be confirmed by letter immediately afterwards.

Dear Miss Wildman

Offer the job and include a commencement date — I am pleased to confirm the offer we made to you yesterday of the post of Senior Secretary to the Training Manager, commencing on 1 August 200—.

Specify the duties or enclose Job Description — Your duties will be as outlined at the interview and as described on the attached Job Description.

Include details of salary and holidays — This appointment carries a commencing salary of £15,000 per annum, rising to £16,500 after one year's service and thereafter by annual review. You will be entitled to 4 weeks' annual holiday.

Mention termination information — The appointment may be terminated at any time by either side giving 2 months' notice in writing.

Ask for confirmation — Please confirm that you accept this appointment on the terms stated and that you will be able to commence your duties on 1 August.

Yours sincerely

22.28 Letter offering appointment

When the appointment is not made at the interview, the offer will be made by letter to the selected applicant as soon as possible.

Dear Miss Jennings

Thank you for attending the interview yesterday. I am pleased to offer you the post of Secretary in our Sales Department at a starting salary of S$1200 (Singapore dollars) per month. Your commencement date will be Monday 1 October.

As discussed, office hours are 0900 to 1730 with one hour for lunch. You will be entitled to 3 weeks' annual paid holiday.

Please confirm in writing by return that you accept this appointment on these terms and that you can take up your duties on 1 October.

Yours sincerely

22.29 Acceptance of offer of employment

Any offer letter should be accepted in writing immediately.

Dear Miss Tan

Thank you for your letter of 24 August offering me the post of Secretary in your Sales Department.

I am pleased to accept this post on the terms stated in your letter and confirm that I can commence work on 1 October.

I can assure you that I shall do everything I can to make a success of my work.

Yours sincerely

22.30 Declining an offer of employment

If you do not wish to take up the offer of employment you should put this in writing immediately and it is courteous to give a reason for declining the offer. In this way the employer may make a second choice as soon as possible.

Dear Miss Tan

Thank you for your letter of 24 August offering me the post of Secretary to the Sales Department.

I am sorry that I will be unable to take up this position. My present company have discussed with me their plans for expansion and I have been offered the new post of Office Manager. You will appreciate that this post will offer me a challenge which I feel I must accept.

I wish you every success in appointing a suitable candidate.

Yours sincerely

22.31 Letter to unsuitable applicants

As soon as an offer of employment has been accepted by the selected applicant, it is courteous to write letters to the remaining applicants who were interviewed telling them that their application was unsuccessful.

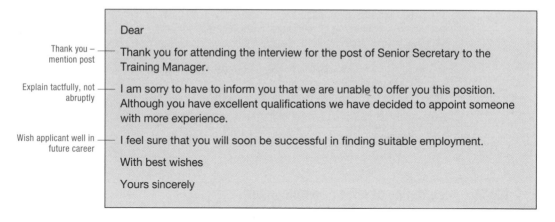

Dear

Thank you — mention post — Thank you for attending the interview for the post of Senior Secretary to the Training Manager.

Explain tactfully, not abruptly — I am sorry to have to inform you that we are unable to offer you this position. Although you have excellent qualifications we have decided to appoint someone with more experience.

Wish applicant well in future career — I feel sure that you will soon be successful in finding suitable employment.

With best wishes

Yours sincerely

TERMINATION OF EMPLOYMENT

22.32 Employee's letter of resignation

A Contract of Employment made for a stated period comes to an end when the period is completed unless both parties agree to an extension. If the contract is for an unstated period it may be ended at any time by either of the parties giving the agreed period of notice.

Dear Miss Ward

I regret to inform you that I wish to give 2 weeks' notice of my resignation from the company. My last day of work will be 30 June 200—.

I have been very happy working here for the past 2 years and found my work challenging and enjoyable. However I have obtained a post in which I will have more responsibilities and greater career prospects.

Thank you for your help and guidance during my employment.

Yours sincerely

22.33 Employer's letter terminating employment (services unsatisfactory)

By the Employment Rights Act 1996 employees who feel they have been unfairly dismissed have the right to appeal to an Industrial Tribunal. An employer must be able to show that the dismissal was justified by referring to the employee's conduct or inability/failure to do the job satisfactorily.

Where it is decided to terminate the employment of a person whose services have been unsatisfactory, it is advisable to do so verbally in the first place. The confirmatory letter should be worded carefully and tactfully.

Dear Miss Anderson

Express regret and give a termination date — Following our discussion earlier this week I regret to inform you that your services with the company will not be required with effect from 31 August 200—.

Give details of employee's unsatisfactory conduct — As you know there have been a number of occasions recently when I have had to point out the unsatisfactory quality of your work. Together with your persistent unpunctuality in spite of several warnings, this has led me to believe that you will

Tactful wording is necessary — perhaps be more successful in a different kind of work.

A carefully worded close is appropriate — I hope you will be successful in finding suitable employment elsewhere. If another employer should wish you to start work before the end of the month, arrangements can be made for you to be released immediately.

Yours sincerely

22.34 Employer's letter terminating employment (services redundant[4])

The Employment Rights Act 1996 states that employees are entitled to *compensation*[5] for loss of employment due to redundancy as in the case of the employer ceasing to carry on business or having no further need of the employee's services. The amount of compensation payable is calculated on the basis of the employee's age, length of service and weekly earnings.

[4] **redundant** laid off, retrenched, out of work
[5] **compensation** payment for loss

Dear Mr White

As you are aware the reorganisation of our office has been the subject of an investigation by a firm of management consultants. They have made a number of recommendations which will result in a decrease in staff.

I very much regret having to inform you that your position as Ledger Clerk is one which will become redundant on 30 June. I am giving you as much notice as possible so that you can immediately begin looking for alternative employment.

You will be entitled to a redundancy payment which will amount to 2 weeks' salary for each of your 5 years' service, at the rate prevailing when your services end. This is calculated as follows:

£200 x 2 x 5 = £2000

I would like to take this opportunity to say that your work has always been entirely satisfactory and I shall be pleased to provide any prospective employer with a reference if required.

I do hope you will soon find another suitable post and wish you all the best for the future.

Yours sincerely

22.35 Warning letter

As a general rule an employee must have received a warning before he or she may be dismissed. The company's rules regarding warnings and dismissal should be laid down in the Conditions of Employment or in the Employment Contract.

In the first place it is good business practice to speak to the employee personally to discuss unsatisfactory work or attitude. A letter should follow as confirmation of what was discussed.

Grounds for dismissal must be specific and if possible measured against the company's general conditions and terms of employment or against the job description. The period of notice served on an employee will depend on the contract of employment. Legal minimum periods of notice for long-serving staff will vary from country to country. These formal requirements should be investigated and considered.

Background details — Dear Mark

Further to our meeting today I am sorry to say that your conduct has been found to be unsatisfactory recently.

Be specific about incidents/dates — There have been two occasions during the past month in which you were found to be breaching our company rules. On 12 March you were found smoking in a prohibited area, and on 24 March you were rude to a customer. On both occasions you received a verbal warning from your supervisor.

Express a hope that conduct will improve — I hope there will be no repeat of either of these incidents, or indeed any other breach of the company's rules or standards of conduct.

State follow-up action — I will review the situation again in one month's time.

Yours sincerely

22.36 Second warning

Dear Mark

At our meeting today I gave you a second warning for unsatisfactory conduct. This occurred after your supervisor informed me that you had been caught taking money from the petty cash till this morning. This follows the 2 previous incidents mentioned in my letter of 12 June.

The sum involved was very small but I stressed to you that integrity and trust are vital in any business. You have appealed to me to give you another chance and against my better judgement I have agreed to do so. However any further unsatisfactory conduct will result in immediate dismissal.

Yours sincerely

22.37 Summary dismissal

Dear Mark

I confirm that you are dismissed from the company with immediate effect following the discovery that you were caught stealing money from a colleague's drawer. This action follows my warning letters dated 25 March and 5 April about unsatisfactory conduct.

Our cheque for one week's salary in lieu of notice is enclosed.

Yours sincerely

22.38 **Letter giving an employee one month's notice**

Dear Mark

I confirm that you have agreed to leave the company at the end of this month, ie 30 June. This follows my warning letters to you dated 25 March and 5 April and further instances of breaching company rules, smoking in prohibited areas and rudeness to customers. All these incidents have been discussed with you and officially reported under the company's general conditions of employment.

If you find another position before the end of the month we will be happy to release you.

Yours sincerely

SUNDRY PERSONNEL MATTERS

Transfer of employee to other work

Where it is necessary to transfer an employee from work which has been enjoyed, the reasons for the transfer must be clearly explained and any advantages must be emphasised. Perhaps there will be the prospect of more interesting and responsible work, more experience, better pay, improved prospects. With tact it should be possible to convey what may be unwelcome or disappointing news to an employee without causing hurt feelings or offence. In this way what might otherwise be received as unwelcome news may almost be turned into good news.

In this case a long-standing employee is happily settled into a routine with no wish to change, but this has been made necessary due to technological changes within the company.

Dear Mr Turner

As Mrs Williamson has already discussed with you, we have arranged to appoint you as Section Supervisor in the Stores Department with effect from Monday 1 July. Your salary will be £19,200 per annum.

In your new post you will report directly to Mr James Freeman, Storekeeper, and you will be responsible for the work of the clerical staff employed in the department.

Your 30 years of loyal service in the Invoice Department have been greatly appreciated by the management, and we are sorry that it is necessary to move you from a department with which you are so familiar. Our only reason for doing so is that invoicing will be completely changed by the introduction of computerised methods. We feel sure that you will understand that it is uneconomic for us to retrain our long-standing employees who might find difficulty in adjusting to new ways of working.

In your new post you will find ample scope for your experience. I know you will do a good job and hope you will find it enjoyable.

Yours sincerely

22.40 Recruitment of staff through an agency

Employers in need of office staff frequently make their requirements known to employment agencies. Such agencies will introduce either full-time, part-time or temporary staff in return for a commission related to the amount of wage or salary paid.

Dear Sir/Madam

I hope you will be able to help me to fill a vacancy which has just arisen in my department.

My Secretary needs secretarial help on a part-time basis. This will be an interesting post and ideal for someone who wishes to work for only a few hours each week. Applicants should be able to undertake normal secretarial duties and have shorthand and typewriting speeds of about 100 and 45 wpm respectively. Applicants of any age would be considered, but willingness and reliability are preferable to someone with high qualifications.

The successful applicant will be required to work for 3 hours on 5 mornings each week. We would be willing to consider an alternative arrangement if necessary.

I propose payment based on an hourly rate of £5 to £6 according to age and experience.

Please let me know whether you have anyone on your register who would be suitable.

Yours faithfully

22.41 Request for an increase in salary

Any letter requesting an increase in salary should be worded very carefully. You should explain tactfully the reason why you feel a salary increase is justified.

Dear Mr Browning

My present appointment carries an annual salary of £18,500; this was reviewed in March last year.

During my 5 years with this company I feel I have carried out my duties conscientiously and have recently acquired additional responsibilities.

I feel that my qualifications and the nature of my work justify a higher salary and I have already been offered a similar position with another company at a salary of £20,000 per annum.

My present duties are interesting and I thoroughly enjoy my work. Although I have no wish to leave the company, I cannot afford to turn down the present offer unless some improvement in my salary can be arranged.

I hope a salary increase will be possible, otherwise my only course will be to accept the offer made to me.

Yours sincerely

22.42 Letter of resignation

When you decide to leave a company you must hand in your notice. It is usual to do so with a formal letter of resignation in accordance with the company's conditions of employment.

Dear Mr McKewan

Please accept notice of my intention to leave the company in one month's time, ie 28 July.

As I have discussed with you I have accepted a position with another company which will allow me greater responsibilities and improved opportunities for advancement.

Thank you for your support during my 2 years with Turner Communications. I have gained a lot of valuable experience which will be very useful.

Yours sincerely

22.43 Welcome letter to new employee

It is with great pleasure that I welcome you as a new employee to SingComm Pte Ltd, Singapore. I am very pleased that you have chosen to accept our offer of employment and hope that this will be the beginning of a mutually beneficial association.

We encourage our personnel to take advantage of selected courses that are available in Singapore, so as to improve their skills and learn new skills in related areas. The current list of courses and their corresponding registration dates are posted on the employee bulletin board. If you decide to attend one of these courses, please advise your supervisor and s/he will make the necessary arrangements.

If you have any questions at any time that I may be able to answer, please do not hesitate to give me a call on [telephone number].

Once again, welcome to SingComm Pte Ltd.

22.44 Reminder about health and safety policy

In view of the recent unfortunate accident involving a visitor to our premises, I would like to remind you about our health and safety policy.

Whenever you have a visitor to the building, you are responsible for their health and safety at all times. For his/her own safety, a visitor should not be allowed to wander freely around the building. If, for example, a visitor needs to use the washroom, you should accompany them and escort them back.

For security reasons, if you see someone you do not recognise wandering around the building unaccompanied, do not be afraid to ask questions. Ask politely why he or she is here, which member of staff they are visiting, and if that person knows the visitor has arrived.

All SingComm employees have a responsibility to take reasonable care of themselves and others and to ensure a healthy and safe workplace. If you notice any hazard or potential hazard, please bring it to the attention of the Health and Safety Manager, Michael Wilson, who will investigate the issue.

A copy of the company's health and safety policy is attached. Please take a few minutes to read it through to remind yourself of the main points.

Thank you for your help in ensuring the health and safety of all employees and visitors to SingComm.

22.45 Letter regarding outstanding holiday entitlement

In the past it has been a policy of the company that all staff must take their holiday entitlement within one calendar year. Any holiday entitlement not taken before 31 December each year has been forfeited.

It has now been decided to amend this rule to provide staff more flexibility with holidays.

With immediate effect anyone who has up to 5 days' holiday entitlement outstanding at 31 December may carry this over to 31 March the following year. Any days that have not been used by 31 March will be forfeited. Unused holiday entitlement may not be converted to pay in lieu.

The approval of staff leave is still subject to agreement with your manager/supervisor. This will take into account the business and operational needs of the department and especially clashes with other staff.

If you have any questions about this new policy, please telephone Human Resource Department on extension 456.

USEFUL EXPRESSIONS

Application letters

Openings

1 I wish to apply for the post ... advertised in the ... on ...

2 I was interested to see your advertisement in ... and wish to apply for this post.

3 I am writing to enquire whether you have a suitable vacancy for me in your organisation.

4 I understand from Mr ..., one of your suppliers, that there is an opening in your company for ...

5 Mrs ... informs me that she will be leaving your company on ... and if her position has not been filled, I should like to be considered.

Closes

1 I look forward to hearing from you and to being granted the opportunity of an interview.

2 I hope you will consider my application favourably and grant me an interview.

3 I look forward to the opportunity of attending an interview when I can provide further details.

Favourable references

Openings

1 Mr ... has applied to us for the above post/position of ... We should be grateful if you would give us your opinion of his character and abilities.
2 We have received an application from Miss ... who has given your name as a referee.
3 I am very glad of this opportunity to speak in support of Miss ...'s application for a position in your company.
4 In reply to your recent enquiry Ms ... has been employed as ... for the past 2 years.

Closes

1 Any information you can provide will be much appreciated.
2 Any information you are kind enough to provide will be treated in strictest confidence.
3 I am sure you will be more than satisfied with the work of Mr ... .
4 I shall be sorry to lose ... but realise that her abilities demand wider scope than are possible at this company.

Unfavourable references

1 I find it difficult to answer your enquiry about Mr ... He is a very likeable person but I cannot conscientiously recommend him for the vacancy you mention.
2 The work produced by ... was below the standards expected and we found it necessary to release him.
3 Her poor time-keeping was very disturbing and caused some disruption to the work of the department.
4 We found her attitude quite a bad influence on other staff within the department.
5 Although ... possesses the qualifications to perform such work, I have seen no evidence that she has the necessary self-discipline or reliability.

Offers of employment

Openings

1 Thank you for attending the interview last ..., I am pleased to offer you the position of ...
2 I am pleased to confirm the offer we made to you when you came for interview on ...

3 Following your interview with ..., I am pleased to offer you the position of ... commencing on ...

Closes

1 Written confirmation of your acceptance of this post would be appreciated as soon as possible.

2 Please confirm in writing that you accept this appointment on the terms stated and that you can commence your duties on ...

3 We look forward to welcoming you to our staff and hope you will be very happy in your work here.

Termination of employment

Openings

1 I regret that I wish to terminate my services with this company with effect from ...

2 I am writing to confirm that I wish to tender my resignation. My last date of employment will be ...

3 As my family have decided to emigrate I am sorry to have to tender my resignation.

4 It is with regret that I have to inform you that your position with this company will become redundant on ...

5 There has been no improvement in your work performance and attitude despite our letters dated ... and ... . As a result we have no option but to terminate your services with effect from ...

Closes

1 I have been very happy working here and am grateful for your guidance during my employment.

2 I am sorry that these circumstances make it necessary for me to leave the company.

3 We have been extremely satisfied with your services and hope that you will soon find another suitable post.

4 I hope you will soon find alternative employment, and extend my best wishes for your future.

Testimonials

Openings

1 Mr ... has been employed by this company from ... to ...

2 Miss ... worked for this company from leaving college in 200– until she emigrated to Canada in March 200–.

Central section

1 Miss ... enjoys good health and is a good time-keeper.

2 She uses her best endeavours at all times to perform her work expeditiously and has always been a hard-working and conscientious employee.

3 Miss ... made a substantial contribution to the work of the ... department, and always performed her work in a businesslike and reliable manner.

4 Mr ... gave considerable help to his colleagues in improvements of teaching methods and materials and also produced many booklets of guidance which are proving valuable to other teachers.

Closes

1 I have pleasure in recommending ... highly and without hesitation.

2 We hope that ... meets with the success we feel he deserves.

3 I shall be sorry to lose his services but realise that his abilities demand wider scope than are possible at this company.

4 I can recommend Miss ... to you with every confidence.

Travel and hotels

In dealing with business travel it may be necessary to arrange for passports to be supplied or renewed, obtain visas when necessary, book travel by air or sea, and make accommodation reservations. Itineraries will also be necessary for business people who travel. Enquiries about such matters are usually made in the first instance by telephone to a travel agent who will deal with most travel requirements on your behalf. Such arrangements need then only be confirmed in writing. This chapter looks at a variety of letters in connection with travel arrangements, including the essential document for business travellers, the itinerary.

PASSPORTS

A passport is a document of identification issued by the government of a country to ensure protection of its subjects who travel overseas. British subjects of the United Kingdom should obtain a passport application form from any main post office or large travel agent. The completed application form, together with relevant documentary evidence and fee, should be sent to any of the regional offices of the Passport Division of the Foreign Office: London, Liverpool, Peterborough, Glasgow, Newport or Belfast. Postal applications are normally processed within 3–5 weeks of receipt. If a passport is required urgently, a personal visit to a passport office can ensure processing within about 5 days. Standard passports are *valid*[1] for 10 years. New regulations mean that husband and wife passports are no longer issued; any children should be included on the passports of both parties. Full particulars regarding passports are issued with application forms.

23.1 Request for passport application form

> Dear Sir
>
> Early next year I intend to visit a number of countries in the Far East and Australasia. Please send me a passport application form and a list of the addresses to which applications for visas for the various countries should be sent.
>
> I have not previously held or applied for a passport of any description.
>
> Yours faithfully

23.2 Formal application for passport

> Dear Sir
>
> I have completed and enclose my application form for issue of a United Kingdom passport. Also enclosed are two passport photographs (one certified at the back), my birth certificate and a cheque for the passport fee.
>
> I propose to leave England on 15 January. Please ensure that my passport is prepared and sent to me in good time to enable me to obtain the necessary visas.
>
> Yours faithfully

[1] **valid** legally in order

VISAS

Visas are required for travel to many countries. Travel arrangements may be made through a travel agent, who will usually obtain any visa which is necessary. Alternatively, visas may be obtained upon application to the visa department of the high commissioners (for British Commonwealth countries) or consuls (in foreign countries) of the countries concerned. A list of their addresses can be obtained from any passport office.

Applications for visas must be returned with the appropriate fee and any documents requested. These may include the applicant's passport, photograph, vaccination or other health certificate, travel ticket and perhaps a statement from an employer or other sponsor guaranteeing the applicant's financial security during overseas visits.

23.3 Request for visa application form

Dear Sir

Our Sales Director, Mr Robert Dickson, proposes to visit Australia in 2 months' time on company business.

As I understand a visa is necessary, please send me the appropriate application form, together with details of your visa requirements.

Yours faithfully

23.4 Formal application for visa

Dear Sir/Madam

I enclose the completed application form for an entry visa to enable Mr Robert Dickson, Sales Director of this company, to visit Australia.

Mr Dickson will be leaving London on 5 August for a business tour of Singapore and Hong Kong. Subject to issue of the necessary visa, he proposes to fly to Perth, Western Australia, on 7 August. Thereafter he will be visiting Melbourne, Sydney and Cairns.

The purpose of Mr Dickson's visit to Australia is to gain information about recent developments in education there, with special reference to the use of our publications. He intends to visit departments of education, universities, commercial and technical colleges and other educational organisations as well as leading booksellers. This company guarantees Mr Dickson's financial security during his stay as well as payment of all expenses incurred.

The following supporting documents are enclosed:

1   Mr Dickson's passport.

2   A cheque for the visa fee.

3   A registered stamped addressed envelope for return of the passport.

4   A copy of the company's publications catalogue for your reference.

If you require any further information please do not hesitate to let me know.

Yours faithfully

TRAVEL BY AIR/SEA

There are two main types of airline customer – the business traveller and the holidaymaker. Business travellers usually make their arrangements at very short notice and as a rule make their *reservations*[2] direct with the airline, often by telephone. Holidaymakers usually employ travel agents to make their arrangements well in advance.

23.5 Enquiry concerning flights

(a) Request

In this fax the writer enquires with the Reservations Officer of British Airways regarding flights between London and New York.

> My company will be arranging a number of business trips to New York during the next 3 months.
>
> Please send me information concerning flights (outward and return) including departure times and cost of single and return fares.
>
> We are particularly interested in information relating to reduced fares.

(b) Reply

This reply is both courteous and helpful, giving confidence.

> Many thanks for your enquiry of 5 September.
>
> I enclose a timetable giving details of outward and return flights between London and New York together with a price list in which you will find details of both ordinary and discounted fares. As you will see from this list discounted fares can be as little as one-third of the normal fare.
>
> A visa is necessary for all visitors to the United States.
>
> If I can be of any further assistance please call me.

[2] **reservation** booking

23.6 Enquiry concerning car ferry

Car ferries are an alternative to flying to Europe. In this letter the writer requests details of car ferries from a well-known operator.

(a) Enquiry

Dear Sir/Madam

Later this year I propose to tour Western Europe with friends and I wish to take a car with me.

Please send me details of your car ferry service including your terms and conditions for transporting a Mercedes-Benz and three passengers from Dover to Calais.

As this would be my first use of the car ferry service I am not familiar with Customs and other formalities involved. I should be grateful for any information you can provide.

Yours faithfully

(b) Reply

Dear Mr Hanley

Thank you for your letter of 4 August requesting details of our car ferry service.

A brochure is enclosed giving all the information you require together with prices and a timetable.

Formalities for touring Europe by car are now simpler than ever before. All that is necessary is for you to check in at our Dover office one hour before departure time and to produce the following documents:

1 Your travel ticket

2 Your passport

3 Your car registration papers

4 A valid British driving licence

5 An international insurance 'green card'

Your car must carry a GB nationality plate.

If you require further details please contact me. Meanwhile I hope you enjoy travelling with British Car Ferries Ltd.

Yours sincerely

23.7 Enquiry concerning sea journey

In this letter the writer makes enquiries about travel on ocean liners.

(a) Enquiry

Dear Sir/Madam

I am interested in your sailings to New York during August or September this year. Please let me have any available literature giving information about the ships scheduled to sail during this period.

Please also let me have details of fares (single and return) for both first- and second-class travel.

I look forward to hearing from you soon.

Yours faithfully

(b) Reply

Dear Mrs Morrison

Thank you for your letter of 11 June enquiring about sailings to New York.

In the enclosed copy of our Queen Elizabeth 2 sailing list you will find details of sailings and of first-class and tourist fares including excursion fares in both classes.

A valid passport is necessary for all passengers, but an international certificate of vaccination is no longer necessary. All passengers other than United States citizens and holders of re-entry permits will also require a visa issued by a United States consul.

As the company's liability for baggage is limited under the terms of the passenger ticket, we strongly urge passengers to insure against all risks for the full period of their journey. I shall be glad to supply details on request.

Please let me know if I can be of further assistance.

Yours sincerely

(c) Reservation of berths

Dear Sir

Thank you for sending me information about the sailings of Queen Elizabeth 2.

Please make a reservation in my name for a first-class single cabin on 3 August sailing to New York. Full payment is enclosed.

I look forward to receiving confirmation of my reservation, together with travel ticket.

Yours faithfully

23.8 **Enquiry concerning holiday cruises**

In this letter the writer enquires about holiday cruises.

(a) Enquiry

> Dear Sir
>
> I am interested in learning more about 10–14-day holiday cruises offered by your organisation for this summer.
>
> Please let me have the relevant brochure as well as costs for tourist-class travel.
>
> Yours faithfully

(b) Reply

> Dear Mrs McFarlane
>
> Thank you for your enquiry of 10 February.
>
> I have pleasure in enclosing our illustrated brochure which contains full details of our summer cruises, as well as tourist-class fares. Also enclosed is a leaflet showing the accommodation available for the coming summer; as the booking position is constantly changing this leaflet can serve only as a broad guide to what we can offer.
>
> Please let me know if you require further information or help.
>
> Yours sincerely

HOTEL ACCOMMODATION

Most large hotels are organised as companies and enquiries should be addressed to The Manager. Private hotels are much smaller and enquiries should be addressed to The Proprietor, by whom they are usually owned and managed.

When requesting information about a prospective booking be sure to observe the following rules:

- Keep your letter short and to the point.
- State your requirements clearly and concisely. To avoid misunderstanding mention days as well as dates for which accommodation is required, as well as the exact period of your stay if it is known (eg 'from Monday 6 to Friday 10 July inclusive').
- State times of arrival and departure if known.
- Request confirmation of the booking if there is time.

23.9 Booking company accommodation at a hotel

In this enquiry a company writes to the Manager of a London hotel requesting information about accommodation.

(a) Enquiry

Dear Sir/Madam

My company will be displaying products at the forthcoming British Industrial Fair at Earls Court and we shall require hotel accommodation for several members of staff.

Please send me a copy of your current brochure and details of terms for half board.[3] Please also indicate if you have one double and three single rooms available from Monday 13 to Friday 17 May inclusive.

I hope to hear from you soon.

Yours faithfully

(b) Reply

Thank you — Dear Miss Johnson

Thank you for your letter of 15 March.

Enclose brochure — As requested I enclose a copy of our brochure in which you will find all the details required.

Repeat details of rooms and dates to avoid misunderstanding — We presently have one double and three single rooms available from Monday 13 to Friday 17 May inclusive. However as we are now entering the busy season and bookings for this period are likely to be heavy, we suggest that you make your reservation without delay.

Refer to advantages offered by the hotel – this will build up a cordial relationship and could lead to further business — You will see from our brochure that this is a modern hotel and I am sure your staff would be very comfortable here. We are well served by public transport to Earls Court, and it should be possible to reach there within 15 minutes.

I hope to receive confirmation of your reservation soon.

(c) Confirmation of reservation

In the first instance you would normally telephone the hotel to make your reservation. This would be confirmed in writing immediately.

Dear Mr Nelson

Thank you for your letter of 17 March and our telephone conversation today.

I confirm reservation of one double and three single en suite[4] rooms from 13–17 May inclusive, with half-board. Names of guests are:

Mr & Mrs Philip Andersen
Mr Geoffrey Richardson
Miss Lesley Nunn
Mr Jonathan Denby

The account will be settled by Mr Philip Andersen, our Company's General Manager.

Yours sincerely

[3] **half board** breakfast and evening meal only
[4] **en suite** with attached bathroom

23.10 Booking private accommodation

(a) Enquiry

Dear Sir/Madam

I shall be passing through London next week and would like to reserve a single room for Wednesday and Thursday 18 and 19 October.

My previous stays at the Norfolk Hotel have always been very enjoyable; I particularly like the rooms overlooking the gardens. If one of these rooms is available I hope you will reserve it for me.

I expect to arrive at the hotel in time for lunch on the 18th and shall be leaving immediately after breakfast on the 20th.

Yours faithfully

(b) Reply

Dear Mr Robinson

Thank you for your letter of 10 October.

I was glad to learn that you have enjoyed your previous visits to the Norfolk Hotel. Unfortunately a room overlooking the garden is not available for the dates you requested. However I have several pleasant rooms on the south side of the hotel, away from traffic noise and with an open view of the nearby park and lake.

The charge for these rooms is £85 per night. You will find all details in the enclosed brochure.

I have provisionally reserved for you one of the rooms mentioned for the 2 nights of Wednesday and Thursday 18 and 19 October.

Please let me have your confirmation soon.

Yours sincerely

23.11 Booking private accommodation overseas

The writer here writes to a hotel overseas mentioning that the hotel has been recommended by a friend.

(a) Enquiry

Dear Sir/Madam

Your hotel has been highly recommended by a friend who stayed there last year.

I will be arriving in Singapore at 1730 hours on Monday 15 April on flight SQ24, accompanied by 3 friends. We wish to stay in Singapore for 4 nights, ie 15–18 April inclusive before arranging independent travel by land in Malaysia.

Please let me know if 2 twin-bedded rooms are available for this period, and what the charges would be. I also understand that your hotel arranges local tours; full details would be appreciated.

I hope to hear from you soon.

Yours faithfully

(b) Reply

In this reply, the Reservations Officer takes the trouble to point out the benefits in the hotel's position and additions since the enquirer's friend visited.

Dear Mr Hill

I am pleased to learn from your letter of 2 February that The Lion Hotel was recommended to you.

A copy of our illustrated brochure is enclosed showing the hotel's many facilities. You will note the recent improvements made to our pool area, with adjoining gym and leisure facilities.

Our hotel's tour operator is Century Tours and a brochure is attached giving details of their half- and full-day tours. There would be no problem in reserving places on any of these tours when you arrive in Singapore.

I have taken the liberty of making a provisional reservation of 2 twin-bedded rooms from 15–18 April at a cost of S$120 per night. This reservation will be held until 1 March and your confirmation would be appreciated before that date.

Arrangements can be made for our courtesy pick-up service to meet your flight SQ24 at 1730 on 15 April if you mention this at the time of confirming your reservation.

You will find The Lion Hotel very convenient for transport both by MRT (Mass Rapid Transport) and bus. It is also within 5 minutes walking distance of Orchard Road.

I look forward to extending the hospitality of The Lion Hotel to your party and hope to receive confirmation of your reservation before 1 March.

Yours sincerely

HOLIDAY ACCOMMODATION AND ITINERARIES

Information about hotels, guest houses and holiday flats may be obtained from the annual holiday guides prepared by the publicity departments of the holiday resorts. These guides contain details of the resort's attractions – places of interest, entertainments, sport, museums, art galleries and cultural activities. Copies are sent on request usually free of charge.

23.12 Request for holiday guide

Requests for guides need only be very short and formal and unless a payment is required may be made on a postcard. Copies of the guide are usually sent out with a compliments slip instead of a formal letter.

Dear Sirs

Please send me a copy of your official holiday guide and a list of hotels and guest houses.

I enclose a large stamped addressed envelope.

Yours faithfully

23.13 Enquiry for hotel accommodation

(a) Enquiry

Dear Sir/Madam

Introduction mentions background details — I found the name of your private hotel in the holiday guide received from the Bridlington Information Centre.

Mention rooms and dates, and mention specific requirements — Please let me know if you have accommodation for a family of 5 for 2 weeks commencing Saturday 10 August. We shall require 2 twin-bedded rooms and 1 single room – the single room should be on the ground floor or near to the lift as it is for my elderly mother.

Ask for confirmation and further details — If you can provide this accommodation please send me a copy of your brochure and also your terms for full board.[5]

Yours faithfully

(b) Reply

Dear Mr Leeson

Thank you — Thank you for your enquiry dated 15 April.

Confirm rooms are available and repeat dates. Respond to special request — I am pleased to say that the accommodation you require is available for the 2 weeks commencing Saturday 10 August. We can offer you two adjacent[6] twin-bedded rooms on the first floor, with a single room on the same floor conveniently located about 10 metres from the lift. Should this distance present a problem we can place a wheelchair at your disposal.

State why early confirmation is necessary — Early confirmation of this accommodation is necessary as bookings for August are always heavy and I should not wish you to be disappointed.

Enclose brochure and close with a personal touch — A brochure containing details of our charges is enclosed. We hope you will give us the opportunity to welcome your family to the Northcliffe.

Yours sincerely

[5] **full board** including all meals
[6] **adjacent** adjoining

23.14 Enquiry to a small private hotel

(a) Enquiry

Dear Sir/Madam

Your hotel has been recommended to me by Mr & Mrs John Windsor who tell me they spent a very happy fortnight with you last summer.

I am planning to bring my family to St Annes for 2 weeks between mid-July and the end of August, and hope you will be able to accommodate us. We need one double and one twin-bedded room for my wife and myself and our two young children.

Our holiday arrangements are fairly flexible and any 2 consecutive[7] weeks within the period mentioned would be suitable.

An early reply would be appreciated so that our holiday arrangements can be completed as soon as possible.

Yours faithfully

(b) Reply

Dear Mr Wilkinson

Thank you for your letter of 10 April. I remember Mr & Mrs Windsor very well; please pass on my thanks for their recommendation.

We are already fully booked for the month of August but the flexibility of your arrangements enables us to offer you one double and one twin-bedded room for 2 full weeks from Saturday 18 July.

We are provisionally[8] reserving this accommodation for you, but would appreciate your written confirmation within one week.

Our current brochure is enclosed for your information.

We look forward to welcoming you to St Annes and assure you that everything possible will be done to make your stay here a very happy one.

Yours sincerely

23.15 Enquiry to the proprietor of holiday flats

(a) Enquiry

Dear Sir/Madam

We wish to arrange a family holiday for 2 weeks from Saturday 14 August. Please let me know whether you have accommodation available which would be suitable for my husband and myself, as well as our two teenage children. We also wish to bring our dog, a clean and well-trained Irish Setter.

If you are able to accommodate us during this period, please let me know the facilities available in your holiday flats, together with your charges.

Yours faithfully

[7] **consecutive** running together
[8] **provisionally** subject to confirmation

(b) Reply

Dear Mrs Turner

Thank you for your recent enquiry regarding holiday accommodation for your family for 2 weeks from Saturday 14 August.

I am pleased to say that we have a holiday flat available which would be suitable for your family. This flat is on the first floor and comprises one double and two bunk beds, as well as cooker, fridge, sink, wardrobes and bedside drawers.

We do allow dogs in our holiday flats and refer you to the rules contained in our enclosed brochure. Schedules of prices are also shown on the separate leaflet.

We hope to welcome you to Thornton Holiday Flats and advise you to make an early reservation.

Yours sincerely

23.16 Itineraries

An itinerary gives full details of a journey in order of date. It shows all travel arrangements, accommodation and appointments. It is usual to use sub-headings and columns so that the information is displayed attractively and is easy to refer to.

Use plain paper but show the company's name

Include traveller's name, places being visited and duration of trip

© **Turner Communications**

ITINERARY FOR MRS SALLY TURNER

TOUR OF SINGAPORE AND MALAYSIA
7–19 JULY 200—

SUNDAY 7 JULY

1530	Depart London Heathrow (flight SQ101)

Display all dates as shoulder headings

MONDAY 8 JULY

1830	Arrive Singapore Changi Airport (Met by Christine Winters, Communications Asia) Accommodation: Supreme International Hotel, Scotts Road.

TUESDAY 9 JULY

Use a 2- or 3-column format for ease of reference

1030	Miss Joy Chan, Communications Asia, Funan Centre
1430	Mr Andre Misso, TalkTime, Bugis Junction

WEDNESDAY 10 JULY

0930–1730	5th International Telecommunications Conference

SUNDAY 14 JULY

Use 24-hour clock for all times

1545	Depart Singapore Changi Airport Terminal 2 (flight MH989)
1700	Arrive Kuala Lumpur Accommodation: Royal Hotel, Petaling Jaya

MONDAY 15 JULY

1030	Mr Keith Walker, KL Talk
1530	Mrs Ong Lee Fong, Malaysia Communications

TUESDAY 16 JULY

1130	Miss Sylvia Koh, Talklines

FRIDAY 19 JULY

2330	Depart Kuala Lumpur (BA 012)

SATURDAY 20 JULY

0830	Arrive London Heathrow

ST/BT
15 June 200—

USEFUL EXPRESSIONS

Openings

1 I wish to visit … and would be pleased to know if you have a single room available on …

2 I should be grateful if you would forward a copy of your current brochure.

3 Please let me know if you have available a first-class single cabin on the … leaving for … on …

4 I was pleased to hear that our hotel was recommended by … after his visit in …

Closes

1 When replying please include a copy of your current brochure.

2 I hope to receive an early reply.

3 I look forward to hearing that you can provide this accommodation.

4 As we wish to make arrangements in good time I should appreciate an early reply.

Secretarial and administrative correspondence

1
2
3
4
5
6
7
8
9
10
11
12
13
14
15
16
17
18
19
20
21
22
23
24
25
26
27
28
29
30

In any company internal communication plays an important role. The Secretary or PA, sometimes now referred to as the Administrative Assistant, often sends letters, faxes and e-mails. Much of this correspondence related to arranging appointments, meetings, interviews, conferences and other functions.

In this chapter we will look at some of the correspondence that is typically dealt with by today's secretarial or administrative support staff.

For my top tips for the Super Secretary, check out:

www.shirleytaylor.com/learninglinks.html

ARRANGING FUNCTIONS

24.1 Letter requesting appointment

(a) Request 1

Dear Mr Harrison

Our Mr Chapman has informed me that you have returned home from your visit to the Middle East. There are a number of points that have arisen on the book I am writing on <u>Modern Business Organisation.</u> I should like the opportunity to discuss these with you.

I shall be in London from 16 to 19 September and will telephone you on Monday 15 September to arrange a day and time which would be convenient for us to meet.

I look forward to the opportunity of meeting you again.

(b) Reply

Dear Mr Alexander

Thank you for your letter regarding <u>Modern Business Organisation</u>.

I will look forward to meeting you again to discuss this. I note you will be telephoning me on Monday morning and hope that it will be possible to arrange to meet on either Tuesday or Wednesday afternoon.

I look forward to meeting you again.

(c) Request 2

Dear Mr Jones

I am very concerned about the difficulties you are having with the goods we supplied earlier this year.

I should very much like the opportunity to discuss this matter with you personally and wonder whether it would be convenient to see you while I am in your area next month. My secretary will telephone you soon to make a convenient appointment.

(d) Request 3

Dear Mrs Graham

I should very much like to see you to discuss various matters of mutual interest. As I shall be in Bradford next week, I wonder if it will be convenient to meet you on Thursday 12 September.

My secretary will call you within the next few days to confirm this appointment or if necessary arrange an alternative appointment.

I look forward to seeing you.

24.2 Letter inviting speaker to conference

(a) Invitation

Dear Miss Forrester

Mention function, location, dates, number of delegates expected — Our Society will be holding a conference at the Moat House Hotel, Swansea from 4 to 6 October the theme of which will be 'Changes in the Role of the Secretary'. Approximately 100 delegates are expected, comprising mostly practising secretaries as well as some lecturer members.

Include title of talk and timing. Mention any payments which will be made — We would be delighted if, once again, you would accept our invitation to speak on the subject of 'Effective Communication' on 5 October from 1030 to 1130. We would of course be prepared to pay you the usual fee of £100 and your travel expenses.

Enclose detailed programme. Mention overnight accommodation — A copy of the detailed draft programme is enclosed. You will of course, be welcome to attend other sessions of the conference on that day. Overnight accommodation will be provided for you on 4 October.

Request confirmation and details of any equipment needed — We look forward to hearing that you can accept our invitation. At the same time please let us know if you will need any visual aids or other equipment.

Yours sincerely

(b) Programme

CHANGES IN THE ROLE OF THE SECRETARY

DRAFT PROGRAMME

DAY ONE – MONDAY 4 OCTOBER 2004

0800	**Registration and morning coffee**
0900	Chairman's opening remarks (Hayati Abdulla, Core Services)
0915	The new secretary (Sally Turner, Author)
1030	Refreshments
1100	Business writing skills (Janice Lim, STTC Training Consultancy)
1230	Lunch
1400	Working with different cultures (Nigel Lau, StaSearch International)
1530	Refreshments
1600	Convincing presentation skills (Ricky Lien, Mindset Media)
1715	End of Day One

DAY TWO – TUESDAY 5 OCTOBER 2004

0800	Morning coffee
0900	Chairman's opening remarks (Janice Lim, STTC Training Consultancy)
0915	IT and the new economy (Sarah Cowles, D&P International)
1000	Refreshments
1030	Effective communication (Pamela Forrester)
1130	Lunch and fashion show
1400	Effective time management (Ian Norton, Leighton Industries)
1515	Refreshments
1545	Projecting the right image (Louisa Chan, C&G Fashion House)
1630	How to be a super secretary (Sally Turner, Author)
1715	End of Day Two

(c) Reply

Dear Ms Bolan

Thank you — Thank you for your letter inviting me to speak at your conference on 5 October on the subject of 'Effective Communication'.

Acceptance and confirmation — I am delighted to accept your invitation, and confirm that I shall require overnight accommodation on 4 October.

Mention any equipment needed — I will require use of an overhead projector for my presentation and hope this can be made available.

The close includes a personal touch — I look forward to meeting you and other members of your Society again at your conference and wish you every success.

Yours sincerely

(d) Letter declining invitation

Dear Mr Woodhead

I was very pleased to receive your letter of 2 July.

Much as I should like to be able to speak at your conference in October, I am sorry to say that I will be unable to do so as I shall be abroad at the time. I must therefore regretfully decline your kind invitation.

I do hope that the day will be a great success.

Yours sincerely

24.3 Letter regarding conference accommodation

Dear Sir

Our company will be holding a one-day conference on Saturday 18 May from 1000 to 1730, and we are looking for suitable accommodation.

About 200 delegates are expected to attend and our requirements are as follows:

1 A suitable conference room with theatre-style seating

2 A small adjacent room for the display of equipment and accessories

3 A reception area for welcoming and registering delegates

4 Morning coffee at 1130 and afternoon tea at 1530

5 A buffet luncheon to be served from 1300 to 1400

If you have suitable facilities available please let us know the costs involved. At the same time please send specimen menus for a buffet-style luncheon.

We hope to hear from you soon.

Yours faithfully

Margin annotations:
- Mention function, date, timing and reason for writing
- Include number of delegates expected
- Number and list the specific requirements
- Ask for information about facilities and costs

24.4 Conference programme

Company's name

Main heading

Date and venue

Sub-heading states whether programme is provisional or final

Use 24-hour clock, with or without the word 'hours'

List each item in turn with any extra details

Include names of presenters in brackets

Clarify the time at which the event will finish

© **Turner Communications**

5TH ANNIVERSARY CELEBRATIONS

to be held on Wednesday 17 September 200—
at Supreme Hotel, Aston, Sheffield

PROVISIONAL PROGRAMME

1800	Arrival of Directors and staff
1830	Arrival of guests 5th Anniversary folders will be issued to guests on arrival Cocktails will be served
1900	Introduction by Suzanne Sutcliffe, Marketing Manager who will act as Master of Ceremonies
1915	Opening address (Sally Turner, Managing Director)
1930	Slide presentation (Mandy Lim, Administration Manager)
2000	Buffet supper
2130	Toastmaster (John Stevens, Public Relations Manager)
2145	Closing address (Suzanne Sutcliffe, Marketing Manager) Drinks will be served until 2300

SS/ST
5 July 200—

For some good websites for secretaries, check out:

www.deskdemon.com

www.executaryinternational.co.uk

www.pa-assist.com

24.5 E-mail regarding board meeting

Dear All

I confirm that there will be a board meeting on Monday 5 April 2004.

The scheduled board meeting dates for the remainder of 2004 are:

Wednesday 5 May
Wednesday 7 July
Wednesday 1 September
Wednesday 3 November

All meetings will start at 10.30 am and will be held in the board room in Atrium Towers. Lunch will follow the meetings, hosted by the Chairman, Mr Graham Newman.

Please inform your directors of these arrangements.

Mary

24.6 E-mail regarding diary dates

(a) Suggesting dates

Good morning Ladies

The Chairman has decided to hold an extra board meeting in August to discuss urgent issues. The suggested dates are:

Tuesday 10 August
Thursday 12 August
Friday 13 August

Timing: Between 11 am and 2 pm or 2 pm and 5 pm

Please let me know if your director is available.

An urgent response will be appreciated.

Joy

 TIP Don't neglect the common courtesies of a greetng and sign-off, just for the sake of speed.

(b) Reply

Hi Joy

The Finance Director will be available on Thursday 12 or Friday 13 August.
His diary is free all day on both these dates.

Please let me have confirmation of the exact date for this extra board meeting
soon.

Thanks
Sandra

For some good websites from secterarial organisations, check out:

International Association of Administrative Professionals (USA)
www.iaap-hq.org

Institute of Qualified Private Secretaries (UK)
www.iqps.org

Australian Institute of Office Professionals
www.aiop.com.au

Association of Medical Secretaries, Practice Managers, Administrators and
Receptionists (UK)
www.amspar.co.uk

Singapore Association of Professional and Executive Secretaries
www.sapes.org.sg

INVITATIONS

Many companies organise special functions to publicise certain events, for example

- the opening of a new branch office
- the introduction of new products or services
- the retirement of a senior executive
- a special anniversary.

Formal invitations are usually printed on A5 or A6 high quality paper or card.

24.7 ## (a) Formal invitation

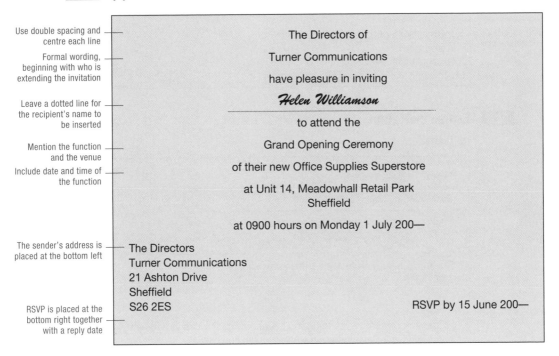

Use double spacing and centre each line ——

Formal wording, beginning with who is extending the invitation ——

Leave a dotted line for the recipient's name to be inserted ——

Mention the function and the venue ——

Include date and time of the function ——

The sender's address is placed at the bottom left ——

RSVP is placed at the bottom right together with a reply date ——

The Directors of

Turner Communications

have pleasure in inviting

Helen Williamson
....

to attend the

Grand Opening Ceremony

of their new Office Supplies Superstore

at Unit 14, Meadowhall Retail Park
Sheffield

at 0900 hours on Monday 1 July 200—

The Directors
Turner Communications
21 Ashton Drive
Sheffield
S26 2ES   RSVP by 15 June 200—

REPLIES TO INVITATIONS

When accepting or refusing an invitation it is usual to do so in a similar style to the invitation which was received. If the invitation is refused it is courteous to give a reason.

24.8 ## Reply to formal invitation

Use a similar formal
style, in double spacing

Use third person and
formal wording

Include all relevant
details from original
invitation

A formal acceptance

The sender's address is
included at the bottom
left and the date at the
right

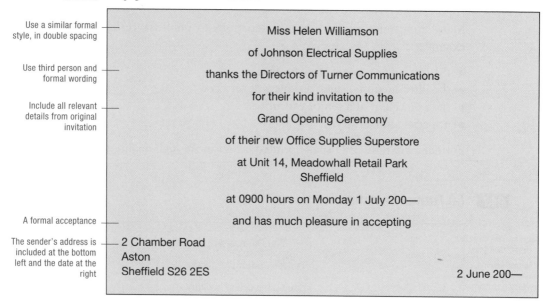

Miss Helen Williamson

of Johnson Electrical Supplies

thanks the Directors of Turner Communications

for their kind invitation to the

Grand Opening Ceremony

of their new Office Supplies Superstore

at Unit 14, Meadowhall Retail Park
Sheffield

at 0900 hours on Monday 1 July 200—

and has much pleasure in accepting

2 Chamber Road
Aston
Sheffield S26 2ES

2 June 200—

24.9 ## E-mail invitation

(a) Invitation

From	sallyturner@marshalls.com.id
Date	2:7:03 16:06:29
To	shirley@shirleytaylor.com
CC	
Subject	Invitation to 10th anniversary dinner

Hi Shirley

I hope you remember meeting me in Jakarta earlier this year when you conducted a 2-day workshop for Marshalls employees.

I was interested to see from your e-newsletter that you will be in Jakarta next month conducting some more workshops. My company will be celebrating its 10th anniversary by holding a dinner at the Aryaduta Hotel on Wednesday 29 August.

It would be great if you could join us at our special celebration. Please let me know as soon as possible so that I can add your name to our VIP list.

Best wishes
Sally Turner
HR Manager
Marshalls Indonesia Sdn Bhd
Telephone: 6782 3742

(b) Reply to e-mail invitation accepting

From	shirley@shirleytaylor.com
Date	3:7:03 17:02:45
To	sallyturner@marshalls.com.id
CC	
Subject	Re: Invitation to 10th anniversary dinner

Hi Sally

Of course I remember meeting you. I really enjoyed my workshop at Marshalls and hope you have seen your photographs in the Photo Gallery on my website.

Thank you so much for your kind invitation to join you at your company's 10th anniversary dinner on Wednesday 29 August. I should normally be flying into Jakarta that evening for some public workshops later that week. However I am going to change my travel plans and fly in one day early so that I can accept your invitation.

I will certainly look forward to seeing you and your colleagues again.

Shirley
http://www.shirleytaylor.com/
Mobile: +65 96355907

(c) Reply to e-mail invitation declining

From	shirley@shirleytaylor.com
Date	3:7:03 17:02:45
To	sallyturner@marshalls.com.id
CC	
Subject	Re: Invitation to 10th anniversary dinner

Hi Sally

Of course I remember meeting you. I really enjoyed my workshop at Marshalls and hope you have seen your photographs in the Photo Gallery on my website.

Thank you so much for your kind invitation to join you at your company's 10th anniversary dinner on Wednesday 29 August. However, I shall only be in Jakarta from Sunday 26th for one night – I have to fly back to Singapore straight after my one-day workshop on the 27th due to commitments in Singapore later that week.

I am so sorry that I cannot join you on what will, I know, be a wonderful evening. Please pass on my apologies to all my friends at Marshalls.

I hope to see you again when I am back in Jakarta for a longer trip.

Best wishes

Shirley
http://www.shirleytaylor.com/
Mobile: +65 96355907

Here is an invitation sent out to invite clients to a special afternoon presentation.

24.10

Invitation to Rendezvous with Shirley

How would you like to transform your business writing style in just 5 simple steps? Learn modern terminology instead of yesterday's jargon? Overcome common problems in today's business writing? Learn the art of writing as you speak?

Imagine all this in just 2 hours!

What's more amazing is that it will cost you nothing except your time. If that's not good enough for you, we will even give you a free book – Shirley Taylor's *Model Business Letters*.

Rendezvous is our way of getting great minds to converge in a pleasant setting. Hopefully we will all learn a thing or two as well, and best of all we can network with peers in an afternoon of learning fun.

Event	Workshop and tea reception
Topic	Make writing your most powerful tool
Venue	Room 1, STTC Training Centre, Wisma Atrium
Date	Friday 26 March 2004
Time	3 to 5 pm

Please secure your place at our Rendezvous early by calling me on 6532341.

See you at Rendezvous.

Unit 4

Classified business letters

Agencies

Many businesses with a large volume of foreign trade do their own buying and selling. A large manufacturing business, for instance, will often have its own export department and if the volume of trade is sufficient may establish branches abroad. However there are many smaller firms which find it more economical to buy and sell through commission agents or commission houses, factors, brokers and other types of agent.

Any company considering appointing an agent should make a thorough investigation into such prospective agent's qualifications, experience and personal qualities beforehand, for example:

- their reliability and financial soundness
- their technical ability to handle the goods to be marketed
- their market connections and the effectiveness of their sales organisation
- the nature and extent of other agencies they hold and in particular whether these are connected with the sale of competing products.

These matters are especially important when foreign agents are appointed, since they will be working without local supervision or control. It is advisable to make a formal appointment of an agent in writing, setting out in detail the terms of the agency.

FINDING AN AGENT

There are useful sources of information for those who want help in finding suitable agents. A British supplier, for instance, wishing to develop trade in an overseas country could make use of one or more of the following:

- the Export Services Division or the appropriate Regional Office of the Department of Trade
- the Consular Section of the appropriate Embassy
- HM Trade Commissioner in the country concerned
- the Chamber of Commerce
- banks
- an advertisement in selected journals in the country concerned.

APPLICATIONS FOR AGENCIES

When seeking an agency the applicant will stress two things:

- the opportunities in the market waiting to be developed
- the particular advantages that may be offered.

The applicant will mention such selling points as knowledge of the market, numerous connections, long-established position and wide experience, the efficiency of their sales organisation, the facilities for display offered by their showrooms and so on. The agent may also give the names of persons or firms who may be referred to and mention the rate of commission expected.

25.1 Application for home agency

(a) Application

Introduction

Background details about why you are writing

Details of experience, staff, facilities

The letter leads logically to a statement of what you want. Suggest a meeting

The close offers references

Dear Sir/Madam

We understand from Knowles Hardware Ltd of Glasgow that you are looking for a reliable firm with good connections in the textile trade to represent you in Scotland.

For some years we have acted as Scottish agents for one of your competitors, Jarvis & Sons of Preston. They have recently registered as a limited company and in the reorganisation decided to establish their own branch in Edinburgh. As they no longer need our services we are now free to offer them to you.

As we have had experience in marketing products similar to your own, we are familiar with customers' needs, and are confident that we could develop a good market for you in Scotland. We have spacious and well-equipped showrooms not only at our Glasgow headquarters but also in Edinburgh and Perth, plus many experienced sales representatives who would energetically promote your business.

We hope you will be interested in our proposal and will let us know on what terms you would be willing to conclude an agreement. I will be visiting your town in 2 weeks' time and hope it will be possible to discuss details with you then.

We can provide first-class references if required, but for general information concerning our standing in the trade we suggest you refer to Knowles Hardware Ltd.

We hope to hear from you soon.

Yours faithfully

(b) Reply

Dear Mrs Matthews

Thank you for your letter of 10 September. We are very interested to discuss further your proposal for an agency in Scotland.

Your work with Jarvis & Co is well known to us and in view of your connections throughout the trade in Scotland we feel there is much you could do to extend our business there.

Our final decision would depend upon the terms and conditions. As you will be visiting our town soon it would be better to discuss these in person rather than to enter upon what may become lengthy correspondence.

Please give me a call on 2684632 to discuss a convenient time to talk.

Yours sincerely

(c) Agency appointed

Dear Mrs Matthews

Refer to meeting and offer the appointment on the terms discussed — It was a pleasure to meet you yesterday. We are now pleased to offer you an appointment as our sole agents for Scotland on the terms and conditions agreed verbally with you.

Give full details of period and commission — This appointment will be for a trial period of 12 months initially. We will pay you a commission of 7% on the net value of all sales against orders received through you, to which would be added a del credere[1] commission of 2½%.

Further details regarding stocks or samples — As we are able to facilitate quick delivery there will be no need for you to maintain stocks of our goods, but we will send you full ranges of samples for display in your showrooms.

Refer to the need for a formal agreement — Please confirm these terms in writing as soon as possible, after which we will arrange for a formal agreement to be drawn up. When this is signed a circular will be prepared for distribution to our customers in Scotland announcing your appointment as our agents.

An encouraging close — We look forward to a successful business relationship.

Yours sincerely

25.2 Application for overseas agency

(a) Electrical engineering

Dear Sir/Madam

Introduction stating why you are writing — I was interested to see your advertisement in *The Daily Telegraph* and wish to offer my services as representative of your company in Morocco.

Background details about your company — I am 35 years old, a chartered electrical engineer, and have a good working knowledge of Spanish and German. For the past 5 years I have acted in Egypt as agent for Moxon & Parkinson, electrical engineers in Warrington, Cheshire. This company has recently been taken over by Digital Equipment Ltd and is now being represented in Egypt by its own representative.

Further details of your experience and abilities — I have been concerned with work in the electronic field[2] since I graduated in physics at Manchester University at the age of 22. During my agency with Moxons I also had first-hand experience of marketing electronic and microprocessing equipment.[3] I feel I am well able to promote the sale of your products in the expanding economies of the African countries.

References — For references I suggest you contact Moxon & Parkinson, as well as the 2 companies named below, both of which I have had close business connections for several years:

Fylde Electronic Laboratories Ltd, 4 Blackpool Road, Preston, Lancs

Suggest a personal interview to discuss further — Sexton Electronic Laboratories Ltd, 25 Deansgate, Manchester

I look forward to being able to give you more information at a personal interview.

Yours faithfully

---

[1] *del credere* **commission** amount paid to an agent who guarantees payment (a *del credere* agent)
[2] **electronic field** the area of electronics
[3] **microprocessing equipment** electronic equipment such as computers which have been greatly reduced in size

(b) Textiles (from an agent abroad)

Dear Sir/Madam

We would like to offer our services as agents for the sale of your products in New Zealand.

Our company was established in 1906 and we are known throughout the trade as agents of the highest standing. We are already represented in several West European countries including France, Germany and Italy.

There is a growing demand in New Zealand for British textiles especially for fancy worsted suitings and printed cotton and lycra fabrics. The prospects for good quality fabrics at competitive prices are very good. According to a recent Chamber of Commerce survey the demand for British textiles is likely to grow considerably during the next 2 or 3 years.

If you would send us details of your ranges with samples and prices, we could inform you of their suitability for the New Zealand market and also indicate the patterns and qualities for which sales are likely to be good. We would then arrange to call on our customers with your collection.

You will naturally wish to have references and may write to Barclays Bank Ltd, 99 Piccadilly, Manchester, or to any of our customers, whose names we will be glad to send you on request.

We feel sure we should have no difficulty in arranging terms to suit us both, and look forward to hearing from you soon.

Yours faithfully

25.3 Application for sole agency

(a) Importer's application

Dear Sir/Madam

We recently attended the International Photographic Exhibition in Cairo and were impressed by the high quality, attractive design and reasonable prices of your cameras. Having since seen your full catalogue, we are convinced that there is a promising market for your products here in Jordan.

If you are not already represented here we should be interested in acting as your sole agents.

As leading importers and distributors of more than 20 years' standing in the photographic trade, we have a good knowledge of the Jordanian market. Through our sales organisation we have good contacts with the leading retailers.

We handle several other agencies in non-competing lines and if our proposal interests you we can supply first-class references from manufacturers in Britain.

We firmly believe that an agency for marketing your products in Jordan would be of considerable benefit to both of us and we look forward to learning that you are interested in our proposal.

Mr Semir Haddad, our Purchasing Director, will be in England during May and will be pleased to call on you if we hear from you positively.

Yours faithfully

(b) Manufacturer's reply

Dear Mr Jamal

Thank you for your letter of 18 March and for your comments on our cameras.

We are still a young company but are expanding rapidly. At present our overseas representation is confined to countries in Western Europe where our cameras are selling well. However we are interested in the chance of developing our trade further afield.

When your Mr Semir Haddad is in England we should certainly like to meet him to discuss your proposal further. If Mr Haddad will get in touch with me to arrange a meeting, I can also arrange for him to look around our factory and see for himself the quality of the materials and workmanship put into our cameras.

Yours sincerely

25.4 Offer to act as *del credere* agent

In addition to the normal duties sometimes an agent will be held personally liable for goods sold for the principal should the buyer fail to pay. Such agents are known as *del credere* agents and are entitled to an extra commission for undertaking this additional risk.

(a) Offer

Dear Sir/Madam

The demand for toiletries in the United Arab Emirates has shown a marked increase in recent years. We are convinced that there is a considerable market here for your products.

There is every sign that an advertising campaign, even on a modest scale, would produce very good results if backed by an efficient system of distribution.

We are well-known distributors of over 15 years' standing with branches in most of the principal towns. With knowledge of the local conditions we feel we have the experience and the resources necessary to bring about a market development of your trade in this country. Reference to the Embassy of the United Arab Emirates and to Middle East Services and Sales Limited would enable you to verify our statements.

If you were to appoint us as your agents we should be prepared to discuss the rate of commission. However as the early work on development would be heavy we feel that 10% on orders placed during the first 12 months would be a reasonable figure. As the market would be new to you and customers largely unknown we would be quite willing to act on a del credere basis in return for an extra commission of 2½% to cover the additional risk.

We hope you will see a worthwhile opportunity in our proposal, and look forward to your early decision.

Yours faithfully

(b) Reply

Dear

We are interested in your proposals of 8 July and are favourably impressed by your views. However we are concerned that even a modest advertising campaign may not be worthwhile. We therefore suggest that we first test the market by sending you a representative selection of our products for sale on our account.

In the absence of advertising we realise that you would not have an easy task, but the experience gained would provide a valuable guide to future prospects. If the arrangement was successful we would consider your suggestion for a continuing agency.

If you are willing to receive a trial consignment we will allow commission at 12½% cent, with an additional 2½% del credere commission, expenses and commission to be set against your monthly payments.

Please let us know soon if this arrangement is satisfactory to you.

Yours sincerely

25.5 Offer to act as buying agents for importer

Dear Sir/Madam

Introduction gives background details — We understand from our neighbours, Firma Karl Brandt, that you have conducted your past buying of hardware in the German market through Firma Neymeyer and Schmidt of Bremen, and that in view of the collapse of their business you now require a reliable agent to take their place.

Introduce yourself and offer your services — We are well known to manufacturers of hardware in this country and believe we have the experience and connections necessary to meet your needs. We therefore would like to offer our services as your buying agents in Germany.

Give further details of your experience and service — Before transferring our business to Germany we had many years in the English trade. Knowing the particular needs of the English market, we can promise you unrivalled service[4] in matters of prices, discounts and freights.

As Firma Brandt have promised to write to you with a recommendation, we would like to summarise the terms we should be willing to accept if we acted for you:

Separate numbered points ensure clarity —
1 We would have complete freedom in placing your orders.
2 All purchases would be made on your behalf and in your name.
3 All accounts would be passed to you for settlement direct with suppliers.
4 Commission at 5% payable quarterly would be allowed us on cif values[5] of all shipments.
5 You would have full benefit of the very favourable terms we have arranged with the shipping companies and of any special rates we may obtain for insurance.

An encouraging close — We hope you will accept our offer and look forward to receiving your decision very soon.

Yours faithfully

[4] **unrivalled service** service which cannot be equalled
[5] **cif values** values covering cost, insurance and freight

25.6 Manufacturer's confirmation of agency terms

Drafting a formal agreement is a matter which calls for great care. It can be very time-consuming, especially if any terms are disputed when drafting is completed. The terms and conditions to be included must, therefore, be clearly agreed by the parties before the agreement is drafted. A precaution similar to that illustrated in the following letter is one to be recommended. The legal touches can be added at the time of drafting.

Dear Sirs

Refer to fax and meeting with the representative — We were pleased to learn from your fax of 14 November that you are willing to accept an agency for marketing our goods in Saudi Arabia. Set out below are the terms discussed and agreed with your Mr Williams when he called here earlier this month, but before drafting the formal agreement we should like you to confirm them.

1   The agency will operate as from 1 January 200— for a period of 3 years, subject to renewal.

2   The agency will be a sole agency for marketing our goods in Saudi Arabia.

List the terms clearly and simply — 3   No sales of competing products will be made in Saudi Arabia either on your own account or on account of any other firm or company.

4   All customers' orders will be transmitted to us immediately for supply direct.

5   Credit terms will not be given or promised to any customer without our <u>express consent</u>.[6]

6   All goods supplied will be invoiced by us direct to customers with copies to you.

7   A commission of 5% based on <u>fob values</u>[7] of all goods shipped to Saudi Arabia, whether on orders placed through you or not, will be payable at the end of each quarter.

8   A special <u>del credere</u> commission of 2½% will be added.

9   Customers will be required to settle their accounts with us direct. A statement will be sent to you at the end of each month of all payments received by us.

10   All questions of difference arising under our agreement will be referred to arbitration.

Request confirmation — Please confirm your agreement to these terms. A formal agreement will then be drafted and copies sent for your signature.

Yours faithfully

---

[6] **express consent** permission clearly stated
[7] **fob values** values cover cost of placing goods on board ship

OFFERS OF AGENCIES

Sometimes a person seeking an agent will take the first step and make an offer to some person already known or recommended. Like the applicant seeking an agency, reference will be made to the market waiting to be developed but concentration will rest on the special merits of the product in the efforts to persuade a correspondent to handle it. It is important to convince the prospective agent that the product is bound to sell well because of its exceptional quality, its particular uses, its novelty, its moderate price, etc, and because of the publicity with which it will be supported.

When offering an agency it is not possible to include all the details but enough information must be given to enable the correspondent to assess the worth of the offer. Failure to include essential basic information will result in unnecessary correspondence.

25.7 Offer of a provincial agency

(a) Offer

Dear Sirs

We have recently received a number of enquiries from dealers in the North of England for information about our range of haberdashery.[8] This leads us to believe there is a promising market waiting to be developed in that part of the country. Sales of our goods in other parts of the United Kingdom have greatly exceeded our expectations, but the absence of an agency in the North has meant poor sales in that region to date.

From our experience elsewhere we believe that an active agent would have little difficulty in expanding sales of our goods in the North of England. As we understand you are well experienced and have good connections in this area we would like to know if you are interested in accepting a sole agency. We are prepared to offer you a 2-year agreement with a commission of 7½% on net invoice values.

As we wish to reach a quick decision I hope you can let me know whether this offer interests you. If so then I suggest an early meeting at which details of an arrangement agreeable to both of us could be discussed.

Yours faithfully

---

[8] **haberdashery** ribbons, lace and other small articles of dress

(b) Reply

Dear Mr Thompson

Thank you for your letter of 5 April offering us the sole agency for your haberdashery products in the North of England.

We are very interested in your proposal and are confident that we should be able to develop a good demand for your products.

Your basic terms are agreeable so please let me know when it will be convenient for me to call on you. It would be helpful if you could offer a choice of dates.

I look forward to meeting you.

Yours sincerely

25.8 Offer of an overseas agency

(a) Offer

Dear Sir/Madam

We understand that you deal in stationery and related products, and would like to know if you are interested in marketing our products in your country on a commission basis.

We are a large and well-established firm specialising in the manufacture of stationery of all kinds. Our products sell well in many parts of the world. The enclosed catalogue will show you the wide range of our products, for which enquiries suggest a promising market for many of them waiting for development in your country.

If you are interested in our proposal please let us know which of our products are most likely to appeal to your customers, and also terms for commission and other charges on which you would be willing to represent us. Please give us some idea of the market prospects for our products and suggest ways in which we could help you to develop the market.

We hope to hear favourably from you soon.

Yours faithfully

(b) Acceptance

Dear

I read with interest your letter of 15 May enclosing a copy of your catalogue and inviting me to undertake the marketing of your products in Zambia.

Provided we can agree on terms and conditions, I shall be pleased to accept your offer.

I already represent Batson & Sons of Manchester in office equipment. As my customers include many of the principal dealers in Zambia I am sure they would provide a promising outlet for stationery and related products of the kind described in your catalogue.

I shall be in London in July and would like to take the opportunity to discuss arrangements with you in detail. Meanwhile I suggest the following terms and conditions as the basis for a formal agreement:

1   All goods supplied to be invoiced direct to buyers with copies sent to me.
2   Accounts to be made up and statements sent to me monthly, in duplicate, for distribution to buyers.
3   An agency commission of 5% to be payable on net amounts invoiced.
4   A del credere commission of 2½% in return for my guarantee of payments due on all accounts.

As initial expenses of introducing your products are likely to be heavy, I feel it reasonable to suggest an agreement extending over at least 3 years, but this is a matter we can discuss when we meet.

Please let me know if you are in general agreement with these suggestions.

Yours sincerely

25.9 Offer of a *del credere* agency

Where the agent acts on a *del credere* basis the principal must be satisfied as to the agent's financial standing. Sometimes references from, for example, the agent's banker may be sufficient. In other cases the agent may have to either provide a guarantor or deposit security, as in the following letter:

Dear

Thank you for your letter of 20 June. We are pleased to hear that you think a good market can be found for our goods in your country. We must confess, however, that credit on the scale you mention opens up a far from attractive prospect.

Nevertheless, we are willing to offer you an appointment on a del credere basis of 12% commission on the net value of all orders received through you, provided you are willing to lodge adequate security with our bankers here.

If security is deposited we shall be willing to protect your interests by entering into a formal agreement giving you the sole agency for a period of 5 years.

Please let me know if you are willing to accept the agency on these terms.

Yours sincerely

FORMAL AGENCY AGREEMENTS

The terms of agency are sometimes set out in correspondence between the parties but where dealings are on a large scale a formal agreement may be desirable. This should be drafted by a solicitor or by one of the parties in consultation with the other. Matters to be covered in such an agreement may include all, or some, of the following:

- the nature and duration of the agency (ie sole agency, *del credere* agency for merely transmitting orders)
- the territory to be covered
- the duties of agent and principal
- the method of purchase and sale (eg whether the agent is to buy for their own account or '*on consignment*'[9])
- details of commission and expenses to be allowed
- the law of the country by which the agreement is governed
- the sending of reports, accounts and payments
- the arrangements of *arbitration*[10] in the event of disputes.

The following illustrates the construction of a typical agency agreement, and is reproduced from *Specimen Agency Agreements for Exporters* by kind permission of the Institute of Export.

25.10 **Specimen Agency Agreement suitable for exclusive and sole agents representing manufacturers overseas**

SPECIMEN AGREEMENT 1

Suitable for exclusive and sole agents representing manufacturers overseas

AN AGREEMENT made this   day of
200   BETWEEN
whose Registered office is situate at
                                                                          (hereinafter
called 'the Principal') of the one part and
                                                                          (hereinafter
called 'the Agent') of the other part

WHEREBY IT IS AGREED as follows:

I.   The Principal appoints the Agent as and from the
     to be its sole Agent in
     (hereinafter called 'the area') for the sale of manufactured by the Principal
     and such other goods and merchandise (all of which are hereinafter referred to as
     'the goods') as may hereafter be mutually agreed between them.

[9] **on consignment** for sale on exporter's behalf
[10] **arbitration** settlement of disputes by an independent person or body

2. The Agent will during the term of   years (and thereafter until determined by either party giving three months' previous notice in writing) diligently and faithfully serve the Principal as its Agent and will endeavour to extend the sale of the goods of the Principal within the area and will not do anything that may prevent such sale or interfere with the development of the Principal's trade in the area.

3. The Principal will from time to time furnish the Agent with a statement of the minimum prices at which the goods are respectively to be sold and the Agent shall not sell below such minimum price but shall endeavour in each case to obtain the best price obtainable.

4. The Agent shall not sell any of the goods to any person, company, or firm residing outside the area, nor shall he knowingly sell any of the goods to any person, company, or firm residing within the area with a view to their exportation to any other country or area without the consent in writing of the Principal.

5. The Agent shall not during the continuance of the Agency hereby constituted sell goods of a similar class or such as would or might compete or interfere with the sale of the Principal's goods either on his own account or on behalf of any other person, company, or firm whomsoever.

6. Upon receipt by the Agent of any order for the goods the Agent will immediately transmit such order to the Principal who (if such order is accepted by the Principal) will execute the same by supplying the goods direct to the customer.

7. Upon the execution of any such order the Principal shall forward to the Agent a duplicate copy of the invoice sent with the goods to the customer and in like manner shall from time to time inform the Agent when payment is made by the customer to the Principal.

8. The Agent shall duly keep an account of all orders obtained by him and shall every three months send in a copy of such account to the Principal.

9. The Principal shall allow the Agent the following commissions (based on fob United Kingdom values) in respect of all orders obtained direct by the Agent in the area which have been accepted and executed by the Principal. The said commission shall be payable every three months on the amounts actually received by the Principal from the customers.

10. The Agent shall be entitled to commission on the terms and conditions mentioned in the last preceding clause on all export orders for the goods received by the Principal through Export Merchants Indent Houses, Branch Buying offices of customers, and Head Offices of customers situate in the United Kingdom of Great Britain, Northern Ireland and Eire for export into the area. Export orders in this clause mentioned shall not include orders for the goods received by the Principal from and sold delivered to customers' principal place of business outside the area although such goods may subsequently be exported by such customers into the area, excepting where there is conclusive evidence that such orders which may actually be transmitted via the Head Office in England are resultant from work done by the Agent with the customers.

11. Should any dispute arise as to the amount of commission payable by the Principal to the Agent the same shall be settled by the Auditors for the time being of the Principal whose certificate shall be final and binding on both the Principal and the Agent.

12. The Agent shall not in any way pledge the credit of the Principal.

13. The Agent shall not give any warranty in respect of the goods without the authority in writing of the Principal.

14. The Agent shall not without the authority of the Principal collect any moneys from customers.

15. The Agent shall not give credit to or deal with any person, company or firm which the Principal shall from time to time direct him not to give credit to or deal with.

16. The Principal shall have the right to refuse to execute or accept any order obtained by the Agent or any part thereof and the Agent shall not be entitled to any commission in respect of any such refused order or part thereof so refused.

17. All questions of difference whatsoever which may at any time hereafter arise between the parties hereto or their respective representatives touching these presents or the subject matter thereof or arising out of or in relation thereto respectively and whether as to construction or otherwise shall be referred to arbitration in England in accordance with the provision of the Arbitration Act 1950 or any re enactment or statutory modification thereof for the time being in force.

18. This Agreement shall in all respects be interpreted in accordance with the Laws of England.

AS WITNESS the hands of the parties hereto the day and year first hereinbefore written.

(Signatures)

APPOINTING AN AGENT – TYPICAL PROCEDURE

In this section we will look at a series of correspondence which evolves through a publishing company's desire to find a suitable agent to market its publications in Lebanon.

The publishing company decides to approach its bank in order to obtain the relevant information. The various letters shown can be adapted in order to apply to enquiries through other sources.

25.11 Publisher's letter to bank (addressed to the Manager)

Dear Sir

At a meeting of our Directors yesterday it was decided to try to develop our trade with the Lebanon. We hope to appoint an agent with an efficient sales organisation in that country to help us to market our publications.

I wonder if your correspondents in Beirut would be able to put us in touch with a suitable and reliable firm. Any help you can provide will be appreciated.

I hope to hear from you soon.

Yours faithfully

25.12 Bank's reply to publishers

Dear Miss Roberts

Thank you for your letter of 24 August regarding the possibility of appointing a local agent in the Lebanon.

Our correspondents in Beirut are the Banque Nationale whose postal address is:

Banque Nationale
PO Box 25643
Beirut

I have today sent a fax to their Manager explaining that you intend to appoint an agent in the Lebanon and asking him to provide you with any assistance possible.

No doubt you will now write to them direct and I have told them to expect to hear from you.

Yours sincerely

25.13 Publisher's thanks to the bank

Dear Mr Johnson

Thank you for your letter of 26 August and for introducing our name to your correspondents in Beirut.

I have today written to the Banque Nationale, and would like to thank you very much for your help.

Yours sincerely

25.14 Publisher's fax message to Beirut bank (addressed to the Manager)

The Manager of Midminster Bank Ltd, London, has kindly given us your name. We are interested in appointing an agent to represent our interests in the Lebanon and wonder if you can recommend a reliable person or company.

We specialise in publishing educational books, including students' text books and workbooks. If you could put us in touch with a distributor who has good connections with booksellers, libraries and educational institutions, we would be very grateful.

Thank you in advance for any help you can provide.

25.15 Reply from Beirut bank

Dear Miss Roberts

Thank you for your fax of 28 August. The Manager of Midminster Bank, London, has already faxed me to explain your proposal to appoint a representative to further your trading interests in the Lebanon.

We are pleased to introduce you to Habib Suleiman Ghanem & Co of Beirut. This company has been our customer for many years. They are a well-known, old-established and highly reputable firm with some 20 years' experience of the book trade in this part of the world. We can recommend them to you with the certain knowledge that they would serve you well.

We have taken the opportunity to contact Mr Faisal Ghanem, General Manager, who has expressed interest in your proposal. I believe he will be writing to you soon.

I wish you much success in your venture, and if I can be of any further help please do not hesitate to contact me.

Yours sincerely

25.16 Publisher's acknowledgement to Beirut bank

Dear Mr Jenkins

Thank you for your fax of 30 August giving us the name of Habib Suleiman Ghanem & Co. I wish to express my company's sincere thanks for your recommendation and the trouble you have so kindly taken to help us.

This company appears to be well equipped to provide the kind of service we need in the Lebanon, and we shall now look forward to hearing from them.

Yours sincerely

25.17 Fax from prospective agents

Dear Miss Roberts

Introduction giving background details — Our bankers, the Banque Nationale, inform us that you require an agent to assist in marketing your publications in the Lebanon. Subject to satisfactory arrangements as to terms and conditions we should be pleased to represent you.

Details of your experience and knowledge — As publishers and distributors in Syria and the Lebanon for over 20 years we have a thorough knowledge of the market. We are proud to boast an extensive sales organisation and well-established connections with booksellers, libraries and educational institutions in these 2 countries.

Associated interests are stated, and prospects for future business — We must mention that we are already acting as <u>sole representatives</u>[11] of several other publishers, including two American companies. However, as the preference in the educational field here is for books by British publishers, the prospects for your own publications are excellent, especially those intended for the student market. Adequate publicity would of course be necessary.

Request details of commission and terms — Before making any commitment we shall require details of your proposals for commission and terms of payment, and also some idea of the amount you are prepared to invest in <u>initial publicity</u>.[12]

We look forward to receiving this information from you very soon.

Yours sincerely

[11] **sole representatives** the only representatives
[12] **initial publicity** advertising in the early stages

25.18 Publisher's fax reply to prospective agents

Refer to fax	Dear Mr Ghanem
	I was pleased to learn from your fax of 3 September that you will consider an appointment as our agent.
Background information about previous trading in the area	Although we transact a moderate amount of business in the Middle East we have so far not had much success in the Lebanon and are now hoping to develop our interests there.
Send catalogue and prices	I am sending by Swiftair today a copy of our complete catalogue of publications. The published prices quoted are subject to the usual trade discounts.
	I would reply to your various points as follows:
Numbered points with subheadings ensure clarity	1 COMMISSION
	The commission at present allowed to our other agents is 10% on the invoice value of all orders, payable quarterly, and we offer you the same terms. We presume your customers would be able to settle their accounts direct with us on the basis of <u>cash against documents</u>,[13] except of course for supplies from your own stocks.
	2 PUBLICITY
	We feel that perhaps an initial expenditure of approximately £4000 to cover the first 3 months' publicity would be reasonable. However as we are not familiar with conditions in your country this is a matter on which we would welcome your views.
State next step if terms are accepted	If you accept these proposals we will send by courier 2 copies of our standard agency contract. I am enclosing a copy for your reference and comments.
Encouraging close	We look forward to the prospect of welcoming you as our agents.
	Yours sincerely

25.19 Fax accepting agency

	Dear
Refer to fax and thank for documents received	Thank you for your fax of 10 September enclosing a copy of your standard form of agency agreement and for the copy of your catalogue which arrived very promptly. The catalogue covers an extensive range of interesting titles which appear to be very reasonably priced.
Comment on information provided	With the proposed initial expenditure of £4000 on advertising, backed by active support from our own sales staff, we feel that the prospects for many of your titles are very good, particularly where they are suitable for use in schools and colleges. We take it that you are prepared to leave the choice of <u>advertising media</u>[14] to us.
State whether terms are acceptable and ask for agreement to be sent	We are grateful for this opportunity to take up your agency here. As your proposed terms are satisfactory we shall be pleased to accept the conditions in the agreement. I presume you will forward this to me without delay.
	Yours sincerely

[13] **cash against documents** payment made upon delivery of shipping documents
[14] **advertising media** forms of publicity

25.20 Publisher acknowledges acceptance of agreement

Dear Mr Ghanem

Thank you for returning a signed copy of the agency contract with your letter of 26 September.

It is important that you carry stocks of those titles for which there is likely to be a steady demand. When you have had an opportunity to assess the market please let us know the titles and quantities you feel will be needed to enable you to meet small orders quickly.

We will follow the development of our trade with keen interest and look forward to a happy and lasting working relationship with you.

Yours sincerely

CORRESPONDENCE WITH AGENTS

25.21 Agent requests increased commission

To ask for more money is never easy and to get it is often more difficult, especially when the amount payable has been fixed and included in an agreement freely entered into. Any request for increased commission must, therefore, be well founded and tactfully presented.

In the letter which follows the agent presents the case convincingly and with restraint. This ensures that it will have a fair hearing. No one receiving such a letter would wish to lose the goodwill clearly shown.

(a) Agent's request

Dear Sir/Madam

Tactfully introduce the subject and explain

We would like to request your consideration of some revision in our present rate of commission. This may strike you as unusual since the increase in sales last year resulted in a corresponding increase in our total commission.

Give further details and fully explain the situation

Marketing your goods has proved to be more difficult than could have been expected when we undertook to represent you. Since then German and American competitors have entered the market and firmly established themselves. Consequently we have been able to maintain our position in the market only by enlarging our force of sales staff and increasing our expenditure on advertising.

Tact is required. Clear justification must be given

We are quite willing to incur[15] the additional expense and even to increase it still further because we firmly believe that the required effort will result in increased business. However we feel we should not be expected to bear the whole of the additional cost without some form of compensation. After carefully calculating the increase in our selling costs we suggest an increase in the rate of commission by say, 2%.

An encouraging close requesting consideration

You have always been considerate in your dealings with us and we know we can rely on you to consider our present request with understanding.

Yours faithfully

[15] **incur** be responsible for

(b) Principal's reply

Dear

Refer to fax and show an appreciation of problems being experienced — Thank you for your fax of 28 August.

We note the unexpected problems presented by our competitors and appreciate the extra efforts you have made with such satisfactory results.

Comment on facts provided in agent's letter — We feel sure that, <u>in the long run</u>,[16] the high quality of our goods and the very competitive prices at which they are offered will ensure steadily increasing sales despite the competition from other manufacturers. At the same time we realise that, in the short term, this competition must be met by more active advertising and agree that it would not be reasonable to expect you to bear the full cost.

Suggest how the matter can be rectified — To increase commission would be difficult as our prices leave us with only a very small profit. Instead we propose to allow you an advertising credit of £4000 in the current year towards your additional costs. This amount will be reviewed in 6 months' time and adjusted according to circumstances.

We hope you will be happy with this arrangement and look forward to your
Request confirmation — confirmation.

Yours sincerely

25.22 Principal proposes reduced rate of commission

Any proposal by a principal to reduce an agent's commission must be well founded and carefully presented, otherwise it would create ill-feeling and strain business relations. If the rate of commission is included in a legally binding agreement it cannot be varied without the agent's consent, and even that consent is not binding unless the principal gives the agent some concession in return.

Dear

It is with regret that I must ask you to accept a temporary reduction in the agreed rate of commission. I make this request because of an increase in manufacturing costs due to additional duties on our imported raw materials, and to our inability either to <u>absorb these higher costs</u>[17] or to pass them on to consumers. In the event, our profits have been reduced to a level which no longer justifies continued production.

This situation is disturbing but we feel sure it will be purely temporary. In the circumstances we hope you will accept a small reduction of, say, 1½% in the agreed rate of commission. You have our promise that as soon as trade improves sufficiently we shall return to the rate originally agreed.

Yours sincerely

[16] **in the long run** eventually
[17] **absorb these higher costs** accept without raising prices

25.23 Agent complains of slow delivery

When a buyer is thinking of placing an order the 3 things which are of interest are quality, price and delivery. Often more importance is attached to the certainty of prompt delivery than to low price, but both are important. Therefore, in an increasingly competitive world, a manufacturer who regularly falls down on delivery dates is placed at a disadvantage and runs the risk of being forced out of business.

Dear

We enclose our statement showing sales made on your account during March and commission and expenses payable. If you will confirm our figures we will credit you with the amount due.

These sales are most disappointing but this is due entirely to late arrival of goods we ordered from you last January. Not having received the goods by mid-February, we faxed you on the 18th but found on enquiry that the goods were not shipped until 3 March and consequently did not reach us until 20 March.

This delay in delivery is most unfortunate as the local agents of several of our competitors have been particularly active during the past few weeks and have taken a good deal of the trade that would normally have come our way had the goods been here. What is more disturbing is that these rival firms have now gained a good hold on the market which until now has been largely our own.

We have reminded you on a previous occasion of the competition from Japanese manufacturers, whose low prices and quick deliveries are having a striking effect on local buyers. If you wish to keep your hold on this market prompt delivery of orders we place with you is essential.

Yours sincerely

25.24 Agent recommends lower price policy

An important reason for appointing a foreign agent is the gain in knowledge of local conditions and of the market for operation. Your agent will know what goods are best suited to the area and what prices the market will bear. Only an unwise exporter would ignore the advice of an agent on these and other matters of which they have special knowledge.

Dear

We are enclosing our customer's order number 252 for card-index and filing equipment.

To secure this order has not been easy because your quoted prices were higher than those which our customer had been prepared for. The quotation was eventually accepted on the grounds of your reputation for quality, but I think we should warn you of the growing competition in the office-equipment market here.

Agents of German and Japanese manufacturers are now active in the market, and as their products are of good quality and in some cases cheaper than yours we shall find it very difficult to maintain our past volume of sales unless you can reduce your prices. For your guidance we are sending you copies of the price lists of competing firms.

Concerning the present shipment please send a draft bill of exchange for acceptance at 2 months for the net value of your invoice after allowing for commission and expenses.

Yours

25.25 Agent recommends credit dealings

(a) Agent's recommendation

Dear

We have studied the catalogue and price list received with your letter of 31 March, and have no doubt that we could obtain good orders for many of the items. However, we feel that it would not be advantageous to either of our companies to adopt a cash settlement basis.

Nearly all business here is done on credit, the period varying from 3 to 6 months. Your prices are reasonable and your products sound in both design and quality. We therefore believe that you could afford to raise your prices sufficiently to cover the cost and fall into line with your competitors in the matter of credit.

In our experience this would be sound policy and would greatly strengthen your hold on the market. With the best will in the world to serve you, we are afraid it would be neither worth your while nor ours to continue business on a cash basis.

If it would help you at all we should be quite willing to assume full responsibility for unsettled accounts and to act as <u>del credere</u> agents for an additional commission of 2½%.

We hope to hear from you soon.

Yours

(b) Manufacturer's reply

Dear

Thank you for your letter of 10 April. We are glad that you think a satisfactory market could be found for our goods but are not altogether happy at the prospect of transacting all our business on a credit basis.

To some extent your offer to act in a <u>del credere</u> capacity meets our objectives, and for a trial period we are prepared to accept on the terms stated, namely an extra commission of 2½%. We make the condition, however, that you are willing either to provide a guarantor acceptable to us or to lodge adequate security with our bankers.

Please let us know your decision on this matter.

Yours sincerely

25.26 Principal complaints to agent

It is always unpleasant to have to make complaints but if a criticism is necessary it must be written with care and restraint. Never assume that the agent, or whoever the other party may be, is at fault. A letter written with courtesy and understanding will usually bring a considerate reply and obtain the co-operation needed to put matters right.

(a) Poor sales

Dear Sirs

We are very concerned that your sales in recent months have fallen considerably. At first we thought this might be due to the disturbed political situation in your country. However, on looking into the matter more closely we find that the general trend of trade during this period has been upwards.

Of course, it is possible that you are facing difficulties of which we are not aware. If so, we should like to know of them since it may be possible for us to help. Please let us have a detailed report on the situation and also any suggestions of ways in which you feel we may be of some help in restoring our sales to at least their former level.

Yours faithfully

(b) High expenses

> Dear Sirs
>
> We have received your October statement of sales and are concerned at the high figure included for expenses. This figure seems much too high for the volume of business done.
>
> It is of course possible that there are special reasons for these high charges. If so we feel it is reasonable to ask you to explain them. We are particularly concerned because, under pressure of competition, the prices at which we offered the goods was cut to a level which left us with only a very small profit.
>
> We shall be glad to receive your explanation and your assurance that expenses on future sales can be reduced. If for any reason this is not possible we should be left with no choice but to discontinue our business with you, for which we sincerely hope there will be no need.
>
> Yours faithfully

 When crossing international boundaries in your e-mail communications, it is better to err on the side of caution and use a more formal tone for your messages. It will then be easy to progress to a more friendly tone as you get to know your recipient better.

USEFUL EXPRESSIONS

Agency applications

Openings

1 We should be glad if you would consider our application to act as agents for the sale of your ...

2 Thank you for your letter of ... asking if we are represented ...

3 We have received your letter of ... and should be glad to offer you a sole agency for the sale of our products in ...

Closes

1 We hope to hear favourably from you and feel sure we should have no difficulty in arranging terms.

2 If you give us this agency we should spare no effort to further your interests.

3 If required, we can provide first-class references.

Agency appointments

Openings

1 Thank you for your letter of ... offering us the sole agency for your products in ...

2 We thank you for your letter of ... and are favourably impressed by your proposal for a sole agency.

3 Thank you for offering us the agency in ... we appreciate the confidence you have placed in us.

Closes

1 We hope to receive a favourable response and can assure you of our very best service.

2 We look forward to a happy and successful working relationship with you.

International trade

Some exporters will deal direct with overseas buyers, but it is more usual for transactions to take place in any of the following ways:

1 The overseas buyer employs a commission agent in the exporter's country.

2 The exporter employs an agent living in the buyer's country.

3 The exporter sends the goods to a *factor*[1] in the importing country for sale 'on consignment'.

The exporter is known as the consignor and the importer is known as the consignee.

Correspondence concerned with buying and selling overseas is generally carried out through fax for obvious reasons of speed. New technology has now given us EDI (Electronic Data Interchange) which substantially reduces the amount of paperwork which needs to be sent between the parties concerned. If both exporter and importer have compatible systems EDI results in huge savings in time, documentation and paperwork.

IMPORT/EXPORT FLOW CHART

This flow chart in Fig. 26.1 shows the traditional documentation and procedures involved in purchasing goods from abroad.

[1] **factor** any agent who deals in their own name and has possession of the goods they are required to sell

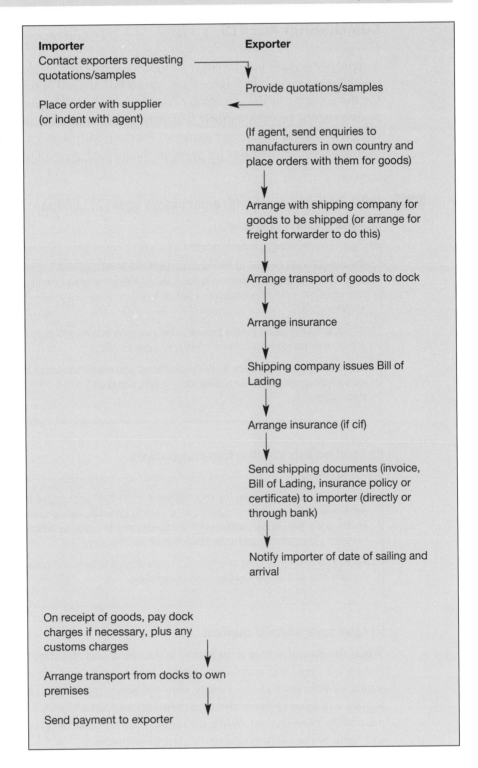

Importer
Contact exporters requesting
quotations/samples

Exporter

Provide quotations/samples

Place order with supplier
(or indent with agent)

(If agent, send enquiries to
manufacturers in own country and
place orders with them for goods)

Arrange with shipping company for
goods to be shipped (or arrange for
freight forwarder to do this)

Arrange transport of goods to dock

Arrange insurance

Shipping company issues Bill of
Lading

Arrange insurance (if cif)

Send shipping documents (invoice,
Bill of Lading, insurance policy or
certificate) to importer (directly or
through bank)

Notify importer of date of sailing and
arrival

On receipt of goods, pay dock
charges if necessary, plus any
customs charges

Arrange transport from docks to own
premises

Send payment to exporter

Figure 26.1 Flow chart showing a typical transaction relating to purchase of goods
from abroad

COMMISSION AGENTS

A commission agent may be either an individual or a firm employed to buy or to sell for a principal. In foreign trade, agents buy and sell in their own names for the accounts of the principals. Their tasks include obtaining quotations, placing orders, supervising their fulfilment and arranging for the despatch of the goods. Agents also collect payments for the principal and sometimes hold themselves personally liable for payment should the buyer fail to pay.

26.1 Bahraini buyer deals with commission agent in London

(a) Agent acknowledges order

> Your order number C75 of 10 February for 1500 fibreglass wash basins in assorted colours will be placed without delay. We have already written to a manufacturer in North London and will do everything we can to ensure early shipment.
>
> We note your request for the basins to be arranged in tens and packed in cartons rather than wooden containers in order to save freight.
>
> We shall arrange insurance on the usual terms and the certificate of insurance will be sent to you through our bankers along with our draft bill and other shipping documents.

(b) Agent requests quotation from manufacturers

> We have received an order for 1500 (fifteen hundred) 40 cm circular fibreglass wash basins in assorted colours for shipment to Bahrain. Please quote your lowest price fob London and state the earliest possible date by which you can have the consignment ready for collection at your factory.
>
> Your price should include arrangement of the basins in tens and packing in cartons of a size convenient for manual handling.

(c) Agent sends advice of shipment

When the manufacturer's quotation is accepted and the date of delivery is known the agent will telephone a freight forwarder to find out details of ships sailing to Bahrain and the closing date for accepting cargo. The freight for-warder will need to know the measurements concerned as well as weight and price of the consignment. When the required information is received, the agent will write to the client giving particulars of shipment.

> YOUR ORDER NUMBER C75
>
> The 1500 fibreglass wash basins which you ordered on 10 February will be shipped to you by the SS <u>Tigris</u> sailing from London on 25 March and due to arrive in Bahrain on 15 April.
>
> The bill of lading, commercial invoice, <u>consular invoice</u>[2] and certificate of insurance, together with our <u>draft</u>[3] drawn at <u>sixty (60) days sight</u>,[4] have been passed to the Barminster Bank Ltd, London, and should reach you within a few days. The enclosed copy of the invoice will give you advance information of the consignment.
>
> We hope the goods will prove to be satisfactory.

(d) Agent passes documents to banker

Payment for the transaction is to be made by bill of exchange drawn at 60 days and sent through the agent's bank to the foreign buyer. The banker's correspondent in Bahrain will not hand over the shipping documents until the buyer accepts the bill as a sign of willingness to meet it when it is presented for payment in 60 days.

On receipt of the letter (see 26.1) the client's bank in Bahrain would present the documents to the client and obtain a signature on the back of the bill of exchange saying that the payment terms are accepted. The documents will then be released and the goods may be collected.

> We enclose a bill of lading, consular invoice, certificate of insurance and our invoice relating to a consignment of fibreglass wash basins for shipment by SS <u>Tigris</u> to Mr Ahmed Ashkar of Bahrain.
>
> Please forward these documents to your correspondent in Bahrain with instructions to hand them to the consignee against acceptance of our 60 days draft, also enclosed.

GOODS ON CONSIGNMENT

Goods on consignment are goods which an exporter sends to an importer, but an invoice will not immediately be issued. The importer will hold the goods in stock until they are sold, at which point the exporter will draw up an invoice for whatever stock has been sold.

---

[2] **consular invoice** an invoice signed by the consul of the country to which goods are exported
[3] **draft** a bill of exchange requiring acceptance
[4] **sixty (60) days sight** for payment within 60 days of acceptance

26.2 Company in Nairobi requests goods on consignment

(a) Buyer's request

Introduce yourself and give background details — We are the largest department store in Nairobi and have recently received a number of enquiries for your stainless steel cutlery. There are very good prospects for the sale of this cutlery, but as it is presently unknown here we do not feel able to make purchases on our own account.

Propose how an agreement would work — We would like to suggest that you send us a trial delivery for sale on consignment terms. When the market is established we would hope to place firm orders.

Further details regarding payment, expenses, commission and references — If you agree we would render monthly accounts of sales and send you the payments due after deducting expenses and commission at a rate to be agreed. Our bankers are the Nairobi branch of Midminster Bank Ltd, with whom you may check our standing.[5]

An encouraging close — We believe our proposal offers good prospects and hope you will be willing to agree to a trial.

(b) Seller's acceptance

Thank agent for letter — Thank you for your letter proposing to receive a trial delivery of our cutlery on consignment which we have carefully considered.

Enclose sample goods. State whether agent's proposal is acceptable. Mention commission — We are sending you a representative selection[6] of our most popular lines and hope you will find a ready sale for them. Your suggestion to submit accounts and to make payments monthly is quite satisfactory, and we will allow you commission at 10% calculated on gross profits.

Details of consignment and documents — The consignment is being shipped by SS Eastern Prince, leaving Southampton for Mombasa on 25 January. We will send the bill of lading and other shipping documents as soon as we receive them. Meanwhile a pro forma invoice is enclosed showing prices at which the goods should be offered for sale.

An encouraging close — We are confident that this cutlery will prove popular in your country and look forward to trading with you.

(c) Agent submits account sales

When the agent has sold the goods an account sales (Fig. 26.2) will be sent to the exporter showing the goods sold and the prices realised, together with the net amount due to the exporter after deducting commission and any charges or expenses incurred. The net amount may be placed to the credit of the exporter in the importing country, or it may be forwarded by means of a banker's draft (unless other means of payment, discussed in Chapter 11 are adopted).

[5] **check our standing** enquire as to our position in business
[6] **representative selection** a selection covering all types of goods

We enclose our account sales for the month ending 31 March showing a balance of £379.20 due to you after deducting commission and charges. If you will draw on us for this amount at two months we will add our acceptance and return the draft immediately.

ACCOUNT SALES
by U Patel & Co
15–17 Rhodes Avenue, Nairobi

25 October 200—

In the matter of stainless steel cutlery ex SS <u>Eastern Prince</u> sold for account of E Hughes & Co Ltd, Victoria Works, Kingsway, Sheffield.

Quantity	Description	@ per 100 £	£
100	Knives	170.00	170.00
100	Forks	170.00	170.00
50	Table Spoons	150.00	75.00
200	Tea Spoons	105.00	210.00
			625.00

Charges:

Ocean Freight	92.55	
Dock Dues and Cartage	37.40	
Marine Insurance	20.50	
Customs Dues	32.85	
Commission	62.50	
		245.80

Net proceeds, as per banker's draft enclosed   379.20

Nairobi, 28 October 200—
(signed) U Patel & Co

E & OE

Figure 26.2   **Account sales.** The account sales is a statement of goods sold by an agent for the consignor. It shows the amount due to the consignor after deduction of charges and agency commission.

(d) Principal sends payment

> Thank you for sending your account sales for March. Our draft for the balance shown of £379.20 is enclosed.

INDENTS

When foreign buyers place orders through commission agents or *commission houses*[7] in the supplier's country their orders are known as indents (see Fig. 26.3). They give details of the goods required, their prices, packing and shipping instructions and method of payment. An indent is not an order for goods; it is an order to an agent to buy goods on behalf of the foreign buyer.

If the indent names the manufacturer who is to supply the goods it is known as a 'closed' or 'specific' indent. If selection is left to the agent the indent is said to be 'open' and the agent will then obtain quotations from a number of manufacturers before placing an order.

26.3 Foreign buyer deals with commission house

(a) Buyer (in Egypt) sends indent to commission house (in England)

> We have received the manufacturer's price list and samples you sent us last month and now enclose our indent number 762 for goods to be shipped by the SS *Merchant Prince* due to leave Liverpool for Alexandria on 25 July. The indent contains full instructions as to packing, insurance and shipping documents.
>
> It is important for the goods to be shipped either by the vessel named, or by an earlier vessel; if there are any items which cannot be supplied in time for this shipment they should be cancelled. When we receive the goods we shall pay you the agreed agency commission of 5%. The account for the goods will be settled direct with the manufacturers.
>
> This is a trial order and if it is met satisfactorily we shall probably place further orders.

---

[7] **commission houses** a commission agency organised as a firm or company

INDENT
No 64

N WHARFE & CO LTD
19–21 Victoria Street
CAIRO, EGYPT

10 February 200–

H Hopkinson & Co
Commission Agents and Shippers
41 King Street
MANCHESTER
M60 2HB

Dear Sirs

Please purchase and ship on our account for delivery not later than 31 March the following goods or as many of them as possible. Insurance should be arranged for the amount of your invoice plus 10% to cover estimated profit and your charges.

Yours faithfully
for N WHARFE & CO LTD

J G Gartside
Director

Identification Marks etc	Quantity	Description of Goods	Remarks
NW 64 Nos 1–12	48	HMV Stereo Model 1636 Walnut finish	Pack 4 per case
NW 64 Nos 13–37	25 bales	Grey Shirting Medium weight About 1,000 metres per bale	Pack in oil bags
NW 64 Nos 38–39	500 pairs	Assorted House Slippers Men's (200) Women's (200) Children's (100)	Pack in plain wooden cases

Ship: By Manchester Liners Ltd
Delivery: cif Alexandria
Payment: Draw at 60 days from sight of documents through Royal Bank, London

Figure 26.3 **Indent.** An indent is an order sent to a commission agent to arrange for the purchase of goods for the principal.

(b) Agent places order with a firm in Manchester

> We have just received an order from Jean Riachi & Co of Mansura, Egypt. Particulars are shown in the enclosed official order form together with details of packing and forwarding, case marks, etc.
>
> The goods are to be ready for collection at your warehouse in time to be shipped to Alexandria by SS <u>Merchant Prince</u> due to sail from Liverpool on 25 July or by an earlier vessel if possible. Prompt delivery is essential and if there are any items which cannot be included in the consignment they should be cancelled.
>
> Invoices priced ex warehouse should be in triplicate and sent to us for forwarding to our customers with the shipping documents. The account will be settled by our customers direct with you. As <u>del credere</u> agents, we undertake to be responsible should the buyer fail to pay.
>
> This is a trial order and if it is completed satisfactorily it is likely to lead to further business. Your special care would therefore be appreciated.
>
> Please confirm by return that you can accept this order, and arrange to inform us when the goods are ready for collection.

BILLS OF LADING

The bill of lading, prepared by the shipping company, sets out the terms of the contract of carriage with the shipping company. It serves as the consignor's receipt for the goods taken on board ship. The bill of lading is also a document of title so that when it is transferred to the consignee it also gives the right to claim the goods to which it refers.

A bill of lading is usually prepared in a set of 3 originals and 3 copies. It will state the name of the vessel, the time of sailing, marks and identification on the cargo, the delivery address and also the statement 'clean shipped on board', meaning the goods are not damaged and they are actually on board ship.

On issue of the bill of lading the consignor must check that all details are correct and that it has been signed by the ship's captain. The bill of lading then goes, with other documents, to the bank to be forwarded to the consignee.

 TIP Check out *Essential Communication Skills – the Ultimate Guide to Successful Business Communication*, a self-study guide to help you develop and improve your business writing skills.

IMPORT DOCUMENTATION AND PROCEDURE

Whether goods are imported on consignment or against orders, import procedure is much the same. Before the ship arrives the importer (who will be either a merchant dealing on their own account or an agent) will usually have received the shipping documents. The original documents would go through the bank, but it is normal practice for photocopies to be despatched by a courier service so that the importer can, in advance, go through the import procedures before the goods actually arrive. This makes things easier for the importer and saves a lot of time.

Shipping documents include:

1 An advice of shipment specifying the goods and stating the name of the carrying ship, its date of sailing and probable date of arrival.

2 A bill of lading.

3 An invoice (pro forma if the goods are imported on consignment).

When the ship arrives the importer must obtain release for the bill of lading and proceed as follows:

1 The importer must *endorse*[8] the bill of lading and present it to the shipping company, or their representative, at the port.

2 The freight must be paid (if not already prepaid by the exporter) and any other charges due to the shipping company.

3 The importer must prepare and submit the necessary import entries on official forms provided by the appropriate Customs authorities.

Import duties may either be specific (ie charged on quantity, as on wines and tobacco) or *ad valorem* (ie charged on invoice value, as on television sets and other manufactured goods). If the goods, or any of them, are required for immediate use, duty must be paid before they may be taken away.

Some goods imported into the United Kingdom are liable to VAT (value added tax) and this should generally be paid when the goods are cleared through customs.

26.4 An import transaction

(a) Importer (London) places order (Japan)

> Our order for 20 Super Hitachi Hi-Fi Systems (SDT 400) is enclosed at the cif price of £550 each, as quoted in your letter of 10 June.
>
> Through the Midminster Bank Ltd, 65 Aldwych, London WC2, we have arranged with the Bank of Japan, Tokyo, to open a credit in your favour for £6000 (six thousand pounds) to be available until 30 September next.
>
> Please let us know when the consignment is shipped.

(b) Importer opens credit

The importer writes to the Midminster Bank in London opening credit.

> I have completed and enclose your form for an irrevocable credit of £6000 to be opened with the Bank of Japan, Tokyo, in favour of Kikuki, Shiki & Co, Tokyo, for a consignment of music systems, the credit to be valid until 30 September next.
>
> When the consignment is shipped the company will draw on the Bank of Japan at 30 days after sight; the draft will be accompanied by bills of lading (3/3), invoice and certificate or policy of insurance.
>
> Please confirm that the credit will be arranged.

[8] **endorse** sign on the back

(c) Supplier in Japan presents documents to Bank of Japan, Tokyo

We enclose a 30 days' sight draft together with bill of lading (3/3), invoice, letter of credit and certificate of insurance relating to a consignment of music centres for shipment by SS Yamagata to Videohire Ltd, London.

Please send draft and documents to the Midminster Bank Ltd, 65 Aldwych, London WC2 4LS, with instructions to hand over the documents to Videohire Ltd against their acceptance of the draft.

(d) Supplier sends advice of shipment

YOUR ORDER NO 825

We thank you for your order for 20 Super Hitachi Music Centres. I am glad to say we can supply these immediately from stock. We have arranged to ship them to your London warehouse at St Katharine Docks, London by SS Yamagata sailing from Tokyo on 3 August and due to arrive in London on or about the 25th.

The shipping documents will be delivered to you through the Aldwych Branch of the Midminster Bank Ltd against your acceptance of the 30 days' sight draft as agreed in our earlier correspondence.

We hope you will find everything satisfactory.

(e) Importer acknowledges consignment

ORDER NO 825

Your consignment of Music Centres reached London on 27 August.

Thank you for the care and promptness with which you have fulfilled our first order. We expect to place further orders soon.

BONDED WAREHOUSES

If imported goods on which duty is payable are not wanted immediately they may be placed in a bonded warehouse, that is a warehouse whose owners have entered into a bond with the Customs authorities as a guarantee that the goods will not be removed until duty on them has been paid.

This system enables payment of duty to be *deferred*[9] until the goods, which may be withdrawn by *instalments*,[10] are needed. The main commodities dealt with in this way are tea, tobacco, beer, wines and spirits.

[9] **deferred** delayed
[10] **instalments** in separate lots

When goods are placed in a warehouse, bonded or free, the owner of the goods is given either a warehouse warrant or a warehousekeeper's receipt. A delivery order, signed by the owner of the goods, must be completed when goods are withdrawn.

26.5 Clearance of goods from warehouse

This letter is from a tea blender to their broker, who has bought a quantity of tea and holds the delivery order issued by the importer.

> We refer to the 12 chests of Assam, ex City of Bombay, which you bought for us at the auctions yesterday and for which we understand you hold the delivery order.
>
> Please clear all 12 chests at once and arrange with Williams Transport Ltd to deliver them to our Leman Street warehouse.

USEFUL EXPRESSIONS

Enquiries and orders

Openings

1 Thank you for your quotation of ... and for the samples you sent me.

2 One of our best customers has asked us to arrange to purchase ...

3 Your letter of ... enclosing indent for ... arrived yesterday.

Closes

1 Please deal with this order as one of special urgency.

2 We look forward to receiving further indents from you.

3 We thank you for giving us this trial order and promise that we will give it our careful attention.

Consignments

Openings

1 We regret that we cannot handle your goods on our own account, but would be willing to take them on a consignment basis.

2 We have today sent a consignment of ... by SS *Empress Victoria*, and enclose the shipping documents.

3 The consignment you sent us has been sold at very good prices.

Closes

1 Please of course credit our account with the amount due.

2 We look forward to hearing that you have been able to obtain satisfactory prices.

3 We will send you our account sales, with banker's draft, in a few days.

4 We enclose our account sales and shall be glad if you will draw on us at 2 months for the amount due.

Banking
(home business)

Commercial banks offer four main services:

1 They accept customers' deposits.
2 They pay cheques drawn on them by their customers.
3 They grant advances to customers.
4 They provide a payments mechanism for the transfer of funds between its own customers and those of other banks.

KINDS OF BANK ACCOUNT

Current accounts are the most usual type of bank account. Deposits in the account can be withdrawn on demand. This is the main method by which customers may utilise the full money transfer facilities of the bank, involving the use of cheques, credit transfers, *standing orders*[1] and *direct debits*.[2] Traditionally the current account holder did not receive interest on funds but some banks now pay a small rate of credit interest. Besides their main services banks offers customers a wide range of miscellaneous services including safe custody and night safe facilities, the provision of references, executor and trustee, and pension and insurance services plus advice on how to start up a business.

Deposit accounts have been used by banks in recent years to attract customers. A range of deposit accounts are offered paying various rates of interest as well as the ordinary deposit account. On ordinary deposit accounts withdrawals are subject to 7 days' notice. Generally the amount of interest depends on the amount of money deposited and to some extent on the length of notice of withdrawal required.

Opening accounts

Anyone wishing to open an account should legally provide satisfactory references or be introduced by an established customer of the bank. In practice, however, some banks do not necessarily take personal references in respect of customers but may rely on proof of identity and some form of credit referencing.

Statements

Periodic loose-leaf statements are provided to customers. These statements record all transactions affecting the customer's current account and the balance after each day's transactions.

---

[1] **standing order** an order to make certain payments at stated times
[2] **direct debit** similar to standing orders but instead of the customer stating the amounts and when to pay them the company tells the bank what to pay and when

Cheques

Cheques are a widely accepted form of payment today. Their acceptability has increased since the introduction of the cheque guarantee card in 1965, which guaranteed the payment of a cheque up to a stated amount (often £50).

A banker is entitled to refuse payment of a cheque in any of the following circumstances:

- When the drawer has countermanded payment.
- When the balance on the drawer's account is insufficient to meet the cheque.
- When the cheque is post-dated, ie dated ahead of time.
- When the cheque has become 'stale', ie over 6 months old.
- When the cheque contains some irregularity, eg a forgery or an unsigned alteration.
- When the banker is aware that the drawer has died or committed an act of bankruptcy.

In any of these circumstances the cheque would be returned to the payee or other holder marked with the reason for its non-payment.

Bank charges

As long as personal customers keep their accounts in credit they are not liable to any bank charges.

Business customers will normally negotiate their charges with their bankers. Such charges are generally applied quarterly.

CORRESPONDENCE WITH BANKS

Correspondence between the bank and its customers tends to be standardised and quite formal, as shown in the range of correspondence in this chapter.

CURRENT ACCOUNTS

27.1 Notification of signatures to bank

Only officers authorised by a company's board of directors may sign cheques for the company. The bank will want to see a copy of the board's resolution authorising the opening of an account and stating the manner in which cheques are to be signed and by whom, with specimens of their signatures.

> Dear Sir
>
> At a meeting of the Board yesterday it was decided that cheques drawn on the company's account must bear two signatures instead of one as formerly.
>
> One of the signatures must be that of the Chairman or Secretary; the other may be any member of the Board. This change takes place as of today's date.
>
> There have been no changes in membership of the Board since specimen signatures were issued to you in July.
>
> A certified copy of the Board's resolution is attached.
>
> Yours faithfully

27.2 Account overdrawn – correspondence with bank

The following is the kind of letter a bank manager would send to a customer who has overdrawn on their account. While being polite, courteous and helpful the letter conveys to the customer the seriousness of an unauthorised overdraft.

(a) Letter from bank

> Dear Mrs Wilson
>
> On a number of occasions recently your account has been overdrawn. The amount overdrawn at close of business yesterday was £150.72. Please arrange for the credits necessary to clear this balance to be paid in as soon as possible.
>
> Overdrafts are allowed to customers only by previous arrangement and as I notice that your account has recently been running on a very small balance, it occurs to me that you may wish to come to some arrangement for overdraft facilities. If so perhaps you will call to discuss the matter. In the absence of such an arrangement I am afraid it will not be possible to honour future cheques drawn against insufficient balances.
>
> Yours sincerely

(b) Customer's reply

> Dear
>
> Thank you for your letter of yesterday. I have today paid into my account cheques totalling £80.42. I realise that this leaves only a small balance to my credit and as I am likely to be faced with fairly heavy payments in the coming months I should like to discuss arrangements for overdraft facilities.
>
> I have recently entered into a number of very favourable contracts, which involve the early purchase of raw materials. As payments under the contracts will not be made until the work is completed I am really in need of overdraft facilities up to about £1500 for 6 months or so.
>
> I will call your secretary in the next few days to arrange a convenient time for me to call to see you.
>
> Yours sincerely

27.3 Drawer stops payment of cheque

When a payment of a cheque is stopped, as for example where the cheque has been lost in the post, payment is said to be *countermanded*.[3] Only the drawer of the cheque can countermand payment. This is done by notifying the bank in writing. An *oral notification*,[4] even when made by the drawer in person, is not by itself enough and, as with a notification by telephone, it should be immediately confirmed in writing.

Dear Sir

I wish to confirm my telephone call of this morning to ask you to stop payment of cheque number 67582 for the sum of £96.25 payable to the St Annes Electrical Co Ltd.

This cheque appears to have been lost in the post and a further cheque has now been drawn to replace it.

Please confirm receipt of this authority to stop the payment.

Yours faithfully

27.4 Complaint concerning dishonoured cheque

(a) Customer's letter to bank

Dear Sir

The Alexandria Radio & Television Co Ltd inform me that you have refused payment of my cheque number 527610 of 15 August for £285.75. The returned cheque is marked 'Effects not cleared'. I believe this refers to the cheques I paid in on 11 August, the amount of which was more than enough to cover the dishonoured cheque.

As there appears to have been ample time for you to collect and credit the sums due on the cheques paid in, please let me know why payment of cheque number 527610 was refused.

Yours faithfully

---

[3] **countermanded** cancelled
[4] **oral notification** a verbal message

(b) Reply from bank

> Dear
>
> In reply to your letter of yesterday, I am sorry that we were not able to allow payment against your cheque number 527610. One of the cheques paid in on 11 August – the cheque drawn in your favour by M Tippett & Co – was post-dated to 25 August and that the amount cannot be credited to your account before that date.
>
> To honour your cheque would have created an overdraft of more than £100 and in the absence of previous arrangement I am afraid we could not grant credit for such a sum.
>
> I trust this explanation clarifies this matter.
>
> Yours sincerely

27.5 Request for bank reference

Bankers will not give information to private enquirers about their customers. When a buyer, in seeking credit from a supplier, gives the bank as a reference the suppliers must approach their own bank, not the buyer's bank, and ask them to make the necessary enquiries. As a rule the information supplied in answer to such requests is brief, formal and much less personal than that obtainable through a trade reference.

(a) Supplier's request to bank

> Dear Sir
>
> We have received an order for £1200 from Messrs Joynson and Hicks of 18 Drake Street, Sheffield. They ask for credit and have given the Commonwealth Bank, 10 Albert Street, Sheffield S14 5QP, as a reference.
>
> Please make enquiries and let us know whether the reputation and financial standing of this firm justify a credit of the above amount.
>
> Yours faithfully

(b) Reply from bank

> Dear Sir
>
> As requested in your letter of 18 April we have made enquiries as to the reputation and standing of the Sheffield firm mentioned.
>
> The firm was established in 1942 and its commitments have been met regularly. The directors are reported to be efficient and reliable and a credit of £1200 is considered sound.
>
> This information is supplied free from all responsibility on our part.
>
> Yours faithfully

BANK LOANS AND OVERDRAFTS

When granting an advance to a personal customer, especially an overdraft, the bank may require some form of acceptable security. The security should be easy to value, easy for the bank to obtain a good legal title, and it should be readily marketable or realisable. The most common types of security accepted are life policies, shares, mortgages of land and guarantees.

Normally a bank will not require security from a customer to support a personal loan.

Interest on an overdraft is charged on a daily basis, while interest on a personal loan is calculated on the full amount borrowed.

27.6 Request for overdraft facilities

(a) Customer's request

> Dear Sir
>
> With the approach of Christmas I am expecting a big increase in <u>turnover</u>,[5] but unfortunately my present stocks are not nearly enough for this. Because my business is fairly new wholesalers are unwilling to give me anything but short-term credit.
>
> I hope you will be able to help me by making me an advance on overdraft until the end of this year.
>
> As security I am willing to offer a life policy, and of course will allow you to inspect my accounts, from which you will see that I have promptly met all my obligations.
>
> Please let me know when it will be convenient to discuss this matter personally with you.
>
> Yours faithfully

(b) Banker's reply

> Dear Mr Wilson
>
> Thank you for your recent letter requesting overdraft facilities.
>
> We are prepared to consider an overdraft over the period you mention, and have made an appointment for you to see me next Friday 11 November at 2.30 pm. Please bring with you the life policy mentioned together with your company's accounts.
>
> Yours sincerely

[5] **turnover** total sales

27.7 • Request for loan without security

Dear Sir

In April 200— you were good enough to grant me a credit of £5000, which was repaid within the agreed period. I now require a further loan to enable me to proceed with work under a contract with the Waterfoot Borough Council for building an extension to their King's Road School.

I need the loan to purchase building materials at a cost of about £6000. The contract price is £20,000, payable immediately upon satisfactory completion of the work on or before 30 September next.

I hope you will be able to grant me a loan of £5000 for a period of 9 months.

I enclose a copy of my latest audited balance sheet and shall be glad to call at the bank at your convenience to discuss the matter.

Yours faithfully

27.8 • Request for loan with security

Dear Sir

I am considering a large extension of business with several firms in Japan and as the terms of dealings will involve additional working capital,[6] I should be glad if you would arrange to grant me a loan of, say, £6000 for a period of 6 months.

You already hold for safe keeping on my behalf £5000 Australian 3% stock and £4500 4% consols.[7] I am willing to pledge these as security. At current market prices I believe they would provide sufficient cover for the loan.

You would be able to rely upon repayment of the loan at maturity[8] as, apart from other income, I have arranged to take into the business a partner who, under the terms of the partnership agreement, will introduce £5000 capital at or before the end of the present year.

If you will arrange a day and time when I may visit you, I will bring with me evidence supporting my request.

Yours faithfully

---

[6] **working capital** the capital needed to keep a business running
[7] **consols** short for 'consolidated annuities' – a form of British Government stock
[8] **at maturity** when it becomes due

27.9 Request for extension of loan

Dear Sir

On 1 August you granted me a loan of £2500 which is due for repayment at the end of this month.

I have already taken steps to prepare for this repayment but due to a fire at my warehouse 2 weeks ago I have been faced with heavy unexpected payments. Damage from the fire is thought to be about £4000 and is fully covered by insurance. However, as my claim is unlikely to be settled before the end of next month, I hope the period of the loan can be extended until then.

I am sure you will realise that the fire has presented me with serious problems and that repayment of the loan before settlement of my claim could be made only with the greatest difficulty.

Yours faithfully

27.10 Request to clear unauthorised overdraft

(a) Request by bank

Dear Mr Hendon

I notice that since the beginning of last September there have been a number of occasions on which your current account has been overdrawn.[9] As you know it is not the custom of the bank to allow overdrafts except by special arrangement and usually against security.[10]

Two cheques drawn by you have been presented for payment today, one by Insurance Brokers Ltd for £27.50 and one by John Musgrave & Sons for £87.10. As you are one of our oldest customers I gave instructions for the cheques to be paid although the balance on your current account, namely £56.40, was insufficient to meet them.

I am well aware that there is a substantial credit balance on your deposit account. If overdraft facilities on your current account are likely to be needed in future, I suggest that you give the bank the necessary authority to hold the balance on deposit as overdrawn security.

Yours sincerely

[9] **overdrawn** withdrawn in excess of balance available
[10] **security** bonds, certificates or other property pledged to cover a debt

(b) Customer's reply

Dear Mr Stannard

Thank you for your letter of 2 December.

I am sorry to have given you cause to write to me concerning recent overdrafts on my current account. Although the amounts involved are not large I agree that overdraft facilities should have been discussed with you in advance and regret that this was not done. I am afraid I had overlooked the fact that the balance carried on my current account in recent months had been smaller than usual.

Later this month I expect to receive payment for several large contracts now nearing completion. No question of overdraft facilities will then arise. Meanwhile I am pleased to authorise you to treat the balance on my deposit account as security for any overdraft incurred on my current account. Once again my apologies for the inconvenience caused.

Yours sincerely

OTHER BANKING CORRESPONDENCE

27.11 • Customer service

Dear Miss Turner

It has been 4 months since you opened your account with us. I trust that the service you have experienced during this time has been of the highest standard.

Customer Service is a top priority at the Royal International Bank, and that is why we invite all our customers to have a Customer Service Review. This service can take place in person at this branch or over the telephone. It gives customers the opportunity to ensure that they have the most suitable accounts to meet their requirements.

This review is free of charge. If you would like to take advantage of this service, or to discuss any other matters, please contact Kelly Sherman on 01245 343234 to arrange a mutually convenient appointment.

I look forward to speaking to you very soon.

Yours sincerely

27.12 **Offers**

Dear Miss Wright

MAXIMUM SAVINGS, MINIMUM EFFORT

Now that you have opened a Bonus 90 Account, why not build up your savings the hassle-free way with a standing order?

This simple arrangement makes everything so easy – just decide how much you would like to transfer from your current account each month, then complete and sign the attached form. We will do the rest. There is no need to visit your branch, and no need to send any cheques.

WATCH YOUR SAVINGS GROW

If you pay money regularly into a savings account with a high interest rate, you will be surprised at how quickly your nest egg builds up. With tiered rates of interest, you will earn more depending on how much you save.

Take advantage of this great opportunity now by completing the standing order form below and returning it in the enclosed reply-paid envelope.

We really can make saving simple!

Yours sincerely

USEFUL EXPRESSIONS

Openings

1 I have entered into partnership with Mr ... and we wish to open a current account in the name of ...

2 I enclose a standing order for payment of £15 on the first day of each month to ...

3 I shall be moving to ... at the end of this month and should be glad if you would transfer my account to your branch in that town.

4 According to the statement received from you yesterday ...

5 The statement you sent me recently shows that my account was overdrawn ... during July.

6 On referring to the statement just received I notice that ...

7 This is to confirm my telephone message this morning asking you to stop payment of cheque number ...

8 I am writing to ask you to consider a loan of £ ... for a period of ... months.

9 Please arrange to buy for me the following securities within the price ranges shown:

Closes

1 If you require further information please let me know.

2 I shall be glad to call on you should you need any further information.

3 I feel that the charges are excessive and should be glad of your explanation.

4 I should be most grateful if you could grant the credit asked for.

5 If you require a guarantor Mr ... of ... has kindly consented to act.

Banking
(international business)

Cheques are the main means of settling business debts in the home trade. They are not suitable for payments in international trade since a cheque is payable only in the drawer's country. Settlement of overseas debts may be made in a number of ways:

- by banker's draft, banker's transfer (mail, telex and telegraphic)
- letters of credit
- bill of exchange and promissory note.

The method of payment used by the importer will depend upon the arrangement made with the exporter when the order is placed. This will depend on the exporter's knowledge of the importer and the extent of trust existing between them.

In recent years SWIFT has come into operation (Society for Worldwide Inter Bank Financial Telecommunication). All major banks throughout the world are members of SWIFT. This is an electronic mechanism which enables bankers all over the world to communicate with each other, thus speeding up the fund transfer mechanism and cutting down on paperwork. However, the traditional methods of payment mentioned above still exist and will be dealt with in this chapter.

BANKER'S DRAFTS

Like cheques, banker's drafts are payable on demand but unlike cheques they carry little or no risk since they are backed by the assets of the bank issuing them. An importer wishing to pay by draft would buy it at a local bank and send it to the exporter who would simply pay it into their own bank account.

28.1 Payment by banker's draft

(a) Exporter's request for payment

We enclose your statement for the month of November showing an outstanding balance of £580.50.

We assume you will settle this outstanding amount by banker's draft in UK Pounds Sterling and hope to receive payment soon.

(b) Importer's reply

Thank you for your letter together with our November statement.

Our banker's draft for UK Pounds five hundred and eighty and 50 pence (UK£580.50) is enclosed.

BANKER'S TRANSFERS (MAIL, TELEX AND TELEGRAPHIC TRANSFERS)

The banker's transfer is a simple transfer of funds from the bank account of a debtor in their own country to the creditor's bank account in the creditor's country. This is one of the safest methods of sending money abroad. All the debtor has to do is to instruct their bank, either by letter or on a special form, to make the transfer. The debtor's bank then arranges for the creditor's bank to be credited with an amount in local currency equal to the sum transferred. The calculation is made at the current rate of exchange.

As these transfers are arranged direct between the two banks losses are impossible. However, as delays may occur when the transfers are made by mail, it is now customary for banks to communicate either by fax and telegraphic transfer as well as by Internet. Exchange rates for these transfers are quoted in the daily press.

28.2 Payment by telegraphic transfer

> Dear Sir
>
> We have received your statement for the quarter ended 30 September and find that it agrees with our books. As requested we have instructed our bankers, the Midland Bank Ltd, 2 Deansgate, Manchester, to telegraph the sum of £2182.89 for the credit of your account at the Bank Nationalé, Sweden.
>
> This payment clears your account up to 31 August. The unpaid balance of £623.42 for goods supplied during September will be telegraphed by our bankers on or before 15 November.
>
> Yours faithfully

BILLS OF EXCHANGE

A bill of exchange is a written order by a creditor (the drawer) to the debtor (the drawee) requiring payment of the sum of money stated in the order to a named person or firm (the payee), usually on a stated future date. Dealings in bills of exchange are now almost entirely confined to international trade, though even here they have now been largely replaced by other forms of payment, especially by the system of bank credits.

A drawee who agrees to the terms of the bill 'accepts' (ie undertakes to pay) and signs it; they then become liable to meet the bill when it falls due for payment.

In this example:
the *drawer* is: Trevor Gartside,
the *drawee* is: C. Mazzawi,
the *payee* is: E. Hughes & Co.

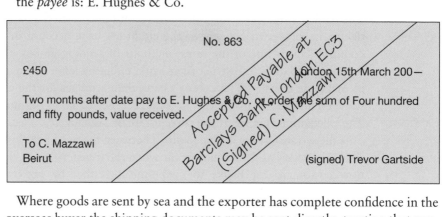

No. 863

£450

Two months after date pay to E. Hughes & Co. or order the sum of Four hundred and fifty pounds, value received.

To C. Mazzawi
Beirut

London 15th March 200—

Accepted Payable at Barclays Bank London EC3 (Signed) C. Mazzawi

(signed) Trevor Gartside

Where goods are sent by sea and the exporter has complete confidence in the overseas buyer the shipping documents may be sent directly, trusting that payment will be made for them according to the terms of the contract. Where these provide for the buyer's acceptance of the exporter's draft bill of exchange, the buyer is entitled to retain the documents when the goods have been accepted and returns the draft.

The exporter frequently requires the importer to arrange for the bill to be accepted by a bank or other financial house. This gives greater security to the person who holds the bill. Even when the importer accepts the bill, the exporter may require that it be marked payable at a named bank as in the above illustration. The holder must then present it to that bank for payment. This is called 'domiciling' a bill. Bills *domiciled in London*[1] are readily taken by the Bank of England for *rediscounting.*[2]

28.3 Payment by bill of exchange

(a) Direct transaction with a trusted customer

Dear Sir

We thank you for your order of 25 June for 1000 metres of poplin shirting at the quoted price of £0.86 per metre.

The shirting is now ready for despatch and will be shipped by the SS *Tripoli* sailing from Liverpool on 18 July.

We are pleased to enclose shipping documents. Also enclosed is our <u>sight draft</u>[3] drawn at 30 days as agreed. Please accept and return it immediately.

Yours faithfully

[1] **domiciled in London** marked as payable in London
[2] **rediscounting** to discount a bill is to obtain payment for it before the due date, at a figure below face value
[3] **sight draft** a bill of exchange payable immediately upon acceptance

(b) Direct transaction with unknown customer

> Dear Sirs
>
> We are pleased to inform you that we can supply the fancy leather goods included in your order number 582 of 6 August and in accordance with our draft at 30 days for acceptance by your bankers.
>
> Immediately we receive the accepted draft we will arrange to ship the goods. Meanwhile we are holding them for you.
>
> Yours faithfully

28.4 Buyer requests extension of time

(a) Buyer's request

> Dear Sirs
>
> You informed me on 25 November that you intended to draw on me at 2 months for the amount due on your invoice number S 256, namely £961.54.
>
> Until now I have had no difficulty in meeting my obligations and have always settled my accounts promptly. I could have done so now had it not been for the bankruptcy of one of my most important customers. I should therefore be most grateful if you could draw your bill at 3 months instead of the proposed 2. This would enable me to meet a temporarily difficult situation which has been forced upon me by circumstances that could not be foreseen.
>
> Yours faithfully

(b) Seller's reply granting request

> Dear Sir
>
> I am replying to your letter of 30 November in which you ask for an extension of the tenor[4] of my draft from 2 to 3 months.
>
> In the special circumstances you mention and because of the promptness with which you have settled your accounts in the past, we are willing to grant the request. Our draft, drawn at 3 months, is enclosed. Please add your acceptance and return it to me.
>
> Yours faithfully

---

[4] **tenor** the period for which a bill of exchange is drawn

(c) Seller's reply refusing request

When refusing a request it is easy to give offence and lose a customer. This example is a tactful and understanding letter and while it will give rise to disappointment it is unlikely to cause offence.

Dear Sir

I am sorry to learn from your letter of 30 November of the difficulty in which the bankruptcy of an important customer has placed you. I should like to say at once that I fully appreciate your wish for an extension of my draft and would very much like to help you. Unfortunately, I cannot do so because of commitments which I have to meet in 2 months' time.

In the circumstances you mention your request is not at all unreasonable. If it had been at all possible I would gladly have done so. As matters stand I am left with no choice but to ask you to accept the draft, as drawn at 2 months. This is enclosed for your signature and return.

Yours faithfully

28.5　Bill dishonoured at maturity

When a buyer who has accepted a bill fails to meet it *at maturity*[5] the bill is said to be 'dishonoured' and the debt for which it was drawn is immediately revived. Dishonour entitles the drawer or other holder of the bill to take legal action against the acceptor either (a) on the bill or (b) on the debt for which it was drawn.

(a) Drawer requests explanation

Dear Sirs

We were very surprised this morning when our bankers returned the bill we drew on you for £325 on 5 August marked 'Refer to drawer'.

Since we are aware from personal knowledge that your firm is financially sound, we presume that failure to honour the bill was due to some mistake. We shall therefore be glad if you will explain the reason. At the same time we must ask you to send by return the sum due on the bill.

Yours faithfully

---

[5] **at maturity** when payment becomes due

(b) Drawer threatens legal action

> Dear Sir
>
> I regret to say that our bill number 670 for £462.72 of 15 December was not met when we presented it to the bank today.
>
> In view of your earlier promise to meet your obligations on the bill, we are both surprised and disappointed that payment has not been made. We should like to feel that there has been some misunderstanding and ask you to explain why the bill was not <u>honoured</u>.[6]
>
> At the same time we are making a formal request for payment of the sum due and shall be glad to receive your remittance. If payment is not made I am afraid we shall have no choice but to start proceedings for dishonour.
>
> Yours faithfully

28.6 Dishonoured bill protested

When a foreign bill (but not an inland bill) is dishonoured it must be 'protested' as a preliminary to legal action. A 'protest' is a formal declaration by a *notary public*[7] that the terms of the bill have not been fulfilled. Its purpose is to prevent the drawee (the acceptor) from denying that the bill was presented for payment (or for acceptance if it is dishonoured by non-acceptance).

In the following letter the supplier gives the buyer a further opportunity to pay, even after protest.

> Dear Sir
>
> Although you gave your <u>unqualified acceptance</u>[8] to our bill number 670 of 15 December for £462.72, this was not met when presented for payment yesterday.
>
> Non-payment has obliged us to make formal protest of the bill. We now offer you this final opportunity to meet your obligations by payment of the sum of £465.22 to cover the amount for which the bill was accepted and the expenses of protest as follows:
>
> | | |
> |---|---|
> | Nominal value of the bill | £462.72 |
> | Expenses of protest | 2.50 |
>
> We hope to receive payment within the next few days so as to avoid our having to take further proceedings.
>
> Yours faithfully

---

[6] **honoured** paid when due
[7] **notary public** usually a solicitor specially authorised to witness deeds and other important documents
[8] **unqualified acceptance** a full and complete acceptance

DOCUMENTARY BILLS

The above examples refer to transactions conducted between importer and exporter direct, but it is more usual for the exporter to gain protection by using the services of the banks. There are three main methods, each requiring the exporter to prepare a documentary bill (ie a draft bill of exchange with shipping documents attached) and to leave it with the bank, which passes it to its foreign branch or correspondent, who then deals with the importer.

1 The importer is ordered to pay the draft either to the exporter, to their order, or to the bank.

2 The exporter again draws on the importer, but asks the bank to discount the draft against the security of the shipping documents, which are passed to the banker.

3 The exporter requires the importer to arrange for a letter of credit, the purpose of which is to enable the exporter to draw on a named bank when the shipping documents are presented. The letter of credit against which the bill is drawn must state the maximum amount and the duration of the credit, the usance (ie the term) of the bill and the shipping documents that are to be sent with the bill.

Where the draft on the importer is drawn for a term, say 60 days, the banker presenting it will hand over the shipping documents only against acceptance (*D/A terms*[9]), but where it is drawn payable on demand, this will be done only against payment (*D/P terms*[10]).

In practice, instructions to the banks are usually given on special forms provided by the banks themselves, thus making certain that all important points are covered. In the correspondence that follows instructions to the banks are given in letters of the kind that would be sent where special forms are not provided.

[9] **D/A terms** documents against acceptance terms.
[10] **D/P terms** documents against payment terms.

28.7 Documentary bill presented through bank

(a) Exporter's letter to importer, D/P terms

Dear Sirs

We were pleased to receive your faxed order of 29 June and have arranged to ship the electric shavers by SS Tyrania leaving London on 6 July and due to arrive at Sidon on the 24th.

As the urgency of your order left no time to make the usual enquiries, we are compelled to place this transaction on a cash basis and have drawn on you through Midminster Bank Ltd for the amount of the enclosed invoice. The bank will instruct their correspondent in Sidon to pass the bill of lading to you against payment of the draft.

Special care has been taken to select items suited to your local conditions. We hope you will find them satisfactory and that your present order will be the first of many.

Yours faithfully

(b) Exporter's letter to importer, D/A terms

Dear Sirs

YOU ORDER NO B 614

We are pleased to inform you that arrangements have now been made to ship the dress goods you ordered on 15 October. The consignment will leave London on 1 November by SS Manchester Trader and is due to arrive at Quebec on the 22nd.

In keeping with our usual terms of payment we have drawn on you at 60 days and passed the draft and shipping documents to our bankers. The documents will be presented to you by the National Bank of Canada against your acceptance of the draft in the usual way.

Yours faithfully

28.8 Exporter's instructions to bank (D/P terms) (to be read with 28.7(a))

Dear Sirs

On 6 July we are shipping a consignment of 2000 electric shavers to the Sidon Electrical Co of whom we have little knowledge and whose standing we have been unable to check. We therefore think it would be unwise to surrender the enclosed documents on a D/A basis and enclose a sight draft on the consignees, with bill of lading and insurance certificate attached.

Will you please arrange for your correspondent in Sidon to obtain payment of the amount due before handing over the documents, and let us know when payment has been made.

Yours faithfully

28.9 Documentary bill sent through exporter's bank

Exporters sometimes send the documentary bill direct to a bank in the importer's country but they more usually deal with their own bank, who arrange for the bill to be presented to the foreign buyer by their branch or correspondent abroad.

(a) Exporter's letter to bank

Dear Sirs

We have today shipped by SS Seafarer a consignment of haberdashery to the Nigerian Trading Co, Lagos. Since the standing of this company is unknown to us we do not wish to hand over the shipping documents against their mere acceptance of a bill of exchange. Therefore we enclose a sight draft on them, together with bill of lading and the other shipping documents. In the circumstances we shall require payment of the draft in full before the documents are handed over. Please instruct your correspondent in Lagos to arrange for this.

Yours faithfully

(b) Exporters advice of shipment to Nigerian Trading Co

When sending the above letter to their bankers, the exporters will send advice of shipment to the Nigerian Trading Co and explain the arrangements made for payment.

Dear Sirs

The goods which you ordered on 2 October have been shipped to you today by SS Seafarer, due at Lagos on 2 December.

We have taken special care to include in the consignment only items suited to conditions in Nigeria. We hope you will be pleased with our selection and that your first order will lead to further business between us.

From the enclosed copy invoice you will see that the price of £865.75 is well within the maximum figure you stated. We have drawn on you for this amount at sight through the Barminster Bank, who have been instructed to hand over documents against payment of the draft. We hope you will understand that the urgency of your order left us with insufficient time to make the usual enquiries. Therefore we had no choice but to follow our standard practice with new customers of placing the transaction on a cash basis.

We look forward to your further orders. Subject to satisfactory references and regular dealings, we would be prepared to consider open-account terms[11] with quarterly settlements.

Yours faithfully

[11] **open-account terms** credit terms with periodic settlement

28.10 Documentary bill sent direct to importer's bank

Dear Sir

We enclose shipping documents for 10,000 bags of rice shipped by SS <u>Thailand</u> which left Bangkok for London on 15 October.

Please hand the documents to Messrs B Stephenson & Co of London EC2P 2AA, as soon as they are ready to take them up against payment of £4260 (four thousand two hundred and sixty pounds) less interest at 2½% from date of payment to 31 December next. Our account should be credited with the proceeds after deducting your charges.

Yours faithfully

An exporter in need of immediate funds will sometimes ask their bank to advance money on a documentary bill. The bank will in return require their execution of a letter of hypothecation. This is a letter authorising the bank to sell the goods should the bill be dishonoured by the importer. An exporter who regularly obtains such advances often signs a general letter of hypothecation which covers all future transactions.

BANKER'S COMMERCIAL CREDITS

From the exporter's point of view the documentary bill suffers from the defect that the foreign buyer may fail to honour the bill. To avoid this risk a system of *banker's commercial credits* or *documentary credits* has been developed. The system is now widely used and works in the following manner.

1 Importers ask their own bank to open a credit in favour of the exporter, usually on a specially printed application form.

2 The importer's bank then sends a letter of credit to the exporter or, more usually, arranges for one of its branches or correspondents in the exporter's country to do so.

3 From this point the exporter deals with the correspondent bank and when the goods are shipped prepares the shipping documents and presents them (more often than not with a bill of exchange drawn on the correspondent bank) to the correspondent bank, which 'pays' for them within the limits of the authorised credit and sends them to the importer's bank.

4 The importer's bank in turn passes the documents to the importer either against payment or against an acceptance of a bill of exchange, if one accompanies the documents.

In effect, the importer's bank is temporarily providing the funds from which the exporter is paid, though it will usually require the importer to maintain a sufficient balance in their account to cover the credit.

The credit can be either *revocable*[12] or *irrevocable*.[13] Under a revocable letter of credit the importer is free to modify or even cancel the credit without so much as giving notice to the exporter, but an irrevocable credit can be neither amended nor withdrawn without the permission of the exporter to whom it is granted; the exporter can therefore rely on being paid.

Within the broad pattern illustrated above there may sometimes be slight differences, but they do not affect the general principles on which the system works. Correspondence connected with these credits is very technical; this is evident from the complicated nature of the printed forms used by the banks, and should be handled by someone who is thoroughly familiar with the practice.

28.11 A documentary credit – stages in transactions

Perhaps the best way to study the system of bank commercial or documentary credits is to follow a transaction through. In this transaction, Messrs A H Brooks & Son are a firm of London fur dealers. They have agreed to take monthly deliveries of furs from the North American Trading Company over a period of 6 months and to open a credit on which the company can draw as shipments are made. Correspondence would take place on the following lines:

(a) Buyer approaches bank

> Dear Sirs
>
> We have just concluded an agreement to purchase monthly shipments of furs from Canada over the next 6 months and would like to make use of foreign-payment facilities by opening a series of monthly credits for £2000 each in favour of the North American Trading Company. It has been agreed that we provide credits with a bank in Quebec against which our suppliers would draw for the value of shipments as they are made.
>
> Please let us know on what terms your bank would be prepared to arrange necessary credits and to handle the shipping documents for us.
>
> Yours faithfully

---

[12] **revocable** can be altered or cancelled
[13] **irrevocable** cannot be altered or cancelled

(b) Bank offers to provide credits

Dear

Thank you for your enquiry of 15 March. We shall be pleased to handle the shipments and to arrange for the necessary documentary credits with our Quebec branch against deposit of bill of lading and other shipping documents. Please complete and return the enclosed form so that we can make the arrangements.

Our commission charges for revocable documentary credits would be $\frac{1}{8}$ to $\frac{1}{4}$% on each of the monthly credits, to which must be added $\frac{1}{4}$% for irrevocable credits and also our charges for such items as telegrams and postages. In return for these charges you have our assurance that your interests would be carefully protected.

Yours sincerely

(c) Buyer instructs bank

Dear

Thank you for your letter of 17 March. I have completed and enclose the form of application for a documentary credit. Please arrange to open for our account with your office in Quebec irrevocable credits for £2000 a month in favour of the North American Trading Company, the credits to be valid until 30 September next.

To enable them to use the credits the company must present the following documents: bills of lading in triplicate, one copy of the invoice, the certificate or policy of insurance and certificate of origin, and draw on your Quebec office at 60 days after sight for each consignment. The documents relate to five cases of mixed furs in each consignment at the value of about £350 per case, cif London.

Yours sincerely

(d) Bank agrees to open credit

If the bank agrees to open a credit they will usually notify the buyer on one of their own standard printed forms. If this is done by letter instead, they would write in some such terms as the following.

Dear

As instructed in your letter of 20 March we are arranging to open a documentary credit with our branch in Quebec in favour of the North American Trading Company, valid until 30 September. Enclosed is a copy of our instruction opening the credit. Please check it to ensure that it agrees with your instructions. As soon as the credits are used we shall debit your account with the amount notified to us as having been drawn against them.

We shall take all necessary steps to make sure that your instructions are carefully carried out. Please note, however, that we cannot assume any responsibility for the safety of the goods or for delays in delivery since these are matters beyond our control.

Yours sincerely

(e) Buyer notifies exporter

The bank in London now sends to its Quebec office a copy of the form completed by Brooks & Son to authorise the opening of the credit.

Dear

We have opened irrevocable credits in your favour for £2000 a month with the Royal Bank of Canada, Quebec, valid until 30 September next.

The terms of the credit authorise you to draw at 60 days on the bank in Quebec for the amount of your invoices after each shipment of five cases. Before accepting the draft, which should include all charges to London, the bank will require you to produce the following documents: bills of lading in triplicate, one copy of the invoice covering cif London, a certificate or policy of insurance and certificate of origin. We will expect your first consignment around the middle of next month.

Yours sincerely

(f) Bank issues letter of credit

The next step is for the Quebec office of the bank to notify the North American Trading Company that the credit is available. They may use a printed form for the purpose. If they were to send the advice by letter or fax and if the London office had requested them to confirm the credit, the message would be something like the following.

Dear

On instructions from Messrs A H Brooks & Son received through our London office, we have opened monthly irrevocable credits for £2000 in your favour valid until 30 September next. You have authority to draw on us at 60 days against these credits for the amount of your invoices upon shipment of furs to Messrs A H Brooks & Son.

Your draws must be accompanied by the following documents which are to be delivered to us against our acceptance of the drafts: bills of lading in triplicate, commercial invoice, insurance certificate or policy and certificate of origin.

Provided you fulfil the terms of the credit we will accept and pay at maturity the drafts presented to us under these credits and, if required, provide discounting facilities at current rates.

Yours sincerely

In this letter the irrevocable credit is issued by the London Branch of the Royal Bank of Canada and is 'confirmed' by the Quebec branch of the same bank in the final paragraph of its letter to the exporter. Where the bank issuing the credit does not have a branch of its own in the exporter's country it will arrange for the credit to be notified to the exporter through a correspondent bank. Unless the issuing bank has authorised or requested its correspondent to confirm the credit, and it does so, the correspondent is under no obligation to accept the exporter's drafts. If it does confirm the credit, it enters into a definite undertaking with the exporter to accept drafts drawn under the credit, provided they conform to its terms. This undertaking is independent of, and in addition to, that of the bank issuing the irrevocable credit, thus providing the exporter with a twofold assurance of payment.

(g) Exporter presents documents

Dear

Referring to your advice of 30 March, we enclose shipping documents for the first of the monthly consignments to Messrs A H Brooks & Son.

As required by them we have included all charges in our invoice, which amounts to £1725.71 and enclose our draft at 60 days for this sum. We shall be glad if, after acceptance, you will discount it at the current rate and send the net amount to our account with the Banque de France, Quebec.

We thank you for your help in this matter.

Yours sincerely

Note: The Quebec office now sends the shipping documents to its London office with a statement of the amount of the draft charged against the credit.

(h) Bank debits buyers

Dear Mr Jones

As instructed by your letter of 20 March, our Quebec office has just accepted for your account a bill for £1725.71 drawn by the North American Trading Company for a first consignment of furs to you by SS <u>Columbia</u>. We have debited your account with this amount and our charges amounting to £15.30.

The ship left Quebec on 22 April and is due to arrive in London on 2 May. The shipping documents for this consignment are now with us and we shall be glad if you will arrange to collect them.

Yours sincerely

USEFUL EXPRESSIONS

Buyer to exporter

Openings

1 We have received your invoice number ... and agree to accept your draft at 60 days after sight for the amount due.

2 As requested in your letter of ... we have instructed the ... Bank to open a credit for £... in your favour.

3 We are sorry to have to ask for the term of your bill dated ... to be extended for one month.

4 I regret that at the moment I cannot meet in full my acceptance, which is due for payment on ...

Closes

1 Please let us know whether you are prepared to give us open-account terms.

2 Please draw on us for the amount due and attach the shipping documents to your draft.

3 We should like to pay by bill of exchange at 60 days after sight and should be glad if you would agree to this.

4 As requested we will arrange to open an irrevocable credit in your favour.

5 Our acceptance will be honoured upon presentation of the bill at the ... branch of the ... Bank.

Exporter to buyer

Openings

1 We have considered your letter of ... and are pleased to grant the open-account terms asked for.

2 As requested in your letter of ... we have drawn on you for the amount of our April account at 3 months from ...

3 As agreed in our earlier correspondence we have drawn on you for the amount of the invoice enclosed.

Closes

1 Please accept the draft and return it as soon as you can.

2 We are quite willing to put your account on a documents-against-acceptance basis.

3 We have instructed our bank to hand over the shipping documents against acceptance (payment) of our draft.

4 Shipping documents, and our draft for acceptance, have been passed to the ... Bank.

5 As arranged, we have instructed our bank to surrender (hand over) the documents against payment (acceptance) of our draft.

6 As soon as the credit is confirmed, we will ship the goods.

Buyer to bank

Openings

1 I enclose accepted bill, drawn on me by ..., and should now be glad to receive the shipping documents.

2 Please accept and pay the following drafts for me and, at maturity, debit them to my account.

3 Please arrange with your correspondents in ... to open a credit in favour of ...

Closes

1 Please accept the above draft for me and debit your charges to my account.

2 Please state the amount of your charges for arranging the necessary credits.

Exporter to bank

Openings

1 We enclose our sight draft on ... of ... and also the shipping documents.

2 Please surrender the enclosed documents to ... of ... when they accept our draft, also enclosed.

3 Please instruct your correspondent in ... to release the documents only on payment of our sight draft for £...

Closes

1 Please obtain acceptance of this draft before surrendering the shipping documents.

2 Please present the bill for acceptance and then discount it for the credit of our account.

3 Please present this acceptance for payment at maturity and credit us with the proceeds.

Transport

CARRIAGE BY SEA

Transporting goods by sea is still attractive in view of the increase in size and speed of ships and the greatly increased use of the container. Ships are now built specifically to carry particular types of bulk cargoes such as oil, mineral ores, meat and fruit.

Liners and tramps

It is usual to classify ships into liners (ships which sail at regular times on set routes) and tramps (ships which have no set times or routes, but go wherever they can find suitable cargoes). Hardly any tramps are used these days for long distance hauls except within the United Kingdom. Tramps are essentially cargo boats, ready at any time to make any particular voyage.

Liners may be either passenger liners or cargo liners. Passenger liners usually take a certain amount of miscellaneous cargo, while cargo liners often provide a limited amount of accommodation for passengers.

The contracts entered into between shipowner and shipper (ie the consignor) may take the form of *either*

a charter party (where a complete ship is hired)

or

a bill of lading (where the ship carries cargoes belonging to various different shippers).

Chartering of ships

When goods are shipped in large consignments, and this applies especially to *bulk cargoes*,[1] it may be an advantage to hire or charter a complete ship either for a particular voyage (a voyage charter) or for an agreed period of time (a time charter). The documents setting out the terms and conditions of the contract between the shipowner who provides the ship and the merchant (the charterer) who hires it is called a charter party. Standard forms of charter party have been drawn up but many shipowners prefer to draw up their own forms.

Ship chartering is usually arranged through shipbrokers; in London the Baltic Exchange acts as a special centre where these brokers conduct business.

The shipping conference system

A shipping conference is an association formed by British and foreign shipping lines, serving a particular sea route. There are some 300 of these conferences,

[1] **bulk cargoes** those not packed but loaded loose

each serving its own particular route or area, eg North Atlantic, South African and Australian. The purpose of the conference is to fix and maintain *freight rates*[2] at a profitable level, and to ensure that a sufficient minimum of cargo is always forthcoming to feed the regular sailings they undertake to provide. They do this by establishing 'ties' between shippers and themselves. The 'tie' may take the form of a *deferred rebate*[3] to shippers who confine their shipment to vessels owned by members of the conference; but the rebate system has now been largely replaced by a *preferential rate system*.[4]

The conference system has advantages for both shipper and shipowner. For the shipper it provides the certainty of regular sailings and reliable delivery dates; for the shipowner it ensures that, in return for undertaking to maintain regular sailings, shippers will place their cargoes with him rather than elsewhere. This helps the conference shipowner to keep ships employed.

The container service

The use of containers provides a highly efficient form of transport by road, rail and air. Its fullest benefits are felt in shipping where costs may be considerably reduced. Containers are constructed in metal and are of standard lengths ranging from 10 to 40 feet (approximately 3–12 metres).

The container service has the following advantages:

- Containers can be loaded and locked at factory premises at nearby container bases making *pilferage*[5] more difficult.
- There is reduced risk of goods getting lost or mislaid in transit.
- Handling is greatly reduced with lower costs and less risk of danger.
- Mechanical handling enables cargoes to be loaded in a matter of hours rather than days, thus reducing the time ships spend in port and greatly increasing the number of sailings.
- Temperature-controlled containers are provided for types of cargo which need them.

[2] **freight rates** transport charges
[3] **deferred rebate** a discount to be allowed later
[4] **preferential rate system** a system offering lower freight rates to conference members
[5] **pilferage** small thefts

29.1 Enquiry for sailings and freight rates

Enquiries of this nature will normally be conducted by telephone or fax. The consignor (or agent) will need to know freight rates and dates of sailings.

> We shall shortly have ready for shipment from Liverpool to Alexandria, 4 cases of crockery. The cases measure 1¼ x 1¼ x l m, each weighing 70 kg.
>
> Please quote your rate for freight and send us details of your sailings and the time usually taken for the voyage.

29.2 Shipping company's reply to enquiry in 29.1

> The SS <u>Princess Victoria</u> will be loading at number 2 dock from 8 to 13 July inclusive. Following her is the SS <u>Merchant Prince</u>, loading at number 5 dock from 20 to 24 July inclusive.
>
> The voyage to Alexandria normally takes 14 days. The freight rate for crockery packed in wooden cases is £97.00 per tonne.
>
> We shall be glad to book your 4 cases for either of these vessels and enclose our shipping form. Please complete it and return it as soon as possible.

29.3 Agent issues forwarding instructions

When notified by the supplier that the goods are ready, the agent either arranges to collect them and despatch them to the docks or will ask the supplier to do so. The shipping form is then returned to the shipping company making arrangements for the goods to be received at the docks.

(a) Agent's advice to supplier

> Thank you for informing us that the items ordered on 16 June are now ready for collection.
>
> Please arrange to send the consignment by road to Liverpool for shipment by SS <u>Merchant Prince</u> due to sail for Alexandria on 25 July and to load at number 5 dock from 20 to 24 July inclusive. All cases should be clearly marked and numbered as shown in our official order. Invoices, in triplicate, and your account for transport charges should be sent to us.
>
> All the necessary arrangements have been made with the shipping company.

(b) Agent's instruction to shipping company

We have today arranged for H J Cooper & Co. Ltd, Manchester, to forward to you by road the following cases to be shipped to Alexandria by SS <u>Merchant Prince</u> on 25 July.

4 cases of crockery, marked ⟨JP⟩ numbers 1–4

The completed shipping form is enclosed together with 4 copies of the bill of lading. Please sign and return 3 copies of the bill and charge the amount to our account.

Shipping and forwarding agents

A shipping and forwarding agent carries out all the duties connected with collecting and delivering the client's goods. These services are particularly valuable in foreign trade because of the complicated arrangements which have to be made. For exporters, the shipping company collects the goods, makes all the arrangements for shipping them, and notifies their despatch to the forwarding agent in the importing country. The latter takes delivery of the goods and either forwards them to the buyer or arranges for them to be warehoused if the buyer does not want them immediately.

Packing, shipping and forwarding agents are specialists; they know the best methods of packing particular types of goods and the most suitable form of packing to use for the country to which the goods are being sent.

By assembling and repacking in larger lots, small consignments intended for the same destination, the forwarding agent can obtain lower freight rates. It is therefore often cheaper, and certainly much simpler, for suppliers to employ a forwarding agent than to deal directly with the shipping and road transport organisations. Many importers and exporters, however, prefer to reduce their costs by dealing direct with clearing or forwarding agents in the countries of their suppliers (if they are importers) or of their customers (if they are exporters).

29.4 Advice of shipment to forwarding agent in buyer's country (Alexandria)

Please note that we have shipped the following goods to you by SS <u>Merchant Prince</u> which left Liverpool yesterday and is due to arrive at Alexandria on 9 August.

Mark and Numbers	Goods	Gross Weight	Value
JR 1–4	4 cases crockery	280 kg	£3250

Insurance in the sum of £2200 is provided as far as Alexandria only.

A copy of the bill of lading and the invoice are enclosed. Please arrange to handle the consignment and deliver it to Messrs Jean Riachi & Co, Mansura, who will be responsible for all charges.

The consignment is urgently required so your prompt attention will be appreciated.

29.5 Advice of shipment to buyer

When the consignment has been shipped and the buyer's forwarding agent notified, the agent will write to inform the buyer of receipt of the consignment. The letter takes the form of an advice of despatch.

YOUR INDENT N0 762

We are pleased to inform you that all goods ordered on your above indent have now been shipped by SS <u>Merchant Prince</u> which sailed from Liverpool yesterday and is due to arrive in Alexandria on 9 August.

The consignment will be handled on arrival by Messrs Behren & Co who will make all the arrangements for delivery.

The bill of lading, invoice, and our account for commission and charges are enclosed. The suppliers have been informed that you will settle their account direct.

We hope to hear from you soon that the goods have arrived safely.

Forwarding agents

Where exporters arrange shipment through a forwarding agent in their own country, the agent handles the whole transaction. This includes arranging for the goods to be collected and transported to the docks and paying the charges, making the arrangements with the shipping company, paying the freight, insuring the goods, preparing the bill of lading and dealing with any other documents which may be necessary (eg consular invoice, *certificate of origin*,[6] certificate of value and weight, export licence, etc). When the goods have been shipped the exporter's agent advises the shipping and forwarding agent in the buyer's country, who deals with them when they arrive at the port. In short, a forwarding agent does everything and, as a specialist in the business, does it well.

29.6 Supplier seeks forwarding agent's services

> We have a consignment of tape recorders now waiting to be shipped to Messrs Tan & Co of Kuala Lumpur. Will you please arrange for the consignment to be collected from the above address and arrange shipment to Klang by the first possible sailing. When it arrives at Klang the consignment will be handled for our customers by Mr J Collins with whom you should make the necessary arrangements.
>
> The recorders are packed in 3 cases and the enclosed copy of the invoice shows quantities and a total value of £2800. Insurance should be taken out for £2900 to include cover for expenses.
>
> When the goods are shipped please send the original bill of lading and one copy to us, together with the certificate or policy of insurance and any other necessary documents.

CARRIAGE BY AIR

Bills of lading are used for consignments by sea. They are not used for consignments by air because the goods usually reach their destination before a bill of lading could be prepared. Instead the consignor is required to prepare an airway bill giving particulars of the consignment. This normally consists of a number of copies, some of which are treated as originals, one for the issuing air carrier, one for the consignee and one for the consignor. The remaining copies serve for other possible carriers and for Customs and record purposes.

It is common practice for the airline or its agent to prepare the airway bill from details supplied by the consignor on a special form – an Instructions for Despatch of Goods form – provided by the airline or by the forwarding agents.

Like the bill of lading, the airway bill serves as a receipt for the goods taken on board and is evidence of the contract of carriage, the terms of which are set out in detail on the back. Unlike the bill of lading, however, the airway bill is not a document of title.

With carriage by air, the consignor may also use the services of a forwarding agent or may deal with the airline direct through its cargo-booking section. The more usual practice is to use an agent.

---

[6] **certificate of origin** a document entitling importer to preferential Customs duties

Air cargo is charged by weight except for bulky commodities which are charged by volume. To encourage movement of traffic by air, special rates are charged for a wide range of enumerated articles. Valuables are subject to a surcharge to cover extra handling costs.

29.7 Enquiry for air freight rates (through agent)

We shall shortly have a consignment of electric shavers, weighing about 20 kg, for a customer in Damascus. We wish to send this by air from London.

Please let us have details of the cost and any formalities to be observed. The invoice value of the consignment is £1550 and we should require insurance cover for this amount plus the costs of sending the consignment.

29.8 Forwarding agent's reply

Thank you for your enquiry regarding your consignment to Damascus. All our charges including freight, airway bill fee, insurance and our own commission are shown on the attached schedule.

To enable us to prepare your airway bill we shall need the information requested in the enclosed form. Three copies of a certified commercial invoice and a certificate of origin will also be necessary.

Your consignment should be in our hands by 10 am on the morning of departure day. Please telephone me when you are ready to deliver the consignment to our officer at the airport so that we can prepare to receive it and deal with it promptly. Alternatively we can make arrangements to collect the goods.

We hope to receive instructions from you soon.

CARRIAGE BY ROAD

Road transport is generally cheaper than rail for both passengers and goods, although rail is cheaper for such bulk commodities as oil, sand and timber.

The most important features of road transport are:

- the ease with which it adapts itself to different situations and the fact that a direct delivery service is provided
- routes are easily varied according to traffic flow
- it is safer for fragile goods and calls for simpler packing than for goods sent by rail
- it is particularly suitable for short distance traffic, mainly because small truck loads can be dealt with easily and quickly.

Documents used

When goods are handed to a carrier the contract of carriage takes the form of a consignment note or waybill (if transport is by road, rail or air). The originals of these documents are handed to the *consignors*[7] and serve as their receipts. The carrier keeps a copy for himself and a further copy is passed on to the *consignee*[8] with the goods.

29.9 Enquiry for freight rates

Early next month we shall have a consignment of motor-car spares for delivery from our warehouse to a company in Aberdeen.

These spares will be packed in 2 wooden cases, each measuring 1 x 1 x 0·75 m and weighing about 80 kg.

Please let us know as soon as possible:

1 Your charge for collecting and delivering these cases.

2 If you can collect them on the 3rd of next month.

3 When delivery would be made to the consignee.

An early reply would be appreciated.

29.10 Supplier notifies despatch of goods

Your Order No 825

We have today despatched by Williams Transport Ltd 2 wooden cases containing the motor-car spares which you ordered recently.

Would you please unpack and examine them as soon as possible after delivery and in the event of any damage notify us and also the carriers at once.

We understand the goods will be delivered to you in 3 days' time.

29.11 Buyer notifies receipt of goods

Our Order No 825

The 2 cases of motor-car spares despatched with Williams Transport Ltd were delivered yesterday in good condition.

The cases are being returned to you by Williams Transport. Please credit us with the amount charged for them on your invoice.

[7] **consignor** the one who sends the goods
[8] **consignee** the one to whom the goods are sent

29.12 **Removal of household furniture**

(a) Request for quotation

> Early next month we will be moving from the above address to 110 Normanshire Drive, Chingford. I would like a quotation on the cost of your removal services.
>
> Our present house has 6 rooms, all of which are fully furnished. You will no doubt wish to inspect our furniture so please arrange for one of your representatives to call as soon as possible.
>
> I hope to hear from you soon.

(b) Quotation

> We are writing to confirm the removal of your furniture from St Annes to Chingford on 3 May.
>
> Our charge for the removal will be £950, including insurance cover in the sum of £45,000. We enclose an agreement form setting out the terms and conditions and shall be glad if you will sign and return it.
>
> Our van with three workmen will arrive at your house at 7.30 am on 3 May. The loading should be completed in about three hours. We should be able to deliver to your Chingford address and complete unloading by 4.30 pm on the following day.
>
> Please let me know if you have any queries.

(c) Claim for damage to property during removal

> When your workmen removed the furniture from my house in St Annes on 3 May the staircase was badly damaged. The new owner of this house has obtained an estimate for the repair in the sum of £220 and he is now claiming this amount from me.
>
> I realise the insurance policy you provided only covered damage to furniture. However, as the damage now reported is claimed to have been caused by your workmen I have advised the new owner to contact you directly.

CARRIAGE BY RAIL

Over long distances and for bulk commodities such as oil, sand and timber rail is cheaper than road. However, unlike road transport, it cannot collect and deliver without the help of some other form of transport. This sometimes causes delay, involves double handling, calls for more complicated packing, increases the risk of theft and damage, and consequently increases costs. The railways are increasingly meeting these problems by using 'containers'.

Goods may be carried either at owner's risk or at company's risk, rates for the former being lower. Rates also vary with the class of goods.

Unless otherwise agreed between buyer and seller, responsibility for collecting and transporting the purchases lies with the buyer. If a carrier is engaged, then the carrier becomes the buyer's agent. Once the goods have been taken over by the agent, the seller's responsibility for them ceases and the buyer becomes liable for any loss or damage which may be suffered.

29.13 Claim for losses due to pilferage

(a) Buyer's complaint

> OUR ORDER NO 328
>
> The consignment of cotton shirts despatched on 21 June was delivered yesterday in a very unsatisfactory condition.
>
> It was clear that 2 of the cases (numbers 4 and 7) had been tampered with.[9] Upon checking the contents we found that case number 4 contained only 372 shirts and case number 7 contained only 375 shirts instead of the 400 invoiced for each case.
>
> Before reporting the matter to the railway please confirm that each of these cases contained the invoiced quantity when they left your warehouse. At the same time please replace the 53 missing shirts with others of the same quality.
>
> You will no doubt be claiming compensation[10] from the railway, in which case we shall be glad to assist you with any information we can provide. Meanwhile, the cases are being held for inspection, together with the contents.

(b) Supplier's reply

> We were sorry to learn from your letter of 27 June that 2 of the cases sent to you on 21 June had been tampered with. We confirm that when they left our warehouse each of these cases contained the full quantity of 400 shirts. The cases were in good order when they left our premises; in support of this we hold the carrier's clean receipt.
>
> As we sent the goods by rail at your request, the railway company must be regarded as your agents. We cannot, therefore, accept any responsibility for the losses and can only suggest that you make the claim for compensation directly with the railway company. We are quite willing to support your claim in whatever way we can.
>
> The 53 missing shirts will be replaced but we will have to charge them to your account. In the circumstances we will allow you an extra discount of 10%.
>
> Please let us know in what way we can help in your claim for compensation.

[9] **tampered with** improperly interfered with
[10] **compensation** an amount of money that makes good the loss

(c) Buyer's claim on railway

We regret to report that 2 of the cases covered by your consignment receipt number S5321 were delivered to us in a condition that left no doubt of their having been broken into during transit. The cases in question are numbers 4 and 7.

This was noticed when the cases were delivered by your carrier and accordingly we added to our receipt 'Cases 4 and 7 damaged; contents not examined'. A later check of the contents revealed a shortage of 53 shirts.

The consignment was sent by our suppliers on carrier's risk terms. Therefore we must hold you responsible for the loss. Our claim is enclosed for the invoiced value of the missing shirts (at £4.00 each) which is £212.00. In support of our claim we enclose a certified copy of our supplier's invoice.

The 2 cases and their contents have been put aside to await your inspection.

USEFUL EXPRESSIONS

Openings

Enquiries

1 Thank you for your enquiry of ... we are pleased to quote as follows for the shipment of ... to ...

2 Thank you for your enquiry regarding sailings to Johannesburg in August.

3 We are due to ship a large quantity of ... to ... and need you to obtain a ship of about ... tons capacity.

4 Please let us know the current rates of freight for the following:

5 Please quote an inclusive rate for collection and delivery of ... from ...

Goods despatched

1 We have today sent to you a consignment of ... by SS ...

2 We have given instructions to ... to forward the following consignment to you by rail:

Closes

1 Please inform us of the date on which the ship closes for cargo.

2 Please complete and return the enclosed instructions form with a signed copy of the invoice.

3 We hope to receive your shipping instructions by return.

Insurance

Insurance is provided as a kind of security to cover almost any kind of occurrence which may result in loss. Its purpose is to make compensation available for those who suffer from loss or damage, in other words a contract to restore to their original position a person who suffers loss.

An insurance claim cannot pay out more than the value of what is lost, and nothing is to be gained from insuring a sum greater than the value of the good(s) insured. If, for example, a ship worth £50,000 is insured for £60,000, the owner would receive only £50,000 if the ship is lost and a claim put forward.

A different kind of insurance is that which provides for payment of a fixed sum in advance to a person when they reach a given age, or to any dependants upon their death. In Britain, this type of insurance is called assurance. Unlike insurance, which is concerned with compensation for loss that may or may not occur, assurance is concerned with providing security for events that are certain to occur.

THE INSURANCE CONTRACT

A contract of insurance is taken out between two parties:

(i)   The *insurer* is the party who agrees to accept the risk; and

(ii) The *insured* is the party who seeks protection from the risk.

In return for payment of a *premium*[1] the insurer agrees to pay the insured a stated sum (or a proportion of it) should the event insured against occur. Premiums are quoted as a percentage of the sum insured – in Britain, at so many pence per £100 (eg 25p%).

A person wishing to take out life assurance or accident insurance must usually submit a *proposal form*[2] containing questions which must be answered truthfully. The insured must also make known any other information that is likely to influence the insurer's judgement regarding the risk. If this is not done, the insurer may void the contract. In marine insurance it is not the practice to use proposal forms. They are only rarely used in fire insurance. However, as with other forms of insurance, all information affecting the risk must be disclosed.

If the proposal is accepted the insurer is required by law to issue a policy. This policy sets out the terms of the contract including the risk to be covered, the sum insured and the premium to be paid. If at a later date it is decided to alter the terms of the insurance, this is usually done by *endorsing*[3] the existing policy rather than by issuing a new one.

A person cannot legally insure a risk for which there is no legal interest. Anyone may insure their own property but not that of a neighbour. Anyone may insure the life of a person who owes them money but only up to the amount owing. Ship owners may insure their ships but not the cargo carried, except for the value of the *freight*[4] lost if the cargo were lost.

[1] **premium** the payment made for insurance
[2] **proposal form** a written request for insurance cover
[3] **endorsing** writing on the back of a document – varying the cover stated in the policy by an additional clause
[4] **freight** the charge for carriage of goods

30.1 Enquiries for insurance rates

(a) Cash in transit

Background details about business and banking

Use numbered points for clarity

Request a reply regarding terms

Dear Sirs

We normally pay into the bank each morning our takings for the preceding business day. The sums involved are sometimes considerable especially at the weekends: takings on a Saturday may amount to as much as £6000.

We bank with the local branch of the Barminster Bank on West Street, Milton – about half a mile from our premises.

We therefore wish to take out insurance cover for the following:

1 Against loss of cash on the premises, by fire, theft, or burglary.

2 Against loss of cash in transit between our premises and the bank.

3 Against accident or injury to staff while engaged in taking money to the bank, or bringing it from the bank.

Please let us know on what terms you can provide cover for the risks mentioned.

Yours faithfully

(b) Goods sent by sea

Dear Sirs

We will shortly have a consignment of tape recorders, valued at £50,000 cif Quebec, to be shipped from Manchester by a vessel of Manchester Liners Ltd.

We wish to cover the consignment against all risks from our warehouse at the above address to the port of Quebec. Will you please quote your rate for the cover.

Yours faithfully

(c) Request for special rate

Dear Sirs

We regularly ship consignments of bottled sherry to Australia by both passenger and cargo liners of the Enterprise Shipping Line. We are interested to know whether you can issue an all-risks policy for these shipments and, if so, on what terms. In particular we wish to know whether you can give a special rate in return for the promise of regular monthly shipments.

I hope to hear from you soon.

Yours faithfully

30.2 Applications for insurance cover

(a) Continuation of 30.1(c)

Dear Mr Johnson

We thank you for your reply to our enquiry of 6 June. The terms you quote, namely 35p%, less 5% special discount for regular shipments, are acceptable. We understand that these terms will apply to all our shipments of bottled sherry by regular liners to Australian ports and cover all risks, including breakages and pilferage.[5]

Our first shipment will be on 2 July for 20 cases of sherry valued at £6000. Please arrange open-account terms[6] with quarterly settlements.

I look forward to receiving the policy within the next few days.

Yours sincerely

(b) Insurance of warehouse stock

(i) Application

Dear Mr Wilson

Thank you for your letter of 15 April quoting rates for insurance cover for stock stored in our warehouse at the above address.

The value of the stock held varies with the season but does not normally exceed £100,000 at any time.

Please arrange cover in this sum for all the risks mentioned in your letter and on the terms quoted, namely 50p% per annum. Cover should take effect from 1 May next.

Yours sincerely

(ii) Acknowledgement

Dear Mr Smith

Thank you for your recent letter. We shall be glad to provide cover in the sum of £50,000 at 50p% per annum on stock in your warehouse at 25 Topping Street, Lusaka. This will take effect from 1 May.

The policy is now being prepared and it should reach you in about a week's time.

Please let me know if I can provide any further help.

Yours sincerely

---

[5] **pilferage** small thefts
[6] **open-account terms** credit terms with periodic statements

(c) Cargo insurance

Dear Sirs

Please arrange full a.a.r.[7] cover in the sum of £5000 for shipment of 20 hi-fi music centres to Quebec by MV Merchant Shipper, scheduled to sail from Manchester on 2 July. The goods are packed in 5 cases marked AHB 1–5, now lying in our warehouse at 25 Manchester Road, Salford.

Please let us have the policy, and one certified copy, not later than 30 June. The charge should be billed to our account.

Yours faithfully

INSURANCE BROKERS

Insurance of business risks, and especially of *maritime*[8] risks, calls for special knowledge. The advice and help of a qualified insurance broker is often of great advantage. A broker advises clients on the risks they should cover, recommends the kinds of insurance best suited to their particular needs and places the risks with the most suitable insurers.

30.3 Requests to brokers to arrange insurance

(a) Example 1

Dear Sir

Will you please arrange to take out an all-risks insurance for us on the following consignment of cameras from our warehouse at the above address to Valletta:

6 c/s cameras due to leave Liverpool on 18 August by SS Endeavour.

The invoiced value of the consignment, including freight and insurance, is £11,460.

Please contact me if you have any queries.

Yours faithfully

---

[7] **a.a.r.** against all risks
[8] **maritime** relating to the sea

(b) Example 2

Dear Miss Taylor

Thank you for calling me this morning. I confirm that we have decided to accept the quotation of 60p% by the Britannia Insurance Co for insurance to cover the transit by road of two 1¼ tonne boilers on 15 July. The consignment will be taken from our works in Birmingham to the Acme Engineering Co, Bristol.

Please arrange the necessary cover and send us the policy as soon as possible.

Yours faithfully

INSURANCE PREMIUMS

Statistics enable insurers to assess the extent of particular risks with considerable accuracy. This helps them to fix their premiums at levels that are fair both to themselves and to the insured. Since premiums vary with the degree of risk, lower rates are charged when protective measures such as fire alarms, *automatic sprinklers,*[9] *fire extinguishers*[10] and fire-resistant materials are used.

30.4 Request for reduction in premium

Dear Mr Maxwell

POLICY NO F 623104

Refer to telephone conversation. Request a review – give full details of the premium concerned

Further to our telephone conversation I should be obliged if you would review the rate of premium charged under the above fire policy for goods in our transit shed[11] at No 4 Dock. As you know, the shed is also used as a bonded store[12] and storage warehouse.

State main reason for request

As we discussed I feel that not enough weight may have been given to the following conditions when the present rate of premium was fixed:

Numbered points ensure clarity and ease of reference

1   The shed is not artificially heated.

2   No power of any kind is used.

3   All rooms are provided with automatic sprinklers, fireproof doors and fire extinguishers of the latest type.

4   A water main runs round the entire dockside and can be tapped[13] at several points within easy distance of the shed.

Tactfully request a reduction

When these conditions are taken into account I believe the present rate of premium seems to be unreasonably high. I hope you will agree to reduce it sufficiently to bring it more into line with the extent of the risk insured under the policy.

I look forward to hearing from you soon.

Yours

[9] **automatic sprinklers** a system which, when overheated, releases water
[10] **fire extinguisher** an appliance for putting out fires
[11] **transit shed** a shed through which goods pass
[12] **bonded store** a warehouse for goods liable to Customs duty
[13] **tapped** used for drawing water

HOUSEHOLDERS' POLICIES

Most fire insurance companies offer a wide range of cover on the buildings and contents of private dwellings under what are known as 'Householders' or 'All-risk' policies. These are designed to give protection in one document from a variety of risks besides those usually covered by a fire policy, including storms, riots, burst pipes, burglary, theft, accidents to servants, liability to third parties, accidental breakage of mirrors, etc, but not losses due to war. It is a condition of such cover that both buildings and contents are insured for their full value.

30.5 Application for householder's insurance

(a) Application

Dear Sirs

I have recently bought the property at the above address with possession as from 1 July and wish to take out comprehensive cover on both building and contents in the sums of £120,000 and £30,000 respectively.[14] The former figure represents the estimated rebuilding cost of the property and the latter the full value of the contents.

Please send me particulars of your terms and conditions for the policy and a proposal form if required.

Yours faithfully

(b) Reply

Dear Mrs Turner

HOUSEHOLDERS' COMPREHENSIVE INSURANCE

Thank you for your enquiry of 19 June. A copy of our prospectus containing particulars of our policies for householders is enclosed.

You will see that we offer two types of cover for buildings. Cover 'B' (premium rate 21p%) is similar to cover 'A' (premium rate 24p%) but excludes cover for accidental damage. For contents we provide only one type of cover at a rate of 70p% per annum. As you will see from the prospectus, our comprehensive policies provide a very wide range of cover.

I enclose a proposal form. Please complete and return it not later than 7 days before the date from which the policy is to run.

Please give me a call if you have any queries.

Yours sincerely

[14] **respectively** relating to each in turn

30.6 Request for increase in cover

Dear Sirs

HOUSE CONTENTS POLICY NO H 96154

On 2 June I sent you a cheque for £175.00 as the premium due for renewal of the above policy.

I now wish to increase the amount of cover from its current figure of £25,000 to £30,000 (thirty thousand pounds) with immediate effect. Please confirm that you have arranged for this and send me the customary endorsement indicating the charge for inclusion in the policy schedule.

From the conditions that apply to your householders' policies I understand that no charge for this increased cover will be made before my next renewal date.

I look forward to receiving your confirmation soon.

Yours faithfully

30.7 Notice of increase in premiums

Some insurance companies encourage household policy-holders to increase the amount of cover for buildings and contents by deferring payment of the higher rate of premium until the next renewal of the policy, as in the above letter. Under this arrangement it is possible for the insured to obtain extra cover free of charge for a period of up to 12 months under a policy that is renewable annually.

The following is a circular letter from an insurance company to its household policy-holders referring to under-insurance due to inflation.

Dear

Unfortunately, our efforts to encourage household policy-holders to revise the sums insured to take account of inflation[15] have been poorly supported. In the past 5 years the monetary value of property[16] and contents has more than doubled, but most householders have failed to provide for this and as a result are grossly[17] underinsured. The problem of underinsurance has often been made worse because the initial cover[18] was inadequate[19]. On some recent claims research shows that the amount of underinsurance has been well over 50%.

In this situation we have been reluctantly compelled[20] to introduce in all household insurance a provision[21] automatically increasing the amount of cover at each renewal of the policy. The increase, currently[22] 6%, will be reflected[23] in the amount of premium payable. Allowance for this will be made in your next renewal notice.

If you have any queries please contact me.

Yours sincerely

[15] **inflation** a rise in the general level of prices
[16] **property** premises
[17] **grossly** very much; considerably
[18] **initial cover** the value insured at the beginning
[19] **inadequate** insufficient
[20] **reluctantly compelled** forced unwillingly
[21] **provision** a term or condition in an agreement
[22] **currently** at the present time
[23] **reflected** included; covered by

30.8 **Request for information concerning cover**

Dear

POLICY NO MH 816/89068

Upon receiving your renewal notice on 21 July I sent you a cheque for £250.75 to extend cover of my premises under the above policy. Unfortunately, I have no record of the amount of cover provided by the premium paid and should be obliged if you would let me have this information as soon as possible.

Should the amount of the cover be less than £50,000 I should like to increase it to this amount with immediate effect. Please arrange for this if necessary and send me your account for the amount of additional premium payable. I will then send you a cheque in payment.

Yours sincerely

HOLIDAY INSURANCE

When a holiday is to be taken abroad it is a wise precaution to insure not only against loss of baggage and other personal property but also against personal accident and illness while away from home.

The costs of medical and hospital care when on holiday must be borne privately and can be very high. In return for a small premium many insurance companies now provide cover for this. Travel agencies are usually willing to make the necessary arrangements.

30.9 **Holiday insurance – application and claim**

(a) Application

Dear Sirs

I shall be touring Italy and Sicily in a 1996 Peugeot 405 GL for 4 weeks commencing 3 July.

Please let me know the terms and conditions on which you could issue a policy to cover loss of and damage to baggage and other personal property. I should also like to consider cover against personal accident and illness, and should be glad if you would send me particulars. The car is already separately insured.

I hope to hear from you soon.

Yours faithfully

(b) Insurer's reply

Dear Mr Sanderson

Thank you for your letter of 8 June regarding insurance to cover your tour of Italy and Sicily.

I enclose a leaflet setting out the terms and conditions of the insurance for both personal property and injury and illness, and also a proposal form. The cover for injury and illness extends to the full cost of medical and hospital treatment and of any special arrangements that may be necessary for your return home.

Please complete and return the proposal form by 26 June at the latest, so that we can be sure of issuing the policy in time.

Yours sincerely

FIDELITY INSURANCE

An employer often seeks protection from the dishonesty of persons employed in positions of trust by taking out a 'Fidelity Guarantee' policy. Employees may be insured either individually or on a group basis under a collective policy guaranteeing a separate amount for each employee. Alternatively, a floating policy may be taken out in which the names of the various employees appear but with one amount of guarantee for the whole.

30.10 **Enquiry for a Fidelity Guarantee policy**

Dear Sirs

We have recently appointed Mrs Tessa Campbell as our chief accountant. She came to us with excellent references, but as a purely precautionary measure we wish to cover her by a fidelity bond for £100,000.

Please let me know on what terms you can provide this cover and send me a proposal form if required.

Yours faithfully

TEMPORARY COVER

No contract comes into effect until the proposal made is accepted by the insurer. However, where a person wants immediate cover while the proposal is being considered, the insurer is usually willing to grant temporary protection and to issue a *cover note*[24] upon request. The note is usually expressed to provide cover up to a stated date.

In the following correspondence the insurer does not issue a cover note, but nevertheless makes it clear that in fact the property is covered.

30.11 Request for cover pending issue of policy

(a) Householder's request

Dear Sirs

1 MARGATE ROAD, ST ANNES-ON-SEA, LANCS

I have recently bought the property at the above address. A covenant[25] in the deeds requires the property to be insured with your company against fire. In a letter to me dated 30 October the solicitors handling the transfer for me stated that you would be getting in touch with me about this.

As I have not yet heard from you, I am writing as a matter of urgency to ask you to insure the property under your usual full-cover householder's policy in the sum of £100,000 as from 7 December inclusive. This is the date fixed for the legal transfer of the property to me. This sum covers the purchase price of £80,000 and estimated rebuilding costs.

In view of the urgency I hope to receive your assurance that you will hold the property covered as from and including next Thursday 7 December. I ask this because I am in no position to accept the risks of non-insurance while the policy is being prepared.

Yours faithfully

(b) Insurer's reply

Dear Mr Brown

COMPREHENSIVE INSURANCE
1 MARGATE ROAD, ST ANNES-ON-SEA, LANCS

Thank you for your letter of 3rd November. I am pleased to inform you that we will hold this property covered for £100,000 as from 7 December on the terms and conditions of the company's comprehensive policy.

A proposal form is enclosed. Please complete it and return it to me immediately.

Yours sincerely

---

[24] **cover note** a document giving temporary insurance cover pending issue of policy
[25] **covenant** a clause in a deed (a sealed contract)

CLAIMS

Claims for loss or damage should always be made promptly by letter and supported by whatever information or evidence can be offered at the time. If a claim relates to goods delivered it should be made immediately the loss or damage is discovered:

1 To the insurer, if the goods have been insured by the buyer.

2 To the seller, where the insurance has been taken out by them.

30.12 Claim for damage to house property

When a claim is made it is usually necessary for a claim form to be completed, as in this correspondence.

(a) Householder's claim

Dear Sirs

POLICY NO PK 850046

I am sorry to have to report a slight accident to the work surface of the sink-unit work-table. This was burnt and cracked when an electric iron was accidentally knocked over on it.

I have made enquiries and am informed that replacement cost of the damaged work surface will be about £80 (eighty pounds). There will also be an additional charge for fixing.

I hope to receive your permission to arrange for the work to be carried out. Should you wish to inspect the damage I am at home on most days, but it would be helpful to know when to expect your representative.

Yours faithfully

State policy number Give details of the incident

State cost involved in repair

Tactfully request permission to proceed with the work

(b) Insurer's reply

Dear Mrs Crowther

POLICY NO PK 850046

I refer to your letter of 14 September and our representative's recent call on you. Our claim form is enclosed. Please complete and return this to me as soon as possible with the contractor's estimate for replacement of the damaged work surface. I will then deal with the matter immediately.

Yours sincerely

ER, MISS JONES, CONTACT THE INSURERS WOULD YOU...

30.13 Insurer requests further information

Sometimes a person suffering a loss gives incomplete or even inaccurate information, hoping that by doing so excessive compensation may be recovered. In such cases the insurer will either ask for further information, as in the following letter, or will *dispute*[26] the claim. Such cases are fairly numerous and varied, and the following is only one of the many kinds of letter the insurer may send. It relates to a claim by a contractor for loss of business suffered as a result of damage to a lorry in a road accident.

A person who suffers loss must do whatever possible to limit the loss, otherwise they may fail to get full compensation.

> Dear
>
> I refer to your claim of 17 February for £1500 as compensation for loss of business due to damage to your lorry.
>
> Before I can deal with your claim I shall need the following further information from you:
>
> 1   What is the actual financial loss suffered as a result of the accident, and how is it calculated?
>
> 2   What steps, if any, were taken to hire a suitable lorry until the damaged lorry could be replaced?
>
> 3   If no steps to hire were taken, please give the reason.
>
> As soon as I receive this information I will deal with your claim immediately.
>
> Yours sincerely

[26] **dispute** to contest; oppose

30.14 Buyer requests seller to make claim

Where, on behalf of the buyer, the seller insures goods in transit, the buyer will report the loss or damage to the seller and ask him to make the claim, as in the following letter.

Dear

OUR ORDER NO C 541

When the SS _Lancastria_ arrived at Famagusta on 10 November, it was noticed that one side of case number 12 containing radio receivers was split. Therefore the case was opened and the contents were examined by a local insurance surveyor in the presence of the shipping company's agents. The case was invoiced as containing 24 Hacker 'Mayflower' radio receivers, 8 of which were badly damaged.

The surveyor's report is enclosed with statement from the shipping agent.

As you hold the insurance policy I should be grateful if you would take up this matter with the insurers.

Eight replacement receivers will be required. Please arrange to supply these as soon as possible and charge them to our account.

Thank you in advance for your trouble on our behalf. If there are any queries please do not hesitate to call me.

Yours faithfully

30.15 Claim for damage by fire

(a) Claim

Dear Sirs

POLICY NO AR 3854

I regret to report that a fire broke out in our factory stores last night. The cause is not yet known but we estimate the damage to stock to be about £100,000. Fortunately no records were destroyed so there should be no difficulty in assessing the value of the loss.

Please arrange for your representative to call and let me have your instructions regarding salvage.[27]

Yours faithfully

---

[27] **salvage** items that can be recovered

(b) Insurer's reply

> Dear
>
> FIRE POLICY NO AR 3854
>
> Thank you for your letter of 21 May. I was sorry to hear about the fire in your factory stores.
>
> As a first step will you please make your claim on the enclosed form. Meanwhile, I am arranging for Mr John Watson, a loss adjuster, to call and assess the damage. He will be in touch with you soon.
>
> If you need help in completing the claim form Mr Watson will be able to assist you.
>
> Yours sincerely

30.16 Insurer declines to meet claim in full (continuation of 30.15)

Sometimes it is necessary for a letter to convey disappointing or unwelcome news, as when a claim is rejected, or in any other circumstances likely to cause disappointment. In such a letter the opening paragraph should be in terms that prepare the receiver for what is coming and soften the blow when it does come. This indirect approach to unwelcome news is used in the following letter.

> Dear
>
> POLICY NO AR 3854
>
> When we received your letter of 5 June we sent Mr John Watson to inspect and report on the damage caused by the fire. He has now submitted his report, which confirms your claim that the damage is extensive. He reports, however, that much of the stock damaged or destroyed was either obsolete[28] or obsolescent.[29]
>
> We therefore regret that we cannot accept as a fair estimate of the loss the figure of £100,000 mentioned in your letter – a figure which we understand is based on the actual cost of the goods.
>
> Our own estimate of the stock damaged or destroyed, based on present market values, does not exceed £60,000. We feel that this valuation is a very generous one, but are prepared to pay on the basis of it under the policy. Please let me know if you will accept this in full settlement of your claim for the value of the stock lost.
>
> Yours sincerely

[28] **obsolete** out of date
[29] **obsolescent** becoming out of date

30.17 Claim for injury to worker

(a) Claim

Dear Sirs

POLICY NO 56241

Our foreman, Mr James MacDonald, met with an accident on 2 March. He crushed his thumb when operating a machine. At the time we did not think the accident was serious enough to report: however, after an absence of 3 weeks Mr MacDonald has returned to his work and is still unable to carry on his normal duties.

We therefore wish to make a claim under the above policy. Please send the necessary claim form to me as soon as possible.

Yours faithfully

(b) Insurer's reply

Dear

POLICY NO 56241

Refer to claim received — Thank you for your letter of 27 March regarding your claim for the accident to Mr J MacDonald.

Tactfully comment on details provided — Under the terms of the policy his claim should have been submitted within 3 days of the accident. As more than 3 weeks have now passed, your claim for compensation under the policy has been forfeited.

The insurer does not have to meet the claim, but he does so as a gesture of goodwill. This is tactfully explained here — Nevertheless, as a gesture of goodwill we have decided to overlook this late submission. However we feel it should have been clear from Mr MacDonald's prolonged absence from work that his accident was more serious than you had thought and that there seems to be no good reason why the claim should not have been made earlier.

Enclose claim form. Clearly state position in the future — I enclose a claim form as requested but must emphasise that future claims cannot be entertained where the terms of the policy are not complied with.

Yours sincerely

30.18 Request to support illness claim

Claims arising from accident, sickness or similar causes must be supported by medical evidence either from the attendant doctor or from the institution treating the patient.

A patient recovering from an operation is required by their insurance company to provide evidence of any stay in hospital. In the following letter a doctor is asked to complete the form received from the company. By providing the details and enclosing an addressed envelope the patient tries to help a busy doctor.

Dear Dr Edwards

The London Life Insurance Co Ltd, of which I am a policy holder, have asked for completion of the enclosed claim form for benefits for the period I was in your hospital and later the Avala Nursing Home.

I have pencilled in the details requested on the side of the form which the company wish you to complete; this may assist you.

I have attached 4 accounts covering both hospital and nursing home accommodation for 6 weeks as follows:

Hospital (23 April to 7 May 200—)
Nursing Home (7 May to 2 June 200—)

The company would like you to return the completed claim form to them. I enclose an addressed envelope for this purpose.

Please give me a call if you have any queries.

Yours sincerely

MARINE INSURANCE

Most of the world's business in marine insurance is centred in London though there are other important markets. At the heart of these activities is Lloyd's, a London corporation of insurers who issue most kinds of policy but are especially active in marine insurance. Lloyd's membership comprises insurers (or underwriters as they are called) and brokers. The underwriters work in *syndicates*[30] specialising in different types of risk. All insurance business with underwriter members must be placed through Lloyd's brokers, but anyone who chooses to place business with insurance companies rather than with Lloyd's may employ any broker, or may deal with the matter directly.

Under the Marine Insurance Act of 1906 all marine insurance contracts must be in the form of a policy. Marine policies may be either *valued* or *unvalued*, both classes being further subdivided into *voyage policies*, *time policies*, *mixed policies* and *floating* or *open policies*. A *valued policy* is one based on values agreed in advance and stated in the policy. With an *unvalued policy* the value of any loss (within the limit of the sum insured) is left to be assessed at the time of the loss.

A *voyage policy*, like a voyage charter, covers a particular ship for a stated voyage (eg London to Melbourne). A *time policy*, like a time charter, covers a particular ship for an agreed period of time not exceeding 12 months (eg from noon 5 April 1997 to noon 5 April 1998). A *mixed policy* combines the features of both time and voyage policies.

Policies may be issued to cover 'All risks', or they may contain clauses relieving the underwriter of certain risks. The premium for an all-risks policy is naturally higher than that for a policy with exemptions.

[30] **syndicates** groups formed for a common purpose

30.19 **Request for an all-risks policy**

(a) Request

Dear Sir/Madam

We wish to insure the following consignment against all risks for the sum of £10,000.

4 c/s Fancy Leather Goods, marked $\boxed{\text{AS}}$ 1–4

These goods are now held at Number 2 Dock, Liverpool, waiting to be shipped by SS Rajputana due to leave for Bombay on Friday 23 June.

We require immediate cover as far as Bombay. Please let us have the policy as soon as it is ready. In the meantime please confirm that you hold the consignment covered.

Yours faithfully

(b) Reply

Dear

Thank you for your letter of 16 June asking us to cover the consignment of 4 cases of fancy leather goods from Liverpool to Bombay.

The premium for this cover is at the rate of £2.30% of the declared value of £10,000. The policy is being prepared and will be sent to you within a few days. Meanwhile, I confirm that we hold the consignment covered as from today.

Yours sincerely

30.20 **Request to insure goods at docks**

Dear Sir

Please arrange to insure for one calendar month from today the following consignment ex SS Ansdell from Hamburg:

2 cases Cameras, marked ⟨AR⟩ value £30,000 and now held at Royal Victoria Dock.

Please confirm that you hold the consignment covered and, when send the policy as soon as possible, together with your account for the premium.

Yours faithfully

FLOATING AND OPEN-COVER POLICIES

Floating policies are sometimes used by merchants engaged in regular overseas trade. A policy of this kind covers a number of shipments by any ship to any port or ports that may be agreed. The merchant takes out a policy for a round sum, say £100,000. As each consignment is shipped it is 'declared' on a special form provided by the underwriter who records the value on a duplicate copy of the policy and issues a *certificate of insurance* stating that the consignment is covered. When the sum insured has been fully declared (or, used up), a new policy is taken out.

Floating policies are sometimes referred to as 'Open' or 'Declaration' policies; but they are not greatly used today, being largely replaced by long-term policies issued on open cover. These open-cover policies extend the floating policy principle and cover all shipments for certain voyages or trades for an extended period, usually a year, *irrespective of their aggregate value*,[31] which may not be known, but with a specified limit for each shipment. The arrangement avoids any risk that a shipment will be left uninsured through oversight.

30.21 Enquiry for open-policy terms

(a) Enquiry

Dear Sirs

Please quote your rate for an all-risks open policy for £100,000 to cover shipments of general merchandise[32] by Manchester Liners Ltd, from Manchester and Liverpool to Atlantic ports in Canada and the United States.

As shipments are due to begin on 30 June, please let us have your quotation by return.

Yours faithfully

(b) Reply

Dear Mr Yates

Thank you for your enquiry of yesterday. Our rate for a £100,000 A R open policy on general merchandise by Manchester Liners from Manchester and Liverpool to Atlantic ports in Canada and the United States is £2.10% of declared value.

This is an exceptionally low rate and we trust you will give us the opportunity to handle your insurance business.

Yours sincerely

---

[31] **irrespective of their aggregate value** apart from their total worth
[32] **merchandise** articles of commerce

(c) Acceptance

Dear Mr Summers

Thank you for your letter of 19 June quoting your rate for an open policy of £100,000 covering consignments on the routes named.

The rate of £2.10% is satisfactory. Please prepare and send us the policy as soon as possible. Meanwhile please let us have your cover note and statement of charges for our first shipment under the policy, which is:

3 c/s General Merchandise (Textiles), marked Value £2500.

I hope to hear from you soon.

Yours sincerely

30.22 Application for an open policy

Dear Sirs

We will shortly be making regular shipments of fancy leather goods to South America by approved ships. I should be glad if you would issue an a/r open policy for, say, £75,000 to cover these shipments from our warehouse at the above address to port of destination.

All goods will be packed in wooden cases and despatched by road to Southampton and, less frequently, to Liverpool.

Yours faithfully

30.23 Declaration of shipment of open policy

When accepting the application in 30.22 the underwriter will send the original policy to the merchant and also a supply of declaration forms, one of which the merchant will complete and send to the underwriter each time goods are shipped.

Dear Sirs

POLICY NO 18752

Please note that under the above open policy, dated 18 March 200—, we have today shipped a third consignment, valued at £1620, by SS Durham Castle, due to sail from Southampton tomorrow. The necessary declaration form is enclosed.

This leaves an undeclared value on the policy of £48,380. Please confirm this figure as soon as possible.

Yours faithfully

30.24 Renewal of an open policy (continuation of 30.23)

Dear Sir

POLICY NO 18752

We enclose a completed form declaring a further consignment, valued £2325.

This will be the last full declaration under the above policy as the undeclared balance now stands at only £825, which will not be sufficient to cover our next consignment in December. Therefore please issue a new policy on the same terms and for the same amount, namely £75,000, as the current policy.

When we make the next shipment, we shall declare it against the present policy for £825 and against the new policy for the amount by which the value of the shipment exceeds this amount.

Yours faithfully

AVERAGE

Average is a term used in marine insurance to refer to partial losses. *Particular average* means partial loss or damage caused by accident to the ship or to some particular cargo. Such losses are borne by the owner of the particular property suffering the damage. *General average* on the other hand refers to loss or damage carried out intentionally for the common good at a time when a ship and its cargo are in danger, as when cargo is thrown overboard to save the ship in a storm. Losses of this kind are shared by all who have a financial interest in the *venture*[33] in *proportion to*[34] the value of their interests.

As a rule, the manufacturer or merchant insures goods 'against all risks' and receives a WA policy containing a 'with average' clause. This means that the underwriters pay for partial losses. Under an FPA policy, which contains a 'free from particular average' clause, the underwriters pay only for total losses. An FPA policy will therefore be issued for a lower premium than a WA policy.

MOTOR INSURANCE

The owner of a motor vehicle must possess a current road licence and is also required by law to insure against accidents to third parties, against death and bodily injury, and up to £250,000 for damages to property (1988 Road Traffic Act). It is customary, but not compulsory, to insure against loss or damage to the vehicle. All these risks may be covered by what is termed a 'comprehensive' policy, ie a single policy providing all-inclusive cover.

---

[33] **venture** the voyage and its risks
[34] **in proportion to** as relative share of the whole

30.25 Renewal of policy

Dear Mr Wrenshall

POLICY NO M 346871

Your policy and certificate of insurance as required by the Road Traffic Acts will expire at noon on 3 April next.

To maintain the insurance in force instructions should be given to your broker not later than, but preferably 6 days before, the date on which the policy expires so that you may receive the new certificate of insurance in time. You will realise that it is an offence under the Road Traffic Acts to use a vehicle on the road without a current certificate of insurance.

As a protection to you against any failure to observe the Acts I am enclosing a temporary cover note and certificate of insurance. However, please remember that this extension of cover applies only to that part of the policy which is necessary to comply with[35] the requirements of the Road Traffic Acts, namely third party personal injury liability and damage to third party property.

The temporary cover note should be kept carefully until the certificate of insurance reaches you.

Yours sincerely

[35] **comply with** carry out; observe

USEFUL EXPRESSIONS

Requests for cover

Openings

1 Please quote your lowest All Risks rates for shipments of ... to ...

2 Please hold us covered for the consignment referred to below (on the attached sheet).

3 We should be glad if you would provide cover of £ ... on ..., in transit from ... to...

4 We wish to renew this policy for the same amount and on the same terms as before.

Closes

1 Please inform us on what terms this insurance can be arranged.

2 Please send us the necessary proposal form.

3 We leave the details to you, but wish to have the consignment covered against All Risks.

4 I shall be glad to receive your certificate of insurance as soon as possible.

Replies to requests for cover

Openings

1 Thank you for your letter of ... . We quote below our terms for arranging cover for ...

2. Your letter regarding renewal of open policy number ... covering ...

Closes

1 The policy is being prepared and should reach you by ... . Meanwhile I confirm that we are holding you covered.

2 We undertake all classes of insurance and would welcome the opportunity to transact further business with you.

Claims

Openings

1 I regret to report the loss of ... which is insured with you under the above policy.

2 I regret to report a fire in one of the bedrooms at this address.

3 I have completed and enclose the form of claim for loss of ...

Closes

1 Please let me know any details you need from me when I submit my claim.

2 If you will make out your claim on the enclosed form we will attend to it immediately.

3 Your claim will be carefully considered when we receive the information requested.

Appendix

USEFUL WEBSITES

Everyone who writes needs to use a dictionary or thesaurus from time to time – or at least they should. If you try doing a search on any search engine for 'dictionary' you will see that there are actually hundreds and hundreds of different sites.

Here are my tips for some interesting and useful online dictionaries and language resources on the Internet:

- **www.m-w.com/netdict.htm**
  Merriam-Webster's Collegiate Dictionary, 10th Edition
  Free dictionary and thesaurus, including an online audible pronunciation database.

- **www.one-look.com**
  One-Look Dictionary Search
  Called the 'Faster Finder', this claims to search 700+ online dictionaries simultaneously with a total word count of over 4 million.

- **www.xrefer.com**
  Xrefer Search Engine
  Xrefer's free site contains encyclopaedias, dictionaries, thesauri and books of quotations from the world's leading publishers. All cross-references, all in one place, providing a single information source.

- **www.yourdictionary.com/**
  yourDictionary.com Portal
  This claims to be the most comprehensive and authoritative portal for language and language-related products and services on the Internet, with more than 1800 dictionaries for over 250 languages.

- **www.oed.com/**
  Oxford English Dictionary
  An expensive subscription service, but some background documents and a Word of the Day are free.

- **www.plainenglish.com**
  Plain English Campaign
  This is an independent pressure group fighting for public information to be written in plain English. The site includes useful examples of what is and what is not 'plain English', free guides and much more.

- **www.worldwidewords.org**
  World Wide Words
  This is a fascinating list of English words and phrases, giving not only their meanings but how they came about.

- **www.foreignword.com**
  This is a link to hundreds of online dictionaries and translation engines, and thousands of specialised glossaries.

- **www.wordwizard.com**
  A portal for word lovers. Learn about word meanings, slang, quotations, insults, famous authors. Wordwizard offers a round trip across the English language.

- **www.thesaurus.com**
  Roget's Thesaurus
  An online version of Roget's Thesaurus of English words and phrases.

- **www.dictionary.com**
  An online dictionary and thesaurus.

- **www.ask.elibrary.com**
  A comprehensive digital archive for information seekers.

 Don't forget to check out my website:
www.shirleytaylor.com

SPOKEN AND WRITTEN FORMS OF ADDRESS

This section provides the correct forms of address for many officials, diplomats, religious leaders, royalty and the British peerage. The chart gives the appropriate form or forms to be used in addressing letters, in salutations, in direct conversation and in more formal introductions.

In diplomatic and other public circles, 'Sir' is generally considered an acceptable alternative to the formal address in both written and spoken greetings; this does not apply to religious or titled persons. The use of 'Madam' or 'Ma'am' for a female is less customary but still acceptable, especially for high officeholders ('Madam Governor'). This rule also holds for high officials of foreign countries.

Person	Letter address	Letter greeting	Spoken greeting	Formal introduction
President of the United States	The President The White House Washington, DC 20500	Dear Mr (or Madam) President	Mr (or Madam) President	The President or the President of the United States
Former President	The Honorable Jack Kimball Address	Dear Mr Kimball	Mr Kimball	The Honorable Jack Kimball
Vice President	The Vice President Executive Office Building Washington, DC 20501	Dear Mr (or Madam) Vice President	Mr (or Madam) Vice President	The Vice President or the Vice President of the United States
Cabinet members	The Honorable John (or Jane) Smith The Secretary of xxxxxxxxxx or The Attorney General Washington, DC	Dear Mr (or Madam) Secretary	Mr (or Madam) Secretary	The Secretary of xxxxxxxxx
Chief Justice	The Chief Justice The Supreme Court Washington, DC 20543	Dear Mr (or Madam) Justice or Dear Mr (or Madam) Chief Justice	Mr (or Madam) Chief Justice	The Chief Justice
United States Senator	The Honorable John (or Jane) Smith United States Senate Washington, DC 20510	Dear Senator Smith	Senator Smith	Senator Smith from Nebraska

Person	Letter address	Letter greeting	Spoken greeting	Formal introduction
Ambassador	The Honorable John (or Jane) Smith Ambassador of the United States American Embassy Address	Dear Mr (or Madam) Ambassador	Mr (or Madam) Ambassador	The American Ambassador The Ambassador of The United States of America
Consul-General	The Honorable John (or Jane) Smith American Consul General Address	Dear Mr (or Mrs, Ms) Smith	Mr (or Mrs, Ms) Smith	Mr (or Mrs, Ms) Smith
Foreign Ambassador	His (or Her) Excellency John (or Jane) Smith The Ambassador of xxxxxxxxxxx Address	Excellency or Dear Mr (or Madam) Ambassador	Excellency; or Mr (or Madam) Ambassador	The Ambassador of xxxxxxxxxx
Secretary-General of the United Nations	His (or Her) Excellency Jack (or Jane) Smith Secretary-General of the United Nations United Nations Plaza New York, NY 10017	Dear Mr (or Madam) Secretary-General	Mr (or Madam) Secretary-General	The Secretary-General of the United Nations
Governor	The Honorable Jack (or Jane) Smith Governor of xxxxxxxxxxx State Capitol Address	Dear Governor Smith	Governor or Governor Smith	The Governor of Maine: Governor Smith of Washington
State legislators	The Honorable Jack (or Jane) Smith Address here	Dear Mr (or Mrs, Ms) Smith	Mr (or Mrs, Ms) Smith	Mr (or Mrs, Ms) Smith
Judges	The Honorable John Smith Justice, Appellate Division Supreme Court of the State of xxxxxxxxxxx Address	Dear Judge Smith	Justice or Judge Smith; Madam Justice or Judge Smith	The Honorable Jack (or Jane) Smith; Mr Justice Smith or Judge Smith; Madam Justice Smith or Judge Smith
Mayor	The Honorable Jack (or Jane) Smith; His (or Her) Honor the Mayor City Hall Address	Dear Mayor Smith	Mayor Smith; Mr (or Madam) Mayor; Your Honor	Mayor Smith; The Mayor

Person	Letter address	Letter greeting	Spoken greeting	Formal introduction
The Pope	His Holiness, the Pope or His Holiness, Pope John XII Vatican City Rome, Italy	Your Holiness or Most Holy Father	Your Holiness or Most Holy Father	His Holiness, the Holy Father; the Pope; the Pontiff
Cardinals	His Eminence, Martin Cardinal Brown, Archbishop of xxxxxxxxx Address	Your Eminence or Dear Cardinal Brown	Your Eminence or Cardinal Brown	His Eminence, Cardinal Brown
Bishops	The Most Reverend Martin Brown, Bishop (or Archbishop) of xxxxxxxxxx Address here	Your Excellency or Dear Bishop (Archbishop) Brown	Your Excellency or Bishop (Archbishop) Brown	
Monsignor	The Reverend Monsignor Nigel Frangoulis Address	Reverend Monsignor or Dear Monsignor	Monsignor Frangoulis or Monsignor	Monsignor Frangoulis
Priest	The Reverend Jack Smith Address	Reverend Father or Dear Father Smith	Father or Father Smith	Father Smith
Brother	Brother Jack or Brother Jack Smith Address	Dear Brother Jack or Dear Brother	Brother Jack or Brother	Brother Jack
Sister	Sister Linda Wright	Dear Sister Linda Wright or Dear Sister	Sister Linda Wright or Sister	Sister Linda Wright
Protestant Clergy	The Reverend John (or Jane) James*	Dear Dr (or Mr, Ms) James	Dr (or Mr, Ms) James	The Reverend (or Dr) Jack James
Bishop (Episcopal)	The Right Reverend Jack James* Bishop of xxxxxxx Address	Dear Bishop James	Bishop James	The Right Reverend Jack James, Bishop of xxxxxxxxxxx
Rabbi	Rabbi Arnold (or Amanda) Schwartz Address	Dear Rabbi Schwartz	Rabbi Schwartz or Rabbi	Rabbi Arnold Schwartz
King or Queen	His (Her) Majesty King (Queen) xxxxxxxxxxx Address (letters traditionally are normally sent via the private secretary)	Your Majesty; Sir or Madam	Varies depending on titles, holdings, etc	

Person	Letter address	Letter greeting	Spoken greeting	Formal introduction
Other royalty	His (Her) Royal Highness, the Prince (Princess) of xxxxxxx	Your Royal Highness	Your Royal Highness; Sir or Madam	His (Her) Royal Highness, the Duke (Duchess) of xxxxxx
Duke/Duchess	His/Her Grace, the Duke (Duchess) of xxxxxxx	My Lord Duke/ Madam or Dear Duke of xxxx/Dear Duchess	Your Grace or Duke/Duchess	His/Her Grace, the Duke/Duchess of xxxx
Marquess/Marchioness	The Most Honorable the Marquess (Marchioness) of Newport	My Lord/Madam or Dear Lord/Lady Newport	Lord/Lady Newport	Lord/Lady Newport
Earl	The Right Honorable the Earl of Bangor	My Lord or Dear Lord Bangor	Lord Bangor	Lord Bangor
Countess (wife of an Earl)	The Right Honorable the Countess of Bangor	Madam or Dear Lady Bangor	Lady Bangor	Lady Bangor
Viscount/Viscountess	The Right Honorable the Viscount (Viscountess) Manson	My Lord/Lady or Dear Lord/Lady Manson	Lord/Lady Manson	Lord/Lady Manson
Baron/Baroness	The Right Honourable Lord/Lady Grey	My Lord/Madam or Dear Lord/Lady Grey	Lord/Lady Grey	Lord/Lady Grey
Baronet	Sir Jack Smith, Bt.	Dear Sir or Dear Sir Jack	Sir Jack	Sir Jack Smith
Wife of Baronet	Lady Smith	Dear Madam or Dear Lady Smith	Lady Smith	Lady Smith
Knight	Sir Elton John	Dear Sir or Dear Sir John	Sir John	Sir Elton John
Wife of Knight	Dear Madam or Dear Lady John	Lady John	Lady John	

Index

SHIRLEY TAYLOR'S
TRAINING PROGRAMMES

Power Up your Business Writing Skills (One or Two days)

One of the biggest challenges in business has always been to communicate effectively, especially in writing. This has become even more crucial in today's fast-paced e-world. In this popular workshop, you will learn proven, practical tools and techniques that will make you a better business writer. You will learn how easy it is to make your writing crisper, clearer, more proactive and more interesting to read. You will acquire the basics of organising your words and thought on paper, structuring your messages logically, presenting your documents attractively, and improving the format, style, language and tone of all your written communications. *Using these guidelines, you will learn a set of practical skills that will be useful to you every day for the rest of your life.*

Remember: You are what you write – so you should learn to write well!

"Shirley captivated my attention from the very beginning. She managed to keep the session alive with her witty jokes and experienced delivery of the topics."

"I have gained a lot from Shirley's class. She is a very interesting and dynamic trainer. She uses words that everybody understands. She is very lively and encouraged class participation."

"Shirley's teaching was very precise and detailed. Her workshop really taught me a lot. Not boring at the least."

"It has helped me to realise some of the outdated phrases that we always use."

Enhance your E-mail Skills (One day)

E-mail has become an essential and fundamental part of the way businesses work. When e-mail is used effectively it can be very powerful indeed. But when it is used ineffectively it can be costly, annoying and it can quickly damage a company's reputation. The Internet has made it possible for us to communicate with people from all over the world. The only way those people can form an opinion of us is by looking at the way we write – so it pays to learn to write well! In this practical workshop you will learn how to make technology work for you, not against you, and become a better business writer in the process.

Success Skills for Secretaries and PAs (One day)

It takes years of experience to achieve respect as an indispensable secretary, administrative assistant or support staff member. There are many essential sills that you need if you are to achieve success in business today. In this practical workshop you will learn how to handle the demands of your job with assertiveness, confidence and professionalism. You will learn how to communicate well, how to handle difficult people, how to prioritise, how to manage time and resources, how to handle crises, how to beat stress and much more. This comprehensive one-day workshop shows you how to make your working life more productive, more rewarding, more successful and much more enjoyable.

"It's the most fantastic seminar I've attended, Shirley's course awakened my inner potentials and encouraged me to do my job better."

"Shirley, I enjoy your speeches and presentations. They are simply lively and certainly enriching. I am always amazed by the way you capture the attention of the audience."

SHIRLEY TAYLOR
Training and Consultancy

**Shirley lives in Singapore and travels extensively conducting her popular workshops and seminars.
Contact Shirley to discuss in-house workshops for you company or to discuss speaking at international conferences.**

**Telephone: (+65) 6472 6076 Fax: (+65) 6399 2710
E-mail: shirley@shirleytaylor.com
Website: www.shirleytaylor.com**

OTHER BOOKS BY SHIRLEY TAYLOR

Communication for Business

This a well-established and popular textbook, workbook and reference book. It contains valuable guidelines on how to compose all business communications effectively and efficiently, together with practical assignments. This textbook is widely used by teachers and students all over the world on many courses leading to professional, business and secretarial qualifications.

(Teacher's resource pack available)

Essential Communication Skills

This is a comprehensive textbook and reference guide on the essentials of good communication skills. It explains the principles of effective communication, both oral and written, and provides solid advice and practical guidelines on how to strengthen communication skills and produce better business communication. Perfect for use as a self-study guide, with answers in the back.

(Teacher's resource pack available)

Guide to Effective E-mail

This book contains practical advice on all the essential aspects of e-mail. It aims to establish some 'rules of the road' for e-mail by providing guidelines on common courtesy online, basic rules of netiquette, composing effective messages, using appropriate language, style and structure, the problems and potential of e-mail, managing your e-mail, and much more.